✍ THE ✍
BEDSIDE
BACCALAUREATE

⤳ THE ⤳
BEDSIDE
BACCALAUREATE

EDITED BY DAVID RUBEL

AN AGINCOURT PRESS BOOK

STERLING

New York / London
www.sterlingpublishing.com

STERLING and the distinctive Sterling logo are registered trademarks of Sterling Publishing Co., Inc.

10 9 8 7 6 5 4 3 2 1

AN AGINCOURT PRESS BOOK

Published by Sterling Publishing Co., Inc.
387 Park Avenue South, New York, NY 10016
© 2008 by Agincourt Press

For acknowledgments and image credits, see page 384.

Distributed in Canada by Sterling Publishing
c/o Canadian Manda Group, 165 Dufferin Street
Toronto, Ontario, Canada M6K 3H6
Distributed in the United Kingdom by GMC Distribution Services
Castle Place, 166 High Street, Lewes, East Sussex, England BN7 1XU
Distributed in Australia by Capricorn Link (Australia) Pty. Ltd.
P.O. Box 704, Windsor, NSW 2756, Australia

Book design and layout: Jon Glick/mouse+tiger

Printed in Singapore
All rights reserved

Sterling ISBN 978-1-4027-5632-0

For information about custom editions, special sales, premium and corporate purchases, please contact Sterling Special Sales Department at 800-805-5489 or specialsales@sterlingpublishing.com.

PREFACE

THE DIFFERENCE BETWEEN THIS BOOK and a miscellany is the difference between knowledge and trivia. The appeal of a miscellany lies in its variety; but in achieving breadth, miscellanies often lack depth and fail to promote understanding. *The Bedside Baccalaureate* is more than a miscellany because it presents detailed, focused overviews of subjects with which any well-educated person would want to be familiar.

The goal of *The Bedside Baccalaureate* is not the simple accumulation of facts (some of which you may already know), but the placement of those facts within a framework of knowledge. The twenty courses that make up the book have been created by experts in their respective fields with the intention of making the subjects accessible to nonexpert readers. The interplay among these subjects is intended not merely to inform (and entertain!) but also to encourage the cross-pollination of ideas and to broaden the mind.

No doubt there will be occasions when you have questions that the text, given its brevity, doesn't answer. For this reason, the contributors have provided suggestions for further reading (beginning on page 382), which you can consult. That you'll want to read more should be expected, because learning is contagious; and once you get started, it can be difficult to stop.

HOW TO USE THIS BOOK

- The twenty courses are grouped, five at a time, into four sections, or "syllabi." These sections are easily viewed in the table of contents that follows.

- Each course consists of eighteen single-page lectures that maximize clarity without comprising the integrity of the ideas. The lectures are rotated, rather than clumped together, to add some variety to the reading experience and also to mimic the heady mix of subjects that one encounters in the world of the intellect.

- You can dip into an assortment of subjects by reading just a page at a time; or, if a course really grabs you, you can skip ahead. You'll find the lectures for each course on every fifth page, and roman numerals next to the lecture titles keep track of the sequence for you.

SYLLABUS

I

An overview of the American Civil War from the point of view of Ulysses S. Grant, who began the conflict working as a clerk in his father's general store and ended it as commander of all the Union armies. This course describes the major battles in which Grant fought as well as the North's command structure and its military strategy.

Recent history has seen the ever-closer integration of countries around the world, marked by increased flows of goods and services, people, capital and knowledge. This course takes up the major social and economic issues raised by this integration, including international trade agreements, winners and losers, and the so-called race to the bottom.

Art History
The Hudson River School
KIRSTEN JENSEN

An analysis of the aesthetic, artistic, and cultural commonalities that defined the Hudson River School, the first truly native school of American art. This style of landscape painting differentiated itself from European modes by emphasizing the sublime power of nature as exemplified by the American wilderness. Artists covered include Thomas Cole, the father of American landscape painting; Asher B. Durand; and Frederic Church.

Physical Sciences
The Astronomical Universe
SUSAN DiFRANZO

An introduction to the science of astronomy, this course begins with a brief history of ancient and Renaissance stargazing before moving on to an overview of modern astronomical research, including the latest theories relating to the origin of the universe, its current expansion, and its ultimate fate. In addition to our solar system and stellar life cycles, topics discussed include black holes, neutron stars, quasars, and extraterrestrial life.

Classics
Myths of Ancient Greece and Rome
DANIEL GREMMLER

A survey of the mythology created by the ancient Greeks and later adopted by the ancient Romans. The source texts, which represent written versions of what was originally an oral tradition, are considered from a cultural as well as a literary point of view. Beginning with the creation myth presented in Hesiod's *Theogony* and ending with Romulus, Remus, and the founding myth of Rome, this course answers the question *What is myth?*, pointing out that the Greeks considered their myths neither true nor false while the Romans viewed myth more as literature.

SYLLABUS

II

English and Comparative Literature

Emerson and Transcendentalism

DELANO GREENIDGE-COPPRUE

108

Among the most important intellectual movements in American history, transcendentalism was personified by Ralph Waldo Emerson, who gave up his Unitarian ministry because he found it too limiting. This course follows Emerson on his 1832 trip to Europe, during which he began combining his reformist Christian views with British romanticism and German idealism. The result was a way of thinking that would shape America's image of itself for generations to come.

Physical Science

The History of the Earth

BILL DANIELSON

109

From the formation of the planet out of supernova debris to the emergence of humanity 4.5 billion years later, this course covers the long run of geological time. The first half considers the geological history of Earth, including the formation of the planet's various layers and the movement of its continental plates. The second half describes the emergence and development of life on the planet. Emphasis is placed on the linkages between geological occurrences and the impacts they have had on Earth's biology.

World History
Revolutionary France

NIRA KAPLAN

This course covers the French Revolution from its roots in the ancien régime and the Enlightenment through the Napoleonic period. In addition to describing the major historical events of the period, its lectures pay close attention to the impact of the Revolution's egalitarian ideals on the French populace and the country's monarchical neighbors. In particular, it considers how the Revolution introduced, in the name of human freedom, some of the worst forms of human oppression.

Math and Engineering
The Search for Alternative Energies

MARK HOFF

Opening with a brief history of conventional energy technologies, this course focuses on the development in recent years of alternative ways to meet the world's growing energy demand. Alternative energy sources highlighted include solar, wind, biomass, biofuels, geothermal, tidal energy, and fuel cells. Short- and long-terms strategies for replacing fossil fuels are discussed—especially in light of the global warming phenomenon, which has made these alternative technologies relevant in a new way.

Religion
Schools of Buddhist Thought

PAUL G. HACKETT

An introduction to the study of Buddhism, beginning with an historical overview of the first five hundred years of Buddhist history and continuing with explanations of the basic principles of the Buddhist worldview, especially as they differ from tradition to tradition. The focus here is on the development of Buddhism from its origins in India as practical teachings on the relief of suffering to its current state as a worldwide religious and philosophical system.

SYLLABUS

III

200

The aim of this course is to explain what it takes to design and build rockets. The lectures begin with a description of the basic physical principles involved in rocket-propelled flight, especially as expressed in Newton's laws of motion. Then they take up the engineering issues involved, such as rocket motor design, propulsion, and staging. The course concludes with a discussion of advanced rocket technologies currently in development and the possibilities of interstellar spaceflight.

201

During his lifetime, Karl Marx wrote thousands of pages of social, economic, and political analysis describing a path to social change that revolutionized the world. This course helps students understand what Marx had to say by dividing his work into four periods, loosely defined in time but strongly defined in theme.

Art History
The Impressionists
KIRSTEN JENSEN

In 1874, a group of Parisian painters, in defiance of the official Salon, organized an exhibition of their own. Although their styles differed, their shared rejection of the rigid standards of the French Académie caused them to be grouped together as impressionists—so called because they painted not what the mind knows, but what the eye sees. This course traces the roots and evolution of the impressionist movement as it describes the work of Renoir, Monet, Pissaro, Sisley, Morisot, Degas, Cassatt, and Cézanne.

Social Sciences
Human Origins
THOMAS R. REIN

An examination of the biological bases of human society and culture, this course surveys human evolution from the emergence of the first hominins seven million years ago to the appearance of *Homo sapiens* between one hundred thousand and two hundred thousand years ago. Descriptions of the relevant fossil, archaeological, and genetic evidence underlie a discussion of current classifications and why new fossils tend to spark new controversies within the academic community.

World History
The Holocaust in Europe
BARRY TRACHTENBERG

During its twelve years in power, the Nazi government in Germany, acting in the name of racial purity, attempted to round up and eliminate the Jews of Europe. The Holocaust they carried out remains the most significant effort ever made by a national entity to destroy an entire people, and its incredible scale challenged the Nazis' ability to carry it out. This course describes the situation of the Jews in prewar Europe, how the Nazis came to power in Germany, and what they did with that power once obtained.

SYLLABUS

IV

Although the modern civil rights movement is usually thought to have begun with the Supreme Court's 1954 decision in *Brown v. Board of Education*, this course traces the roots of that movement all the way back to Reconstruction to show how the dramatic events of 1954–65 were merely the crescendo of a struggle long in development. Close attention is paid to not only the national leadership of Martin Luther King, Jr., but also to the role played by the student movement, especially in Mississippi.

An introduction to the basic concepts of empiricism as developed by the three great British empiricists of the seventeenth and eighteenth centuries: John Locke, George Berkeley, and David Hume. Thinking and writing in reaction to the rationalism of Descartes, Leibniz, and others, these British theoreticians began with the premise that all knowledge is based on experience (rather than reason, as the rationalists believed).

Physical Sciences
Einstein and Relativity
SUSAN DIFRANZO

This course takes relativity, one of the most complicated concepts in physics, and explains it in terms that anyone can understand. Beginning with basic Galilean and Newtonian principles, the lectures trace the development of Einstein's ideas, illustrating them with thought experiments similar to those used by Einstein himself. Topics include simultaneity, time dilation, length contraction, and the curvature of space–time.

Religion
The Sects of Islam
MICHAEL PREGILL

Unlike Christian sects, which are distinguished primarily by doctrine, the main sects of Islam vary little in doctrine and practice. Instead, the Sunnis and the Shi'a are separated primarily by a political divide that reaches all the way back to the death of Muhammad in 632. This course examines the differences between Sunni and Shi'ite Islam by investigating the deep roots of both sects in Islamic history and then considering their roles in contemporary Iran, Lebanon, and Iraq.

English and Comparative Literature
Masterworks of Imperial Russia
MARK PETTUS

The nineteenth century is generally considered the golden age of Russian literature because so many great writers flourished during this period. Pushkin, Gogol, Turgenev, Dostoevsky, Tolstoy, Chekhov—the list is as long as it is impressive. This course looks at the major works of the period—including *Dead Souls*, *Notes from the Underground*, *The Brothers Karamazov*, *Anna Karenina*, and *War and Peace*—both as literature and as social documents expressing the deep social divisions that existed under tsarist rule.

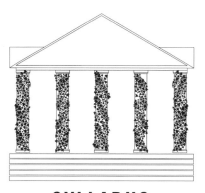

SYLLABUS

I

I. THE UNION ARMY IN 1861

THE UNITED STATES usually prepares for its wars only after getting into them, and the Civil War was no exception. In early 1861, as Pres. James Buchanan struggled to keep the war from beginning on his watch, the US Army numbered just sixteen thousand professional soldiers, nearly all of whom (179 out of 197 companies) were stationed far away on remote outposts in the West. Commanding these men were fewer than one thousand officers, nearly a third of whom resigned to join the Confederacy once states began seceding. As a result, by the time Abraham Lincoln took office in early March, the new president faced dangerous shortages of military manpower and command expertise.

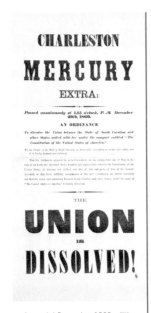

A special December 1860 edition of the *Charleston Mercury*.

The US Army's general in chief at the time was Winfield Scott, a septuagenarian known in the ranks as Old Fuss and Feathers. Scott had commanded the regular army since 1841. During the Mexican War of 1846–48, he and his colonel (brevet) of engineers, Robert E. Lee, had forced Veracruz to capitulate after a three-week siege and then captured Mexico City. Two decades later, however, Scott was not the same man; he suffered now from dropsy and was known to fall asleep during meetings.

At first, Lincoln avoided any action that might provide the South with an excuse for war. On April 15, however, two days after the fall of Fort Sumter, the president issued a proclamation calling for the states to raise seventy-five thousand militia troops for ninety days' federal service. Lincoln asked for just ninety days because he, like most other Northerners, expected the war to be short. After all, the South had merely a third of the North's military-age population and perhaps only a tenth of its manufacturing capacity.

By July 1861, thirty-five thousand troops had assembled in and around Washington, DC Organized into the Army of Northeastern Virginia under Brig. Gen. Irvin McDowell, this force represented the largest field command yet gathered on the North American continent. It was also quite green, however, and when McDowell, pressured by impatient politicians, took it out for its first spin around Virginia, this inexperience proved decisive. On July 21, at the first battle of Bull Run, Confederate troops guarding the important rail junction at Manassas routed the Union force—making it clear that, after all, the war would not be a short one.

In early 1861, *the United States had a tiny professional army. By July, however, Irvin McDowell was commanding the largest troop formation ever seen in North America.*

I. DEFINING GLOBALIZATION

AMONG THE PROMINENT buzzwords of the new millennium, *globalization* is surely the most hotly contested. It seems that every new economic development, favorable or unfavorable, is attributable to this process, and people are quick to take sides for or against it. World leaders hold international meetings to promote globalization, while antiglobalizers protest the effect it is having on the world. Few people, however, whether for or against the process, are able to define specifically what *globalization* means.

Some politicians have defined globalization simply as an increase in world trade, but this definition fails to take into account the many other possible causes for increased trade among nations. If an inventor were to make a technological breakthrough that raised worker productivity, for example, the world supply of goods would also rise. This, in turn, would increase world trade, but not because of globalization.

Others, mainly antiglobalizers, have tried to define globalization by the frictions it creates in the global economy. They make use of politically weighted phrases such as *fair trade* and *race to the bottom*, but these describe their critical opinion of globalization rather than the process itself.

Scholars generally define globalization as an increase in world integration. The emphasis is typically placed on economic integration, because most scholars believe that globalization is triggered by the removal of trade barriers and works primarily through economic channels. Yet they also recognize that the process affects cultural, social, and political systems as well.

As an example of this integration, consider the world market in milk and milk products (such as powdered milk, cheese, and butter). A recent drought in Australia reduced the amount of grass on which Australian dairy cows could feed, thus limiting the amount of milk these cows produced for export. At the same time, a new tax levied by the government of Argentina raised the price of the milk the country exported, thereby decreasing Argentine milk sales worldwide. These two developments produced a supply shortage in the world market, which dairy farmers in Europe couldn't fill because of strict production quotas set by the European Union. In China, meanwhile, demand for milk and milk products increased as rising income levels drove higher per-capita consumption. All these occurrences may have seemed isolated and unimportant to the average consumer, but they were actually closely connected through globalization and resulted in a strong upward pressure on the price of milk everywhere.

Globalization is best defined *as an increase in world integration. It relates most directly to national economies but also affects cultural, social, and political systems.*

I. PRECURSORS

DURING THE COLONIAL PERIOD and into the first few decades of the new republic, the best way to earn a living as an artist in America was to paint portraits. Newly wealthy Americans considered oil portraits of themselves and their families important symbols of social status, and they eagerly commissioned works from John Singleton Copley, Gilbert Stuart, and Charles Willson Peale, among others. One does, however, occasionally find an example of colonial-era landscape work in the background of portraits or historical scenes. Some colonial artists even produced views of cities, such as William Burgis's *A South East View of Ye Great Town of Boston in New England in America* (ca. 1722). But these works were primarily topographical in nature, intended to document a particular place and its inhabitants rather than express an aesthetic point of view.

Attitudes began to change about the time that settlers began moving westward beyond the borders of the original colonies. The spirit of exploration that this migration engendered combined with an increasing awareness of nationhood to produce a new interest in the American landscape as a subject for art. Understandably, the most popular subjects were those landforms perceived to be uniquely (or at least familiarly) American: the Catskill Mountains, the Hudson River Valley, the Adirondacks, the Appalachians. During the early nineteenth century, most of these areas were still wilderness, inspiring a sense of awe but also a desire to domesticate.

Thomas Doughty, *Fanciful Landscape* (1834)

Early landscape painters such as English-born Joshua Shaw and Irish-born William Guy Wall celebrated these rugged landscapes in portfolios of engravings published during the early 1820s. Meanwhile, Thomas Doughty of Philadelphia became the first American-born painter to work exclusively in landscapes, exhibiting frequently at the Pennsylvania Academy of Fine Arts, the National Academy of Design in New York City, and the Boston Athenaeum. Working contemporaneously, Shaw, Wall, and Doughty established the first conventions of American landscape painting, grounded primarily in the European (especially English) landscape tradition.

Portraiture was the predominant mode of painting in America until the early nineteenth century, when a few artists began to focus on the landscape.

I. THE FIRST ASTRONOMERS

SINCE THE DAWN OF TIME, people have gazed up at the sky and marveled at what they saw. Gradually, they discerned patterns and used these patterns to order their daily lives. Some of the earliest astronomical records we have found date from the beginning of the third millennium BCE, when the Egyptians used observed astronomical patterns to anticipate the annual flooding of the Nile. Other cultures recorded similar astronomical patterns in great detail. Typically, these early cultures explained what they saw in terms of the supernatural. By the sixth century BCE, however, Greek astronomers were developing the first scientific models of the universe based largely on earlier work by the Babylonians.

A table of solar eclipses from a Mayan codex.

These early Greek astronomers knew by observation that the Sun and the Moon moved independently across the sky in regular, predictable paths. They also knew that the stars generally moved together as a single group. But they were puzzled by the behavior of a few stars that moved independently of the rest, sometimes even in the opposite direction. They called these stars planets (from the Greek word for "wanderer") and set about trying to explain their odd behavior.

During the fourth century BCE, Eudoxus of Cnidus hypothesized that the objects people saw in the heavens were actually embedded in huge transparent spheres that rotated independently, thus explaining why some of the objects moved independently of others. Because these spheres were all centered on Earth, Euxodus's theory was called geocentric. Not long afterward, around 350 BCE, Aristotle revised Eudoxus's theory to include more spheres and the idea of a divine mover (a god who moves the heavens).

Although this revised theory persisted for the next eighteen hundred years, it did not explain the observed patterns very well. So, about five hundred years after Aristotle, the Greek astronomer Ptolemy proposed a modification of Aristotle's theory. According to Ptolemy, the planets moved in epicycles, or small circles, while continuing to follow their primary Aristotelian paths. The tables of motion that Ptolemy developed based on this theory were used for centuries, but they still didn't match observed behavior very well.

Meanwhile, Aristarchus of Samos, having shown during the third century BCE that the Sun was much larger than Earth, proposed that Earth actually revolved around the Sun; but his heliocentric theory was quickly dismissed as wrongheaded.

The first scientific *models of the universe were developed in ancient Greece, with Aristotle's geocentric theory of heavenly spheres prevailing.*

I. SOME GREEK AND ROMAN HISTORY

BECAUSE GREEK MYTHOLOGY predates written records, it is impossible to know for certain when the mythmaking began. Archaeologists have been able to establish a rough time line based on non-literary sources, such as building techniques and pottery styles, but the farther back one goes in time, the more approximate such dates become. For this reason, Greco-Roman historians speak most often of "eras"—the earliest, of course, having the most uncertain dates.

Zeus, the king of the Greek gods, pictured on a ca. 350 BCE gold coin.

The first truly Greek era was the Mycenaean, which began about 1600 BCE and ended about 1100 BCE. During this period, citadels such as Mycenae, a military stronghold and cultural center, dominated southern Greece. The Mycenaeans believed in the same gods as the later Greeks, but no one knows whether they created similar myths, because they left no written records. What we do know is that the Mycenaeans themselves became fodder for myth, which is why Hesiod refers to their time as the Age of Heroes.

With the decline of Mycenae in the twelfth century BCE, Greece fell into a "dark age" that lasted until the eighth century BCE. During this time, Mycenaean architectural ruins remained highly visible throughout the Aegean world and no doubt contributed to the legends that became the basis for so much Greco-Roman mythology.

The onset of political stability and the expansion of Greek trade during the eighth century BCE marked the end of the dark age and the start of the Archaic era, during which the first written records appear, including the most important works of Greek mythology. These stories were taken quite seriously at that time.

The establishment of democracy at Athens in 505 BCE marks the beginning of the Classical era, which continued until the death of Alexander the Great in 323 BCE. During this period, myths began to be taken less literally.

After the Classical era came the Hellenistic, which lasted until the overthrow of the last independent Greek kingdom in 27 BCE. Meanwhile, the Romans began creating a history of their own, which is typically divided into two major periods: Republic and Empire. The Republican era began about 500 BCE and ended with the defeat of Marc Antony by Octavian (later Augustus Caesar) in 27 BCE.

Classical mythology *spans approximately fifteen hundred years of history, during which time attitudes among the Greeks and Romans toward myth changed considerably.*

II. THE UNION COMMAND STRUCTURE

NOT SURPRISINGLY, the Union and the Confederacy organized their armed forces in the same basic manner. The smallest tactical unit was the company, which consisted of one hundred recruits, usually from the same town or county. Ten companies formed a regiment.

Because these companies often came from neighboring towns, Civil War regiments enjoyed strong unit cohesion, which helped maintain good morale. For similar reasons, recruiters in large cities often organized regiments along ethnic lines. The Sixty-ninth New York Volunteer Infantry, for instance, consisted almost entirely of Irish immigrants. (The number of a regiment referred to the chronological order of its organization.)

Four infantry regiments made up a brigade, commanded by a brigadier general. Three or four brigades made up a division, commanded by a brigadier or a major general. Two or more divisions (typically three) made up a corps, commanded by a major general. A single corps might act in the field as a small army, but most Union armies had at least two corps.

Unlike the infantry, cavalry regiments tended to have twelve companies and were attached to divisions, corps, or armies as the tactical situation required. Artillery batteries, consisting of four to six guns, were attached to brigades, divisions, or corps.

Some regimental officers were appointed by the governor of the state that raised the regiment; others were elected by the citizen-soldiers themselves. As a result, political influence had much to do with who received a command, and many officers thus commissioned proved highly incompetent. The same proved true on the federal level, where generals commissioned by President Lincoln nevertheless had to be confirmed by the Senate. "It seems but little better than murder to give important commands to such men as Banks, Butler, McClernand, Sigel, and Lew Wallace, yet it seems impossible to prevent it," one West Point professional wrote.

Because so few Union officers were professional soldiers, the training given recruits was largely superficial. It consisted mainly of company and regimental drill in basic maneuvers, along with some instruction in skirmishing tactics. But there was little target practice and even less mock combat. The results were predictable, and the day after the first battle of Bull Run, Congress established military examining boards to weed out the worst of the new officers.

The Union suffered *from the poor leadership of "political" officers, who lacked military knowledge and thus were unfit to train inexperienced volunteers.*

The Fifth Vermont Volunteer Infantry Regiment at Camp Griffin, Virginia.

II. WHEN DID GLOBALIZATION BEGIN?

THERE ARE AS MANY different starting dates for globalization as there are definitions of the term, in part because different definitions suggest different starting points. According to Nayan Chanda of the Yale Center for the Study of Globalization, globalization began eight thousand years ago, because by that time all the forces that would push the process forward were already in place. "Essentially," Chanda wrote in his 2007 book *Bound Together*, "the basic motivations that propelled humans to connect with others—the urge to profit by trading, the drive to spread religious belief, the desire to exploit new lands, and the ambition to dominate others by armed might—all had been assembled by 6000 BCE to start the process we now call globalization."

Other proposed starting dates include Christopher Columbus's discovery of the New World in 1492; the first circumnavigation of the globe, completed in 1522; the Industrial Revolution, which began during the late eighteenth century; the adoption of the prime meridian and the international date line in 1884; and the fall of the Berlin Wall in 1989.

According to the World Bank, there have been three "waves" of globalization. The first began in 1870 and lasted until the start of World War I in 1914. Brought about by reductions in trade barriers and advances in transportation technology, it resulted in vast migrations of people amounting to 10 percent of the world's population. The second wave, which lasted from 1950 to 1980, was characterized by multilateral trade agreements among developed nations that essentially left out the developing world. In contrast, the third (and current) wave of globalization, which began in 1980, has been characterized by the willingness of large developing countries to adopt trade liberalization in order to attract foreign capital.

In a 2002 *European Review of Economic History* article, economists Kevin H. O'Rourke and Jeffrey G. Williamson attempted to calculate a starting date for globalization by analyzing four centuries of historical data. Their premise was that in a globalized world, the prices of goods and services would be determined solely by global supply and demand. Therefore, as globalization progressed, price levels in different countries should converge. Using data from 1565 to 1936, O'Rourke and Williamson found that price convergence began around 1820.

This starting date of 1820 is as reasonable as any, and it fits the current academic consensus that globalization—narrowly defined as world economic integration—began sometime between 1820 and 1870.

The starting date given to globalization depends on one's definition of the term, but most scholars agree that the process began between 1820 and 1870.

II. EUROPEAN ROOTS

AMERICAN LANDSCAPE PAINTERS of the early nineteenth century, new to the genre, understandably turned to Europe for inspiration. What they found was the cultural movement known as romanticism, then sweeping the Continent. A reaction to the Enlightenment, which emphasized the scientific rationalization of nature, romanticism stressed emotional responses—especially trepidation, horror,

J. M. W. Turner, *Snow Storm, Hannibal and His Army Crossing the Alps* (ca. 1812)

and awe—to the sublime power of the natural world. In terms of landscape painting, the romantic movement informed three crucial aesthetic ideals that guided American painters: the pastoral (also known as the beautiful), the sublime, and the picturesque.

Pastoral landscapes present nature in an idealized form, as a paradise, and the human figures they contain are integrated into the landscape in such a way as to suggest strongly a harmony between man and nature. The seventeenth-century French painter Claude Lorrain is generally credited with formalizing this approach, which profoundly influenced the work of English artists during the eighteenth century.

Opposed to the pastoral in aesthetic terms is the sublime, which presents nature as so great and awesome as to be dangerous and terrifying. In sublime landscapes, man has little significance. Instead, steep cliffs, craggy peaks, threatening clouds, and trees blasted by lightning evoke the desolation and solitude of the wilderness. Seventeenth-century Italian painter Salvatore Rosa believed that contemplation of the sublime led to a more elevated experience of nature verging on the spiritual. His work became an important source for the English artist J. M. W. Turner and later the American Thomas Cole.

The concept of the picturesque was first articulated by English clergyman William Gilpin in his 1768 "Essay on Prints," which defined the picturesque as "that kind of beauty which is agreeable in a picture." Essentially, picturesque paintings are defined by the pleasure one takes in viewing them. In more formal terms, the picturesque borrows from both the pastoral and the sublime, taking from the pastoral an idealized, humanized nature and from the sublime a sense of drama. The landscapes of English artist John Constable show particularly well the balance valued by the picturesque ideal.

American artists became aware of these concepts through study abroad and the reading of English works on aesthetics. They made use of all three sets of conventions in their work but were especially taken with the sublime and the picturesque.

The roots of American landscape painting *can be found in eighteenth-century European aesthetics, especially in the concepts of the pastoral, the sublime, and the picturesque.*

II. ASTRONOMERS OF THE RENAISSANCE

EARLY IN THE SIXTEENTH CENTURY, the Polish astronomer Nicolaus Copernicus quietly revived the heliocentric theory proposed by Aristarchus. Using a Sun-centered model better explained why planets appeared to move backward against the motion of the stars, and it also allowed Copernicus to work out the distance to each planet and its orbital period (the time necessary to complete a single revolution around the Sun). Yet Copernicus was reluctant to publish his work because he feared repercussions. Although fellow astronomers might be prepared to embrace his heliocentrism, he knew that the Roman Catholic Church, which dominated Europe politically as well as religiously, was not. The church considered heliocentrism a form of heresy, and it punished such heretics with persecution and even death.

Brahe used this sextant to measure the altitude of astronomical bodies above the horizon.

Tycho Brahe, a son of Danish nobility, was fourteen years old in 1560, when he witnessed a solar eclipse. The event so impressed him that he decided to dedicate the remainder of his life to astronomy. Early in his career, Brahe noticed that Ptolemy's planetary tables were severely in error, so he set about devising more accurate tables. Because the telescope had not yet been invented, he constructed huge quadrants (as large as small houses) to record precisely the changing positions of the planets and the stars. In doing so, he was able to make the connection between a supernova he observed in 1572 and the star he had previously observed at the same location. His conclusion—that stars were not constant but changed over time—was revolutionary.

Brahe also introduced the idea that comets had elliptical orbits that passed through the orbits of the planets. Although he didn't favor heliocentrism himself, Brahe did realize that his comet theory contradicted the prevailing Aristotelian notion of heavenly spheres. Brahe's comet theory, in fact, led him to create a model of the universe quite similar to that of Copernicus—except that in Brahe's model, Earth was at rest. According to Brahe, the planets orbited the Sun, and the Sun orbited Earth.

During the final years of his life, Brahe was assisted by Johannes Kepler. As the result of a childhood illness, Kepler had very poor eyesight, which made him a poor observer, but he was an excellent mathematician. Using Brahe's observations to test his own theories, Kepler developed over many years the Laws of Planetary Motion that made him famous and are still used today to describe the motion of the planets around the Sun.

During the Renaissance, *conceptions of the universe were altered dramatically by the work of Nicolaus Copernicus, Tycho Brahe, and Johannes Kepler.*

II. WHAT IS MYTH?

ANCIENT GREEKS AND ROMANS did not think like twenty-first-century Americans. To understand them, therefore, we need to get inside the "mind" of their cultures and think as they did. Fortunately, the myths that they left behind provide a useful record of their cultural worldviews.

One of the most important differences between ancient and modern is our understanding of what myth actually means. When we hear the word *myth*, we think of something fictional, a fantastical story filled with magic. The story that we think of is always false, but that is not how myth was understood in the ancient world.

The English word *myth* is derived from the Greek word *muthos*, which meant "story" or "narrative." Significantly, the Greek word has no truth-value attached to it. Referring to a story as a myth in ancient Greece said nothing about whether it was true or not. It could have been both, either, or neither. Greeks simply didn't make a distinction.

In Archaic Greece, there was no history, no mathematics, no philosophy as we know these disciplines today. There was only myth, which took the form of sung poetry. The poems weren't even written down at first but passed from generation to generation as an oral tradition. The stories contained in the myths recorded the "fames," or great deeds, of Greek culture. There were two types: *klea andrōn*, the fames of men, and *klea theōn*, the fames of gods.

During the Classical period, the Greeks developed two new disciplines of thought, history and philosophy, both of which asserted a specific truth-value. They were *not* fiction and thus defined themselves in opposition to poetic myth. Philosophy, for instance, was based on verifiable reason (*logos* in Greek, from which the English word *logic* is derived), whereas myth was deemed unverifiable.

As the Classical era came to a close, the ancient myths remained very popular, but they had lost much of their mystical power. For the most part, they had become forms of entertainment, allegories and satires, rather than tales of import.

The Greek word muthos *(from which we derive the English word* myth*) meant "story," but not necessarily a false one.*

A detail from a sixth-century BCE vase showing a centaur.

III. GRANT IN 1861

AFTER HIS GRADUATION from West Point in 1843, Lt. Ulysses S. Grant served with distinction in the Mexican War, earning a commendation from Robert E. Lee. He was subsequently promoted to captain and posted to Fort Humboldt, a remote frontier outpost in northern California. In 1854, however, Grant left the army. During the next six years, he tried his hand at a number of business ventures, all of which failed. By 1860, he was forced to accept a job offer from his prosperous father: working as a clerk in a general store the family owned in Galena, Illinois.

Grant had resigned his commission under murky circumstances. Certainly, he had been unhappy at Fort Humboldt. In addition to disliking the post commander and finding the duty extremely boring, he was homesick, separated from his family and lacking the financial resources to bring his wife and children out west. As a result,

Grant fighting in Mexico City during the Mexican War.

he often drank heavily, and there were stories (which Grant could never shake) that the post commander had forced the resignation because of Grant's growing alcoholism.

Following President Lincoln's April 15 call for seventy-five thousand troops, Grant began organizing a company of Galena volunteers, which soon offered him the captaincy. But Grant declined, feeling that he would be humiliated if returned to military service at the same rank that he had held when he left. What Grant most wanted were a colonelcy and command of a regiment.

While a local congressman made Grant's case to Illinois governor Richard Yates, Grant himself wrote to the adjutant general in Washington, applying for a new regular-army commission, adding that he felt "competent to command a regiment." Although Grant never heard back from Washington, Yates soon offered him the job of mustering in new regiments around the state.

A month passed, and with no regiment of his own forthcoming, Grant began to lose hope. In fact, he was preparing to return home to Galena when the junior officers of a regiment he had mustered in, the Twenty-first Illinois, complained to Governor Yates that their colonel was an incompetent drunkard. Recalling with favor the man who had mustered them in several weeks previously, they asked Yates for Grant, and the governor complied, making the necessary appointment on June 15, 1861. Years later, Grant often took pleasure in citing the adage that the man doesn't seek the office, the office seeks the man.

At the time the war broke out, *Ulysses S. Grant was considered a failure in both his military and his civilian careers.*

III. THE BARRIERS TO INTERNATIONAL TRADE

THE MOST COMMON barriers to international trade are tariffs. These are taxes imposed by a country on imported goods (and sometimes exported goods as well). The two main reasons for imposing tariffs are to protect a sector of the domestic economy from foreign competition and to generate revenue for the government.

Import tariffs shield domestic producers from foreign competition by artificially raising the cost of cheaper imported goods. This type of protectionism is often justified by the "infant industry" argument, which holds that new industries need to be sheltered until they reach maturity and only then become able to compete in the ruthless international marketplace.

The revenue-raising aspect of tariffs is negligible in most developed countries, but in the developing world, tariffs are a crucial source of government income. Unlike other taxes, which can be easily avoided, tariffs are collected at the border and thus are much more difficult to evade. In some African countries, tariff revenues account for as much as 30 percent of all government income.

Within a particular country, tariffs redistribute wealth from domestic consumers, who pay higher prices for protected goods, to domestic producers and the government. Overall, however, they shrink a nation's wealth, because they cost consumers more than they benefit producers and the government.

The most common nontariff barriers are import quotas, which cap the quantity of goods that can be imported into a particular country. Sometimes, the threat of an import quota is enough to cause the adoption of "voluntary" restrictions by exporters, which achieve the same result. During the early 1980s, for example, Japan voluntarily limited its automobile exports to the United States in order to forestall threatened US trade sanctions.

Other nontariff barriers work, as tariffs do, to increase the cost of bringing imported goods to market. Local content requirements may specify that domestically sold goods have to contain a certain amount of domestic raw materials and/or domestic labor. In Canada, radio and television stations are required to air a minimum amount of Canadian-made programming. Technical and product standards can also favor domestic goods over foreign imports. The European Union prohibits the importation of any beef produced using growth hormones. The rationale for this standard is the health of the human consumer, but sanitation, product safety, and the health of the environment are also commonly used justifications.

Protectionism can take many forms. Tariffs are the most common, but numerous non-tariff barriers exist as well, such as import quotas and local content requirements.

III. THOMAS COLE

ALTHOUGH NOT THE FIRST American artist to dedicate himself to landscapes, Thomas Cole (1801–48) became known as the father of American landscape painting because he was the first American to combine successfully European romantic aesthetics (particularly the sublime) with subjects that were recognizably American in character. In doing so, Cole founded the first truly native school of American art.

Born in England, he migrated with his family to the United States in 1818. Continuing inland to the frontier, the Coles settled in Ohio, where Thomas learned the rudiments of painting and became, for a time, an itinerant portraitist. By 1825, he had moved to New York City, then as now an artistic center, and that year he took his first trip up the Hudson River to the Catskills. Shortly after his return, Cole exhibited three Catskill scenes in the window of a framer's gallery. When two of these were snapped up by influential members of the New York art establishment—John Trumbull and Asher B. Durand—Cole's work became an overnight sensation.

Cole's focus on American landforms, particularly scenes of the wilderness, came at an opportune time commercially. Middle- and upper-class families faced with rapid urbanization were beginning to see the wilderness as a welcome respite from the crush of cities, and the Catskills, in particular, were becoming a popular vacation destination. Cole's landscapes brought to life this scenery and tapped into a growing national pride in the country's unique and (as yet) unspoiled natural landscape.

Most Europeans at the time viewed the American landscape through the prism of the sublime as awe-inspiring but rough and uncultivated—lacking, that is, the sort of humanized, historical associations that make pastoral and picturesque works attractive. Cole objected to this view and spent the better part of his career refuting it. In the absence of the sort of ancient ruins favored by European landscape artists, Cole frequently included in his paintings natural ruins—for example, tree trunks "blasted" by lightning—to symbolize America's poignant, if brief, history and the majesty of its landscape.

Recognized as the *father of American landscape painting, Thomas Cole adapted European ideals to create his early scenes of the Hudson River Valley and Catskills.*

Thomas Cole, *The Oxbow* (1836)

III. GALILEO AND NEWTON

WHILE BRAHE AND KEPLER worked at the court of Holy
Roman Emperor Rudolf II in Prague, Galileo Galilei
(whom many consider the father of modern science)
was hard at work himself, studying the heavens at his
villa outside Florence. An early proponent of the use of
mathematics to describe physical phenomena, Galileo
rejected the prevailing idea that scientific theories need
only be consistent with church doctrine to be considered

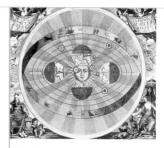

A heliocentric map of the
solar system from 1660.

true. Instead, he believed that theories had to be supported by experimental or
observational evidence if they were to be accepted.

In 1608, Galileo learned of a distance-viewing device recently invented by
Dutch lens maker Hans Lippershey. Working from rough sketches, Galileo refined
Lippershey's design for astronomical use and trained the resulting telescope on the
night sky. Immediately, he saw that the Moon was not a perfectly smooth sphere
as previously supposed but actually a large rock covered with craters. Observing
Jupiter, he saw four small objects orbiting the planet, thus discovering the four
largest Jovian moons. Similarly, he became the first human to observe the rings
of Saturn and the phases of Venus.

Like Kepler, Galileo believed strongly in heliocentrism, and his vocal support
for that theory soon brought him into conflict with the Roman Catholic Church.
Although Galileo possessed influential friends, he was nevertheless forced to stand
trial before the Inquisition in 1633. Found guilty, he was ordered to recant his ideas
(which were banned) and placed under house arrest for the remainder of his life.

Born in 1643, a year after Galileo's death, Isaac Newton eventually rose to
occupy the same pinnacle of physical science that Galileo had. Among Newton's
greatest achievements was his theory of universal gravitation, which described
mathematically the force that holds the planets in orbit around the Sun. In fact,
Newton coined the word *gravity*.

Legend has it that Newton was initially inspired by watching an apple fall
from a tree. His observation led to the idea that the force that had caused the apple
to fall straight down might also be the force that holds planets in orbit. Building on
Kepler's Laws of Planetary Motion and Galileo's discovery that all objects accelerate
at the same rate, Newton was able to define and quantify the gravitational force and
also develop his own laws of motion, which are still used to describe the relationship
between force and motion.

Although Galileo *was imprisoned for advocating heliocentrism, a generation later
Newton was called a genius for his heliocentric Theory of Universal Gravitation.*

III. THE MUSES

COMPOSED DURING THE ARCHAIC PERIOD, Hesiod's *Theogony* was one of the first mythological accounts of the Greco-Roman world. At the time, there was no history, no philosophy, no staged drama. These wouldn't exist for another century or more. There was only poetry. Thus, the works of Hesiod, Homer, and others had to bear the cultural burden of preserving Greek memory, most importantly through myth. In fact, the function of myth was so deeply ingrained in Greek culture that the word for truth was *alētheia*, which meant literally "not forgetting." Truth was that which was remembered, and in a very real sense the preliterate Greeks used myth to "not forget" their past.

The stories in *Theogony* (which means "birth of the gods") explain the creation of the universe, but perhaps the most important section is the poem's long invocation to the Muses. According to Hesiod, the Muses were the nine daughters of Zeus, the king of the Olympian gods, and his aunt Mnēmosynē (Memory). All were patrons of the arts, and Hesiod credits them with teaching him, just a lowly shepherd, how to sing the stories of gods and men.

A carving of the Muses on a second-century CE marble sarcophagus.

The Muses, wrote Hesiod, "sing for Zeus Father / They thrill the great mind deep in Olympos / Telling what is, what will be, and what has been." They also "move in the dance, intoning / The careful ways of the gods, celebrating the customs / Of all the Immortals in a voice enchanting and sweet." In other words, the Muses are responsible for both facilitating memory and doing so in an entertaining fashion. Like all gods, however, they are under no obligation to communicate clearly to mortals: "We know how to tell many believable lies. / But also, when we want to, how to speak the plain truth."

To the ancient Greeks, poets acted as agents of the Muses in the human world. Like seers and oracles, they were not considered creative artists but rather vessels for the knowledge and creativity of the gods. Their gift of "sweet-tongued words," to use Hesiod's famous phrase, reflected a magical power to call upon the Muses for memories of the past, which the poets sang about in their songs. However, because the information came from the gods, its meaning could be deceptive.

It was through poetry, *inspired by the Muses, that Archaic Greeks remembered both their history and their culture.*

IV. GRANT IN COMMAND

GRANT'S FIRST TASK as commanding officer of the Twenty-first Illinois Volunteer Infantry was to transform its 1,250 men from an armed gang into a disciplined military force. His strategy was to be quiet but firm. He began by removing the armed guards that his predecessor had stationed around the perimeter of the camp to keep the men from coming and going as they pleased. Then he issued orders for thrice-daily drills, at which every man in the regiment would have to be present. During the first few days of this new regime, truants filled the guardhouse, but quickly the men got Grant's message: The new colonel meant business.

Grant as a newly promoted brigadier general.

After just three weeks of drill under Grant, the regiment was sent on its first mission: to subdue a band of secessionists across the Mississippi River in northern Missouri. These irregular home guards, under the command of Col. Thomas Harris, were reportedly encamped outside the town of Florida.

Despite the extensive combat experience he had gained during the Mexican War, Grant was apprehensive. He had never served as top commander during a battle before and thus felt unsure about his capabilities. "As we approached the brow of the hill," he wrote in his memoirs,

> my heart kept getting higher and higher until it felt to me as though it was in my throat. I would have given anything then to have been back in Illinois, but I had not the moral courage to halt and consider what to do; I kept right on. When we reached a point from which the valley below was in full view I halted. The place where Harris had been encamped a few days before was still there and the marks of a recent encampment were plainly visible, but the troops were gone. My heart resumed its place. It occurred to me at once that Harris had been as much afraid of me as I had been of him. This was a view of the question I had never taken before; but it was one I never forgot afterwards. From that event until the close of the war, I never experienced trepidation upon confronting an enemy, though I always felt more or less anxiety. I never forgot that he had as much reason to fear my forces as I had his. The lesson was valuable.

Grant was a quiet *but firm commander who understood that the enemy feared him as much as he might fear the enemy.*

IV. MEASURING GLOBALIZATION

GLOBALIZATION STATISTICS are usually grouped into four categories: the flow of goods and services, the flow of capital, the flow of people, and the flow of knowledge. Typically, these statistics are kept by national governments and therefore relate to a particular country rather than to the global economy as a whole. For example, the flow of goods and services is usually measured by adding together the value of a country's imports and exports and then expressing the sum as a percentage of national income. The flows of capital and people are measured in a similar but slightly different way: These reflect net migration (inflows minus outflows), expressed as percentages of total national income and total national population, respectively. The flow of knowledge is much more difficult to measure, which is why proxies such as patent registrations are often used.

Two well-known indices use these statistics to compile annual globalization rankings. The index compiled by the Swiss think tank KOF measures three economic, social, and political factors. The economic component incorporates data not only on trade and capital flow but also on trade and capital restrictions, such as tariffs and banking regulations. The social component reflects data on personal contacts (such as international telephone traffic), information flow (such as the amount of Internet access in a particular country), and cultural proximity, which measures the extent to which the residents of different countries feel that they share a common identity. (This sense of affinity can be measured, for example, in the proliferation of McDonald's restaurants.) The political component makes use of diplomatic data, such as the number of embassies in a particular country and its participation in UN Security Council missions. According to the 2007 KOF index, the five most globalized countries were Belgium, Austria, Sweden, the United Kingdom, and the Netherlands. The five least globalized were Burundi, the Central African Republic, Myanmar, Haiti, and Rwanda.

The second major globalization index, published jointly by management consultants A. T. Kearney and *Foreign Policy* magazine, tracks four factors: political engagement, technological connectivity, personal contact, and economic integration. Making use of somewhat different data, the 2007 ATK/FP index ranked Singapore, Hong Kong, the Netherlands, Switzerland, and Ireland as the five most globalized countries. The five least globalized were Iran, India, Algeria, Indonesia, and Venezuela. It doesn't take much effort to recognize that there is almost no overlap at the top and bottom of the two indices. Therefore, although such rankings may be handy, their reliability is open to question.

Because most statistics are kept by national governments, they relate primarily to the country keeping them, and thus their applicability to the global economy is limited.

IV. THE COURSE OF EMPIRE

COLE'S EARLY SUCCESS gave him the confidence and wherewithal to pursue what he called a "higher kind of landscape." Thus, as his career developed, he moved away from depictions of specifically American scenery to works that were more imaginary in scope. This shift in styles, though it led to a decline in his public popularity, only enhanced his influence among his fellow artists.

Cole's transformation began during a trip he made to England in 1829, during which he visited the studios of John Martin and J. M. W. Turner. Viewing their latest work inspired Cole to think about a new approach to landscape painting in which the details of the natural landscape become a backdrop for scenes with religious, moral, and even mythological themes. In 1831, Cole returned to Europe, this time visiting Italy, where he spent days sketching Roman ruins while conceiving a historical cycle of paintings that would chronicle the rise and fall of a civilization. When the five canvases were finally completed, he titled the series The Course of Empire.

The cycle, whose central theme is mankind's relationship to nature, presents man's emergence, his creation of a Roman-style civilization, its rise to power and glory, its fall into decadence, and ultimately its destruction. In the first canvas, *The Savage State*, man and nature are shown to be in conflict, but by the second canvas, *The Pastoral* or *Arcadian State*, man and nature appear in harmony. In the third canvas, *The Consummation of Empire*, man has subordinated nature, which disappears almost entirely from the scene. The fourth canvas, *Destruction*, is a masterpiece of the apocalyptic sublime, with swirling vortexes of clouds, darkened skies, and dramatic lighting effects. In the final painting, *Desolation*, it is now man who leaves the scene as nature gradually reclaims the ruins of civilization.

Thomas Cole, *Destruction* (1836)

In addition to being a masterpiece of artistic skill, Cole's cycle demonstrated conclusively that American landscape painters could, like their European counterparts, display both aesthetic quality and intellectual ambition. After visiting the first exhibition of the cycle in 1836 at the National Academy of Design, James Fenimore Cooper described *The Course of Empire* as "the work of the highest genius this country has ever produced."

Thomas Cole's *series demonstrates his belief that landscape painting should have not merely an aesthetic purpose but also a moral or spiritual quality.*

IV. OBSERVING THE UNIVERSE: LIGHT

NEARLY EVERYTHING that we know about the universe we've learned from light that arrives here on Earth in one form or another. Although light can also be thought of as packets of energy, in the astronomical sense it is defined as an electromagnetic wave with a wavelength and a frequency. Wavelength is the distance between corresponding adjacent points on a wave, such as from peak to subsequent peak or trough to subsequent trough. Frequency refers to the number of wavelengths that pass through a particular point in a given time (usually measured in cycles per second). Multiplying these two quantities together yields the speed of a wave.

The speed of light in a vacuum never changes. It's always 3.0×10^8 meters per second (m/s), or approximately 186,000 miles per second. Because this speed remains constant, so must the product of the light's wavelength and frequency. Therefore, these two quantities are inversely proportional—that is, as one goes up, the other goes down.

Normally, when people speak of light, they mean visible light. But light actually comes in a much broader range called the electromagnetic spectrum. At the low-energy end of the spectrum, light waves have low frequencies and large wavelengths. At the high-energy end, they have high frequencies and correspondingly small wavelengths. Waves of the lowest energy are called radio waves. The next three classes of light moving up the spectrum in energy are microwaves, infrared waves, and visible light. Within visible light, the colors range from red at the low-energy end through orange, yellow, green, and blue to violet at the high-energy end.

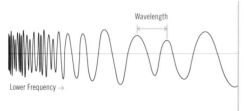

Wavelength

Lower Frequency →

A schematic of a modulating-frequency wave.

Continuing to move up in energy, the next class of light is ultraviolet. From this point on, light becomes ionizing, which means that it can alter molecules. It does this by exciting electrons in the outer shells of atoms, causing them to break free, leaving the atoms charged, or ionized. The UV radiation in sunlight, for example, can penetrate the outermost layers of your skin and cause damage that may lead to skin cancer.

Above UV light on the electromagnetic spectrum, we find X-rays, which are more energetic and therefore even more penetrating. The ability of X-rays to penetrate deeply into our bodies makes them an excellent diagnostic tool but also a dangerous one. Finally, above X-rays are gamma rays, the highest-energy light waves.

Light is the means *by which we observe the universe. Traveling at a constant speed, it is described in terms of wavelength and frequency.*

IV. THE FORMATION OF THE WORLD

THE FAMES OF GODS contained in Hesiod's *Theogony* are primarily aetiological myths, which explain the origins of things. Such myths explain human inventions (such as musical instruments), naturally existing phenomena (such as mountain ranges), and even such intangibles as desire.

The earliest deities cited by Hesiod had dual functions, acting both as personalities and as the substance of the cosmos. In the beginning, there was Chaos (the Greek word for "abyss" or "emptiness"). Out of Chaos, there emerged Gaia, Tartaros, and Eros.

When translated into English, the name *Gaia* means "Earth." *Tartaros* has no direct English translation, but it similarly refers to a place. Often, Tartaros is likened to the Judeo-Christian Hell, but more accurately it is the "bottom" of the world—as far beneath the earth as the sky is above it. *Eros*, the name of the third primordial god, means "desire." Sexual desire is certainly an important aspect of Eros, but he also embodies the desire for something different from what already exists and thus fosters change.

Soon after her own appearance, Gaia gave birth (immaculately) to Ouronos, whose name means "sky" or "heaven." Ouronos's creation thus completed the basic plan of the world. Gaia subsequently bore two more children, the mountains that frame the earth and the raging sea, after which it fell to Eros to fill in the rest.

Eros did so by filling Ouronos with an irresistible desire for Gaia, which caused them to procreate. Their children included Oceanos (Ocean)—which, unlike the primordial Sea, the Greeks thought of as a giant river circling the earth and providing all of its fresh water. Other important children were Mnēmosynē (Memory), Themis (Eternal Law), Hyperion (the Sun), and Cronos (Time).

Finally, Ouronos and Gaia gave birth to three Cyclopes, ill-tempered creatures with a single eye in the center of their foreheads, and to three other beings of enormous strength with fifty heads and one hundred hands. Usually referred to simply as the Hundred-Handers, these latter creatures were so gruesome and terrifying that Ouronos hid them in Tartaros.

Aetiological myths explain the origins of objects found in the world as well as the creation of the natural world itself.

V. GRANT IN THE WEST

REPORTS OF GRANT'S effectiveness at maintaining discipline spread quickly, and in August 1861 he was promoted unexpectedly to brigadier general. The appointment came directly from President Lincoln, who knew nothing of Grant but had asked several Illinois congressmen for a recommendation.

Given command of southeastern Missouri, Grant made his headquarters at Cape Girardeau. At first, the assignment seemed inconsequential, but on September 3, Brig. Gen. Gideon Pillow led a Rebel force into neutral Kentucky, seizing the Mississippi River towns of Hickman and Columbus. While Kentucky governor Beriah Magoffin protested the invasion and demanded Pillow's withdrawal, Grant entered Kentucky himself, crossing the Ohio River and occupying Paducah.

A Currier & Ives lithograph of Grant storming Fort Donelson.

This display of initiative caught the attention of Grant's superiors, who put him in charge of a large river expedition being planned for the spring. Its immediate purpose was to reduce two troublesome forts, Henry and Donelson, which guarded the Tennessee and Cumberland Rivers, respectively. The two forts sat across from each other on a well-defended peninsula just south of the rivers' convergence on the Kentucky-Tennessee border. Their capture would open up a path for Union troops straight into the heart of Tennessee.

Fort Henry succumbed easily on February 6, but Donelson—with a garrison of fifteen thousand men under Pillow, John B. Floyd, and Simon Bolivar Buckner—proved much more resistant. Grant had used four ironclads to overwhelm Henry, and on February 14 he sent the same gunboats against Donelson. This time, they were driven off, and the next day a Rebel counterattack punched a hole in the Union lines, opening an escape route. This hard-won window closed, however, when Grant filled the gap before the Southern commanders took advantage of it.

That night, Floyd and Pillow fled. In the morning, Buckner, hoping for some leniency from his West Point classmate, asked Grant for a truce. Grant's reply was so unbending that it begat a famous nickname. "Sir: Yours of this date, proposing armistice and appointment of Commissioners to settle terms of capitulation, is just received. No terms except an unconditional and immediate surrender can be accepted. I propose to move immediately upon your works. Your obedient servant, U. S. Grant." Henceforth, the general was known as "Unconditional Surrender" Grant.

Early successes in Kentucky and Tennessee earned Grant a reputation as one of the most aggressive commanders in the western theater.

V. THE BENEFITS OF TRADE

INTERNATIONAL TRADE offers each participating country the opportunity to specialize in goods and services that it can produce at a relative cost advantage compared with other countries. For example, with regard to wine production, a country with a grape-friendly climate, such as France, has a comparative advantage over an arid country, such as Israel. On the other hand, Israel's hot climate gives it a comparative advantage over France in citrus fruit production.

Without international trade, each country would have to meet all of its needs domestically. In other words, France would have to grow its own oranges, and Israel would have to make its own Beaujolais. Even if this were possible, it would clearly be inefficient. Instead, it makes much more sense for France to specialize in wine, for Israel to specialize in citrus, and for the two countries to trade. In this way, productivity is maximized, and the standards of living in both countries rise.

With specialization, of course, comes greater efficiency, allowing countries that specialize to produce more goods at a lower cost. At the same time, access to foreign markets helps smaller countries achieve economies of scale that domestic markets could not support. The market for cocoa in Ghana, for example, is relatively small, but the fact that Ghanaian cocoa producers have access to foreign markets enables them to benefit from the reduced costs that mass production brings.

Trade between the developed and the developing world is usually based on the comparative advantages that developed countries have in technology and developing countries have in raw materials and labor. Developed countries tend to import from developing countries natural resources (such as oil), agricultural staples, and simple manufactured goods (such as textiles). In exchange, they export a lot of high-tech machinery (such as manufacturing equipment) and consumer goods (such as cell phones). These exchanges are indispensable for the economies involved, rich and poor alike.

Other benefits of trade include a wider range of choices for consumers. Were it not for international trade, North Americans wouldn't be able to purchase bananas during the winter or chocolate at any time. Yet there is more to the global economy than simply the international market in goods and services. Global trade is also a marketplace in which ideas, technologies, and lifestyles are exchanged. Some argue that, while influencing taste and broadening cultural boundaries, global interchange also encourages peace—because openness to trade promotes economic development, which promotes prosperity, which promotes peace.

International trade *allows nations to specialize in particular industries by relieving them of the need to meet all of their domestic requirements with domestic goods.*

V. KINDRED SPIRITS

IN 1811, at the age of seventeen, William Cullen Bryant wrote the poem "Thanatopsis." Its publication six years later earned Bryant national acclaim. By that time, however, he had begun building a career for himself as a lawyer in

Asher B. Durand, *Kindred Spirits* (1849)

Great Barrington, Massachusetts. Still, he never gave up the dream of earning a living as a writer, and in 1825 he moved to New York City to work as the editor of a short-lived literary review.

That same year, Bryant met Thomas Cole after Cole's return from the Catskills. The two young intellectuals became fast friends and soon welcomed into their circle the engraver Asher B. Durand, who had already made his reputation by engraving John Trumbull's *Declaration of Independence* (which now appears on the one-dollar bill). It was this friendship, which meant so much to America's intellectual and artistic development, that Durand memorialized in his 1849 painting *Kindred Spirits*.

The painting, one of the most beloved of American landscapes, was commissioned in 1848, the year of Cole's death, to commemorate the funeral oration delivered by Bryant at the National Academy of Design. Bryant's eulogy memorialized Cole as a national hero for his role in developing a uniquely American school of art. In *Kindred Spirits*, Durand places Cole and Bryant atop a promontory commanding a spectacular view of magnificent Catskill scenery. The painting eschews the overt religious and moral symbolism that characterized Cole's later work but still conveys the idea that solace and spiritual enlightenment can be found in the sublime American wilderness.

In this way, Durand's painting expresses the shared approach of the three men to nature and the American landscape. All three saw the country's unspoiled wilderness as a sacred place, close communion with which could bring not only joy but also enlightenment. This larger meaning of nature had been the message of Bryant's "Thanatopsis," and it was also the point of writings by Cole and Durand, whose essays on nature and the American landscape were published widely.

Even though *Kindred Spirits* ostensibly commemorated Cole's contribution to American landscape art, it simultaneously marked the passing of Cole's mantle to Durand, the new dean of what later became known as the Hudson River School.

Cole, Durand, and Bryant *were close friends who believed that nature contained an underlying spirituality capable of improving mankind through close association.*

V. OBSERVING THE UNIVERSE: TELESCOPES

THE FIRST TELESCOPE developed by Galileo was a simple affair that used a series of lenses to focus visible light into an eyepiece. This type of telescope was called a refracting telescope because it refracted, or bent, light. As time went on, astronomers fitted refracting telescopes with larger and larger lenses to gather more light and see objects more clearly. However, refracting telescopes had an important limitation: Because each color in the visible spectrum refracts at a slightly different angle, larger lenses began to produce a slight distortion called chromatic aberration.

To eliminate this distortion, astronomers designed a new telescope that used mirrors to reflect light instead of lenses to bend it. In these reflecting telescopes, light was reflected off a curved mirror at the back of the telescope onto smaller mirrors that, in turn, bounced the waves into an eyepiece.

Eventually, astronomers realized that they needn't limit themselves to visible light when the rest of the electromagnetic spectrum was also available to them. Radio telescopes, for instance, produced tremendous advances in observational astronomy after coming online in the 1930s. Visible light is sometimes absorbed by gas clouds or blocked by space dust, but radio waves simply pass through these obstacles. Therefore, they can reveal much more about the universe than visible light does.

A radio telescope consists of a large dish antenna that collects radio waves and transmits them to a computer, which records and analyzes the signals. Often multiple dishes are linked to form an array, which allows the signals they receive to be analyzed together. One such array, among the largest in the world, links ten radio telescopes in locations from the Virgin Islands to Hawaii, a distance of five thousand miles.

Sometimes, Earth's atmosphere restricts what a telescope can see. Although generally transparent to both radio and visible light waves, the atmosphere is opaque to most other electromagnetic waves, and even visible light can be blocked by water vapor (clouds) and light pollution. So, during the last quarter century, astronomers began looking beyond ground-based telescopes to space-based instruments. Examples now include the Chandra X-Ray Observatory, the Compton Gamma-Ray Observatory, and the Hubble Space Telescope. Since its launch in 1990, the Hubble has collected infrared, visible light, and ultraviolet radiation, from which it has formed images of astronomical objects never seen before.

The Eagle Nebula as seen by the Hubble Space Telescope.

Astronomers observe *the universe using telescopes that receive and analyze light ranging across the electromagnetic spectrum, from radio waves to X-rays.*

V. THE TITANS

THE WORLD under Ouronos was a wild, savage place, and the sky god was far from benevolent. In addition to hiding the Hundred-Handers in Tartaros, he mistreated several other of his children with Gaia, burying them in their mother's belly. Hesiod gives no reason for this practice other than Ouronos's own savage pleasure.

Pained by Ouronos's cruelty, Gaia crafted a blade of flint to be wielded against him. Her son Cronos volunteered to use it; and when his father came to bed his mother one night, Cronos used the blade to cut off his father's genitalia. Thus rendered impotent, Ouronos had no choice but to cede his rule of the world to Cronos.

Zeus, Hera, and Athena battle the Titans on a fifth-century BCE vase.

Cronos and his siblings, whom Ouronos henceforth termed Titans (meaning "overreachers"), turned out to be just as violent as their father. Under their rule, for example, justice was absolute and unmitigated. According to Hesiod, when Cronos cut Ouronos, some of his father's blood fell on his mother, giving birth to the Erinyes (Furies). These grotesque, winged females became the epitome of unmitigated Titan justice. They relentlessly pursued those guilty of crimes against their own blood and punished them without mercy or end.

Meanwhile, Cronos became concerned that one of his own children would one day usurp him, so he devised a plan for maintaining his rule. Whenever his consort, Rhea, gave birth, Cronos swallowed the child whole. This savage act understandably troubled Rhea, who managed to save her last child, Zeus, by substituting a rock for him. When Cronos swallowed the rock, it troubled his digestive system, causing him to regurgitate the twelve children he had previously swallowed.

An all-consuming war ensued, with the entire world forced to choose sides between Zeus and Cronos. Those allying themselves with Zeus included Prometheus (among other Titan offspring) and the three Cyclopes, who furnished Zeus with an important new weapon, the thunderbolt. Eventually, Zeus freed the Hundred-Handers from Tartaros and with their help overwhelmed Cronos. Zeus subsequently cast the Titans into Tartaros, charging the Hundred-Handers with guarding the gate.

Zeus's victory was so complete that it ended the chain of reciprocal family violence that had dominated the cosmos since its creation. Where vengeance and other primal impulses had once dominated, Zeus brought the concept of mitigated justice and other basic values of civilization.

Zeus's victory *in his war with the Titans ended the cycle of savage, reciprocal violence that had previously dominated the cosmos.*

VI. SHILOH

DURING THE FEBRUARY 1862 CAMPAIGN against Forts Henry and Donelson, the Federals took nearly 3,000 casualties, but this figure was dwarfed by the 16,500 Confederates killed or captured. "Unconditional Surrender" Grant became an overnight sensation as newspaper accounts extolled his leadership. Some described how he had directed his brigade to victory not with a sword but with a cigar, so heartened Northerners began showering him with boxes of cigars. Meanwhile, he was promoted to major general, but the applause would be short-lived.

In early April, Grant and approximately forty thousand men waited for thirty-five thousand more Federals under Don Carlos Buell to join them at Pittsburg Landing, a tiny hamlet on the Tennessee River just north of the Mississippi-Tennessee border. Maj. Gen. Henry W. Halleck, commander of all Union forces west of the Appalachians, had devised a plan that called for Halleck himself to lead this combined force against Corinth, a crucial Rebel road and rail hub in northeastern Mississippi.

Grant leads a charge at Shiloh.

Grant knew that, at some point, Confederate generals Albert Sidney Johnston and P. G. T. Beauregard would have to make a stand against this invasion force, but he discounted the notion that Johnston and Beauregard would attack before Buell's men arrived. Thus he took few precautions and so was completely surprised when forty-four thousand Confederates indeed attacked on Sunday morning, April 6. The two-day battle of Shiloh (named for the church around which most of Grant's men were encamped) turned out to be the war's bloodiest fighting yet. Eventually, the Union commander rallied his troops and fought the Confederates to a standstill, but Grant's strategic victory was lost in the horror of the grisly aftermath.

Because Shiloh was the first of the large-scale battles that would soon become commonplace, few were prepared for the accumulation of death. The vast number of casualties—more than twenty thousand, rivaling the war's *total* number to date—shocked the Northern public. A scapegoat was needed, and Grant was the obvious choice. Washington politicians condemned him for his lack of preparedness, and Grant's enemies within the army, aware of his alcoholic past, spread rumors that he had been surprised at Shiloh because he had been drunk. Groundless though these rumors were, the bad publicity prompted Halleck to relieve Grant of his battlefield command and put him on the shelf for a time.

The Confederate *attack at Shiloh, which took Grant by surprise, resulted in the Civil War's bloodiest battle yet.*

VI. THE FLOW OF GOODS AND SERVICE

CENTURIES AGO, when communication and transportation technologies were still primitive, trade among nations was mostly limited to commodities that could endure long journeys (either aboard ships or in caravans), that were relatively valuable with respect to their size, and that were rarities in the markets where they were finally sold. Exotic spices, expensive textiles (such as silk), and precious metals were among the first commodities traded across national boundaries.

The Silk Road, which linked East Asia to Western Europe, was one of the world's first major trade routes. Another was the Spice Road, along which spices traveled from India to the West. Both the silks and the spices were paid for mainly in gold and silver. With the onset of the transportation and communications improvements that marked the beginning of the modern era (ca. 1500), new trade routes developed, and the system expanded.

With the Industrial Revolution, however, the pattern of international trade changed dramatically. Agriculture declined sharply as a percentage of the Western economy, and manufactured goods became the new engine of growth, flowing from the West to the rest of the world in exchange for natural resources. European colonialism supported this new exchange pattern, providing the industrialized West with cheap (or even free) land, natural resources, and unskilled labor.

As time passed, however, the technology associated with mass production began to spread around the world. Once developing nations acquired this technology, they gained a comparative advantage over developed nations because of their cheap labor, and the flow of trade in simple manufactured goods changed direction. Under the new pattern of trade, which continues today, developed nations exchange high-tech products and services, produced by skilled labor, for textiles and other cheap manufactures that were once produced by the West but are now produced by the unskilled labor of developing countries.

Underlying this basic pattern, however, are a multitude of complicating factors that have made international trade increasingly difficult to model. For instance, as the populations of large developing nations such as China and India have become more highly educated, they've begun to compete with similarly trained workers in Europe and the United States. Also, manufactured goods can often contain component parts produced in several different countries, and labeling regulations usually fail to identify adequately who made what. One thing is certain, however: The world economy is not becoming simpler.

Exchange patterns *have shifted over time, with flows sometimes changing direction, but there has nevertheless been a steady increase in the complexity of trade.*

VI. ASHER B. DURAND

ASHER BROWN DURAND (1796–1886) grew up in northern New Jersey, seventeen miles from New York City. When he was sixteen, his family apprenticed him to an engraver, and Durand's ensuing success at that work supported his later rise to prominence as a painter. In 1825, the year that he met Cole and Bryant, Durand became a founding member of the National Academy of Design, which soon emerged as one of the leading American venues for art exhibition and education. At the time, Durand was painting portraits and genre scenes, but Cole gradually persuaded him to shift his focus to landscapes.

Another important influence on Durand (and on many other American landscape painters) was the English writer John Ruskin, who contended that truthfulness to nature was essential for art. While Cole reduced the level of naturalistic detail in his later paintings to emphasize their spiritual elements, Durand reveled in detail as he sought to record as much as possible about nature through direct observation.

Durand later translated Ruskin's ideas into a distinctly American aesthetic. Specifically, he urged American artists to use objectivity in approaching nature— rather than subjectivity, which Durand associated with European styles. In 1855, he published his advice in a series of essays, "Letters on Landscape Painting," which appeared in *The Crayon*, a New York City art periodical. These highly influential essays suggested that American artists should sketch with pencil and paper out of doors until "the natural variety of form" became ingrained in their minds. Durand also opined that American artists should no longer look to Europe for subject matter "while the virgin charms of our native land have claims upon your deepest affections."

These twin emphases—on the close observation of nature and on the primacy of the American landscape—essentially codified the style of what became known as the Hudson River School. There was an additional element, however, that underlay most American landscape painting: an abiding belief in nature's innate spirituality and the power of that spirituality to elevate viewers to a higher moral plane.

Asher B. Durand's *"Letters on Landscape Painting" codified the ideals and stylistic character of the Hudson River School.*

Asher B. Durand, *The American Wilderness* (1864)

VI. PLANETS

THE EIGHT PLANETS in our solar system are usually divided into two types. Those closer to the Sun are called terrestrial, or rocky, planets because they are primarily composed of solid rock and metal. The four terrestrial planets in our solar system are Mercury, Venus, Earth, and Mars. The planets farther from the Sun are the jovian planets, or gas giants. The four jovian planets in our solar system are Jupiter, Saturn, Uranus, and Neptune. Although the jovian planets have small rocky cores, they principally consist of gaseous hydrogen and helium, a few organic compounds, and some volatile ices. They range in size from four to eleven times the size of Earth, which is the largest of the terrestrial planets.

The planet Mars.

Astronomers currently assume that other solar systems contain planets similar to those found in our own. The first extrasolar planet ever detected was Gamma Cephei Ab, discovered in 1988. In 2007, a planet that seems to be terrestrial was discovered orbiting the star Gliese 581. Even so, of the approximately 250 planets thus far detected, nearly all have been gas giants the size of Jupiter or larger. The reason for this may be that terrestrial planets are rare, but more likely it relates to the methods astronomers use to detect extrasolar planets.

Because planets are generally much smaller than stars and don't emit their own light, they are very difficult to see. Therefore, astronomers usually look to stars for indirect evidence of orbiting planets. Stars that have planets orbiting them tend to wobble on their axes as the planets pull them one way and then another. When wobbles are detected, astronomers can approximate the size of the planet by estimating the mass necessary to cause such a wobble. However, this method is only useful for detecting gas giants because only large jovian planets are massive enough to cause a star to wobble.

Another way that astronomers look for planets involves monitoring the brightness of a star. When a planet crosses in front of a star, its brightness is dimmed, if ever so slightly. If the brightness of a star seems to wax and wane on a regular basis, this could be evidence of a planet orbiting that star. Although the minuscule change in brightness caused by an Earth-sized planet can't presently be detected, the next generation of space-based telescopes is expected to have this capability.

There are two types *of planets: terrestrial planets, which occupy the inner solar system, and jovian planets, which occupy the outer solar system.*

VI. THE THREE WIVES OF ZEUS

ALTHOUGH HE FATHERED numerous children, both mortal and immortal, Zeus took just three wives. According to Hesiod, "Zeus made Metis his first wife, / Wiser than any other god, or any mortal man." Like Prometheus, Metis (meaning "cunning intelligence") was a second-generation Titan, the daughter of Oceanos and Tethys. Zeus's first marriage thus associated him with intelligence. But when Zeus learned that Metis's second child was prophesied to be greater than his father, Zeus ingested Metis. This act recalls the manner in which Cronos disposed of Zeus's siblings, but more importantly it symbolizes Zeus's internalization of Metis's intelligence.

Because Metis was pregnant at the time, Zeus himself became pregnant upon ingesting her. He carried the child to term, and Athena, the goddess of wisdom, was born from his brow. Appearing in full armor, she became the goddess with whom Zeus most often shared his mind. Because she was born without the "hindrance" of a female, Athena remained untroubled by the emotionality that swayed other females. She was beautiful yet almost asexual.

Zeus's second wife was Themis ("established custom"), and their marriage produced Eunomia (Lawfulness), Eirene (Peace), the Moirai (Fates), and Dikē (Justice). Like most of the early gods, these children were personifications of their names.

Zeus's third wife, Hera, was different. Rather than representing any trait, she played the role of female and wife in Greek mythology. As the goddess of marriage, she was especially intolerant of Zeus's many infidelities, and the jealous rage that she felt toward the children of these affairs inspired many a myth.

Zeus's marriage to Hera produced three children: Hebe, the goddess of youth; Eileithyia, the goddess of childbirth; and most importantly Ares, the god of war. Ares, in particular, signified the tumultuous relationship between Zeus and Hera.

Even with the ascendance of Zeus and the establishment of his and Hera's rule atop Mount Olympos, there remained monsters in the world. These remnants of the age of the Titans epitomized the Titans' wild and savage nature, and they had to be eliminated (or at least subdued) if the world was to be truly tamed and civilized. This task fell initially to the Olympians and later to human heroes, but it couldn't have proceeded without the stabilizing influence provided by the three marriages of Zeus.

Zeus's three marriages *and the offspring they produced furthered the establishment of order in the cosmos.*

A Roman copy of a fifth-century BCE bust of Hera.

VII. THE SIEGE OF VICKSBURG

AFTER SHILOH, several months passed before Grant was given another command. During that time, he meditated on the battle and concluded that even a sharp blow to the South wouldn't collapse the resilient Confederacy. "I gave up the idea of saving the Union except by complete conquest," he wrote later.

At the war's outset, the North's military planners had identified three primary goals: the destruction of the Southern economy, against which a naval blockade had been deployed; the capture of Richmond; and the seizure of the Mississippi River, which would cut off Louisiana, Texas, and Arkansas from the rest of the Confederacy. During the fall of 1862, the first two goals still seemed distant, but not so the third. The chief remaining obstacle was Vicksburg, which sat high on a bluff above the river's eastern bank.

In October 1862, Grant took command of the Army of the Tennessee and three months later moved his forty-five thousand men to Young's Point, a location twenty miles above Vicksburg on the opposite bank. There, he rendezvoused with a corps of thirty-two thousand men under Maj. Gen. William Tecumseh Sherman. For the next ten weeks, Grant struggled to find a way across the river that wouldn't expose his men to Vicksburg's powerful guns. He tried digging a canal and navigating the jungle-like Yazoo River delta, but both attempts failed, the latter ending with the nervous breakdown of the naval commander involved.

Finally, with newspapers accusing him of sloth and stupidity, Grant developed a risky new plan: He would march downriver, cross below Vicksburg, and approach the city from the south. The risks were that, in order to ferry the troops, the Union flotilla would first have to run the Vicksburg guns, and, once Grant's troops crossed the river, they'd be cut off from their supply lines.

The main crossing took place on April 30, and three weeks of hard fighting later Grant reached the outskirts of Vicksburg, The first direct assault took place on May 19, followed by another on May 22. When the Rebel lines held, Grant dug in for a siege. Over the next forty-seven days, the steady barrage of Union artillery forced Vicksburg's residents to abandon their homes and occupy temporary shelters newly dug into the hillside. Some of these "caves" held two hundred people, but they were hardly adequate, and on July 4, 1863, the starving, disheartened populace finally capitulated.

Many historians cite Grant's capture of Vicksburg as the military turning point of the war, rather than the concurrent Union victory at Gettysburg.

Union troops raise the US flag outside the Vicksburg courthouse on July 4, 1863.

VII. THE FLOW OF CAPITAL

THE MOVEMENT OF CAPITAL across national borders has a profound effect on economic growth. Without foreign capital, investment in a particular country would depend solely on that nation's ability to save. Whatever resources are not consumed in a country are saved and made available for investment through the country's financial system. In developing countries, however, where the margin between available resources and subsistence is often thin, saving is nearly impossible.

The availability of foreign capital enables poor countries to develop much faster than they could on their own. The motivation of foreign investors is, of course, not altruistic. Their incentive is the higher rate of return that investing in a developing country can bring (because of the higher growth rates that one finds in the developing world).

The flow of money from rich to poor countries can take one of several forms. By far the most common are foreign direct investment, portfolio investment, foreign aid, and foreign loans. *Foreign direct investment (FDI)* refers to the purchase of physical assets in another country, either to start a new business or to gain an ownership interest in an existing foreign company. For statistical purposes, the United Nations defines FDI as an ownership interest of at least 10 percent. Interests that fall below this threshold are considered *portfolio investment*. For the most part, portfolio investment takes the form of short-term investment in foreign stocks and bonds rather than a long-term investment in foreign economic development.

Because the poorest countries have few assets and tend to be financially (and often politically) unstable, they attract almost no portfolio investment and little FDI. Instead, the capital they receive comes in the form of *foreign aid* or through *foreign loans*. Sometimes these loans are made by private-sector banks, but the primary lenders are international financial institutions (such as the World Bank) and wealthier governments.

The conventional wisdom is that the flow of international capital improves global economic efficiency. Lately, however, some economists have called into question the benefit of short-term capital inflows. This "hot money" flows into developing nations in search of high rates of return; but, unlike investments in factories and other illiquid long-term assets, it's much more mobile and fickle. At the first sign of instability (or the prospect of a better deal elsewhere), it will take flight, sometimes destabilizing the financial market in which it was invested.

The flow of international capital *makes it possible for poor countries to invest in long-term economic development. Short-term capital inflows, however, can be problematic.*

VII. COMMONALITIES

THE TERM *Hudson River School* emerged during the 1870s to describe a group of American landscape painters who became active (and popular) during the mid-

John F. Kensett, *The White Mountains from North Conway* (1851)

1840s. These painters, nearly all of whom were native born, were inspired by Thomas Cole and Asher B. Durand, and they assiduously followed Durand's dictate to seek out and represent on canvas the natural beauty and sublime wonder of the American wilderness.

For painters living in New York City, the *American wilderness* still meant, largely, the Hudson River Valley, but the White Mountains of New Hampshire were quickly becoming popular as a destination for both tourists and artists. Some painters were even attaching themselves to government-sponsored mapping expeditions venturing out into the West.

Beyond this basic commonality of subject matter, artists associated with the Hudson River School also tended to paint in similar styles and favor similar themes. Following Durand, they valued "objective" responses to nature and thus recorded the minutest details of a scene, including the leaves on the trees, the moss on the rocks, and even individual blades of grass. By the mid-1840s, the availability of oils in tin tubes made it possible to sketch using oil paint as well as pencil. As a result, hours were spent out of doors studying nature firsthand and directly recording aspects of the scenery that were later transferred to larger canvases back in the studio. (This practice differs from plein air painting, favored by artists of a later period, in which the ultimate work is painted out of doors.)

Hudson River School artists also tended to idealize nature, employing conventions of the sublime and the picturesque to elevate the landscape and heighten the experience of viewing it. Accordingly, their paintings often employed composite subjects featuring realistic detail but presenting imagined scenes composed of many different actual sites. A particularly common theme was the sublime wilderness and its rapid transformation into cultivated land. Another popular theme was the changing quality of light that could be seen in passing thunderstorms or at dawn or dusk. Using these two themes in combination enabled artists to employ both the sublime and the picturesque in the same painting.

Although painters *associated with the Hudson River School were rather diverse in some ways, their close observation of nature was a hallmark characteristic.*

VII. DWARF PLANETS, ASTEROIDS, AND COMETS

IN ADDITION TO PLANETS, star systems contain a variety of objects made up of the "stuff" left over from planet formation. Dwarf planets, for example, are large, rocky objects too small to be classified as true planets. Scientifically, they are defined in terms of gravity. The difference between a dwarf planet and a true planet is that true planets are gravitationally dominant in their orbits—that is, there is nothing of significant size left in their orbits not under their gravitational control. Nevertheless, the dwarf planets—which in our solar system include Pluto, Ceres, and Eris—do have sufficient mass for their own gravity to pull them into spherical shapes, much like true planets.

Asteroids are smaller rocky objects of irregular shape. In our solar system, many can be found in the asteroid belt that lies between the orbits of Mars and Jupiter. Because of the asteroid belt's position, astronomers once theorized that it contained the remains of a destroyed planet. Now it is believed that this material never formed a planet because of the strong gravitational influence of nearby Jupiter.

Thirty-five-mile-long asteroid Ida, located in the belt between Mars and Jupiter.

Other asteroids orbit the Sun in paths that cross the orbits of the planets. Although planets and asteroids rarely occupy these points of intersection at the same time, there could be, and likely have been, collisions with devastating consequences.

Unlike asteroids, which tend to congregate in the inner solar system, comets have their origin in the solar system's outskirts. Beginning just outside the orbit of Neptune and extending far out into space is a huge collection of icy objects, consisting primarily of frozen gases that were pushed out of the inner solar system by a massive stellar wind (the flow of charged particles from a sun) shortly after the formation of the planets. Most of these trans-neptunian objects remain outside Neptune, but a few have highly elliptical orbits that bring them occasionally into the inner reaches of the solar system.

Nearly all the time, these objects exist as large dirty snowballs moving through space, but for the short time that one's orbit brings it closer to the Sun, it heats up, causing it to emit a stream of dust particles and gaseous vapors. This is the comet's "tail," which is always pointed away from the Sun, indicating the prevailing solar wind.

Although not gravitationally dominant like the planets, the remaining objects in a solar system still have significant impact.

VII. ZEUS'S PROGENY

ALTHOUGH ZEUS had three wives, he nevertheless slept with numerous other females, both mortal and immortal, including most of his sisters. The children of these liaisons figure prominently in Greco-Roman myth, and a few are extremely important.

Because of her particularly close association with her half brother Ares (the god of war), Aphrodite (the goddess of love) made it clear that, even under the sway of Zeus, the world would not be without pain. While Hesiod attributed her birth to the foam created when Ouronos's genitalia fell into the sea, Homer and later authors wrote that she was actually the child of Zeus and the nymph Dione. Although less poetic, this latter version makes more sense because, within the larger scheme of Greek cosmology, Aphrodite was an Olympian, and Olympians tended to be either the siblings or the progeny of Zeus. Moreover, Aphrodite clearly belongs to the new world order under Zeus and not to the savage past of the Titans.

To Zeus and the second-generation Titan Leto were born the twin archer gods, Apollo and Artemis. Apollo is especially important in Greek mythology and may be the most conspicuous god in the Olympic pantheon. He and Athena were particular favorites of Zeus and knew his will better than any other Olympians (including, to her displeasure, Hera). They served as their father's left and right hands and interacted frequently with human heroes.

Italian Renaissance artist Sandro Botticelli's *The Birth of Venus* (ca. 1486).

Apollo, nominally a sun god, was even more important as an oracular deity. In Greek culture, oracles were either gods themselves or priests associated with gods who thereby had access to divine knowledge. Their role was to share this knowledge with the wider community, which they did—but often cryptically. Most of the oracles in Greek mythology were associated in some way with Apollo, and his sanctuary at Delphi was considered the holiest place in the Greek world.

Hermes, another youthful Olympian, was the child of Zeus and the nymph Maia, who lived alone in a cave (which was not unusual for nymphs). Her son, however, wanted more, and his boldness quickly earned him the attention first of Apollo and later of Zeus, who made Hermes his herald. Interestingly, Hermes's progeny were the most prolific thieves in Greco-Roman myth.

Zeus sired innumerable children, both mortal and immortal. All are part of Greek mythology, but some feature more prominently than others.

VIII. THE MILITARY DIVISION OF THE MISSISSIPPI

AFTER THE FALL OF VICKSBURG, the North pressed its advantage in the western theater, organizing an offensive in central Tennessee. Maj. Gen. William S. Rosecrans's Army of the Cumberland led the push, opposed by Gen. Braxton Bragg's Army of Tennessee. (Northern armies were typically named for rivers; Southern armies, for states.)

Bragg, whose primary mission was to protect the Rebel rail hub at Chattanooga, spent most of August 1863 pleading with Confederate president Jefferson Davis for more troops. Yet only those belonging to the Union general Rosecrans came, albeit slowly. When Rosecrans's army finally neared Chattanooga in early September, Bragg abandoned the city, which Rosecrans occupied on September 9. That same day, Davis finally decided to send help, detaching Lt. Gen. James Longstreet's corps from Gen. Robert E. Lee's Army of Northern Virginia and speeding it west.

Meanwhile, Rosecrans sent one of his own corps under Maj. Gen. George H. Thomas to probe for Bragg's army south of Chattanooga. On September 19, Thomas encountered the dismounted cavalry of Maj. Gen. Nathan Bedford Forrest along a stretch of Chickamauga Creek. Unaware that Longstreet's corps had just arrived, Thomas decided to attack.

The flag of the Thirty-eighth Alabama Infantry, which fought at Chickamauga.

In the Cherokee language, *chickamauga* means "river of death," and the two-day battle of Chickamauga turned out to be one of the war's deadliest, with casualties totaling thirty-five thousand. In the end, the Confederates routed the Federals, but Bragg's reluctance to press his advantage permitted the Federals to withdraw and regroup behind Chattanooga's fortifications. Bragg then laid siege to the city, establishing strong lines atop Lookout Mountain and along Missionary Ridge.

On October 16, President Lincoln chose Grant to command the new Military Division of the Mississippi, which included the Armies of the Cumberland, the Ohio, and the Tennessee. The next day, Grant put Thomas in charge of the Army of the Cumberland and made arrangements to travel to Chattanooga himself.

Grant arrived on October 23 and, within a week, opened up a badly needed supply line. Meanwhile, he ordered Sherman (now commanding the Army of the Tennessee) to join him. With the might of two armies behind him, Grant attacked on November 23, the key assault coming two days later along Missionary Ridge. Weakened by the November 4 transfer of Longstreet's corps to Tennessee, Bragg couldn't hold out. Instead, he gave up the siege and retreated into Georgia.

With the Army *of the Cumberland trapped in Chattanooga, Lincoln put Grant in charge of the new Military Division of the Mississippi.*

VIII. THE FLOW OF PEOPLE

JUST AS CAPITAL FLOWS to markets that offer a greater rate of return, so does labor. The mass international migration of 1846–1939 is a historical case in point. During that period, fifty-one million people left Europe for the New World, especially the United States, because they judged the employment prospects to be better there. After World War II, a similar migration took place within Europe, as southern Europeans left their homes to take jobs in the reindustrialized north. West Germany, the United Kingdom, and France were the primary host countries, with Italy, Greece, Spain, Yugoslavia, Poland, Albania, and Turkey providing most of the guest workers.

The experience of Turks in West Germany was rather typical. In 1961, the West German government, facing an acute labor shortage, formally invited Turkish workers to relocate to Germany. Most of those who responded were unskilled and unemployed in their home country, where a labor surplus existed. In West Germany, however, the Turkish workers received relatively high wages and even sent home a portion of their earnings. These transfers, known as remittances, became important sources of income for the guest workers' families in Turkey— covering day-to-day living expenses, providing a cushion against emergencies, and even funding small investments. Today, more than 2.7 million people of Turkish origin live and work in Germany.

Yet labor doesn't always flow quite so easily. Immigration laws can severely restrict the free movement of labor, especially when that labor is unskilled. Current European Union laws, for example, block the flow of unskilled labor from developing countries. On the other hand, equally strict US laws have proven largely ineffective because, faced with below-subsistence wages at home, workers from poor countries simply ignore the laws and immigrate illegally.

Skilled labor, in contrast, is treated preferentially because it is almost universally in demand. When skilled workers in developing countries take advantage of their mobility and migrate to richer countries where they can enjoy higher standards of living, they contribute to a phenomenon known as brain drain. Because developed nations object to illegal immigration and developing nations object just as strongly to brain drain, labor mobility continues to be one of the most sensitive topics in international trade talks.

Like capital, *labor wants to flow across national boundaries toward opportunities for greater return. Its mobility is limited, however, by immigration laws.*

VIII. NATURE VS. PROGRESS

MOST AMERICAN LANDSCAPE PAINTERS of the mid-nineteenth century shared the country's obsession with "progress" and accepted, more or less, the general viewpoint that industrialization was necessary for the health and growth of the nation. But they also felt conflicted, finding it difficult to ignore the damage being done to the landscape in the name of economic expansion. For example, during the 1850s, the tanning industry took over the Catskill Mountains. The reason was the hemlock trees that grew plentifully on the region's slopes. Hemlock bark contained tannin, a chemical essential for the tanning of animal hides. As a result, within a generation of Thomas Cole's first visit to the mountains, parts of the Catskills were transformed from forested wilderness into landscapes of tree stumps and tanning factories.

Cole professed faith in human progress and man's role in cultivating the wilderness, but he also worried that Americans were acting as conquerors, rather than as stewards, of nature. In viewing *The Course of Empire*, one can hardly help sensing an inescapable pessimism: America might be enjoying the Arcadian stage of its civilization, but destruction lay not far in the future.

The next generation of landscape painters, notably Sanford Robinson Gifford and George Inness, expressed their ambivalence in more direct ways. In *Lackawanna Valley* (1856), for instance, which the Delaware, Lackawanna & Western Railroad commissioned for advertising purposes, Inness depicts the early development of the railroad system. He exaggerates the prominence of a railroad roundhouse to emphasize the industrial progress being made but, more to the point, includes a profusion of tree stumps in the foreground to show his ultimate disregard for the effect of machinery on the natural environment.

George Inness, *Lackawanna Valley* (ca. 1856)

Other artists took positions that were even more extreme. Frederic Church, for instance, became convinced that man could not inhabit a landscape without destroying it, so in canvases such as *Twilight in the Wilderness* (1860), he omitted all signs of human life, focusing instead on the sublime power of the pure, uninhabited wilderness. Perhaps not surprisingly, this period also saw the beginning of the first campaign to save the vanishing wilderness. Through such efforts, environmentalists were able to establish Yellowstone, the first national park, in 1872.

Members of the Hudson River School *were deeply ambivalent about the effects of human progress on the American landscape.*

VIII. STARS

THE MOST IMPORTANT object in a solar system is the star, or stars, around which all the other objects orbit. Some solar systems, such as our own, have just one star; others (possibly most) have more than one. Binary star systems, for instance, contain two stars, while the closest star system to Earth, Alpha Centauri, has three stars.

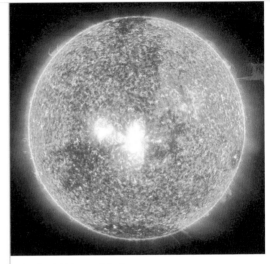

An ultraviolet image of the Sun.

The light that stars emit is always the result of nuclear fusion, the process by which two or more atomic nuclei are fused together under extreme high-energy conditions to produce a single, larger nucleus. In the fusion reaction that takes place most often within stars, two hydrogen nuclei are joined together to form a single helium nucleus. In the process, energy is released, which the star emits as waves of light across the entire electromagnetic spectrum.

The more massive a star, the greater its gravitational pull—and this, in turn, affects the rate at which it consumes its nuclear fuel. A supermassive star, by virtue of its enormous gravitational pull, experiences such high-energy conditions in its core that it consumes its nuclear fuel quite rapidly. A medium-sized star, such as our own Sun, might take ten billion years to fuse all of the hydrogen in its core, but a supermassive star (between 40 and 120 times the size of the Sun) might run out of nuclear fuel in just ten million years.

Stars are primarily classified by spectral type (a measure of their temperature), which is determined by the visible light they emit. The most intense light emitted by the hottest stars tends toward the blue end of the visible spectrum, while the light reaching us from cooler stars tends toward the red end. Stars in the middle of the range, such as the Sun, emit a yellow light. Arranged from hottest to coolest, the spectral types are O, B, A, F, G, K, and M. (A convenient mnemonic is "Oh, be a fine girl, kiss me!") The Sun is a G-class star.

The size of a star *directly affects the way it evolves, with large stars consuming their nuclear fuels much more quickly than smaller stars.*

VIII. THE FIVE AGES OF MANKIND

THE FIVE AGES OF MANKIND explain the (de)evolution of human civilization. With each succeeding age, for example, the life span of humanity decreases—similar to the decline experienced in the Judeo-Christian tradition by the biblical generations of Adam and Eve, Cain and Abel, Abraham and Sarah, and so on, with similarly increasing degrees of ignorance, pain, evil deeds, and culpability.

In the Greek hierarchy, the Golden Age came first. It began during the reign of Cronos when, according to Hesiod, humans "lived like gods, not a care in the world." There was no grief, no "miserable old age," and humans died quickly and painlessly.

During the Silver Age, the Olympian gods created a new race of humans who were "not nearly so fine as the first," requiring one hundred years of nurture before reaching a short-lived adulthood. Even then, they brought on their own deaths with a reckless ignorance: "They just could not stop / Hurting each other and could not bring themselves / To serve the Immortals." This angered Zeus, who destroyed them.

Bronze Age humans were even worse. Whereas Silver Age mortals brought about their own destruction through ignorance, those of the Bronze Age destroyed themselves. According to Hesiod, "they killed each other off with their own hands." They also failed to cultivate crops, a common marker of civilized behavior in Greek myth.

Later, "Zeus fashioned a fourth race / To live off the land, juster and nobler, / The divine race of Heroes, also called Demigods." Known as the Age of Heroes, this fourth age of mankind featured humans who were mortal children of the gods as well as other "heroes" with close connections to divinity and kingship. The most famous (and last) generation of these heroes fought the Trojan War. "When Death's veil had covered them over," Hesiod wrote, "Zeus granted them a life apart from other men…free from care… / In the Isles of the Blest."

Hesiod himself lived during the comparatively destitute Iron Age. According to the poet, "The gods send us terrible pain and vexation." But it is not all bad: "Still, there will be some good mixed in with the evil."

Each successive *age of mankind represents a further separation from the gods.*

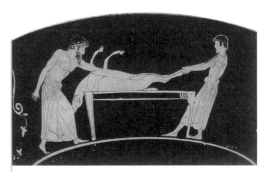

The ritual sacrifice of a deer to the gods, as shown on a a fifth-century BCE vase.

IX. MEANWHILE IN THE EAST

LESS THAN A WEEK after the July 1861 disaster at Bull Run, President Lincoln made the first of several command changes that would mark his early conduct of the war. He fired Brig. Gen. Irvin McDowell and replaced him with George B. McClellan. Promoted to major general just two months earlier, the thirty-four-year-old McClellan had already made a name for himself as an administrator, and he eagerly set to work equipping and training the new Army of the Potomac (formed out of what had been the Army of Northeastern Virginia).

While this organizational work continued, McClellan developed an elaborate plan for the capture of Richmond. It called for the transfer of ninety thousand troops by ship to Fortress Monroe, a Union toehold on the Virginia peninsula formed by the York and James Rivers. From there, the Army of the Potomac was to march up the James to Richmond. On March 17, 1862, McClellan began loading his troops onto transports.

Maj. Gen. George B. McClellan

Meanwhile, anticipating the Union offensive, Gen. Joseph E. Johnston began withdrawing Confederate forces from Manassas and transferring them to Richmond.

McClellan's Peninsular Campaign made some overall sense, but it neglected to take into account the marshy conditions, exacerbated by spring rains, that made travel on the peninsula time-consuming and difficult. In addition, as a field commander, McClellan left much to be desired. Despite an enormous advantage in numbers, he advanced so cautiously that it seemed he believed his army was the weaker force. On April 9, an already frustrated Lincoln urged the general to attack, but McClellan merely plodded along, taking two more months to move his leading forces within six miles of Richmond. As a result, it wasn't until the end of May that the Union and Confederate armies became fully engaged.

During the first major battle, fought on May 31 at Seven Pines (also known as Fair Oaks), Johnston was severely wounded, necessitating his replacement as the top Confederate field commander in Virginia. To fill this crucial vacancy, Jefferson Davis chose Robert E. Lee.

On June 25, Lee launched what became known as the Seven Days' Campaign. He pushed this offensive hard because, having already committed sixty thousand troops to the attack, he couldn't allow McClellan the opportunity to mount a counterattack against Richmond's dangerously depleted defenses. Nevertheless, such an opportunity did present itself, but McClellan quailed and instead ordered a general retreat down the peninsula. It would be another two years before a Union army again came so close to Richmond.

While Bull Run *showed the Union that winning the war wouldn't be easy, the Seven Days' Campaign brought into question whether the Union would win at all.*

IX. OUTSOURCING

IN THE PAST, surplus labor flowed to where the jobs were. Recently, however, a new trend has emerged: jobs flowing to where the surplus labor is. This trend is part of a broader practice known as outsourcing. Economists define outsourcing as the purchasing of goods or the subcontracting of services that would otherwise be produced in-house.

Outsourcing needn't be international. It can refer to a Michigan automobile company purchasing leather seats from a vendor in Colorado or a New York magazine publisher subcontracting its customer service to a call center in Illinois. The benefits of such outsourcing, both domestic and international, are obvious: Purchasing a product made efficiently by another company will result in greater wealth for everyone.

As economist Gregory Mankiw explained in 2004 while serving as chairman of the Council of Economic Advisors, outsourcing "is probably a plus for the economy in the long run. We're very used to goods being produced abroad and being shipped here on ships or planes. What we are not used to is services being produced abroad and being sent here over the Internet or telephone wires. But does it matter from an economic standpoint whether values of items produced abroad come on planes and ships or over fiber-optic cables? Well, no, the economics is basically the same."

A good example of services more efficiently subcontracted than provided oneself are those offered by call centers in India. The declining cost of international telephone traffic and the availability of high-speed Internet access has made it possible for some workers, such as customer service personnel, to export their services around the world. India has become an obvious choice for American outsourcing because its workers are relatively well educated, speak fluent English, and earn much less than comparable American workers.

Yet many Americans, especially those who have lost their jobs to outsourcing, dispute Mankiw's favorable opinion of the practice. Economically, there can be no debate: Outsourcing clearly benefits the companies involved and the global economy as a whole. But it does raise important questions of social justice that have yet to be answered. For example, are any of the profits made through outsourcing being used to compensate and retrain the outsourced workers, and are these profits being shared equitably with the workers who remain employed?

Outsourcing has clear *economic advantages that help domestic companies remain competitive , but it also raises questions of social justice that have yet to be answered.*

IX. FREDERIC CHURCH

FREDERIC EDWIN CHURCH (1826–1900) was probably the most famous and successful American artist of the 1850s and 1860s. Rivaled only by the works of Albert Bierstadt, Church's paintings won him extreme popularity at home and abroad and often commanded record-breaking sums.

Family wealth made it possible for Church to study art from an early age, and at eighteen he became a pupil of Thomas Cole. (In fact, Church was the only known formal student that Cole ever had.) Working under Cole, Church learned to temper his teacher's romanticism and moralism with a more objective and scientific approach to nature.

Like Cole, Church had an excellent eye for naturalistic detail, but he took it much farther—even, at times, to the level of articulating individual blades of grass. Church also had a strong inclination toward grandeur, which made his canvases remarkable in macrocosm as well as microcosm. For example, Church's masterpiece *Niagara* (1857), which measures about three feet high and seven feet wide, can be appreciated both through a magnifying glass and from a great distance. Its sweeping panorama so well captures the awesome expansiveness of Niagara Falls that one experiences, while viewing the painting, the feeling of standing at the water's edge, gazing out into the frothy chasm.

Frederic E. Church, *Niagara* (1857)

Church's determination to depict both the details and the grand scope of a scene was strongly influenced by the writings of the German scientist and explorer Alexander von Humboldt, whose multivolume work *Kosmos* (1845–62) was widely read in Europe and America. In *Kosmos*, Humboldt urged landscape painters to consider their subjects not only as specific scenes but also as part of a larger natural whole. Thus, in *Niagara*, Church contrasted the extremely realistic detail of the water in the foreground with the broad strokes of the sky beyond. In this way, he balanced his own interest in scientific detail with a faith he inherited from Cole in the inherent spirituality of the landscape and its larger divine purpose.

Frederic Church, *who was Thomas Cole's only formal pupil, translated Cole's European romanticism into a more modern American aesthetic.*

IX. STELLAR BIRTH

BECAUSE NUCLEAR FUSION can occur only under conditions of extraordinarily high pressure, the gravitational pull of a very massive body is necessary for star formation to take place. According to current theory, the process begins with a huge cloud of gas and dust called a nebula. At some point, a shock wave, perhaps generated by a nearby supernova, disturbs the equilibrium of the nebula, causing it to contract under the pull of its own gravity. If the nebula starts out with even a small rotation (as most do), it begins to rotate faster now, just as an ice skater spins faster as she pulls her arms into her body.

As the nebula contracts more and more and spins faster and faster, a great deal of the matter within it concentrates in the center and flattens out into a disk. Particles that were once far apart move closer together, and the resulting pressure causes the particles to heat up. Eventually, a protostar is formed, which begins radiating heat outward, creating a thermal push that counters the prevailing gravitational pull.

Meanwhile, other, smaller clumps of matter form elsewhere in the nebula. As these condense under the pull of their own gravity, they tend to combine with other clumps in their path. Eventually, they grow large enough to attract other matter in their vicinity and form planets in orbit around the protostar.

A star-forming cloud in the Christmas Tree Cluster.

A protostar reaches critical mass when the pressure and temperature at the center become sufficiently high for nuclear fusion to begin. At this point, the protostar becomes a star. Solar systems with more than one star are thought to be the result of density fluctuations within the original nebula. In other words, before the precipitating shock, there were regions in the nebula that were already slightly more dense than other regions. As the nebula contracts, each of these denser regions compresses to form its own protostar.

Once nuclear fusion begins, the new star produces an enormous stellar wind, much more powerful than that generated by an established star. This wind picks up all the matter left over from planet formation and carries it well outside the orbit of the outermost planet. From these bits and pieces, comets form.

Stars evolve *along similar lines from their earliest beginnings as nebulae through the protostar stage until fusion begins.*

IX. PANDORA

GREEK MYTHOLOGY provides an interesting contrast with the way the origin of the sexes is explained in the Bible. In both systems, men were created first, with women created later *for* men. According to the Judeo-Christian tradition, woman was created as a companion for man. In Greek mythology, however, Zeus created the first woman as a curse to punish men for the actions of another god.

Although Prometheus sided with Zeus during the war with the Titans, as a second-generation Titan himself he was still considered something of a rival to Zeus. Once, according to Hesiod, while "the gods and mortal men were negotiating," Prometheus played a trick on Zeus. It resulted in larger portions of food being served to the mortals than to the king of the gods. An insulted Zeus decided to punish Prometheus by taking the gift of fire away from the mortals, of whom Prometheus was known to be fond. This action indeed upset Prometheus, who used his crafty wit to return fire to humans, thus becoming the patron god of mankind. But Prometheus's disobedience did not pass unnoticed, and again Zeus chose to punish him indirectly, this time by cursing the race of men with the first woman, Pandora.

The creation of Pandora ("gift from all of the gods") turned into a joint Olympian venture, with each god providing a different aspect of her physique or personality. Aphrodite, for example, gave her physical attractiveness; Hermes, a liar's tongue. "And they were stunned," Hesiod wrote. "Immortal gods and mortal men, when they saw / The sheer deception, irresistible to men. / From her is the race of female women, / The deadly race and population of women, / A great infestation among mortal men."

The myth of Pandora elucidates two important aspects of the Greek worldview. First, it shows how the ancient Greeks wove misogyny into the very fabric of their universe. It also demonstrates, in Zeus's willingness to punish innocent mortals, the degree to which humans were merely pawns in the power struggles of gods.

Even so, despite such unfair treatment, the ancient Greeks revered Zeus above all other gods and invoked his beneficence more often than that of any other god in the pantheon.

The story of the creation *of woman demonstrates the ambiguous relationship in Greek myth between humans and the gods.*

X. LEE'S SUCCESS

AFTER RECUPERATING for six weeks under the protection of the Union navy's powerful guns, the Army of the Potomac (now reinforced to 120,000 men) evacuated the peninsula to join forces with Maj. Gen. John Pope's 63,000-man Army of Virginia near Alexandria. Lee, meanwhile, had begun planning an invasion of the North that he and Jefferson Davis hoped would force the Union into peace talks. Such an invasion could not succeed, however, if the Army of the Potomac was permitted to reinforce Pope.

Gen. Robert E. Lee

Lee's accelerated plan called for Maj. Gen. Thomas J. "Stonewall" Jackson to lead the left wing of the Army of Northern Virginia around Pope's camp on the Rappahannock River for an August 26, 1862, strike on the Orange & Alexandria Railroad, Pope's main supply line. Next, on August 27, Jackson would attack the huge Union supply depot at Manassas Junction.

Both operations went according to plan, and, just as Lee had anticipated, these jabs flushed out Pope, who attacked Jackson without realizing that Lee had quietly sent his army's right wing (under Longstreet) to attack Pope's flank. Longstreet's surprise appearance on August 30 sparked yet another Federal flight across Bull Run. This time, however, the Confederates kept marching north, crossing into Maryland on September 4.

On September 9, Lee issued orders sending two-thirds of his army (under Jackson) to capture Harpers Ferry. Although dividing one's forces is always risky, Lee judged that, because of McClellan's proven reluctance to attack, the risk was acceptable. Likely this would have been the case had not Union soldiers discovered by chance a mislaid copy of Lee's orders. "Now I know what to do!" McClellan reportedly exclaimed, and though he continued to move slowly, he proceeded much faster than he would have otherwise (and much faster than Lee had expected).

On September 15, after capturing Harpers Ferry, Jackson headed back to Lee's position near Sharpsburg. Had McClellan struck while Jackson was still on the move, Lee's army might have been divided and destroyed. Instead, McClellan waited until September 17 to send his Federals against the Rebels deployed along Antietam Creek. This delay made all the difference. The fighting that followed was fierce, and more than six thousand soldiers died; but Lee's army survived, and when McClellan failed to renew his attack the next day, Lee limped back into Virginia.

As a military commander, *Robert E. Lee was known for his ability to judge an opponent's qualities and his willingness to take risks.*

X. WINNERS AND LOSERS

As described earlier, when a country specializes in a particular good or service and then exchanges that good or service with other countries, all of the participants benefit. Yet these gains from trade are never distributed evenly across an entire national economy. Always, there are winners and losers.

When identifying winners and losers, it's useful to distinguish between the short-term and long-term effects of international trade. Short-term winners include companies that produce exportable goods and consumers who purchase imports. For example, American producers benefit to the extent that they can expand their markets overseas, while American consumers benefit to the extent that they pay less for imports than they would for domestic manufactures.

Short-term losers include domestic producers of importable goods, whose products must now compete with foreign imports, and domestic consumers of exportable goods, who end up paying more than they would otherwise because of the additional international demand. When Chinese textiles are sold in the United States, for example, the losers are American textile manufacturers and Chinese textile consumers—the former because the Chinese imports are cheaper than American manufactures, and the latter because strong US demand drives up the price of textiles in China.

In the long term, however, there are different winners and losers. For example, let's say that, in exchange for the textiles it exports to the United States, China begins importing a large amount of cheap American wheat. In the short term, the winners are US wheat producers and Chinese wheat consumers and the losers are Chinese wheat producers and US wheat consumers. The long-term winners and losers, however, will depend on what economists call the factors of production—primarily capital, land, and labor.

The key to understanding the long-term effects of a textile–wheat exchange is that textile production requires a great deal of labor and little land, while wheat production requires a great deal of land and little labor. The long-term winners in this example will be American landowners and Chinese workers, while the long-term losers will be Chinese landowners and American workers. Here's why: In the United States, where wheat production will grow and textile production will shrink, many textile workers will be laid off, driving down wages. At the same time, much more land will be placed into wheat cultivation, driving up rents. This process will work in reverse in China, where farmers will take land out of wheat production and textile manufacturers will hire more workers.

The short-term winners *and losers of international trade are not necessarily the same parties that experience its long-term gains and losses.*

X. THE HEART OF THE ANDES

IN THEIR SEARCH for new subject matter, the artists of the Hudson River School eventually moved well beyond the Hudson River Valley. Frederic Church, for example, was an avid explorer, and his wanderlust took him to South America (in 1853 and again in 1857), to the Arctic (in the early 1860s), and to Italy, Greece, and the Near East (during the late 1860s). Church's two trips to South America, in particular, produced some of his most memorable and best-known work.

Like his mentor Cole and his colleague Asher B. Durand, Church believed in celebrating the American landscape, but until the western mapping and geological expeditions in the late

Frederic E. Church, *The Heart of the Andes* (1859)

1850s (in which Albert Bierstadt participated), access to the Rocky Mountain West was still limited and rather dangerous. So, in search of heroic scenery that could convey a sense of both history and timelessness, Church traveled instead to South America, inspired in part by Alexander von Humboldt, who had traveled there in 1799–1804 and written about the journey in the first volume of *Kosmos*.

The vast scale of the Andes had a significant effect on Church's paintings, which became larger, more grandiose, and much more concerned with dramatic lighting effects. In *The Heart of the Andes* (1859), which measures about five feet wide by ten feet tall, Church used the immense scale to create a complete natural world. Like Durand's *Kindred Spirits*, the scene is a composite. In the foreground, Church shows Ecuador's lush greenery populated with finely rendered birds and flowers. In the middle ground, a river winds lazily through a broad plain. The grand snowy peaks of the Andes dominate the background. A few critics complained that the painting contained too much detail, but they missed the point that Church was using the detail to convey the boundlessness of God's creation in the New World.

Church exhibited *The Heart of the Andes* in a frame that mimicked a window so that viewers could imagine themselves looking out onto the Ecuadorian landscape. After a successful showing in New York City, Church sent the painting to London, where it was greeted with reviews that compared Church favorably to the great British romantic J. M. W. Turner. This acclaim deeply impressed the still-provincial American art world and persuaded artists such as Bierstadt and Thomas Moran to emulate Church's success with what became known as the Great Picture.

Before western exploration *revealed the majesty of the Rocky Mountains, artists such as Frederic Church frequently traveled abroad in search of timeless, monumental scenery.*

X. STELLAR EVOLUTION

AMONG THE BEST astronomical tools is the Hertzsprung-Russell (HR) diagram, which uses the relationship between a star's brightness and its spectral type (i.e., temperature) to organize the different stages in stellar evolution. As the HR diagram shows, stars tend to cluster around similar characteristics. The most obvious cluster is the diagonal band of stars that stretches from the upper left of the HR diagram to its lower right. Most stars enter this band, known as the main sequence, once fusion begins in their cores. As stars age, however, they move off the main sequence into other HR groupings.

The future of a star depends largely on its mass. All stars start out fusing hydrogen into helium, with the outward thermal pressure of the fusion reaction balancing the inward gravitational pull. When a star begins to run out of hydrogen, however, fusion slows, and this lowers the star's temperature. As a result, the star begins to contract, because there's no longer enough outward thermal pressure to balance the inward gravitational pull. As the star is compressed, however, the pressure inside it increases, and its temperature rises as well.

For a medium-sized yellow star like the Sun, this increase in temperature is sufficient to ignite the hydrogen in the star's outer layers. As these outer layers heat up, they expand outward, forming a different kind of star called a red giant. (It's red because it emits light with less energy.) At this point, the star leaves the main sequence and moves onto the horizontal band marked III on some HR diagrams.

Later, when all the hydrogen in the star's outer layers is used up, it compresses again, increasing its temperature again. If the star is massive enough, this increase in temperature is sufficient for the fusion of helium into carbon to begin. For a medium-sized star, however, this is as far as the process can go. Once its helium is used up, it contracts into a white dwarf, quietly radiating its remaining energy into space.

For more massive stars, the pattern of contraction and reignition continues. Once all of the helium in the core has been fused into carbon, the carbon begins fusing into neon, then oxygen, then silicon, and finally iron. At this point, the process ends, because iron can't be fused into anything else. The resulting star has an iron core, surrounded by successive shells of silicon, oxygen, neon, carbon, helium, and hydrogen.

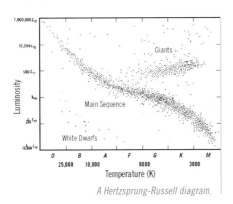

A Hertzsprung-Russell diagram.

When fusion begins, *stars enter the main sequence described by the Hertzsprung-Russell diagram.*

X. THE HOUSE OF TANTALUS

THE STORY OF THE house of Tantalus begins with the tale of Tantalus himself. This mortal child of Zeus invited the Olympians to a feast, during which he surreptitiously served them a dish containing his son Pelops, whom he had cut up and boiled. When the gods discovered Tantalus's deception, they restored Pelops and punished Tantalus by placing him in Hades (the forbidding Greek underworld) in a pool of water beneath a fruit tree. Whenever the parched, hungry Tantalus bent down for a drink of water, the pool receded; whenever he reached up for a piece of fruit, the tree raised its branches. In this way, Tantalus was "tantalized" for all eternity.

A later episode of the saga describes how Pelops pursued Hippodamia, the daughter of King Oenomaus of Pisa, who didn't want her to marry and had already killed thirteen of her suitors after beating them in chariot races. Pelops was given the same opportunity: He could race the king, and if he won, he could marry Hippodamia. If he lost, his life would be forfeit. Pelops accepted these terms and then bribed Myrtilus, the king's charioteer, to remove the linchpins of the king's chariot. It crashed, killing Oenomaus. But when Myrtilus attempted to claim his bribe, Pelops pushed him off a cliff into the sea. As he fell, Myrtilus cursed Pelops.

The curse had little immediate effect on Pelops, who inherited the southern Greek peninsula thereafter known as the Peloponnesus ("Pelops's island"), but his children suffered greatly. After two of his sons, Atreus and Thyestes, killed their half brother, Pelops banished them. Taken in by the Mycenaean king Eurystheus, Atreus and Thyestes inherited Eurystheus's kingdom upon his death, but they feuded bitterly over the throne. When Atreus prevailed, he exiled Thyestes.

Apollo purifies Orestes in a scene from a fourth-century BCE vase.

Years later, an apparently regretful Atreus welcomed Thyestes back with a feast. Afterward, however, Atreus revealed to his brother that Thyestes had, in fact, eaten two of his own sons, whom Atreus had killed and secretly served to his brother. Later, Thyestes's surviving son, Aegisthus, avenged this atrocity by killing Atreus's son Agamemnon. It then fell to Agamemnon's son, Orestes, to slay Aegisthus. With no one left to avenge Aegisthus, the Furies rose from Hades to hound Orestes. Eventually, Athena and Apollo chose to intervene, establishing a law court at Athens, where Orestes was tried and vindicated. Respecting this judgment, Zeus dismissed the Furies and, through his mitigating justice, ended the reciprocal violence that had plagued the descendants of Tantalus.

The story of *Tantalus describes the cycle of reciprocal violence that haunted his ancestors for generations until the beneficence of Olympian justice restored the social order.*

XI. A MAN WHO WILL FIGHT

Lincoln meets with McClellan at Antietam after the battle.

ON OCTOBER 25, 1862, five weeks after Antietam, Major General McClellan sent President Lincoln a request for more horses. The president replied with this acid note: "I have just read your despatch about sore-tongued and fatigued horses. Will you pardon me for asking what the horses of your army have done since the battle of Antietam that fatigue anything?" Two weeks later, Lincoln relieved McClellan of command, replacing him with Maj. Gen. Ambrose Burnside.

Although a competent general, Burnside was far from ambitious, and it was only with reluctance that he accepted leadership of the Army of the Potomac. His plan was to cross the Rappahannock River at Fredericksburg with 120,000 men and continue south to Richmond. But when Burnside reached Fredericksburg on December 12, he found Lee and 78,000 Confederates waiting for him. The ensuing battle produced a resounding Rebel victory, and a month later Lincoln relieved Burnside of command.

The president next turned to one of Burnside's division commanders, Maj. Gen. Joseph Hooker. In April 1863, "Fighting Joe" Hooker led the Army of the Potomac again across the Rappahannock, but this time well above and below Lee's position in Fredericksburg. Hooker's plan was to outflank Lee, but he wasn't quick enough. After learning of the threat on April 30 (two days after Union troops began crossing the river), Lee sent forty-five thousand men to block Hooker's exit from a densely wooded area west of Fredericksburg known as the Wilderness. Four days later, a bloodied Hooker began pulling back across the Rappahannock, and Lincoln began looking for another general. Unfortunately, Lee was already preparing another invasion of the North, and by June 28, when Lincoln finally settled on Maj. Gen. George G. Meade as Hooker's replacement, Lee's army was already marching into southern Pennsylvania.

The climactic battle of this campaign was fought at Gettysburg on July 1–3, with Meade arranging his forces in a defensive line that took advantage of the available high ground. Costly Confederate assaults on July 2 failed to dislodge him, and more failures on July 3, including the famously unsuccessful attack known as Pickett's Charge, sealed the outcome. (In all, Federal casualties topped twenty-three thousand, with the Confederate number uncertain but similarly high.) Meade performed well enough, but his reluctance to pursue Lee back into Virginia and his subsequent unwillingness to attack entrenched positions during two fall 1863 campaigns persuaded Lincoln that he still hadn't found the man who would fight.

When McClellan failed *to pursue Lee after Antietam, Lincoln's patience ran out, and the president began his long search for a commander who would fight.*

XI. THE WORLD TRADE ORGANIZATION

THE 151-MEMBER World Trade Organization (WTO) was established in 1995 specifically to resolve issues arising out of global trade. At its heart is a set of negotiated agreements, signed and ratified by nearly all of the world's trading nations, which the WTO bureaucracy uses to define and interpret the rules of international trade. The organization's self-stated goal is "to improve the welfare of the peoples of its member countries [by] ensuring that trade flows as smoothly, predictably and freely as possible."

The WTO evolved out of the General Agreement on Tariffs and Trade (GATT), an international treaty negotiated at the end of World War II with the goal of limiting barriers to trade in the postwar world. Initially, the GATT was merely one aspect of a larger economic reconstruction and recovery plan, but it developed a life of its own. With subsequent rounds of trade negotiation, it became the basis of the multilateral trading system currently in effect.

During the first few rounds of GATT talks, negotiators focused their attention on lowering import tariffs. As a result, the average tariff rate fell from about 40 percent in 1947, when the GATT took effect, to about 4 percent during the mid-1990s. (The main exception to this remarkable reduction, agriculture, continues to be protected.) In the mid-1980s, however—during the eighth, or Uruguay, round of talks—the emphasis of the negotiations shifted to nontariff barriers (such as import quotas) and issues unrelated to goods (such as services and intellectual property). Out of these negotiations came the WTO.

According to the WTO, the organization "is a place where member governments [can] go to try to sort out the trade problems they face with each other." Antiglobalizers, however, routinely condemn the WTO because it symbolizes to them the social inequities wrought by globalization. Because the WTO strongly supports trade liberalization, antiglobalizers consider it a cause of job losses in developed countries and of labor and natural resource exploitation in developing ones. Large disruptive protests outside the organization's November 1999 meetings in Seattle produced little policy change but did result in much greater public awareness of these controversial issues.

After Seattle, the WTO launched a public relations campaign to explain that its mandate was not exclusively the liberalization of trade. Under some circumstances, for instance, such as the protection of consumers or the prevention of the spread of disease, WTO rules support the imposition or maintenance of artificial trade barriers.

The World Trade Organization, *which evolved out of the General Agreement on Tariffs and Trade, defines and interprets the rules of international trade.*

XI. ALBERT BIERSTADT

ALTHOUGH BEST KNOWN for his western landscapes, Albert Bierstadt (1830–1902) is still considered one of the masters of the Hudson River School because of his interest in naturalistic detail, his grand manner of painting, and his idealized view of nature. In meticulously rendered canvases, Bierstadt used dramatic, almost sublime, light effects; panoramic views; and plunging perspectives to wow his audience with the grandeur of his subject matter.

Bierstadt's family emigrated from Germany to New Bedford, Massachusetts, while he was still an infant. In 1853, however, the twenty-three-year-old returned to Germany for four years of artistic training at the Düsseldorf Academy, where the Düsseldorf School of painting had risen to international prominence during the 1830s and 1840s. The leading members of the Düsseldorf School, which formed an important part of the German romantic movement, advocated plein air painting and produced heroic, highly articulated landscapes that underpinned Germany's emerging national consciousness. Upon his return to America, Bierstadt began painting similarly idealized, heroic landscapes grounded in American nationalism, especially the idea of manifest destiny.

Albert Bierstadt, *Rocky Mountains, Lander's Peak* (1863)

In 1859, Bierstadt joined an expedition traveling west to map the Rocky Mountains. He later painted several Great Pictures in the manner of Church based on sketches made during this trip. The most important of these works—*Rocky Mountains, Lander's Peak* (1863)—proved popular enough to merit a national tour. Although there is no such peak as Lander's—the scene is ideal, not actual—the landscape nevertheless evokes the larger truth that is the grandeur of the region.

In 1863, Bierstadt traveled even farther west to Yosemite, and though his paintings of El Capitan and Cathedral Rocks show actual places, they are no less dramatic. In all, Bierstadt's views of the West provided easterners with their first views of American scenery that matched the best of what Europe had to offer. During the late 1860s, however, Bierstadt's popularity, along with that of the Hudson River School, faltered. Especially after the Civil War, painting in the grand style began to seem melodramatic as the public moved toward a more private, introspective appreciation of nature.

Albert Bierstadt's *highly dramatic scenes of the West were grounded in uniquely American ideas about manifest destiny.*

XI. STELLAR DEATH

THE MORE MASSIVE the star, the faster it fuses its nuclear fuel. A small star may remain on the main sequence for trillions of years before gradually contracting into a white dwarf. A medium-sized star may stay on the main sequence for billions of years before turning into a red giant and then a white dwarf. (After radiating all their energy into space, white dwarfs subsequently become cold black dwarfs.) Large stars, however, consume their fuel much more quickly, remaining on the main sequence for only a few million years before experiencing exciting, cataclysmic ends.

When fusion stops, stars cease generating outward thermal pressure. So gravity takes over, and the stars contract. The pull of this gravity is so strong in large stars that they become compressed beyond the point of stability. The result is an explosion caused by the repulsive forces generated by the nuclei in the star's compressed core. Such explosions, called supernovas, are responsible for some of the most beautiful sights in the universe. The Crab Nebula, for instance, was created about one thousand years ago by a supernova. In time, it will likely give birth to a star of its own.

Once a supernova has blasted away the outer layers of a star, the remaining core, if it's small, becomes a white dwarf. Otherwise, it undergoes yet another transformation. First, you need to know that our Sun, by definition, has a solar mass of 1. If the remaining core of a supernova has a solar mass between about 1.4 and 2, it will continue to contract until it becomes a neutron star. This happens because, during contraction, the protons and electrons in the star's core combine under pressure to form neutrons. As a result, neutron stars are incredibly dense. If our Sun contracted into a neutron star, it would shrink to less than ten kilometers across, and a teaspoonful of it would weigh about one hundred million metric tons.

However, if the core left over from a supernova has a solar mass of 2 or more, not even the repulsive forces generated by nuclei under pressure can withstand the pull of its gravity. In these cases, the cores inevitably collapse into singularities, or single points, called black holes.

A Milky War star in the process of becoming a white dwarf.

Once a star *can no longer support fusion, it collapses and, depending on its mass, winds up as a white dwarf, a neutron star, or a black hole.*

XI. THE RAPE OF PERSEPHONE

THE STORY OF PERSEPHONE has been preserved in the collection of poems known as the Homeric Hymns. Although these hymns were not actually composed by Homer, they do emulate his style and diction. Historians believe that they were composed at different times throughout the Archaic, Classical, and Hellenistic periods.

A detail from a Greek vase showing Persephone and Hades.

Persephone was the daughter of Zeus and the grain goddess Demeter. One day, while she was enjoying a leisurely stroll through Greece, Hades rose up from the underworld in his chariot and kidnapped her. Learning what had happened, a deeply distraught Demeter petitioned Zeus for the return of her missing child. She found out, however, that Zeus had already made a marriage agreement with Hades (which is why Zeus had allowed Hades to kidnap Persephone in the first place).

As this myth makes clear, marriages in the ancient Greek world were arranged by men (fathers and/or grooms), not by the couple themselves. Similarly, rape (in this sense meaning "the carrying away of a person by force") was considered a crime committed by one man against another man, rather than an offense against the woman involved. Nevertheless, Demeter's distress shows the very real consequences of suppressed female autonomy, and her reaction to her situation reflects the deep fear of female irrationality that pervaded Greek myth.

Unwilling to accept Zeus's judgment, Demeter protested the marriage by preventing the harvesting of crops—knowing that without crops, humans would have nothing to offer in sacrifice to the gods. The gods didn't eat grain, of course, but they required honors from humans, so the ending of the sacrifices—in addition to threatening humanity with extinction—brought the world of the gods to a grinding halt. (Evidently, the relationship between human beings and gods was not entirely one-sided.)

To placate Demeter, whose motherly rage was now disrupting the entire cosmos, Zeus agreed to allow Persephone to spend two-thirds of the year on Olympos with her mother. During the remainder of the year, she would return to her husband in the underworld. Thus we have the two seasons of the Greek year: While Persephone resides on Olympos, a happy Demeter permits crops to grow. During Persephone's absence, her mother mourns, and the earth is barren.

In this aetiological myth, *the kidnapping of Persephone by Hades and Demeter's subsequent protest lead to the establishment of the seasons.*

XII. THREE STARS

DURING THE WINTER OF 1863–64, political considerations dominated the war councils in Washington and Richmond. The North would be holding a presidential election in the fall, and Lincoln's chances didn't seem very good because of the stalemate that prevailed in the East. Despite all the recent carnage, the Army of the Potomac and the Army of Northern Virginia occupied essentially the same positions they had a year earlier, and this suited the South fine. The Confederate strategy was simple: Hold out until November, when war-weary Northerners would surely throw out the Republicans and elect Peace Democrats inclined to negotiate Southern independence.

Meanwhile, in February 1864, Congress passed a bill reinstating the rank of lieutenant general, last held by George Washington. The popular choice for the new top job was Grant, the Hero of Chattanooga, but Lincoln delayed the appointment because of widespread rumors that Grant was planning to run for president himself. After receiving assurances through intermediaries that Grant had no political aspirations, Lincoln presented the general with his third star at a White House ceremony on March 9. As a fellow guest at Willard's Hotel described Grant, "His face has three expressions: deep thought; extreme determination; and great simplicity and calmness."

Determined to command from the field rather than from a desk, the new general in chief traveled the very next day to Brandy Station, Virginia, where the Army of the Potomac had made its winter camp. After meeting with Major General Meade, Grant made two key decisions. First, he would remain in the East rather than return to the West, as he had previously intended. Second, he would make his headquarters with the Army of the Potomac while retaining Meade as its commander—subject, of course, to Grant's orders.

Grant photographed while visiting Washington to receive his third star.

Aware of the South's waiting game, Grant decided that the best way to thwart the Confederacy's political strategy would be to crush the Rebel armies and thus win the war before November. In the past, he observed, the Union armies in the East and West had "acted independently and without concert, like a balky team, no two ever pulling together." Now they would follow a coordinated strategy designed to prevent Rebel armies from reinforcing one another. Sherman, whom Grant named as his successor in the West, would drive from Chattanooga toward Atlanta, while Grant himself took on Lee.

When Lincoln gave *Grant control of all Union armies in March 1864, the general had to broaden his view to include the eastern theater as well as the western.*

XII. THE WORLD BANK AND THE IMF

IN JULY 1944, financial experts from forty-four countries attended the United Nations Monetary and Financial Conference held in Bretton Woods, New Hampshire. The purpose of the conference was to make financial arrangements for the postwar world. The participants knew that the two most pressing needs would be capital for long-term reconstruction and loans for short-term currency stabilization. Therefore, they recommended the creation of two institutions to meet those needs: the International Bank for Reconstruction and Development (IBRD) and the International Monetary Fund (IMF).

The purpose of the IBRD was to finance the reconstruction of Europe and Japan, whose cities and industries had been devastated by aerial bombing. After achieving this goal, the IBRD redefined itself. Its new mission was to alleviate poverty and support growth in the developing world. In 1960, the International Development Association (IDA) was formed to complement the work of the IBRD. The IDA's mission was to make loans to the world's poorest countries on terms more flexible than those offered by the IBRD. Together, these two institutions constitute the World Bank, which today provides low-interest loans, interest-free credit, and grants to the developing world.

Meanwhile, the IMF continues to pursue the work it was assigned at Bretton Woods: stabilizing exchange rates and overseeing the world's international payment system (which national governments use to transfer funds to one another). While the World Bank provides long-term help with education, health care, and other infrastructure projects, the IMF acts as a lender of last resort, providing short-term loans to countries with large trade imbalances that would otherwise have to employ draconian measures in order to pay off their creditors. The IMF also helps these countries reorganize their economies so that they can pay off their debt.

Like the WTO, however, the IMF and the World Bank have both been attacked by critics of globalization, who hold the IMF responsible for worsening the 1997 Asian financial crisis and who fault the World Bank for its lack of success in fighting global poverty. An often-heard complaint is that both institutions have a one-size-fits-all approach that does more harm than good because it fails to take into account germane differences among developing nations. As a result, a few of those nations have refused IMF loans, and some development experts have begun to question the need for a World Bank. Others, however, contine to believe that the IMF and the World Bank can play important roles as international safety nets and lenders of last resort.

The World Bank and the IMF were created at the end of World War II to manage the postwar global economy. As the world changed, however, so did their missions.

XII. LUMINISM

LUMINISM IS A TERM that modern art historians use to describe a style prevalent in American landscape painting between the 1850s and the 1870s. As the name implies, luminist painters were interested in light, especially brilliant or glowing light, and the effect it had on the atmosphere of a landscape. Typically, luminist landscapes also possessed a sense of serenity that art historian Barbara Novak has called "the still small voice" (in contrast with the "grand operas" of Church and Bierstadt).

Fitz Henry Lane, *New York Harbor* (1850)

Like the artists of the Hudson River School, luminists believed deeply in the spiritual quality of nature and read extensively among the works of transcendentalists, especially Ralph Waldo Emerson and Henry David Thoreau. In his 1836 book *Nature*, Emerson wrote of an experience he had had during which he felt the physical and spiritual worlds merge. He became, in his own words, a "transparent eyeball." In this condition, seeing coincides with being, and Emerson became able, he said, to apprehend absolute spiritual truths.

The hushed calm, infinite space, and clarity of vision that characterized luminist painting is often viewed as an artistic parallel to Emerson's transcendentalist state. Other critics, however, see the tranquility of luminist paintings as fundamentally an artistic response to the national strife then engulfing the country—the idealized landscapes offering nostalgic passage back to a simpler time before civil war.

Important precursors of American luminism include the landscapes of European artists Claude Lorrain and J. M. W. Turner, whose evocative and atmospheric paintings were well known to American artists through published engravings and their own travels abroad. Domestically, the marine landscapes of Robert Salmon, an English artist who immigrated to Boston in 1828, made use of light in a way that influenced Fitz Henry Lane, a leading luminist of the 1850s. Although many artists of the period incorporated aspects of luminism into their work, the painters most closely associated with the style were Lane, Martin Johnson Heade, John Frederick Kensett, and Sanford Robinson Gifford.

A painting style *concurrent with the Hudson River School, luminism emphasized atmosphere, especially the use of light, over topography.*

XII. BLACK HOLES

THE COLLAPSE OF LARGE astronomical objects into black holes was first predicted by Albert Einstein's General Theory of Relativity, published in 1915. At the time, Einstein's theory seemed fantastic, but it has since been shown that black holes do exist and play an important role in the universe. At the center of every black hole is a singularity, where the entire mass of the black hole is concentrated at a single point in space. Over time, this central mass can grow as the black hole pulls in more matter.

Moving outward from the singularity, we come to the event horizon, sometimes called the point of no return. Light waves within the event horizon cannot escape the tremendous pull of the singularity's gravity, so black holes are invisible. The size of the event horizon depends on the mass of the singularity.

If you approached a black hole in a spaceship, you would begin to feel its gravitational pull long before you reached the event horizon. The acceleration you would experience due to this gravity would increase your speed, pulling you in faster and faster. As you approached the event horizon, the rate of this acceleration would increase greatly, even over small distances. In fact, the front of your spaceship would begin accelerating much faster than the rear. As a result, the spaceship (and you) would be stretched out by the awesome gravitational force—an effect called spaghettification.

An artist's view of a black hole at the center of a galaxy.

Although black holes are not visible, they can be located by the effects that they have on the surrounding space. When a black hole forms in a binary star system, for example, it begins pulling in matter from its companion star. Typically, this matter is hydrogen and helium from the companion star's outer layers, but, if the star is close enough, the entire core can be sucked in. As the matter spirals down into the black hole (like water running down a drain), friction among the particles generates heat that is radiated outward as X-rays. Because these X-rays are generated beyond the event horizon, they can be easily detected.

Black holes can also be detected by the effect they have on light. When light passes near to a black hole, its path is bent slightly by the black hole's gravity, as though it were passing through an optical lens. For this reason, the effect is called gravitational lensing, and it is also detectable.

Although black holes *were once considered purely theoretical, they are now accepted as genuine phenomena whose influence is found everywhere in the universe.*

XII. THE SANCTUARIES OF APOLLO

PERHAPS THE TWO most sacred places in the entire Greek world were Delphi, located northwest of Thebes on the Greek mainland, and Delos, an island in the southern Aegean. Neither had any military value, but both were important politically because of their mythological origins, descriptions of which can be found in the long Homeric Hymn to Apollo.

A Greek king consults the oracle at Delphi.

The story of Delos begins with Leto, whom a jealous Hera persecuted for sleeping with Zeus. In fact, Hera caused every place on earth to shun the pregnant Leto. Finally, Leto came to the barren little island of Delos, to which she swore an oath. If the island permitted her to give birth there, she would ensure that it became home to fame and honor. Delos agreed, and Leto gave birth on the island to the twins Artemis and Apollo. Because Delos was so small and barren, it couldn't sustain on its own any sort of human settlement, but Apollo fulfilled his mother's promise by establishing an oracular sanctuary on the island that was supported and honored by all the city-states of the Greek world, despite the various enmities they often harbored toward one another.

With regard to Delphi, Apollo made his way one day to the slopes of Mount Parnassus, where he intended to establish a temple. The land, however, was guarded by the giant snake Pytho, a remnant of the Titan age when the site had been home to oracles associated with the goddess Themis. Apollo then killed Pytho, providing yet another example of an Olympian taming the primordial wild.

After slaying the snake, Apollo left the area, transformed himself into a dolphin, and leapt aboard a ship manned by sailors from Crete. While the sailors marveled at the magical dolphin, Apollo guided their ship around the Peloponnesus to Crisa, a port on the Gulf of Corinth near Mount Parnassus. At this point, the dolphin disappeared, and Apollo appeared before the men in human form, commanding them to become the priests of his new sanctuary at Delphi (after *delphinos*, the Greek word for "dolphin"). In exchange for dedicating the rest of their lives to him, Apollo promised the men that they would never have to toil for sustenance because the entire Greek world would provide for them in his honor.

Two loosely related *mythological events explain the importance of Delphi and Delos in the Greek world.*

XIII. PRISONER EXCHANGES

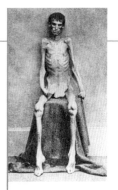

An emaciated
Andersonville prisoner.

EARLY IN THE WAR, prisoners weren't much of an issue. The few
who were taken were easily held in county jails and converted
warehouses until informally exchanged. During the winter of
1861–62, however, Confederate officials began pressing for a
formal exchange cartel because, already beginning to run low
on food, they didn't want the responsibility of feeding Union
prisoners. At first, the Lincoln administration resisted because
it didn't want to confer any sort of diplomatic recognition on
the Confederacy, but the Seven Days' Campaign forced a change in this policy.
With thousands of prisoners pouring into new, highly inadequate POW camps,
Lincoln came under a great deal of public pressure to hasten repatriation. In July
1862, therefore, he agreed to formal exchanges on a man-for-man basis with rank
weighting. (A general, for example, was worth sixty privates.) Excess prisoners on
one side were paroled after promising not to take up arms again until "exchanged"
for prisoners taken later by the other side.

This situation prevailed until Lincoln issued the Emancipation Proclamation
in January 1863, prompting a large number of runaway slaves and free blacks to
join the Union ranks. The Confederate government responded in May 1863 with
an announcement that, henceforth, all captured black soldiers would be either
reenslaved or executed. The North's next move was to halt all prisoner exchanges
so that it could hold Southern prisoners hostage to this threat.

By the time Grant took command in March 1864, the prisoner-of-war issue
had turned critical. As Northern newspapers reported daily, tens of thousands of
Union soldiers were suffering horribly in abominable prisoner-of-war camps such
as the notorious Andersonville in southern Georgia. Nevertheless, on April 17,
Grant formalized the exchange ban. His decision was immediately attacked as
inhumane, but its subsequent impact on the war was undeniable.

Unlike the North, the South faced a severe manpower shortage. It couldn't
afford to have any of its pieces taken off the game board, and Grant's aggressiveness
in the field—more dead, more wounded, more *prisoners*—only intensified the
pressure. Many thousands of Union POWs would die terrible deaths in places like
Andersonville, but withholding an equal number of Southern soldiers from the
battlefield unquestionably shortened the war. "It is hard on our men held in
Southern prisons not to exchange them," Grant wrote a few months later, "but
it is humanity to those left in our ranks to fight our battles."

By refusing to *exchange prisoners, Grant condemned many thousands of men to death
in abominable camps. However, his policy undoubtedly shortened the war.*

XIII. THE WASHINGTON CONSENSUS

THE PHRASE *Washington consensus* was originated in 1989 by economist John Williamson, who used it to describe the commonalities that he found in the economic policies being promoted by Washington-based international institutions, such as the World Bank and the IMF. Williamson's analysis focused specifically on the recommendations these institutions were making to Latin American countries to help them recover from the financial crises they experienced during the 1980s, but the idea turned out to have a much wider application.

Among the ten elements that Williamson identified as the basis of the Washington consensus were: fiscal discipline, so that a country didn't spend more than its revenues; reorientation of public spending, from unproductive sectors to strategic national targets such as education or public health; tax reform, to minimize evasion and enhance the business environment; financial liberalization, especially the deregulation of foreign capital and reform of the domestic financial sector; and trade liberalization, including the removal of both tariff and nontariff barriers to trade.

Over time, this policy agenda came to be seen, especially by antiglobalizers, as a set of rules that international financial institutions were imposing in order to promote and regulate globalization so that multinational companies could exploit the developing world. As Williamson himself noted, "There are people who cannot utter the term [*Washington consensus*] without foaming at the mouth."

In response to these criticisms, several supplementary policies were added, resulting in what Harvard economist Dani Rodrik has called the "augmented" Washington consensus. Among the ten additional elements that Rodrik identified are: corporate reform, containment of corruption, negotiation of more and stronger WTO agreements, social safety nets, and targeted poverty reduction. The basic difference between the original and the augmented consensus is that the augmented consensus places a greater emphasis on institutional reform. Yet Rodrik believes strongly that the augmented Washington consensus is bound to fail because it's "infeasible, inappropriate, and irrelevant" and because it continues to reflect a one-size-fits-all mentality that leaves no room for individually tailored local strategies. According to Rodrik, its "rules" describe the behavior of developed countries but not how to become one.

As Rodrik's argument suggests, a more useful discussion might be whether there should be a consensus at all. Handling the different problems that arise in different countries using a single list of remedies would seem analogous to prescribing the same regimen of medicines to a variety of patients with widely differing diseases.

The phrase Washington consensus, *often used pejoratively, refers to the policy commonalities of Washington-based international economic institutions.*

XIII. KENSETT AND GIFFORD

JOHN FREDERICK KENSETT and Sanford Robinson Gifford were both landscape artists associated with the Hudson River School style during the early phases of their careers. Traveling separately in Europe, however, both men became familiar with the work of the French Barbizon painters, especially Jean-Baptiste-Camille Corot, whose plein air canvases were bathed in a soft natural light. Seeing Corot's work persuaded both men to give up the sharp, objective, detailed descriptions of nature that were characteristic of Hudson River School painting and instead begin creating in a luminist style that was softer and more poetic—in other words, more subjective.

Like his friend Asher B. Durand, Kensett (1816–72) had originally trained as an engraver but shifted to painting after 1840. His early landscapes were filled with picturesque detail, but as he matured, his paintings gravitated toward a luminist aesthetic in their simplicity of form, attention to atmosphere, and use of brilliant midday light. Kensett's subjects also changed from the mountain scenery he favored early in his career to tranquil coastal scenes in which still water provided an ideal reflective medium for the shimmering light that became his stylistic hallmark. A prime example of Kensett's mature style is the serene *Beacon Rock at Newport Harbor* (1857), one of many scenes of the Newport, Rhode Island, coastline that Kensett painted over the years. In *Beacon Rock*, the landscape has been reduced to an expanse of sky, some placid water, and a solid mass of rock, all bathed in Kensett's remarkable shimmering light.

Sanford Robinson Gifford, *A Gorge in the Mountains (Kauterskill Clove)* (1862)

Gifford (1823–80)—who grew up in Hudson, New York, a few miles up the river from the Catskill home of Thomas Cole—began his artistic career painting portraits and genre scenes but switched to landscapes during the 1840s. His mature work offers a skillful blending of detail and atmosphere, but the primary focus is always on the light. Gifford is particularly well known for the saturated late-afternoon light that illuminates many of his landscapes. The effect is such that the viewer sees the painted scene as through a gauze curtain, and the heat of the late-afternoon sun becomes palpable. In other works such as *A Gorge in the Mountains (Kauterskill Clove)* (1862), Gifford uses a more pervasive, form-dissolving light to create retinal sensations that make the colors on the canvas seem to flicker and change before one's eyes.

Both Kensett and Gifford *moved from the Hudson River School to luminism as they became more interested in the artistic use of light and atmosphere.*

XIII. GALAXIES

FOR THE SAME REASON that matter in a nebula tends to clump (because of the attractive force of gravity), so do stars tend to cluster. The galaxies that they form come in many different sizes, containing anywhere from ten million to one trillion stars and ranging in diameter from fifteen hundred to three hundred thousand light-years. But there are just three main types of galaxies: spiral, elliptical, and irregular. Our solar system

The spiral galaxy M81.

resides in a large spiral galaxy called the Milky Way, which contains approximately three hundred billion stars and is one hundred thousand light-years across.

At the center of every spiral galaxy is a bulge of stars, around which most of the galaxy's remaining stars rotate in a flat disk. The majority of those stars occupy the two spiral arms that give this type of galaxy its distinctive shape. Surrounding the disk is a roughly spherical shell of stars called the halo. Because spiral galaxies tend to contain a lot of gas and dust, they are excellent stellar nurseries and typically have many younger stars. These tend to congregate in the arms, while the older stars tend to populate the galaxy's central bulge and halo. Even among spiral galaxies, however, there can be some differentiation in shape. In barred spiral galaxies, for example, the arms spiral out from a bar-shaped grouping of stars that spans the center of the disk.

Although most large galaxies are spiral, there are many more elliptical galaxies in the universe, because small galaxies tend to be elliptical and most galaxies tend to be (relatively) small. Unlike spirals, elliptical galaxies have no disk and no arms; nor do they rotate much. Instead, they look like elongated bulges. Because they usually lack the gas and dust necessary for new star formation, they contain primarily older stars.

Irregular galaxies have, as one might expect, irregular shapes. Some have bulges that are off-center. Some have bulges but no spiral arms. Some are even more unusual in shape because they have resulted from the collision of two other galaxies.

Like stars, galaxies also tend to form groups, called clusters. A cluster can contain tens, hundreds, or even thousands of galaxies. Our Milky Way is part of a cluster called the Local Group, which contains about forty galaxies. Clusters themselves form groups, called superclusters. Our Local Group, along with about one hundred other clusters, is part of the Virgo Supercluster.

Stars tend to *cluster in groups called galaxies, which take a variety of shapes and sizes.*

XIII. HERMES BECOMES THE HERALD OF ZEUS

LIKE APOLLO AND ARTEMIS, Hermes came into being as the result of an extramarital affair between Zeus and another immortal—in this case, the nymph Maia, who chose to continue living in her cave rather move to Olympos (despite being on generally friendly terms with the Olympians).

Hermes's birth was unremarkable, and he might have lived on with his mother, unnoticed, had it not been for his unbridled ambition. According to the Homeric Hymn to Hermes, the infant god, from the day of his birth, set out to be mischievous. One day, while Hermes was on his way to steal some cattle from Apollo, a tortoise crossed his path. Hermes marveled at the tortoise and said he would make it sing. Hermes then gutted the tortoise, attached ox's horns to its shell, and strung the horns with sheep gut. The result was the lyre, the primary instrument used by ancient Greeks to accompany their lyric poetry.

After driving off a few cattle, Hermes realized that it might be wise to hide his tracks, so he began herding the cattle back and forth to create multiple trails. Then he fashioned the first pair of sandals to disguise his own footprints. These tricks delayed Apollo, but they couldn't prevent him eventually tracing the stolen cattle back to Maia's cave. In the meantime, Hermes had slaughtered two of Apollo's cows.

Of course, being a god, Hermes did not eat meat, but he craved its aroma, so after butchering the cows, he took some fat, wrapped it around a bone, and burned the result, creating exceedingly sweet vapors that he and the other gods found highly pleasing. This arrangement of fat and bone became the "gods' portion," and all sacrifices made by humans thereafter were performed in the manner invented by Hermes.

By the time Apollo caught up with the infant, he had already returned to his crib, so Apollo left, returning later with Zeus. Keeping to his wily ways, Hermes told a series of convincing lies that impressed Zeus with their guile and with the nerve Hermes showed in lying to his father. Eventually, Zeus ordered his two sons to make peace, and Hermes did so by presenting Apollo with the newly invented lyre. Zeus then made Hermes his herald because the child was so obviously comfortable traveling around the countryside. This story also suggests why Hermes became the patron god of thieves and liars.

The story of *how Hermes became Zeus's herald explains the creation of the lyre and Hermes's invention of the proper ritual for making sacrifices to the gods.*

A musician plays a lyre in this third-century CE Roman mosaic.

XIV. THE WILDERNESS CAMPAIGN

AS GRANT WAITED for the spring rains to subside, he and Lincoln agreed on a new target for the Army of the Potomac. Previous Union commanders had set their sights on the capture of Richmond. Each time they pushed south, however, Lee bloodied their noses, and they pulled back across the nearest river, usually the Rappahannock. But Grant wasn't much interested in the Confederate capital. He wanted to destroy Lee's army, and his pursuit of this goal was brutally single-minded.

Grant's first Virginia offensive began in early May 1864, with Lee still encamped at Orange Court House on the Rapidan, a tributary of the Rappahannock. On May 3, Grant directed Meade to take the Army of the Potomac across the Rapidan and march it around Lee's right flank. Grant had 122,000 men; Lee, just 66,000. But as Fighting Joe Hooker had learned exactly one year earlier, the densely forested area known as the Wilderness, through which Meade had to pass, was a powerful force equalizer.

The second Battle of the Wilderness began on May 5, with some fierce but inconclusive fighting on the Orange Turnpike and Orange Plank Road. The next morning, the battle was rejoined, with much the same result. Over those two days in the Wilderness—which began a long, hard tug-of-war between Grant and Lee—the Union lost 17,000 men (compared with 11,000 for the Confederacy), but Grant refused to "skedaddle," as his predecessors had. Instead, apparently indifferent to the conditions and the terrain, he pushed ahead, confronting Lee again and again. "That man will fight us every day and every hour till the end of the war," James Longstreet said.

Unable to best Lee in the Wilderness, Grant next sought to capture the strategic crossroads at Spotsylvania Court House. To block him, Lee marched the Army of Northern Virginia through the night of May 7–8, beating Grant to the spot. During the next two weeks, the slugfest continued, with the two great armies striking each other repeatedly in the general area of Spotsylvania. As in the Wilderness, Union casualties were gruesome (and about 50 percent higher than Confederate casualties), but Grant kept fighting.

One of the Confederate entrenchments at Spotsylvania.

Although badly bloodied *in his first confrontation with Lee, Grant pushed forward— demonstrating that, unlike previous Union commanders, he would not retreat.*

XIV. ENVIRONMENTAL CHALLENGES

ECONOMIC ACTIVITY often results in negative environmental impacts, such as chemical waste and air pollution. Yet the cost of cleaning these up is not always included in the price of the product. In many cases, especially in the developing world, producers take advantage of lax regulation to pollute with impunity.

Some global economists have theorized that this behavior follows a pattern previously identified by economist Simon Kuznets. According to Kuznets, economic inequality increases with per-capita income until a critical income level is reached, after which the inequality declines. The Kuznets curve, which resembles a bell curve, is the graphic representation of Kuznets's theory.

If one applies the same logic to the relationship between income and the environment, the result is an "environmental" Kuznets curve, which shows environmental degradation rising with per-capita income. Once a tipping point is reached, however, higher per-capita income correlates strongly with an improving environment. This makes sense because, at the low per-capita income levels associated with the developing world, less attention is paid to environmental regulation than to more pressing social needs. For a time, more economic activity simply means more pollution. However, as a country becomes more developed, stricter environmental oversight is usually put into place, reversing the trend. Initially, the environmental harm is stabilized; then, as incomes rise further, some of the new wealth is put to work repairing the damage already done.

This theory has important implications for the global warming debate, because it suggests that greenhouse emissions from developing countries (especially India and China) will continue to rise until per-capita income in those countries reaches the Kuznets tipping point. As it turns out, however, very little empirical evidence exists to support this theory. So far, the relationship it describes has been shown to apply only to urban concentrations of sulfur dioxide.

The environmental Kuznets theory rests on two main assumptions: that environmentally friendly production costs more than environmentally unfriendly production, and that poor nations can't afford environmentally friendly production until they reach a certain income level. But these assumptions may be false. Denmark's economy has recently disproven the first assumption, growing 50 percent without any increase in greenhouse emissions. The reason was that Denmark shifted 22 percent of its electricity generation to wind power. The success of market-oriented programs such as ecolabeling, which calls attention to environmentally friendly products, also suggests that economic growth need not always cause environmental harm.

The environmental Kuznets *theory holds that growth in poor countries will always cause adverse environmental impacts until a certain income level is reached.*

XIV. FITZ HENRY LANE AND MARTIN JOHNSON HEADE

IT WAS PRIMARILY the landscapes of Fitz Henry Lane and Martin Johnson Heade that inspired art critic John Baur, then director of the Whitney Museum of American Art, to coin the term *luminism* in 1954. Baur's intention, more than to describe the paintings of Lane and Heade, was to distinguish them from the work of the Hudson River School.

Initially a lithographer, Lane (1804–65) turned to painting later in life, favoring scenes around his native Gloucester as well as views of nearby Boston and the coast of Maine. Lane's choice of coastal landscapes and harbors as the mainstays of his work was highly unusual for the time. Before Lane, marine painting hardly existed in the United States, except as practiced by a few immigrant artists such as the English-born Robert Salmon.

Early Lane paintings such as *Boston Harbor* (1850–55) are highly detailed, precisely defined, and bathed in a light that glows from the center of the composition. Later Lane paintings tend to be more imaginative and atmospheric, becoming nearly abstract. This transformation can be seen in *Brace's Rock, Brace's Cove* (1864), which is little more than a series of horizontal planes interrupted only by the diagonal mast of a wrecked ship. Works like *Brace's Rock*, which seems to suggest a union between man and nature, make Lane the artist most frequently compared to Emerson and the other transcendentalists.

Fitz Henry Lane, *Brace's Rock, Brace's Cove* (1864)

Although Heade (1819–1904) was born in Pennsylvania, he studied in Europe before returning to the United States. In 1858, he moved to New York City, where he struck up relationships with some of the leading landscape painters of the time, including Frederic Church and John Frederick Kensett, whose influence no doubt inspired Heade to begin painting landscapes himself.

Unlike Kensett, Gifford, and Lane, Heade showed more affinity for hushed than brilliant light, and he was particularly interested in fleeting atmospheric effects, which give his paintings a sublime air of mystery and quiet drama. Best known for a series of paintings depicting the dramatic light of approaching thunderstorms, Heade traveled to South America later in life at the urging of Church, who thought his friend might appreciate the scenery. Instead, the experience caused Heade to move away from landscapes and begin painting the lush plants and flowers of the tropics.

Lane and Heade *were the two artists most closely associated with luminist painting.*

XIV. QUASARS

AN INTERESTING PROPERTY of all waves is the Doppler effect, which occurs when the source of a wave and the observer are moving relative to each other. Think of a race car moving around a track. As the car approaches you, the sound waves emitted by its engine compress, thus increasing their frequency, or pitch. As the car passes and moves away from you, the sound waves elongate, and their frequency drops. When children imitate this distinctive sound, they are principally mimicking the Doppler effect.

The same effect holds true for light. If a source of astronomical light, such as a star, is moving toward us, its light will be shifted up in frequency toward the blue end of the visible spectrum. This is called blueshift. Similarly, light emitted by stars moving away from us will be redshifted. The amount of blueshift or redshift that we observe can be used to determine an object's speed. The greater the shift, the greater the speed of the object relative to us.

An artist's rendering of a quasar.

The Doppler effect is particularly relevant to the study of quasars, which is shorthand for QUASi-stellAR radio objectS. When astronomers first began studying quasars during the late 1950s and early 1960s, they were puzzled because quasars looked like stars but emitted light that had unsual wavelengths. Eventually, Dutch astronomer Maarten Schmidt realized that astronomers were really looking at distant ultraviolet light that had been redshifted into the visible spectrum.

Yet even this explanation seemed incomplete. Distant stars moving at such high speeds away from us should be impossible for us to detect, and yet we could detect them. This meant that quasars must be emitting light equivalent to that produced by thousands of galaxies. Eventually, Schmidt realized that quasars weren't stars at all but young, "active" galaxies. Like most large galaxies, they had supermassive black holes at their centers. However, because these galaxies were young, their central black holes were still feeding and thus producing an incredible amount of light. This explained why quasars appear so bright to us.

It has been theorized that, during the early stages of galactic evolution, the supermassive black holes at the center of most large galaxies absorb the innermost star systems. In time, however, the resulting output of energy becomes so great that it pushes the next tier of star systems just out of reach of the black hole. At this point, the galaxy stabilizes and becomes "inactive," like our own.

Quasars are young, *"active" galaxies whose central black holes are still feeding on the innermost star systems.*

XIV. APHRODITE LEARNS A LESSON IN LOVE

IN THE HOMERIC HYMN to Aphrodite, the goddess of love is portrayed as one who takes pleasure in causing other gods to fall in love with mortals. Even all-knowing Zeus can be controlled by Aphrodite in this way, upsetting the patriarchal order of the Greek pantheon. For this reason, according to the hymn, the king of the gods decided to teach the goddess of love a lesson and "into Aphrodite herself Zeus sent sweet desire to sleep with a mortal man."

Zeus caused Aphrodite to fall in love with the Trojan Anchises, and after taking human form she promptly seduced and bedded him. Later, she revealed to Anchises the truth that she was a goddess and the name of the mortal child she would bear him: "Aineias shall be his name, since dread sorrow held me when I came into the bed of a mortal man." By choosing the name *Aineias* (or the more familiar *Aeneas* in Latin), Aphrodite associated the child with the Greek word *ainos*, meaning "dread." But what was the cause of this dread?

Aphrodite rests in a giant shell in this first-century CE wall painting from Pompeii.

The hymn relates that Aphrodite was "in tears" as she seduced Anchises. Clearly, she was embarrassed, which had been Zeus's intention. He didn't want her teasing him any longer about his own mortal bedfellows. But there was also a deeper significance to Aphrodite's tears.

In the earliest Greek myths, rarely are the Olympians called "gods" and the human beings called "humans." Instead, Hesiod and Homer most often refer to human beings as "mortals" and the Olympians as "immortals." This is done to highlight the contrast between the two groups, the implicit difference being death.

Generally, gods exist free of the pain, suffering, and old age that shackle mortals. But when a god falls in love with a mortal or sires a mortal child, the god becomes connected to that human's mortality. Aphrodite shed her tears because she knew that Anchises, whom she loved, would inevitably grow old, lose his strength and physical attractiveness, and die. The same would be true for their son, Aineias. Such a situation was foreign to the gods, who found mortality unsettling, and thus love affairs between gods and mortals were always bittersweet.

The story of Aphrodite's *own experience with love demonstrates that one of the few ways to hurt the immortal gods is to connect them closely to mortals.*

XV. COLD HARBOR

DESPITE THE HIGH CASUALTIES, the fighting around Spotsylvania went rather well for the Union. According to one soldier, although there was "constant marching and fighting, such as the Army of the Potomac [had] never experienced before," the troops remained "spirited and confident of success." During the last week of May, Grant began probing for an opening on the Confederate right flank. With

Grant at Cold Harbor.

Lee sidestepping to block him, the two armies hopscotched south toward Richmond. In early June, they found themselves facing each other at the dusty crossroads of Cold Harbor, near the battlefields of the Seven Days' Campaign.

With 109,000 Federals confronting 59,000 Rebels along a seven-mile front, Grant made plans for a full-scale assault on the morning of June 2, but supply problems, poor communication, and a great deal of fatigue (from all the marching) forced a twenty-four-hour delay. By dawn on June 3, Grant was confident, his men would be ready and properly positioned, but even with this extra time, Union preparations were highly inadequate.

Bickering among the corps commanders had gotten Grant and Meade to fighting as well. As a gesture of reconciliation, Grant allowed Meade to issue the orders for the attack, but these inexplicably contained no overall plan. Instead, Meade let the corps commanders plan their advances independently. Coordination suffered, as did reconnaissance. Apparently, the corps commanders spent most of June 2 squabbling among themselves rather than scouting the Rebel works. Meanwhile, Lee took advantage of the extra day to dig in even deeper. According to one Northern reporter, the Rebels had "lines within lines" and "works within works."

Unlike their commanders, many Union foot soldiers took the time to inspect the Rebel fortifications and knew what they would be up against. On the night of June 2–3, Sixth Corps commander Horatio Wright observed his men "calmly writing their names and home addresses on slips of paper, and pinning them in the backs of their coats, so that their dead bodies might be recognized on the field."

The attack began at 4:30 AM and lasted eight hours until a disgusted Grant, realizing that his command structure had broken down, called it off. Another day passed before reports reached headquarters detailing the extent of the disaster. The Union army lost seven thousand men, or fives times the number of Confederate casualties. There was no doubt now that Lee had won a major victory. No one realized, however, that it would be his last.

At Cold Harbor, a breakdown in the Union command structure led to a shocking defeat, with Union casualties outnumbering Rebel losses by a factor of five.

XV. CHILD LABOR

ONE OF THE MAIN challenges posed by globalization is how to develop a universal standard for workers whose employment situations vary so widely. As critics of globalization are quick to point out, the primary reason that developing nations can produce simple manufactured goods so cheaply is that their workers often toil in substandard conditions. In the worst cases, these workers are impoverished children, who earn just pennies a day.

The United Nations Children's Fund (UNICEF) makes a distinction between *child work*, which is permissible under Convention 138 of the International Labor Organization (ILO), and *child labor*, which is not. *Child work* is defined as the participation of children twelve years old and older in economic activity "that does not negatively affect their health and development or interfere with education." *Child labor*, on the other hand, refers to work performed by children in contravention of this standard—that is, harmful or disruptive work performed by children twelve to fourteen, and any work performed by a child under twelve.

Many different strategies are used to fight child labor. The most common is the "rule of law" approach, which can be implemented either nationally or internationally through the ILO. An especially good arm-twister, the ILO uses the threat of Western boycotts and sanctions to pressure the governments of offending countries into signing compliance agreements, which are then closely monitored.

The "consumer awareness" strategy can also be highly effective when the offense involves a high-profile multinational company. In recent years, Nike, Reebok, Levi Strauss, IKEA, and Disney have all found themselves involved in child labor scandals, often because they failed to investigate the practices of subcontractors in developing countries. Faced with public relations nightmares, each of these companies took swift action once the child labor was exposed, implementing new and more rigorous standards for subcontractors so that future embarrassment might be avoided.

However, neither of these strategies is a complete solution, because neither addresses the underlying problem of extreme poverty. Merely enforcing child labor laws or restricting trade with nations known to tolerate child labor can worsen the situation of the children involved, who need to work because their families are so poor. If factories employing children are closed, then those children may become thieves, prostitutes, or bonded laborers (a form of slavery). For this reason, antipoverty measures, economic growth programs, and access to foreign credit also play important roles in decreasing the incidence of child labor.

Child labor *can be reduced by enforcing international law and increasing consumer awareness—but only if the underlying problem, extreme poverty, is also addressed.*

XV. THOMAS MORAN

THOMAS MORAN WAS BORN in England in 1837. Seven years later—after his father, a hand-loom weaver, lost his job to mechanization—the family immigrated to America, settling outside Philadelphia. Young Thomas attended grammar school and afterward was apprenticed to an engraver, but he soon left that position to work in the studio of his older brother Edward, already a successful artist. Encouraged by Edward and informally instructed by several other Philadelphia painters, Moran began exhibiting his own work in the early 1860s.

Among his favorite artists was J. M. W. Turner, whose work he came to know through engravings. In 1862, however, accompanied by Edward, Moran sailed to England to view Turner's work firsthand. Seeing the paintings in person had a profound effect on the young American, who was deeply impressed by Turner's lighting effects and his dramatic use of color.

Nine years later, Moran made another significant trip, this time joining Ferdinand V. Hayden's 1871 expedition to the Yellowstone region of northwestern Wyoming. It was the paintings that Moran produced following this trip that made his career. The sketches for his enormous canvas *The Grand Canyon of the Yellowstone* (1872), for example, were shown in the US Capitol during the congressional debate over whether to make Yellowstone a national park. Later, the finished painting was purchased by Congress.

Like every other landscape painter of his generation, Moran was strongly influenced by the writings of John Ruskin and thus made many meticulous drawings of the natural phenomena he encountered out West. Influenced by Turner, however, Moran was equally concerned with aesthetic effects, and he displayed a deeper interest in atmosphere, light, brushwork, and pigment than earlier members of the Hudson River School. Indeed, the attention Moran paid to color and paint effects began an important shift in landscape painting from the realistic representation of nature that had dominated American landscapes since the 1830s toward a more poetic aesthetic.

Like Albert Bierstadt, *Thomas Moran is best known for his western landscapes, which began the transition from the Hudson River School to later styles of American landscape painting.*

Thomas Moran, *The Grand Canyon of the Yellowstone* (1872)

XV. COSMOLOGY: THE BEGINNING

MANY THEORIES EXIST about how the universe began. However, because we can neither go back in time to watch nor re-create the event, we will likely never know for certain which theory is true. But this doesn't mean we can't make educated guesses and explore the possibilities based on what we do know.

Most scientists during the first half of the twentieth century believed in the steady state theory, which held that the universe did not change and had always been the way we see it today. Discoveries during the second half of the century, however, proved that the universe was, in fact, changing. The redshifted light emitted by quasars, for example, proved that galaxies were moving farther away from one another.

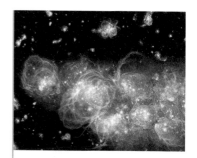

An artist's conception of star formation in the early universe.

Working backward from this idea of an expanding universe, scientists developed another theory. If the universe was indeed expanding, then perhaps its expansion began with a single initial event. The premise of the resulting big bang theory was that all the matter and energy in the universe originated at a single point in space, which suddenly exploded. Physicists have been able to trace this event back to a very small fraction of a second after the big bang, but they can't go back all the way back, so the origin of the singularity and the reason it exploded remain mysteries.

According to the big bang theory, for the first few moments after the explosion the universe remained very small, very dense, and incredibly hot, consisting of a soup of elementary particles moving at very high speeds. The universe then expanded, cooling as it went. As the particles cooled, they slowed down and began to combine, forming atoms. As the universe continued to expand and cool, these atoms began to attract other atoms gravitationally, forming nebulae.

Even so, certain observations relating to the flatness and homogeneity of the universe still didn't fit the big bang theory, so in 1981 American astronomer Alan Guth proposed a revision called the inflationary model. While the original big bang theory posited fairly constant expansion of the universe over time, the inflationary model held that the very early universe expanded at a rate much faster than was previously thought, only to slow down at a later time to the rate we observe today. The effect of this tremendous early expansion was to create a universe approximately as flat and homogeneous as the one we currently occupy.

Scientists have proposed *a variety of theories concerning the origin and early history of the universe, the most current being the big bang theory and the inflationary model.*

XV. DIONYSUS GROWS UP OUTSIDE CIVILIZATION

SEMELE WAS ONE of those unfortunate mortals who, after being seduced by Zeus in his human form, became the object of Hera's jealous wrath. Once impregnated by Zeus, Semele was tricked by Hera into beholding the king of the gods in his true form. This revelation killed her, but even so Hera's jealousy was not assuaged because Zeus saved the fetus, sewing it into his thigh. The immortal child eventually born from Zeus's thigh was called Dionysus.

This story provides an important insight into the way that ancient Greeks conceived of their gods. When Zeus engaged in amorous affairs with mortals, he had to disguise himself—sometimes as a human, sometimes as an animal (such as a bull), sometimes even as drops of rain—because appearing in his true form would destroy the object of his affection.

The same was true for all the gods, who were not simply immortal humans with magical powers. Rather, they were luminous beings whose existence exceeded the physical and intellectual capacities of human beings. The statues of the gods produced by Greek and Roman sculptors were understood to be pale representations, reflecting only those aspects of the divine that the human imagination could comprehend.

A detail from a ca. 490 BCE Greek amphora depicting Dionysus.

As Semele learned, the true form of the gods was a radiance that overwhelmed human life.

Zeus and Semele's son, Dionysus, was a unique god in the Greek pantheon, but not merely because his mother was a mortal. To protect the boy from Hera, Zeus arranged for him to be raised in secrecy by satyrs (half-man, half-goat creatures with insatiable sexual appetites). Because Dionysus was thus raised away from Olympos, he grew up "outside" the civilization of the gods and returned to it only after coming of age.

As a result of his upbringing, Dionysus became the god most closely associated with wine and revelry, and the myths that feature him usually concern the dangerous pleasures of illusion and drunkenness. In these stories, Dionysus typically arrives at a city that subsequently denies his worship because its leader becomes offended by the drunken revelry of the satyrs and maenads (nymphlike worshippers) who always accompany Dionysus. The leader is then savagely punished by Dionysus for denying humanity's inherently wild nature and the need of all humans to satisfy their appetites and desires.

The story of Dionysus teaches *that wildness is a dangerous but necessary aspect of human nature.*

XVI. THE PSYCHOLOGICAL BURDEN

THE BATTLE OF COLD HARBOR ended a seven-week campaign of unprecedented carnage. Before Grant took over in 1864, the Army of the Potomac had fought a few set pieces with no follow-up, retreating when it lost and eschewing pursuit when it won. Now Grant kept it in close contact with Lee's army, fighting a relentless style of warfare that produced sixty-five thousand Union casualties between May 4 and June 4. "For thirty days now, it has been one funeral procession past me," Fifth Corps commander Gouverneur K. Warren exclaimed after Cold Harbor, "and it is too much!"

A pencil sketch of Grant whittling during the Battle of the Wilderness.

Through all the bloodshed, Grant remained stoic. An officer who served with him in the Wilderness described Grant's disposition as a field commander this way: "He keeps his own counsel, padlocks his mouth, while his countenance…indicates nothing—that is, gives no expression of his feelings and no evidence of his intentions. He smokes almost constantly, and…has a habit of whittling with a small knife. He cuts a small stick into small chips, making nothing."

The general's apparent indifference to suffering led some reporters to conclude that he was a "butcher," whose lack of feeling (not to mention ill-conceived battle plans) freely wasted the lives of his men. For many years, Grant had a difficult time shaking this charge, but history has since shown it to be baseless. In the West, for example, with the exception of Shiloh, Grant was quite frugal when it came to the lives of his men, losing fewer during the entire Vicksburg and Chattanooga campaigns than Lee lost in three days at Gettysburg. More to the point, Grant was a realist. "It is at all times a sad and cruel business," he once remarked. "I hate war with all my heart, and nothing but imperative duty could induce me to engage in its work or witness its horrors."

These horrors affected the general much more than he let on. For instance, his son Fred often told of how his father's eyes "filled with tears" when he looked on wounded men during the Vicksburg campaign. Grant also suffered from piercing "sick-headaches" that regularly incapacitated him. No one at the time knew what brought them on, but they are now believed to have been produced by a mixture of grief and stress. According to one aide, the headaches caused Grant "fearful pain such as almost overcomes even his iron stoicism."

Faced with the terrible *carnage in Virginia, Grant barely tolerated the burden of command, suffering often from debilitating "sick-headaches."*

XVI. **CORRUPTION**

AS DEVELOPING NATIONS expand their trade relationships and become more integrated into the global economy, the strength of their governmental and financial institutions is put to the test. The quality of these institutions will generally determine whether a nation benefits from globalization, how much it benefits, and how the attendant gains are distributed throughout society. If the institutions are strong, the potential economic benefits from globalization are great; if they're weak, however, the bulk of the gains are usually lost to corruption.

The economic definition of corruption is the abuse of public office for private gain. According to the German think tank Transparency International, which publishes an annual corruption perception index, corruption is a particular problem among the developing nations of Africa. In 2007, thirty-six of the fifty-two African nations included in the index scored two or below (on a scale of one to ten), indicating that corruption in those countries was perceived to be rampant. Another fourteen African nations scored between three and five, indicating that corruption there was perceived to be a serious challenge. Only two African countries, Botswana and South Africa, scored better than five.

Corruption undermines the potential benefits of globalization in many ways. For example, it increases the cost and risk of doing business in a country, thereby chasing away foreign capital. It also affects foreign aid, which can be cut or even halted if the donor country comes to believe that too much of its money is being skimmed by politicians and bureaucrats. In Uganda, for example, according to one study, only twenty cents of every dollar allocated to education in 1995 made its way into the country's schools. The rest was lost to local patronage politics.

A common rationalization is that corruption in developing counties promotes income redistribution. Traffic policemen, for example, earn minuscule salaries from their governments. If forced to rely on these salaries alone, they would hardly survive. Therefore, in lieu of issuing tickets, they take small bribes—which are a beneficial form of income redistribution, it is argued, because they help the officers survive. This argument is misleading, however, because the officer's petit larceny contributes to a much larger culture of corruption that sanctions grand crimes like rigged multibillion-dollar privatization auctions, which enrich the already wealthy while pushing the poor deeper into poverty. Countries that move toward global integration without first strengthening their domestic institutions run the risk of rewarding the powerful while hurting the rest of the country.

Weak governmental and financial institutions provide a fertile medium in which corruption can grow, undermining the potential benefits of globalization.

XVI. NEW INFLUENCES FROM EUROPE

DURING THE DECADE that preceded the Civil War and throughout most of the 1860s, Hudson River School landscapes, especially those by Church and Bierstadt, sold extremely well and commanded very high prices. During the late 1860s, however, American patrons and collectors began to pass over works by native artists in favor of pictures painted by Europeans, especially those associated with the French Barbizon School.

The hamlet of Barbizon, which sat on the edge of the Fontainebleau forest, was home to a group of artists who, beginning in the 1830s, were drawn there by the beautiful scenery. The leading painter of the group was Jean-Baptiste-Camille Corot, and other notable members included Charles-François Daubigny, Jean-François Millet, and Théodore Rousseau.

Henry Ward Ranger, *Connecticut Woods* (1899)

Rejecting the conventions of landscape painting that required an exact representation of nature, the Barbizon artists substituted for realistic detail an artist's own impression of nature, often based on mood. To this end, they emphasized atmospheric effects and used color harmonies to create emotionally evocative landscapes. Moreover, rather than paint in studios, as their contemporaries typically did, artists of the Barbizon School painted en plein air. This practice led to landscapes that seemed "sketchy," or less finished, to conventional critics, but supporters of the Barbizon painters argued in response that their paintings were, in fact, more powerful than conventionally finished canvases because they were closer to the artist's original impression of nature.

Although a few of the American artists who visited France during the 1840s and 1850s adopted some of the subjective qualities of the Barbizon work, most continued to paint in the objective, realistic style of the Hudson River School. Gradually, however, as the poetic Barbizon landscapes became increasingly popular with American collectors, a new generation of American artists began to seek formal training in France. The effect was swift, and by the end of the 1870s, a more moody and subjective approach to landscape painting, representing an artist's personal response to nature, had eclipsed the last vestiges of the Hudson River School.

After the Civil War, *American landscape painting began to reflect the strong influence of the French Barbizon school.*

XVI. COSMOLOGY: THE END

THE QUESTION OF HOW, or if, the universe will end is another fascinating puzzle. Part of the problem has been that we haven't been sure until recently whether the universe is expanding at a constant rate or slowly decelerating. If the universe's rate of expansion is constant, then it may continue expanding forever. However, if this rate is slowing, then perhaps the expansion will stop and contraction may begin.

The idea that expansion will reverse itself completely, with the universe collapsing back into a singularity, is called the big crunch. (In fact, this may already have happened, with our own universe's big bang resulting from a previous universe's big crunch.) To explore this idea further, astronomers began taking careful measurements to determine the universe's exact rate of expansion. Much to their surprise, they discovered in 1998 that the universe's expansion was actually *accelerating*.

The only force known to act on such a large scale in the universe is gravity. But gravity is an attractive force, which means that it can't explain why objects are moving farther away from one another. In order for the universe to be accelerating outward, some other powerful force must be at work.

The leading candidate is a yet undetected, purely theoretical form of energy called dark energy. It has been estimated that dark energy accounts for about three-quarters of the total mass-energy of the universe. (With his famous equation $e = mc^2$, Einstein showed that mass and energy are essentially equivalent.) According to this theory, dark energy permeates all of space and powers the accelerating expansion of the universe, although no one knows how.

Whatever may be causing this accelerating expansion of space–time, it's pushing distant galaxies away from us at speeds faster than the speed of light. This means that we can no longer see those galaxies, because the light from them can't reach us. (To understand this, picture an ant walking across an infinitely stretchy sheet. As the ant walks, the sheet stretches in the same direction. If the sheet stretches faster than the ant walks, the ant will never get to the other side.) If this accelerating expansion of space–time continues, more galaxies will disappear from our view, followed by own our galaxy and then our own sun. In the end (called the big freeze), the universe around us will go dark, and the ambient temperature will fall below that necessary for new stars to form.

The discovery *that the universe is expanding at an accelerating rate has led to the development of new theories about its possible end.*

XVI. THE LABORS OF HERAKLES

HERA'S JEALOUSY of Zeus's extramarital affairs peaked with the birth of Herakles, the most godlike of Zeus's mortal children. Herakles was the ultimate embodiment of masculine *aretē* ("excellence"), and he spent most of his life ridding the world of monsters while "conquering" women. Yet he was also prone to suffering and error, and his greatest labors were performed as penance for previous mistakes.

As a young man, after fighting a victorious war against the kingdom of Orchomenus, Herakles married the princess Megara. Later, however, he murdered Megara and their children in a fit of madness sent by Hera. Seeking purification, he went to the oracle at Delphi, who told him to settle at Tiryns, where he should serve the Mycenaean king Eurystheus for twelve years. According to one second-century CE source, "She also told him to accomplish the ten labors imposed upon him and said that when the labors were finished, he would become immortal." (Herakles actually performed twelve labors, but two were discounted because he received outside assistance or payment.)

The labors that Eurystheus prescribed seemed impossible. Most involved slaying supernatural creatures, such as the Nemean Lion (whose skin was impenetrable) and the Hydra (a many-headed serpent). In accomplishing these labors, Herakles continued the work of civilizing the savage world left behind by the Titans. He was also commanded by Eurystheus to bring back some of these creatures—the most famous being Cerberus, the giant three-headed dog that guarded the gates of Hades. Once Herakles performed the twelfth labor of capturing Cerberus, Eurystheus had no choice but to release him from servitude.

After being freed, Herakles successfully fought a river god for the hand of the princess Deianeira. When the centaur Nessus tried to steal Deianeira away from him, Herakles shot Nessus with a poisoned arrow. As the centaur lay dying, he told Deianeira to preserve the blood from his wound because it would act be a powerful love potion. Years later, when Herakles fell in love with another princess, Deianeira sent him a cloak dipped in Nessus's blood. Instead of winning Herakles back, however, the cloak melted his skin and bone and caused him to throw himself onto a pyre, where he died in extreme agony.

Herakles had already earned a measure of immortality in tales that would be passed on from one generation to the next. But at the moment of his death he was also granted literal immortality, becoming a god and thereafter living with Zeus on Olympos.

Herakles wrestles a sea serpent in a figure from a ca. 500 BCE vase.

Although a son of Zeus, *Herakles was mortal, and thus his lot in life was toil, ignorance, error, and suffering.*

XVII. THE SIEGE OF PETERSBURG

ON JUNE 12, 1864, nine days after Cold Harbor, Grant began moving his troops quietly across the James River for an attack on Petersburg, which guarded the southern approach to Richmond. In all likelihood, the city (and thus Richmond) would have fallen quickly had it not been for the timidity of several Union field commanders. What these generals saw at Petersburg was a line of defenses much more imposing than anything they had seen at Cold Harbor; what they didn't see was that the earthworks were guarded by a garrison of just twenty-five hundred men. According to Confederate commander P. G. T. Beauregard, "Petersburg at that hour was clearly at [their] mercy." The Union delay, however, gave Lee time to move his own army down to Petersburg, and by June 18, the two sides were settling into trenches each would occupy for the next nine months.

In the short run, meaning the first three or four months, the siege worked to Lee's advantage, blunting Grant's superiority in men and munitions while stoking public dissension in the North. Lee and Confederate president Jefferson Davis knew that their only real hope was a Democratic victory in the 1864 presidential election, which would remove Lincoln from office and lead to a negotiated peace. However, with Sherman's capture of Atlanta in September 1864, Lincoln's reelection was assured, and the complete defeat of the Confederacy became merely a matter of time.

The final Union push began on March 29, when Maj. Gen. Philip Sheridan led nine thousand cavalrymen and two corps of infantry to Five Forks, a strategically vital crossroads through which Lee's most important supply line passed. "Hold Five Forks at all hazards," Lee ordered Maj. Gen. George Pickett on the morning of April 1, but that afternoon Pickett's defenses collapsed under Sheridan's assault. With this defeat, Lee recognized the inevitable and began making plans for the evacuation of Petersburg and Richmond.

A dead Confederate soldier in a Petersburg trench.

At the same time, capitalizing on Sheridan's victory at Five Forks, Grant ordered an all-out offensive along the entire Petersburg front. The attack, which began at 4:40 AM on April 2, was everywhere successful, and forced Lee to accelerate his departure plans. "This is a sad business, colonel," Lee told one of his subordinates. "It has happened as I told them in Richmond it would happen. The line has been stretched until it is broken."

For nearly a year, *the Army of the Potomac camped in front of Petersburg. Then, in April 1865, Grant began the offensive that finally ended the Civil War.*

XVII. THE RACE TO THE BOTTOM

THE PHRASE *race to the bottom* was first used by Supreme Court justice Louis Brandeis in 1933 to describe the Depression-era practice of US states competing with one another to lower taxes and ease regulation in order to attract more business. More recently, the phrase has become popular among antiglobalizers, who argue that globalization encourages poor and rich countries alike to debase themselves in a similarly cutthroat competition for jobs and investment. The "race to the bottom" argument applies to all countries because lower standards in the developing world pressure the developed world to lower its standards in order to remain competitive.

The environment provides a simple case in point: Developing countries with lax environmental standards can produce some goods more cheaply than developed countries because the environmental costs of producing those goods aren't reflected in the prices charged for them. When these cheap goods begin to supplant competing merchandise from developed countries, the governments of those countries begin to feel pressure from domestic manufacturers, who want environmental regulations relaxed so that they can remain internationally competitive. The same logic applies to labor. If the real wages in France (that is, corrected for purchasing power) are higher than those in Morocco (or if France requires employers to spend more on worker health and safety), then Morocco will have a cost advantage over France in the production of most labor-intensive goods.

It would seem that, for French goods to remain competitive, either Morocco would have to pay workers more or France would have to pay workers less. All other factors being equal, the latter is the more likely consequence. However, the race isn't always to the bottom, because all other factors usually aren't equal. For example, French vintners may grow grapes more efficiently than Moroccan vintners, thus offsetting their higher labor costs. Also, French wine may be better than Moroccan wine, thus commanding a higher price.

A more defensible "race to the bottom" argument is that the world's poorest peoples, finding it difficult to compete internationally, choose to poison their environments and destroy important nonrenewable resources in shortsighted spasms of desperation, greed, and despair. The burning of the Amazonian rain forest to create farmland that will quickly be washed away by heavy rains is but one example of this extremely damaging behavior.

The "race to the bottom" *argument holds that, in the presence of poverty, countries will feel pressure to lower labor and environmental standards in order to stay competitive.*

XVII. GEORGE INNESS

GEORGE INNESS (1825–94) was an extremely popular artist throughout his lifetime. He began exhibiting landscapes in the Hudson River School style at the National Academy of Design in 1844, when he was just nineteen years old. He was an exact contemporary of Church, but his style was never in tune with that of his colleague. One reason was Inness's many trips to Europe. The first, in 1851, included visits to Italy and France. Two years later, Inness returned to France and made a memorable visit to Barbizon. By the mid-1850s, he was already integrating aspects of the Barbizon aesthetic into his landscapes.

After visiting Barbizon, Inness moved away from the conventions of the picturesque toward a more intimate view of nature. Through the use of subtle color harmonies and delicate contrasts between light and shadow (learned from the Barbizon painters), he created new, highly subjective landscapes that conveyed an intriguing sense of mystery.

In 1878, Inness joined the utopian Swedenborgian community in Montclair, New Jersey, after which his work became even more spiritual. Swedenborgians (followers of the eighteenth-century Swedish mystic Emanuel Swedenborg) believed that every object in the material world had a corresponding relationship with an object in the spiritual world. Furthermore, through this relationship, objects in the material world received the "influx" from God that they needed to exist.

George Inness, *Sundown* (1894)

The influence of Swedenborgian theology on Inness's paintings can be seen in such canvases as *Sundown* (1894), in which concrete forms of nature such as trees and clouds dissolve into mysterious patterns of atmosphere and light. The key change in Inness's work was that, instead of creating landscapes with familiar natural forms that revealed indirectly a larger divine purpose (as Cole and Church had done), he now painted pictures with muted detail that fused visually the natural and spiritual worlds.

In more formal artistic terms, Inness began using modern European techniques to transform the romantic idealism of the mature Hudson River School into a moody expressionism that had an extraordinary influence on the next generation of American artists, who in turn crafted their own approach to nature and its relationship to art.

It was George Inness, *an artist associated with the Hudson River School early in his career, who most completely integrated aspects of the Barbizon school into his landscapes.*

XVII. LIFE IN THE UNIVERSE

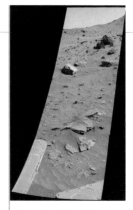

ONE OF THE MOST INTERESTING questions in astronomy is *Are we alone?* Although the existence of extraterrestrial life, especially intelligent extraterrestrial life, has been the subject of eager speculation for more than a century, serious research didn't begin until the early 1960s, when the US government and several private institutions began funding programs collectively known as the Search for Extraterrestrial Intelligence (SETI).

Scientists believe Martian rocks such as these may contain fossilized remains of extraterrestrial life.

Then as now, SETI researchers scan the heavens for radio transmissions that might indicate an intelligent source. None has yet been found, but the search continues. One effort, called SETI@home, links together the personal computers of anyone willing to download the necessary software from the Internet. Once this software is installed, each personal computer becomes part of a vast network used by researchers to analyze signal data from radio telescopes. Linking PCs together in this way creates a virtual machine equivalent to the fastest supercomputer on Earth.

One of the first SETI scientists, Frank Drake, developed an equation in 1960 to estimate the number of civilizations in our galaxy with which we might be able to communicate. As with any equation, the accuracy of the results depends entirely on the accuracy of the inputs. In this case, the inputs are highly speculative, including the percentage of solar systems that have planets, the percentage of those planets capable of supporting life, the percentage of those planets on which life will actually develop, the percentage of such life that will be intelligent, the percentage of such intelligent life that will actually develop the technology necessary for interstellar communication, and the length of time that such civilizations could send messages into space. Depending on the estimates one uses, results can vary from nearly zero to very large numbers indeed. Drake himself got ten as a result, meaning that there should be approximately nine other civilizations in the Milky Way capable of interstellar communication.

In 1974, scientists working at the Arecibo radio telescope in Puerto Rico composed and sent a message into space containing symbolic information about the human race and life on Earth. The message was aimed at a globular star cluster twenty-five thousand light-years away. Even if some advanced civilization were to receive the message, we couldn't expect a response in less than fifty thousand years, because that's how long it would take for light waves to travel there and back.

Humans have long wondered *whether we are alone in the universe, but only recently have researchers begun looking actively for extraterrestrial life.*

XVII. ROMAN MYTHOLOGY

AS THE ROMANS BUILT their empire, they made it a practice to bring back from conquered lands images and artifacts associated with the local religious cults. In this way, they symbolically "adopted" the gods of other cultures. With regard to Greece, however, the process was much more literal.

In its early years, Rome was influenced Etruria by to the north and Latium to the south. The Etruscans and the Latins were, in turn, influenced by their primary trading partners, the Greeks. Through these connections and direct contact as well, the Romans came to associate their own early local traditions with those of the learned Greeks. Thus the early Roman goddess of wisdom—who had a name, Minerva, but no mythological tradition—took on the elaborate narrative background of the Greek goddess Athena.

A sixteenth-century fresco of Apollo driving his chariot across the sky.

For this reason, Greek and Roman myths feature the same basic stories, but there are several key differences between them, such as the naming systems. With the exception of Apollo, the gods of Rome have different names than the gods of Greece. For example, Zeus is Jupiter, Ares is Mars, and Aphrodite is Venus. (In the Roman world, gods and planets were closely associated.) The names of human heroes were similarly transformed, with Herakles becoming Hercules and Odysseus becoming Ulysses.

Roman authors also had a different attitude toward myth than their Greek predecessors. Although Rome was founded during the eighth century BCE, there are no early mythological texts in Latin (whereas Hesiod and Homer predate all other literature in the Greek language). In fact, the Latin canon remains quite sparse until the first century CE, when the two most important works of Latin myth, Ovid's *Metamorphoses* (8 CE) and Vergil's *Aeneid* (15 CE), were composed. By this time, poetry had long since been displaced as the only means of recording history, and most Romans no longer thought of myths as religious or philosophical texts. Instead, by the end of the Republican period, Romans had come to consider poetry as a form of entertainment.

This didn't mean that Romans ceased to believe in their gods—widespread monotheism was still a few centuries away—but it did reflect a steep decline in the power of myth, especially myth as expressed in poetry. Latin authors often invoked the gods but rarely with the seriousness found in Hesiod and Homer. Instead, they focused on personal relations, historical personalities, and politics.

Romans understood *myth more as a form of entertainment than as a means for serious religious or philosophical inquiry.*

XVIII. APPOMATTOX

LATE IN THE AFTERNOON ON APRIL 2, 1865, the Army of Northern Virginia escaped Petersburg and Richmond, heading southwest along the Richmond & Danville Railroad. After securing the Confederate capital, the Army of the Potomac followed in pursuit. On April 6, when the Rebels became dangerously strung out along Sailor's Creek, Sheridan's cavalry attacked the stragglers, capturing an entire corps. The defeat cost Lee nearly a quarter of his strength.

On the evening of April 7, Grant and Lee began exchanging notes. "The results of the last week must convince you of the hopelessness of further resistance on the part of the Army of Northern Virginia in this struggle," Grant wrote. "I feel that it is so, and regard it as my duty to shift from myself the responsibility of any further effusion of blood by asking of you the surrender of that portion of the Confederate States army known as the Army of Northern Virginia."

"I have received your note of this date," Lee replied. "Though not entertaining the opinion you express of the hopelessness of further resistance on the part of the Army of Northern Virginia, I reciprocate your desire to avoid useless effusion of blood, and therefore, before considering your proposition, ask the terms you will offer on condition of its surrender."

The exchange of notes continued throughout the day on April 8. Meanwhile, elements of the Army of the Potomac leapfrogged ahead of Lee and cut off what remained of his army near Appomattox Court House. At dawn on April 9, Lee tried unsuccessfully to break through the Federal lines to the west. When that effort failed, he had no choice but to surrender.

The decisive message reached Grant shortly before noon. For the past several days, he had been suffering from one of his debilitating headaches, but reading Lee's note made the headache disappear. Dismounting, Grant sat down in the road to compose a reply. A few hours later, he and Lee met at the nearby home of retired grocer Wilmer McLean.

In Grant, Lincoln had found a general both able to conceive of "total war" and willing to carry it out. This had made all the difference. But in the end, Grant also showed himself to be a man of peace. The terms that he offered Lee were uncommonly generous. For instance, he allowed Lee's officers to keep their sidearms, and with those sidearms, also their dignity. Thus began the long road to reconciliation.

The surrender ceremony in the parlor of the McLean house in Appomattox Court House.

The generous surrender terms *that Grant offered Lee at Appomattox began the long process of national reconciliation.*

XVIII. CURSE OR CURE?

IN GENERAL, supporters of the "race to the bottom" argument believe that the process of globalization inevitably leads to environmental degradation, child labor, corruption, and other social ills. The particular villains in this scenario are the multinational corporations that antiglobalizers consider the catalysts, if not the instigators, of a "new colonialism," which allows rich Western countries to exploit once again the natural resources and labor forces of poorer African and Asian nations.

Although globalization certainly exacerbates many social problems, it would be unfair to say that globalization *causes* the problems. Their actual source, of course, is poverty. To the extent that globalization increases economic inequality, it contributes to the problems; however, to the extent globalization equitably grows a poor country's economy, it ameliorates them.

Like it or not, the globalization genie is out of its bottle. There is no turning back, and even if a reversal were possible, ripping apart the economic linkages that have developed since World War II would do much more harm than good to globalization's "losers." The most useful discussion to have now is how can losses be minimized, gains maximized, and the net difference shared equitably across all societies.

According to economic theory, the gains to winners always outpace the losses to losers. If this is so, then globalization can be everywhere successful as long as a portion of the winners' gains are used to compensate the losers' losses. The problem, of course, is that such compensation rarely takes place, because merely opening up one's economy isn't sufficient to ensure global economic success. Losers must be supported by a social safety net that winners are compelled to fund; otherwise, globalization will continue to produce more uncompensated losers and more economic inequality.

Globalization is neither a magical cure nor an evil curse. Much like technological progress, it offers new opportunities, from which good or ill or both may come. How individual countries manage those opportunities is what determines their outcome. National leaders will have to decide how to proceed. Clearly, they should do so only after evaluating their country's individual situation and shoring up any weak institutions that they find. If developing countries simply accede to the one-size-fits-all Washington consensus, then they deserve the same criticism that the IMF and the World Bank already receive.

Neither a curse nor a cure, *globalization is an opportunity that can result either in gains for all or in benefits for the winners and deeper poverty for the losers.*

XVIII. THE HUDSON RIVER SCHOOL LEGACY

BY THE END OF THE NINETEENTH CENTURY, American landscape painting had undergone a significant transformation. The Hudson River School was no longer popular, having passed out of fashion. Nevertheless, the tradition begun by Thomas Cole and his followers continued to have relevance as it influenced the development of new American landscape artists. During the 1880s, two new styles of landscape painting supplanted the Hudson River School and its highly detailed representations of nature. One was impressionism; the other, tonalism.

William Merritt Chase, *A City Park* (ca. 1887)

Following the style's French pioneers, American impressionists employed vigorous brushstrokes and often applied paint thickly to their canvases using a technique called impasto. Also like their French counterparts, they painted en plein air and sought to capture the fleeting effects of sunlight and atmosphere, rather than make precise records of natural detail as their Hudson River School predecessors had done. Another important difference was subject matter. Instead of painting the wilderness in the manner of Cole, Durand, Church, and Bierstadt, the American impressionists preferred to paint everyday life, including urban landscapes and scenes of leisure and recreation. The artists most closely associated with American impressionists, which flourished between the 1880s and early 1920s, were Childe Hassam, William Merritt Chase, Theodore Robinson, and Mary Cassatt.

Popular at roughly the same time, tonalism took its name from the tonal harmonies used to create the style's heightened sense of intimacy. Like Inness, whose later works were an important influence, tonalists such as Dwight Tryon and John Twachtman muted the detail in their paintings to create softly contoured representations of nature's more suggestive moments. Especially popular subjects were twilight and dawn, when mist prevailed, light was less distinct, and hues and colors most susceptible to change. Often, tonalist landscapes evoked a nostalgic feeling in contemporary viewers, reflecting a common desire among urbanized Americans of the period to escape their fast-paced lives of steam and steel and return for a moment to the natural, unspoiled world that Thomas Cole experienced on his first trip to the Catskills in 1825.

During the late nineteenth century, *American landscape painting shifted to a pair of styles more concerned with mood, atmosphere, and an emotional response to nature.*

XVIII. THE FUTURE OF ASTRONOMY

IN HIS GENERAL THEORY OF RELATIVITY, Albert Einstein predicted a number of incredible astronomical phenomena that have since been proven real—black holes, for instance. An equally interesting phenomenon predicted by Einstein but not yet detected is the gravity wave.

According to Einstein, just as a tossing a rock into a pool will generate ripples, so should analogous disturbances in space–time produce gravity waves. These waves should occur in two main types: burst waves and periodic waves. A star going supernova should produce the burst-type wave—that is, a huge pulse moving outward from the point of the explosion. Periodic waves, on the other hand, would be generated by very massive, very asymmetric objects rotating in space. For example, two neutron stars orbiting each other should produce periodic waves.

If we could detect these waves, we could learn far more about the universe than we have from electromagnetic waves, because light doesn't give us the full picture of what is happening—especially if so much of the universe is dark energy, as cosmologists suggest. For this reason, the search is on to detect gravity waves.

Unfortunately, the amplitude of a wave (sometimes called its height) depends on the stiffness of the medium through which it travels. The stiffer the medium, the smaller the wave's amplitude. For instance, a towel held loosely can accommodate a big wave, but through a towel held taut, only small waves can pass. In the case of gravity waves, the medium through which they travel is space–time, which is incredibly stiff. As a result, gravity waves can be expected to have very, very small amplitudes, far below what we can currently measure.

Although the detection devices being developed vary greatly in design, a common problem is that everyday seismic activity, which normally fades into the background, produces enormous distortion when we measure on such a delicate scale. For this reason, future attempts to detect gravity waves will likely be made in space, where no such vibrations exist.

Of the two types of gravity waves, the burst type is expected to have the larger amplitude, so research is currently focusing on this one. A limiting factor, however, is that supernovas are relatively infrequent events. We may have to wait a long time before one occurs capable of producing detectable gravity waves, and even then our instruments may not be pointed in the right direction.

A new and perhaps revolutionary *means of observing the universe may come from the gravity waves predicted by Albert Einstein's General Theory of Relativity.*

XVIII. ROMULUS AND REMUS

ROMULUS AND REMUS, the mythological founders of Rome, were children of the war god Mars by Rhea Silvia, a priestess who lived in Alba Longa. Their grandfather, Numitor, had been king of Alba Longa until he was deposed by his tyrannical brother, Amulius. Fearing that Rhea Silvia would produce a rival heir, Amulius had compelled her to become a vestal virgin (a celibate priestess associated with the hearth goddess Vesta).

A famous fifth-century BCE Etruscan bronze of the she-wolf Lupa suckling Romulus and Remus.

Once Romulus and Remus were born, however, an enraged Amulius ordered Rhea Silvia buried alive (the standard punishment for vestal virgins who had betrayed their oath of celibacy) and her newborns cast out into the wilderness. Ordinarily, they would have perished of exposure, but they were saved by the she-wolf Lupa, who suckled them.

This unusual nurturing, in combination with their divine ancestry, produced in Romulus and Remus exceeding strength, beauty, and ferocity. Upon coming of age, they overthrew Amulius and restored their grandfather to the throne. Then they set off to found their own city, accompanied by vagabonds, runaways, and others eager for a new start.

After arguing about the best site for their city, the twins decided to settle the matter with an augury contest (involving the studying of bird signs). Romulus won the contest, but Remus refused to accept the result and struck out at his brother, beginning a fight that ended with Remus's death. Romulus then founded the city, which he called Rome, atop Palatine Hill.

Under Romulus's rule, members of three indigenous tribes came to populate the city: the Etruscans, the Latins, and the Sabines. With Romulus's death, however, the leaders of Etruria began to exercise a disproportionate influence over the city, eventually establishing a line of Etruscan kings.

Resentment peaked when the son of the last Etruscan king, Tarquin, raped the noblewoman Lucretia, who subsequently committed suicide (considered a noble death for dishonored women in the Roman world). Before killing herself, however, Lucretia told her relatives what had happened. This prompted her brother, Brutus, to incite a revolt that deposed Tarquin and transformed Rome from a hereditary monarchy into a republic, governed by the Senate, which ruled Rome for the next five hundred years.

The myth of Rome's founding *tells a story of conflict that reflects the ideology of the imperial period in which the myth was promulgated.*

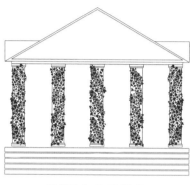

SYLLABUS

II

I. AMERICAN UNITARIANISM

RALPH WALDO EMERSON (1803–82) was born into the profession of divinity. His father's family had been ministers in and around Boston since the early seventeenth century, when the Massachusetts Bay Colony was founded. For 150 years, the

Ralph Waldo Emerson

Reverends Emerson hewed to the orthodox Puritan line, preaching not only predestination (the concept that God had already determined who would be saved and who would be damned) but also innate depravity (the idea that humanity has been corrupt since its fall from grace). By the time of Emerson's birth, however, the family had, like much of eastern Massachusetts, adopted the more liberal faith of Unitarianism. Although there had been Unitarians in Europe since the Protestant Reformation, the faith hadn't taken hold in America until the 1780s, when the Enlightenment was at its height. As scientific explanations of the universe became more popular, so did rationalist accounts of humanity's place in that universe.

American Unitarianism was essentially a rationalist critique of Puritanism. The faith's name referred to its assertion that God was a unity rather than a trinity. Unitarians believed neither in the Holy Ghost (a concept they found unnecessarily mysterious) nor in the divinity of Jesus, although they did follow his teachings. In addition, they rejected the idea that humanity was innately depraved. Instead, they emphasized reason and morality, free will, and the human capacity for good.

After attending Harvard College and Harvard Divinity School, the twenty-five-year-old Emerson was ordained at Boston's Second Church in 1829. He seemed destined (if not predestined) for a career in the family business, yet every new generation harbors some skepticism toward the ideas of its elders, and in Emerson's case this tendency was particularly pronounced. Like a number of other young Unitarian ministers, Emerson was deeply dissatisfied with what he perceived to be Unitarianism's devotion to historical Christianity—that is, the inherited doctrines and practices of the religion—rather than the transcendental truth that such doctrines and practices were meant to convey.

True religion, Emerson believed, wasn't a set of rules imposed by God for humanity to obey but an ongoing process of revelation and discovery. By October 1832, he felt so intellectually limited within Unitarianism that he resigned from the Second Church and made immediate plans for a voyage to Italy, France, and Great Britain, departing on Christmas Day. Emerson thus broke with his past and freed himself to become one of the most original thinkers in the history of American letters.

Unitarianism emerged *in America as a response to the severity of Puritan orthodoxy, but even the more liberal Unitarian faith proved too constraining for Emerson.*

I. BEFORE EARTH

ONCE UPON A TIME, there was a universe but no Earth. We know this from geology, which tells us that Earth is made up of "heavy" elements—that is, elements with relatively high atomic masses. Only a supernova, or exploding star, could have produced these elements. Therefore, such a star must have existed before Earth did.

The core of this argument, the heavy-element evidence, requires a little chemistry and some astrophysics to understand. We'll begin with the basic unit of matter, the atom, and its component parts: protons, electrons, and neutrons. Electrons, which have a negative charge, orbit the nucleus of the atom, where the protons and neutrons reside. Because protons have a positive charge, they would repel one another when grouped together unless buffered by neutrons, which have no charge and act as glue.

The simplest atom, consisting of a single electron orbiting a single proton, is elemental hydrogen. The next step up, elemental helium, consists of two electrons orbiting a nucleus with two protons and two neutrons. Elemental carbon has six electrons, six protons, and six neutrons.

In the early universe, the first and most abundant element was hydrogen. Initially, the hydrogen was probably evenly distributed, but over time it began to clump, the result of

Data from two satellites were used to produce this image of Earth.

random motion and the attractive force of gravity. Eventually, some of these clumps became dense enough for nuclear fusion to begin. (This is the process by which stars "burn" matter to produce energy.)

The simplest nuclear fusion involves two hydrogen atoms being forced together to form a single helium atom. For most stars, fusion ends here, but within the cores of very large stars, fusion continues. Helium is fused into carbon, carbon is fused into oxygen, and so on. The last element in this chain is iron, which cannot be fused.

Once a star uses up all of its nuclear fuel, fusion ceases, and the star begins to contract. The awesome gravitational forces involved eventually compress the core beyond the limit matter will allow, and a supernova results. The energy of the supernova forces more atoms together, producing even heavier elements. Thus, without supernovas, there would be no elements heavier than iron and no Earth. No doubt the late astronomer Carl Sagan had this conclusion in mind when he reflected, "We are all star stuff."

The fact that Earth *is composed of heavy elements created by the explosion of a star demonstrates that, at one point in the early universe, there was no Earth.*

I. THE PARADOX OF THE FRENCH REVOLUTION

FEW EVENTS IN WESTERN HISTORY have been as controversial, influential, and complex as the French Revolution. Between 1789 and 1815, France experienced political and social upheaval on a scale rarely seen, and the events that took place there have left a legacy to inspire as well as horrify the world.

Soldiers (commoners) jeer a cleric and an aristocrat in a 1790 etching.

Most historians view the French Revolution as the moment in time when the West left behind a millennium dominated by monarchy, an aristocratic social order, and feudal village life to enter the modern world of democracy, nation-states, and mass movements. Although the American Revolution (which preceded the French by a few years) espoused similar principles of liberty and equality, the circumstances of the French Revolution made its impact on the world arguably much greater.

Understanding France's situation in 1789, especially the enormous obstacles that political change faced both inside and outside the country, is crucial to understanding the breadth, depth, radicalism, and violence of the Revolution. Unlike distant colonial America, France sat at the center of the eighteenth-century world. It was still governed by an absolute monarch, and it still adhered to the same system of class privilege and social distinctions that had prevailed in Western Europe since the Middle Ages. Furthermore, France was surrounded by similar monarchies just as hostile to the ideals of social freedom.

With the onset of revolution, France's neighbors reacted to preserve their own social orders, yet the warfare that ensued worked out differently than they intended. The French won, and the ideas of their Revolution were exported, through the military might of Napoleon, to the rest of Western Europe and even the New World.

Although the immediate impact of the French Revolution was about as profound as it could be, the quality of its legacy remains more difficult to assess. On the one hand, the deeply held beliefs concerning human potential that inspired the Revolution still inform political debate today. The Declaration of the Rights of Man, for instance, remains a model for human rights activists throughout the world. Yet the Revolution also inspired some of the worst in human behavior, including repression, violence, and the creation of the first authoritarian state. There is a paradox here, and it is only by unraveling the contradictions of the French Revolution that students of history can fully grasp its significance.

The paradox of the French Revolution *is that it introduced, in the name of human freedom, some of the worst forms of human oppression.*

I. THE ECONOMICS OF ENERGY

ENERGY IS THE MOST BASIC COMMODITY ON EARTH. Everyone uses it, directly and indirectly, on a daily basis. As with all commodities, its price is governed by the laws of supply and demand. When supply falls or demand increases, the price of energy rises. Of course, when supply increases or demand falls, the price should go down—but demand for energy rarely falls.

Upward trends in energy prices often lead to changes in energy sources. During the early nineteenth century, for example, the conventional fuel used for home lighting was whale oil, which was cheap and plentiful. However, as demand increased (with the growth of the US population) and supply decreased (with the slaughter of whales), the price of whale oil rose until it eventually surpassed that of a new alternative fuel, kerosene. Once this tipping point was reached, whale oil was phased out, and the alternative fuel kerosene became the new conventional technology.

When energy is cheap and plentiful, most people think little about it. However, when energy becomes expensive or scarce, people get agitated, because they're so dependent on it. This is why energy companies have always focused on delivering as much product as possible at the lowest possible cost to consumers. Not unreasonably, they have based their corporate policies on the premise that the public's desire for plentiful, low-cost energy trumps all other considerations— whether these be related to energy independence, the environment, or social sustainability. (The term *social sustainability* refers to the effects that energy projects have on surrounding communities, from public health issues to occupational safety concerns.)

Yet there is more to the economics of energy than simply the price paid by consumers. Although consumer price has always been the dominant factor in energy decision making, it fails to reflect many hidden costs incurred by society as a whole. Importing large quantities of cheap petroleum may lower the price of gasoline at the pump, but this practice also incurs economic and political costs associated with dependence on potentially unstable foreign suppliers. Similarly, the environmental costs associated with many forms of conventional energy production are usually paid for in tax dollars rather than in consumer dollars. Consider, for example, the cost of the environmental and worker safety issues associated with coal mining. Therefore, comparing the retail kilowatt-hour price of coal-generated electricity with that of solar- or wind-generated electricity isn't really fair, because the hidden costs to society aren't being taken into account.

The basic economic fact *of the energy industry has been that, above all else, most consumers want their energy cheap and plentiful.*

I. BUDDHISM AND THE VEDIC WORLDVIEW

THE VEDIC PERIOD OF INDIAN HISTORY (into which the Buddha was born) began sometime around 1200 BCE. It was named for religious texts known as the Vedas, which set forth the Indic worldview. Written in Sanskrit (a grammatically complex sacred language), these texts came to regulate all aspects of Indian religion and

A page from a fifteenth-century manuscript of the Rig Veda.

society. They specified the four castes (priests, warrior-kings, merchants, and laborers) and cataloged the numerous deities and semiphysical beings whom the Vedic priests sought to appease.

During the sixth century BCE, however, new trends in religious thought and practice began to emerge. These were written down over the course of several hundred years in texts known collectively as the Upaniṣads. Central to the new ideas was a conception of the universe as limitless in space and time. During this limitless time, it was further believed, the universe passed through (and continues to pass through) regular cycles of creation and destruction.

These cycles also applied to living things, which were believed to possess something akin to a soul that migrated across lifetimes from one plane of existence to another (a process called transmigration). Specifically, living things (or, more properly, aspects of their being) transmigrated among the physical world (of humans and animals but not plants), the semiphysical world (where ghosts, spirits, and gods existed), and a world of formless consciousnesses.

Underlying this system was a mechanism of ethical causality. It was believed that an individual's actions and motivations over the course of a lifetime cumulatively determined the nature and quality of that individual's subsequent lives. *Karma* was the name given to this sequence of actions and their ethical consequences, which controlled transmigration.

The semimonastic religious teachers who espoused this Vedic worldview (out of which both Hinduism and Buddhism evolved) advocated a variety of ascetic practices, from self-mortification to elaborate meditative exercises that promoted a renunciation of the material world. The goal of these practices was to attain an ideal existence, the exact definition of which varied from sect to sect. The reward could be bliss during one's current lifetime, physical immortality on earth, or rebirth into a permanent heavenly state. When the Buddha began his religious career during the mid-sixth century BCE, he accepted some of these Vedic ideas, rejected others, and modified much of the rest.

The Vedic worldview *was one of ethical causality, according to which ethical conduct determined the nature and quality of one's subsequent lives.*

II. BRITISH ROMANTICISM

IN CHOOSING TO LEAVE the Unitarian church, Emerson was, like his Puritan forebears, rejecting a religion of observance for a more engaged spiritual life. He didn't yet know what that life would entail, and he still had many questions, but he expected to find some answers abroad—particularly in Great Britain, where he hoped to meet the romantic writers William Wordsworth, Samuel Taylor Coleridge, and Thomas Carlyle, whose work he had been studying closely. These meetings indeed occurred, and Emerson's firsthand exposure to romanticism (especially through the close friendship he established with Carlyle) confirmed its place as one of the pillars of his thought.

An idealized drawing of William Wordsworth at age thirty-six.

Wordsworth, Coleridge, and Carlyle all lamented the effects of the Enlightenment and the Industrial Revolution on the human condition. They believed that as humanity lost its direct connection to nature, its spirituality suffered, because nature was a mirror of the human soul. Wordsworth captured this sentiment in a well-known 1806 poem: "The world is too much with us; late and soon, / Getting and spending, we lay waste our powers; / Little we see in Nature that is ours; / We have given our hearts away, a sordid boon!" In the romantics' view, industrialism had turned humanity coldly rational and mechanistic. Romanticism's task, therefore, was to reverse this process by emphasizing nature as the path to transcendent spiritual truth.

One of the most important documents produced by the romantic movement was the preface to Wordsworth's *Lyrical Ballads* (1798), in which he rejected rigidly classical forms of poetry for a new lyricism that was free of limitations on form and content. Wordsworth believed that poetry should be more natural, almost artless in its art, and instructed his readers accordingly: "While they are perusing this book, they should ask themselves if it contains a natural delineation of human passions, human characters, and human incidents; and if the answer be favorable to the author's wishes, that they should consent to be pleased in spite of that most dreadful enemy to our pleasures, our own pre-established codes of decision." *Natural, human*, and *passion* all became buzzwords for the romantics, who championed the individual's personal relationship with nature and defied anything, especially classical forms of expression, that stood in its way.

Emerson traveled *to Great Britain to learn firsthand about romanticism, which rejected Enlightenment rationalism in favor of a direct connection to nature.*

II. THE DATING GAME

ELEMENTS ARE DEFINED by the number of protons in their nuclei. For instance, an atom with six protons in its nucleus is, by definition, carbon. The number of neutrons, however, can vary. Although most carbon atoms have six neutrons, some have eight, which makes them unstable and radioactive.

Atoms of the same element with different numbers of neutrons are called isotopes. Generally, an isotope is identified by its atomic mass, which is the total number of protons and neutrons in its nucleus. Carbon-12, for example, refers to the stable isotope of carbon with six protons and six neutrons, while carbon-14 is the radioactive isotope with six protons and eight neutrons.

As atoms get larger, it becomes more and more difficult for the neutrons to hold the protons together. Calcium, with 20 protons and 20 neutrons, is the last element whose most stable isotope has protons and neutrons in a 1:1 ratio. Higher up the periodic table, zirconium, with 40 protons, requires 51 neutrons to keep its nucleus together, while lead, the last of the stable elements, needs 125 neutrons to bind together its 82 protons.

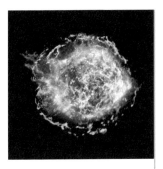

An X-ray image of the remains of an exploding star, or supernova.

Although supernovas can create elements with more than eighty-two protons, no force in nature can keep such large nuclei together indefinitely. Sooner or later, they will split apart into smaller, more stable pieces—a process known as radioactive decay. Although rates of decay vary from isotope to isotope, for a given isotope the rate is a constant, known as the half-life. Specifically, the half-life of a radioactive isotope is the time required for one-half of a sample to decay into a more stable form. This property has led to the development of a geological method known as radiometric dating.

Some relatively stable isotopes have half-lives measured in billions of years, whereas highly unstable isotopes can exist for less than a second. Uranium atoms, for example, have ninety-two protons, which puts them well above the stable limit of eighty-two. Therefore, all isotopes of uranium are radioactive, but some are more stable than others. Relatively unstable uranium-234 has a half-life of 245,000 years, while U-238, more stable because it has more neutrons, has a half-life of 4.5 billion years. Ultimately, both U-234 and U-238 decay into lead-206 (Pb-206). Therefore, a rock containing equal parts U-234 and Pb-206 would be 245,000 years old. A similar rock containing equal amounts of U-238 and Pb-206 would be 4.5 million years old.

Scientists can calculate *the age of certain rocks by comparing the relative amounts of radioactive and stable material found in them.*

II. THE ANCIEN RÉGIME

BEFORE 1789, France was governed (at least ostensibly) by an all-powerful monarch who ruled absolutely over a society defined by birth and privilege. This was the ancien régime (literally, the old regime), created a century earlier by the great French king Louis XIV (1638–1715). Also known as the Sun King, Louis XIV had inherited the throne as a five-year-old boy, and he grew up in a world where

Louis XIV, the Sun King, pictured at the center of the sun.

rebellious nobles held most of the country's political power because it was they who raised the armies that fought the country's wars. The nobles also liked to fight among themselves, however, and by the time Louis took control of the French government in 1661, a lengthy and destructive civil war known as the Fronde had left the nobility in a particularly weakened state.

From the outset of his half-century reign, Louis XIV's goal was to consolidate all political, religious, and social power in the monarchy. He did this primarily by co-opting his two main rivals, the nobility and the clergy. Specifically, he created a large standing army and then appointed important nobles to lead its officer corps; meanwhile, he aligned himself closely with the Roman Catholic Church against France's Protestant population (the Huguenots). With the aid of these new allies and the support of church doctrine asserting the divine right of kings to rule, Louis XIV intimidated local law courts (*parlements*) into following his edicts and established a national bureaucracy through which he collected the taxes that paid for his magnificent new court at Versailles, which became the French capital. The Sun King's overall philosophy of government can be summarized in the dictum, commonly attributed to him, *L'état c'est moi* ("I am the state").

France under Louis XIV was seen as a rigidly hierarchical society divided into three feudal estates: the First Estate (the clergy), the Second Estate (the nobility), and the Third Estate (the commoners). Being elites, the first two estates enjoyed substantial legal privileges, including exemption from state taxation and the power to exact seigneurial dues. (These were the taxes that a lord collected from the commoners living within his seigneury, or feudal fiefdom.) The governing myth in eighteenth-century France was that, as long as each estate tended to its duties and remained in its place, order and harmony would prevail. "It is necessary," the royalists claimed, "that some command and others obey."

The ancien régime, *which Louis XIV established during the seventeenth century, consolidated all political, religious, and social power within the French monarchy.*

II. CONVENTIONAL ENERGY

THE GOAL OF ALL ENERGY TECHNOLOGIES is to convert the energy present in fuel into more useful and efficient forms. The first controlled fires, for example, converted the energy present in biomass fuels such as wood into thermal energy, which could be used for heating, lighting, and cooking. Wood, in fact, became the world's first conventional energy source and remained dominant for tens of thousands of years because it was easy to obtain and met the energy needs of its consumers.

About 6000 BCE, however, residents of the Middle East (where wood wasn't plentiful) began burning asphalt, thus launching the era of fossil fuels. (The term *fossil fuel* refers to energy-rich compounds created by the compression of plant and animal remains over millions of years.) In addition to asphalt, other early fossil fuels included peat and coal. All could be easily found at or near the earth's surface. It

Miners hauling out coal about 1920.

wasn't until the late eighteenth century, however, that engineers began developing the technologies required to exploit fossil fuels buried deep underground.

The first to be exploited was coal. For hundreds of years, coal had been burned in Europe, where it was especially plentiful, but it wasn't until the late eighteenth century that advances in mining technology made coal available in large quantities at dramatically reduced prices. Soon, a new energy technology developed around coal, making the Industrial Revolution possible. By the late nineteenth century, a ton of coal produced four times the energy of a ton of wood at just one-half the cost.

The Industrial Revolution also inspired a new energy-conversion process. As long as users required only thermal energy, fuels were simply burned. With the advent of industrialization, however, mills and factories needed mechanical power to run their machines. Initially, the steam engine accomplished this by burning coal. The heat of the fire, when applied to water in a boiler, generated steam; the steam expanded, exerting force on a piston; and the piston turned a shaft, creating the mechanical energy.

Because the burning took place outside the engine itself, the steam engine is considered an *external* combustion device. The next great technology, of course, was the *internal* combustion engine, fueled by petroleum. When commercial production of petroleum began during the 1850s, most of the output was refined into kerosene; but as the internal combustion engine took off, so did petroleum, and petroleum now fuels most of the energy applications in use today.

Since the late eighteenth century, *conventional energy production has been dominated by the burning of fossil fuels.*

II. THE BUDDHA

PRINCE SIDDHĀRTHA GAUTAMA, who became the Buddha, was born ca. 560 BCE in the area of Lumbini in present-day Nepal. Shortly after his birth, according to Buddhist tradition, his father, the king of the Śākya clan, received a prophecy that Siddhārtha would become either a great monarch or a great religious teacher. Desiring the former, the king attempted to safeguard his son from disturbing sights. Mostly, this meant providing Siddhārtha with the best of everything: a sheltered and luxurious environment, the finest education, rigorous physical training, and an ample harem. In time, Siddhārtha married a suitable princess and fathered a son named Rāhula (Sanskrit for "fetter").

The birth of the Buddha as pictured in an eighteenth-century Thai manuscript.

During his late twenties, however, Siddhārtha became increasingly curious about the outside world and began sneaking out of the palace, accompanied by a few servants. On his first three trips, he saw, respectively, an elderly man, a diseased man, and a corpse. When he asked his charioteer what these sights meant, the servant responded that all human beings were subject to such fates. During Siddhārtha's fourth excursion, he encountered a wandering mendicant. Already despondent over the implications of the charioteer's statement for his own life, Siddhārtha asked for an explication of the beggar's behavior. When he was told that the man was seeking escape from life's endless cycles of suffering, the prince decided to pursue a similar course himself. Leaving the palace again, he rode into the jungle, where he joined a group of ascetics and, at thirty years of age, embarked on a new religious life.

Studying with several teachers, Siddhārtha mastered a number of meditative techniques and for the next six years practiced extreme physical austerity, which weakened his body dramatically. Eventually, he realized that these practices weren't leading him to the liberation he was seeking, and so he decided to separate from his companions and look instead for a "middle way" between asceticism and hedonism. Accepting food from a village girl, he replenished his body and sat down to meditate beneath a tree near the present-day town of Bodhgaya. During the course of the night, according to Buddhist tradition, Siddhārtha became enlightened and gained the knowledge of all his former lives as well as a wide range of new abilities, including clairvoyance, flight, and the ability to know the previous and subsequent lives of others. As a result, he became known as Śākyamuni ("sage of the Śākya clan") Buddha.

Six years after renouncing *his hedonistic royal lifestyle for one of religious asceticism, Siddhārtha Gautama achieved enlightenment and became Śākyamuni Buddha.*

III. GERMAN IDEALISM

ALTHOUGH EMERSON HAD STUDIED the works of the British romantics before his 1832–33 voyage, it wasn't until he reached Scotland and began conversing with Carlyle that he fully appreciated the debt that romanticism owed to German idealism of the late eighteenth century. One reason for this gap in Emerson's understanding was that, while the works of the British romantics were widely available in America, those of the German idealists, translated or not, were nearly impossible to find in New England bookstores. (Harvard College didn't begin offering classes in German until the mid-1820s.)

The basic principle of German idealism was that objects become real only when they take shape in the human mind. The leading proponents of this philosophy were Immanuel Kant (1724–1804), J. G. Fichte (1762–1814), F. W. J. Schelling (1775–1854), and G. W. F. Hegel (1770–1831).

In his *Critique of Pure Reason* (1781), Kant argued that neither reason nor experience is, by itself, capable of generating knowledge. Rather, humans need both experience and reason to gain knowledge of the world. "Thoughts without content are empty," Kant wrote, while "intuitions without concepts are blind."

Kant conceived of objects in the world as surface "representations" that lack depth and require human interpretation for full understanding. He called this approach transcendental idealism—from which the name of its Emersonian offshoot, transcendentalism, derives. Only by transcending experience and logic, Kant (and later Emerson) believed, could one arrive at the deepest spiritual truths.

Schelling's work was another important influence on the British romantics and thus, indirectly, on Emerson. In *System of Transcendental Idealism* (1800) and *Exposition of My System of Philosophy* (1801), Schelling advanced the theory that mind and nature were completely dependent on each other. In Schellingian terms, a person sees a tree, which has an objective reality of its own as well as a separate reality within the mind of the person viewing it. These two realities—subject and object, self and nature—are mutually dependent because both are required to create meaning and knowledge. (This idea closely paralleled the romantic concept of nature as the mirror of the soul.)

In December 1832, Emerson had left Boston feeling shackled by the formulaic conventions of the Unitarian Church. When he returned in October 1833, however, he felt altogether transformed—inspired to write and full of ideas that would shape America's image of itself for generations to come.

The principles of German idealism, *especially the idea that objects achieve full reality only in the human mind, reached Emerson indirectly through the British romantics.*

III. EARTH IS BORN

MORE THAN 4.5 BILLION YEARS AGO, an ancient star exploded in a supernova. The heavy elements it created were spread around the blast zone in their pure form, as well as in cohesive little groups of atoms called molecules. At first, this debris existed only as a vast cloud of gas and dust called a nebula. Over time, though, gravity and the random motion of particles produced clumping, which led to the formation of a new solar system. At the center of the cloud, a new star began to coalesce. Meanwhile, elsewhere in the nebula, other clumps of matter came together, condensing under their own weight and combining with other clumps in their vicinity to form planets in orbit around the new star. This is how our solar system began.

Lighter elements in the outer nebula condensed to form the four gas giants—Jupiter, Saturn, Uranus, and Neptune. At the same time, heavier elements, upon which the Sun's gravity had a more pronounced effect, remained within the inner solar system. These came together to form the four terrestrial planets—Mercury, Venus, Earth, and Mars.

Terrestrial planets tend to accumulate mass through collision. If two objects meet in a head-on collision, the result is usually destructive, but most collisions in space are not head-on. Sometimes the impacts are glancing, and sometimes one object merely overtakes another moving in the same general direction. In these situations, the two objects often merge and become a single larger object more capable of surviving future collisions.

About twenty-five million years after becoming a planet, Earth went through a molten phase, becoming a giant ball of lava. For this reason, no rocks from its planet-building phase survive on Earth, but similar rocks do exist elsewhere in the solar system. The asteroid belt that lies between the orbits of Mars and Jupiter is full of planetary material that never coalesced because of Jupiter's strong gravitational pull. Every now and then, one of these asteroids strikes Earth, giving scientists the chance to study them. Composition analysis has revealed that these rocks contain the same ninety elements commonly found on Earth, while radiometric dating indicates that they are all about 4.5 billion years old. Nothing older has yet been found.

Our solar system *began as a massive cloud of gas and dust, called a nebula, in which matter clumped together to form the Sun and the planets.*

An illustration of the dusty disk surrounding a star out of which planets form.

III. THE LIMITS OF PATRONAGE

THE DIVINE RIGHT OF KINGS NOTWITHSTANDING, the French monarch's real power lay in his ability to award patronage—whether in the form of military commissions, bishoprics, or other public offices. Important courtiers, in turn, used their access to royal patronage to help others gain employment and income, thus obtaining loyal followers themselves. As a result, power within the ancien régime was wielded not publicly through mechanisms of government but privately through personal connections (typically between nobles and their minions).

The cleric at right refuses to give up his money in this 1788 cartoon.

Even so, with the advent of a consumer economy, French society gradually began to reflect distinctions based on wealth as well as on family. Within the nobility and the clergy, huge disparities in wealth arose, and the same was also true among commoners. Artisans, who received economic protection through the monopolistic guild system, became somewhat wealthier and better educated, but the real winners were the core of the new bourgeois—merchants, professionals, and civil servants who used their burgeoning wealth to buy their way into the First and Second Estates. Some of the new bourgeois were even able to purchase for themselves state offices that conferred tax exemptions.

In the end, it was this habitual privatization of the state that doomed the ancien régime. A state based on patronage uses as its currency private gifts. A prosperous France, therefore, meant a country awash in private gifts. Over time, such a system inevitably becomes much too top-heavy. As the monarchy sold off one public office after another during the eighteenth century and privatized such fundamental economic tools as taxation and customs collection, it introduced too many middlemen, and its revenue stream declined—despite the overall financial success of capitalism—because too many people were either exempt from payment or skimming off the top.

Thus, French society was never quite as harmonious or orderly as the myth of the ancien régime implied. Rather, it consisted of many different groups competing for the social status and legal privileges once accorded only on the basis of birth but now available for money as well. Because anyone with enough cash could purchase an exemption, the burden of taxation fell primarily on the peasantry, whose ability to pay (even collectively) was limited. As a result, French monarchs began settling their bills with borrowed funds; and the more that they borrowed, the higher were the interest rates they had to pay. Eventually, they bankrupted the government.

The ancien régime *functioned for a time on patronage, but as members of the new bourgeois bought their way into the system, it became too top-heavy and collapsed.*

III. ALTERNATIVE TECHNOLOGIES

WHAT MAKES A TECHNOLOGY CONVENTIONAL is its widespread use, and what makes it widespread is its low cost and convenience. Therefore, almost by definition, alternative technologies cost more than conventional ones, at least in terms of the price paid by the consumer. For example, among alternative technologies, wind power has come the closest to competing with conventional fossil fuels, yet it still costs about 50 percent more than coal-generated electricity. If, however, one takes into account the hidden costs of conventional energy and the noneconomic benefits of alternative technologies, then the equation changes.

Growing awareness of the environmental costs of conventional energy has led to increased demand for cleaner energy. Global warming, in particular, has altered the way many people think about the energy they consume—which, in turn, has begun to reshape the economic relationship between energy producers and consumers. As more and more consumers sign up for green energy programs and buy hybrid cars (both of which carry additional costs), energy companies are reconsidering whether the conventional wisdom of *cheap, convenient, and plentiful above all else* still applies. Skeptics argue that the demand for cheap, large-scale energy resources will continue to trump the relatively new consumer preference for clean, renewable alternatives. On the other hand, if the era of cheap petroleum-based energy is indeed ending—as shrinking petroleum reserves and rising gasoline prices indicate—then one may not even have to factor in the hidden costs and benefits for today's alternative technologies to become tomorrow's conventional resources.

For the time being, however, solar, wind, biomass, and geothermal energy remain the principal alternative technologies. All are environmentally clean, and all are renewable, meaning that their fuel supply is, for all practical purposes, infinite. For this reason, the terms *alternative energy* and *renewable energy* are often used interchangeably, but they shouldn't be. Hydropower, for example, although a form of renewable energy, is considered a conventional technology because it has been in widespread industrial use for generations. (Nuclear energy is considered conventional for the same reason.)

The most common use to date for solar and wind energy has been electricity generation, with wind having the greater potential for large-scale, grid-connected use and solar currently more suited to local and building-scale installations. Most of the work being done on biomass energy has been focused on small-scale power generation and biofuels (such as ethanol), while the principal application for geothermal energy has been the heating of homes and other buildings.

The primary alternative technologies—*solar, wind, biomass, and geothermal—are all clean and renewable but cost more than conventional energy—at least for now.*

III. THE DHARMA

INITIALLY, the Buddha doubted that anyone else could comprehend what he had realized. Nevertheless, he sought out his former companions in the jungle so that he could tell them of his enlightenment. Finding them in a public park near Varanasi, he offered his first teaching, called the First Turning of the Wheel of Dharma. The Sanskrit word *dharma* has many shades of meaning. In is original Vedic context, it meant "duty" in the sense of social obligation, such as the obligation one feels as a member of a particular caste. In a Buddhist context, however, the meaning of *dharma* is closer to "truth" or "reality" (or even "law," as in *law of nature*).

The Buddha's first teaching asserted four "truths" about the nature of reality. The first was that ordinary life is characterized by suffering—physical suffering, emotional suffering, and a sort of angst inherent in day-to-day existence. The second truth was that the cause of this suffering is the desire that follows from all beings' ignorance of the true nature of reality. The third truth was that it is possible to attain a state of being in which suffering is extinguished. The fourth truth concerned the Eightfold Path leading to that state.

In Vedism, one reached a higher state of being through the mechanism of rebirth. According to the Buddha, however, the path to a higher state of being was not related to rebirth. Instead, the way to elevate oneself was to realize meditatively the truths contained in the First Turning of the Wheel of Dharma. Because the realization of these truths elevated one from an ordinary state of being to a "noble" state, they came to be called the Four Noble Truths.

A statue of the Buddha at Sensoji Temple in Tokyo, Japan.

The fourth truth, which concerned the Buddhist path to enlightenment, described the three stages through which an individual must pass. According to the Buddha, the first stage, calming the body, was attained by following an ethical code of conduct in one's *speech*, *actions*, and *livelihood*. The second stage, calming and focusing the mind, was pursued through a training regimen of *effort*, *mindfulness*, and *concentration*. Only when thus prepared could a person strive for the third stage, cultivating wisdom, by concentrating on proper *intention* and *understanding*. If one followed this Eightfold Path, the Buddha explained, ignorance of the true nature of reality would be eradicated, and suffering would end.

Ordinary human existence *is characterized by suffering rooted in ignorance. By following the Eightfold Path, however, one can gain release from suffering.*

IV. NATURE

An 1839 cartoon in which the artist pictures himself as Emerson's "transparent eyeball."

UPON HIS RETURN to the United States, Emerson settled in Concord, then a small village outside Boston, where he drew upon the insights he had gained in Europe for the texts of his first public lectures. These talks became quite popular—in part because they were witty, engaging, and laced with anecdotes; in part because they offered listeners exciting ideas that ranged well beyond the New England intellectual mainstream. In September 1836, Emerson took the next step, publishing the ninety-five-page manifesto *Nature*, which became the founding document of the transcendentalist movement.

Written in the terse, epigrammatic style that would become a hallmark of his prose, *Nature* combined Emerson's study of British romanticism and German idealism with ideas and experiences of his own to create something altogether new. Beginning with a romantic critique of the Industrial Revolution, Emerson urged his fellow Americans to reengage with nature, which he believed could minister to them in the way that Christ ministered to the Christian faithful. Specifically, he believed that a close connection to nature could ameliorate America's social ills (largely a result of its materialist pursuits) and help its citizens obtain salvation.

In this passage from the first chapter, Emerson drew a clear distinction between nature in a material sense, which held no benefit, and nature as the mirror of the soul: "The charming landscape which I saw this morning is indubitably made up of some twenty or thirty farms. Miller owns this field, Locke that, and Manning the woodland beyond. But none of them owns the landscape. There is a property in the horizon which no man has but he whose eye can integrate all parts, that is, the poet. This is the best part of these men's farms, yet to this their land-deeds give them no title."

In *Nature*'s most famous passage, Emerson described how he came himself to experience transcendent reality (in the Kantian sense) through close observation of nature. "Standing on the bare ground, my head bathed by the blithe air, and uplifted into infinite space," Emerson wrote, "all mean egotism vanishes. I become a transparent eyeball. I am nothing. I see all." Certainly, this way of thinking had little in common with the Calvinism that had dominated American intellectual life for generations and the rationalism that had been lately ascendant. It spoke not for strict logic and predetermined fate but for intuition, individuality, and free will existing outside of civilization.

In Nature, *the founding document of transcendentalism, Emerson urged a close connection to nature, which he believed could help individuals find salvation.*

IV. THE IRON CATASTROPHE

ABOUT TWENTY-FIVE MILLION YEARS AFTER ITS FORMATION, Earth began to melt. Part of the reason was residual energy from the many collisions the young planet was still experiencing. Another source of heat was the ongoing decay of radioactive material left over from the supernova. But the most important contributing factor was gravity. The presence of so much matter in one place created a strong gravitational pull that caused the planet to contract. Over time, this contraction raised the pressure in Earth's core and its temperature as well.

The advent of planetary gravity also created on Earth the phenomenon known as weight. According to its scientific definition, weight is the force that gravity exerts on an object. In the absence of gravity, objects have mass but no weight. That is why objects in space are said to be weightless. For the same reason, only where gravity exists can objects be said to be "heavy."

Because the early Earth was molten, the various elements that made up the planet could move about freely. Furthermore, because of the strong pull of gravity, the lighter elements, such as carbon and magnesium, tended to float to the surface, while the heavier elements, such as iron and nickel, sank to the bottom. The migration of iron turned out to be particularly important for the future of Earth because iron is the most common heavy element on the planet, accounting for about one-third of its total mass. The droplets of iron that began to fall through the newly molten Earth proceeded slowly at first, but as time went on, the process sped up, eventually producing a catastrophe.

The word *catastrophe* originally meant "the culminating act in a drama." Because it was usually applied to tragedies, however, it came to be associated with the disasters that befell tragic heroes. The Iron Catastrophe was no such disaster but a catastrophe in the original sense of the word. Lasting between one hundred million and five hundred million years, it marked the culminating act in Earth's formative drama because it created the layers that characterize the planet's modern structure: a solid iron-nickel inner core (solid because of the great pressure that far down), a molten iron-nickel outer core (molten because the pressure outside the inner core is not quite so great), a dense rocky mantle, and a less dense rocky crust.

Shortly after its formation, *Earth melted. This allowed the planet's component elements to reorganize themselves by weight, creating Earth's iron core.*

IV. THE IMPACT OF THE ENLIGHTENMENT

AS FRENCH URBAN SOCIETY GREW WEALTHIER, it also became more literate. In academies and salons, where social distinctions among the wealthy ceased to be made, nobles and bourgeois began to debate philosophy and science with each other. Even artisans joined reading groups and began paying attention to the newspapers then cropping up all over the country.

This was the height of the Enlightenment, when a group of French writers known as *philosophes* spread the values of free inquiry and open debate throughout France and later across the rest of the Western world. At the core of their beliefs was the idea that reason was the basis for all human improvement. Inspired by the many advances recently made in science, they wanted to apply the same rational method to all forms of human endeavor, including political philosophy.

Because the *philosophes* despised irrationality, they frequently attacked the mysticism and religious intolerance of the Catholic Church. In 1762, for example, Voltaire (1694–1778) launched a public campaign to free Jean Calas, a Huguenot being put to death by the Languedoc *parlement* for allegedly murdering his son to prevent him from embracing Catholicism. Voltaire used the trumped-up Calas case to demonstrate the extent to which French public institutions had become infused with religious bigotry, but he couldn't save Calas.

The *philosophes* also offered a sophisticated critique of ancien régime economic policy, pointing out the irrationality of France's protectionist tariffs and outmoded seigneurial agricultural system. Technological innovation and free trade, they argued, were the keys to future prosperity. So long as France retained its traditional forms of industry and agriculture, so long as social status continued to be accorded on the basis of privilege rather than merit, individuals would continue to fall below their full productive potential.

Voltaire

As for their political beliefs, most *philosophes* condemned absolute monarchy as arbitrary and oppressive. Voltaire and Denis Diderot (1713–84) both argued for a more "enlightened" form of monarchy in which the king used his power to rationalize society. Montesquieu (1689–1755), who considered personal liberty the primary goal of any government, proposed a system of checks and balances to limit oppressive rule. Jean-Jacques Rousseau (1712–78) went farthest of all: He argued that, because sovereignty rested ultimately with the people, the ideal government was a republic—that is, a government elected by the people—in which the citizens themselves acted for the public good. (Most of Rousseau's *philosophe* colleagues found this utopian idea a little too radical.)

The rationalist *philosophes* *encouraged an intellectual climate in which the monarchy's actions could be criticized and its merits debated.*

IV. ENERGY IN THE TWENTIETH CENTURY

ELECTRICITY TRACES its industrial roots back to 1882, when Thomas Edison installed the first public power station in New York City. This development set the stage for a transformation of energy technology that came to define the twentieth century.

Power lines in Suffolk, England.

Electrical power stations made possible the generation of large volumes of energy that could be easily transmitted to distant locations in a universal form suitable for multiple applications. Edison built the first plants to power the electric lightbulb he had invented three years earlier, but the availability of electricity quickly inspired other inventors to develop uses for this new and highly adaptable technology.

Before electrification, which wasn't completed in many rural areas until after World War II, energy sources considered "alternative" today could still be found in use, especially on farms. These traditional technologies included windmills, which converted wind power into mechanical energy for grinding grain, and woodstoves, which converted biomass fuels into thermal energy for home heating. The advent of electricity, however, made these technologies obsolete.

The second great defining element of twentieth-century energy use was the growth of the automobile industry, which reshaped how Americans lived in numerous economic and cultural ways. In particular, the mechanization of farms, the suburbanization of the population, and the construction of the national highway system transformed the United States socially, while making the country dependent on the fossil fuels—petroleum, coal, and natural gas—that powered the country's highly industrialized, highly mobile lifestyle.

Especially during the postwar boom (1945–70), demand for energy became so strong that only large-scale conventional sources could meet it. During those years, growth in electric power demand averaged 8 percent annually (four times the current rate), leading to much electrical infrastructure construction. Because the United States had large stocks of high-quality coal, coal-fired electrical plants were the preferred option, but many large hydroelectric plants and the first nuclear plants were also built. Meanwhile, the oil and natural gas infrastructures expanded at a similarly rapid rate. The most important factor in designing these projects was how quickly they could be built. There were no environmental considerations to speak of, unless one counts the preference for locating power plants near large fossil fuel reserves and alongside rivers or bays, whose water could be used for cooling.

During the twentieth century, *electrification and the rise of the automobile created a huge demand for energy that only massive expansion of the fossil fuel sector could meet.*

IV. THE SAṄGHA

FROM THE START OF HIS TEACHING CAREER, the Buddha ordained students as monks because he believed that renouncing one's worldly life helped a person avoid the entrapments of desire, ignorance, and hatred that were at the root of all suffering. Collectively, the community of Buddhist monks was known as the *saṅgha*. Along with the *dharma* and the Buddha himself, it completed the Three Jewels of Buddhism.

Initially, the Buddha offered few behavioral guidelines for the monks, because his first five hundred disciples had perfected their renunciation over many previous lifetimes. As the Buddha's fame spread, however, he began ordaining monks who lacked such predispositions and sometimes acted in ways that were inappropriate.

The Buddha resolved this problem by offering additional guidelines that, over time, grew into a set of some 250 vows. Many concerned the monks' commitment to renunciation and specified in minute detail what articles they could and could not possess. These rules were important because an insufficient commitment to renunciation could impede a monk's ability to calm his body and his mind.

Other vows were designed to correct behavior that reflected poorly on the *saṅgha* as a whole, because offending laypeople could adversely affect the support they gave to the monks. It was not sufficient for a monk simply to avoid misconduct, the Buddha said; he must avoid even the impression of impropriety. Therefore, the Buddha set down vows to regulate how monks walked, how they ate, and how they behaved in the presence of a woman, so that the sensibilities of the patronizing public would never be offended.

The monks' relationship to women changed dramatically, however, after a group of women approached the Buddha one day and asked him to ordain them as nuns in his order. At first, the Buddha refused, citing two reasons: Maintaining celibacy within a sexually integrated *saṅgha* would place an enormous strain on the community, and granting such social advancement to women would cut against the grain of northern India's patriarchal society. However, when one of his most senior disciples supported the women's request, the Buddha reconsidered and relented (though he did subject the women to a more extensive set of vows in order to protect both them and the *saṅgha* from controversy). While women certainly faced greater social obstacles in pursuing a religious life, there was no inherent difference, the Buddha was forced to admit, between men and women in their capacities for enlightenment.

To help his students *avoid the entrapments of their worldly lives, the Buddha created a monastic community and a set of vows to regulate the monks' and nuns' behavior.*

V. CERTAIN LIKEMINDED PERSONS

DURING THE SPRING OF 1836, several months before the publication of *Nature*, Unitarian minister Convers Francis published *Christianity as a Purely Internal Principle*, a pamphlet that found favor among younger, more liberal Unitarian clergy because it emphasized the idea that religion resided ultimately within the individual. This approach certainly appealed to Emerson and also to Frederic Henry Hedge, a Unitarian minister in Maine, who wrote to Emerson in June 1836 proposing "a meeting, annual or oftener if possible, of certain likeminded persons of our acquaintance for the free discussion of theological & moral subjects."

On September 8, Hedge and Emerson met in Cambridge with two friends, Unitarian ministers George Ripley and George Putnam, to discuss Hedge's idea. The next day, *Nature* appeared in print. Although Emerson published the book anonymously (for reasons known only to him), he was quickly found out because he had been advancing similar ideas in his popular public lectures. In the meantime, the first meeting of the transcendentalists took place at Ripley's home in Boston on September 19.

Although raised as an orthodox Congregationalist (that is, a latter-day Puritan), Ripley had, like Emerson, attended Harvard Divinity School and become a Unitarian minister, employed at Boston's Purchase Street Church. Also like Emerson, Ripley disapproved of Unitarianism's cool rationality and longed for a more transcendent faith. "The truth of religion," he once told his congregation, "does not depend on tradition nor on historical facts, but has an unerring witness in the soul."

Because transcendentalism so strongly emphasized individuality and personal experience, there exists a tendency to think of transcendentalists as loners, living the sort of isolated life that Henry David Thoreau wrote about in *Walden* (1854). In fact, the transcendentalists regularly sought out one another's company because, as Thoreau wrote, "thought breeds thought."

Between 1836 and 1840, Emerson and his friends met about thirty times, most often at Emerson's home in Concord. The forum was open, and the conversation wide-ranging. Among the regular participants—in addition to Emerson, Hedge, and Ripley—were Bronson Alcott, Margaret Fuller, Nathaniel Hawthorne, and Thoreau. At first, Emerson referred to the gatherings as the Symposium; then the name of the group changed to Hedge's Club, because its members typically convened on the occasions Hedge was in town; finally, it became known as the Transcendental Club.

The transcendentalist movement *came together when Emerson began holding private discussions among "likeminded friends." These evolved into the Transcendental Club.*

V. EARTH'S MAGNETIC SHIELD

AS EARTH SLOWLY COOLED, most of its layers solidified. Its outer core, however, remained molten, a development that turned out to have important implications for the future of life on Earth.

When conducting metals such as iron and nickel move about, they generate magnetic fields. Because the entire iron-nickel outer core of Earth is constantly in motion, circulating around the inner core because of a process called convection, it produces an enormous magnetic field that extends many thousands of miles out into space.

The significance of this field to life on Earth becomes obvious when one considers the hazards posed by the Sun, a runaway nuclear reactor located just ninety-three million miles away. The Sun's enormous gravity ensures that most of its exploding matter never gets too far away, but some particles do escape. Collectively, they are known as the solar wind. In order to break free of the Sun's gravity, they have to be moving very fast, about a million miles an hour. This high rate of speed makes them dangerous to anything in their path, including life on Earth. Fortunately, the magnetic field generated by the circulating metals in Earth's outer core shields us from these particles.

The process is easily observed in the nighttime sky above Earth's two magnetic poles. While most of the charged particles are deflected into space, a few do collect at the poles, where they release energy in the form of light. (Think of a truck plowing snow with its windows open. Although most of the snow is pushed aside, a little does get in the windows.) Around the northern magnetic pole, this release of energy is called the aurora borealis, or northern lights. Around the southern pole, it is known as the aurora australis, or southern lights.

The aurora borealis as viewed from orbit.

If not for the shielding effect of Earth's magnetic field, the planet would be subject to a constant bombardment of highly charged particles akin to solar sandblasting. Some scientists believe the effect would be sufficient to strip Earth of its atmosphere and its oceans, leaving the planet as sterile and lifeless as Mars, which has no molten outer core and thus no magnetic shield.

The circulating motion *of the iron and nickel in Earth's molten outer core generates a powerful magnetic field that protects the planet from the dangerous solar wind.*

V. THE REVOLUTION BEGINS

MORE THAN A CENTURY of poor financial management finally came to a head during the mid-1780s. The long and expensive Seven Years' War (1756–63), had inspired a few attempts to reverse the proliferation of exemptions and reform the tax base, but these efforts were no more successful than the war had been. To make matters worse, when the French government sent troops to America to help the rebellious colonists in 1780, it funded the deployment with high-interest, short-term loans that it had no ability to repay.

At first, Louis XVI, whose rather ineffectual reign began in 1774, tried to raise the money by declaring a new tax. For his edict to take affect, however, it had to be written into the registry of laws kept by each provincial *parlement*, and the *parlementaires* (judges with hereditary appointments) refused. Emboldened by Enlightenment ideas and quoting the language of Montesquieu and Rousseau, they shot back that taxation without popular consent was despotism.

The failure of several other schemes eventually persuaded Louis XVI to convene the Estates General. Composed of elected representatives from the three estates, the Estates General was an antiquated institution that hadn't met since 1614 and recalled a hierarchical world that no longer existed. From the outset, there was trouble, especially among members of the bourgeois elite who resented being grouped with other commoners. This important constituency might have listened to the king, except that its pique and overall thirst for political influence made it much

A 1789 etching of the Tennis Court Oath.

more receptive to the rhetoric of Emmanuel Sieyès, who published the influential pamphlet *What Is the Third Estate?* "Everything" was Sieyès's answer. The First and Second Estates were anachronisms, Sieyès wrote; only the Third Estate could claim to represent the entire French nation.

At the opening session of the Estates General in Versailles on May 5, 1789, representatives of the Third Estate proposed that all votes be taken by head rather than by estate. (Previously, each estate had been given a single, collective vote.) When most of the clergy and nobility refused to go along with this, the Third Estate began meeting separately and on June 17 declared itself the National Assembly. Louis XVI immediately ordered its meeting hall closed, but three days later the members of the National Assembly (which now included some reform-minded nobility and clergy) gathered on a tennis court at Versailles to swear an oath: They would not disband until they had written a new constitution for France.

Although the French government's *financial crisis was the proximate cause of the Revolution, the nationalist rhetoric of Emmanuel Sieyès provided the trigger.*

V. **THE OIL SHOCK**

IN 1970, with the US energy infrastructure well developed and functioning efficiently, the energy industry saw no reason to invest in alternative technologies. Even as declining domestic oil production increased the market share of foreign suppliers, the nation's growing reliance on imported oil wasn't seen as a serious problem. Most oil imports came from the Middle East, especially Saudi Arabia, where crude oil could be extracted easily and in large quantities. In 1973, however, imports from the Middle East abruptly stopped.

The reason was the Arab oil embargo, which began in October 1973 in response to US support for Israel during the Yom Kippur War. The effect was immediate and severe. Within three months, petroleum imports fell from thirty-seven million barrels a day to just two million barrels a day. Meanwhile, the price of gasoline rose nearly 40 percent, and supply shortages caused long lines at gasoline stations, further dramatizing the downside of America's dependence on foreign oil.

In response, federal and state governments enacted numerous tax incentives and regulatory modifications designed to reduce demand, reward efficiency, and stimulate investment in new technologies that might bring the nation closer to energy independence. In August 1977, the Department of Energy was created in part to organize these efforts on the national level. Meanwhile, the private sector got involved. Recognizing that US crude oil production had peaked in 1970 and was already in decline, energy companies began investigating alternative technologies that many believed would be the future of the industry. Finally, the nascent environmental movement also played a role in driving the alternative energy boomlet of the 1970s. An offshoot of the 1960s counterculture, the ecology movement (as it was known then) championed the principles of conservation and sustainability, which it held up to corporations and consumers as important standards that needed to be respected.

This combination of spiking petroleum prices, governmental incentives, and growing public awareness of environmental issues led to the funding of much alternative energy research and even some development. Construction of the world's first large-scale wind farm began in 1981 at Altamont Pass near San Francisco, prompted by federal tax credits; small-scale biomass fuels made a huge comeback, as woodstoves became popular again; and some homeowners even installed solar panels for local heat and electricity generation.

The spike in petroleum prices *brought about by the 1973 Arab oil embargo caused both government and private industry to reevaluate US energy dependence.*

V. THE RELIEF OF IGNORANCE

IN DESCRIBING THE FOUR NOBLE TRUTHS, the Buddha identified the main obstacle to enlightenment as ignorance of the true nature of reality. Because this problem was cognitive in nature, solving it required meditation rather than ritual or action. Simply holding the right concepts or viewpoint wasn't enough; if it were, then a person in a coma might be enlightened. Instead, release from suffering required a fundamental transformation of mind achieved through conscious mental activity.

Buddhist thought distinguishes between two types of ignorance. Artificial ignorance refers to socially constructed concepts, such as sexism and racism, that are learned. Like all ignorance, artificial ignorance causes suffering. But in a Buddhist context, the suffering caused by artificial ignorance is considered relatively superficial compared with the suffering caused by innate ignorance. This second, deeper level of ignorance is characterized by passive, uncritical acceptance of the idea that objects are what they appear to be—that is, that they have some form of inherent or intrinsic existence.

The Buddha emphasized the impermanent nature of things, which are always changing from moment to moment and which can always be broken down into component parts or otherwise conceptually divided. Individuals can say that they understand this, but they nevertheless behave as though the objects with which they interact are whole and unchanging—from a favorite chair to a close friend. To the extent that the changeable nature of all things conflicts with the images of permanence held in one's mind, suffering is produced.

Innate ignorance is not learned, but neither, according to the Buddha, is it intrinsic to the nature of the mind, because Buddhists define the mind simply as the capacity for knowing. In other words, even though innate ignorance works on an almost subliminal level, it can be eliminated. Buddhists strive to accomplish this through meditation.

The meditation to relieve innate ignorance makes use of two important techniques (sometimes called *yogas*) to put the individual in a very specific state of mind. Stabilizing meditation (*śamatha*) helps the practitioner to become calm and alert. Insight meditation (*vipaśyana*) promotes focus, attentiveness, and insight. When these two forms of meditation are practiced together, the mind acquires the force necessary to overcome innate ignorance and effect a permanent transformation in the practitioner's consciousness.

Buddhists practice two types *of meditation to relieve innate ignorance: stabilizing, aimed at calming the mind, and insight, which focuses on the nature of reality.*

VI. THE AMERICAN SCHOLAR

Harvard College as it appeared in 1790.

ON AUGUST 31, 1837, Emerson traveled to Cambridge to deliver a ninety-minute address at Harvard College. His audience wasn't the graduating class, whose commencement had taken place the day before, but a distinguished group of teachers, ministers, and other intellectuals gathered together under the auspices of the college's Phi Beta Kappa Society. In the address, now known as "The American Scholar," Emerson applied to academia his most persistent theme: nature (rather than civilization) as the medium through which divine wisdom is transmitted to humanity. The pursuit of knowledge, Emerson told his audience, is "an indestructible instinct" linked closely to nature, but intellectuals are mistaken when they associate this pursuit too closely with academic scholarship. One obvious pitfall is the tendency to imitate. "The scholar," according to Emerson, "is the delegated intellect. In the right state, he is, *Man Thinking*. In the degenerate state, when the victim of society, he tends to become a mere thinker, or, still worse, the parrot of other men's thinking."

Because Emerson believed strongly that each person must cultivate a trust in his or her own mind, the role of intuition is central. "Each age," Emerson said, "must write its own books," but to do so, each new generation must first use intuition (rather than rational thought) to establish an original relationship with the world. The greatest danger, Emerson believed, was to become a bookworm, spending all one's time with the thoughts of older generations rather than exploring nature and experiencing humanity anew. According to Emerson, the European-style scholarship being practiced by the Harvard intelligentsia was much too sheltered—a turning away from what really mattered in life. What America needed, he said, was a generation of courageous, optimistic scholars who could teach the rest of the country how to live authentically.

In closing, Emerson proclaimed, "We have listened too long to the courtly muses of Europe. The spirit of the American freeman is already suspected to be timid, imitative, tame. Public and private avarice make the air we breathe thick and fat. The scholar is decent, indolent, complaisant. See already the tragic consequence. The mind of this country, taught to aim at low objects, eats upon itself." But there was, he said, a remedy: If the American scholar could become truly heroic, he could teach students how to resist the social institutions that throttle their creativity and instead engage with life on an individual basis.

In "The American Scholar," *Emerson applied transcendentalist precepts to academia, asserting that books were of secondary importance compared with one's experience.*

VI. THE BIG SPLASH

ABOUT THIRTY MILLION YEARS into its existence, the early Earth was beginning to take its present shape. The Iron Catastrophe was already well under way, and some of the lighter elements that had floated to Earth's surface were already beginning to cool and form a crust. Even so, the inner solar system remained a very crowded place, with many asteroids still wandering about and perhaps as many as twenty planet-sized objects still vying for permanent status. Inevitably, there were collisions, which gradually reduced the number of competitors to the four inner planets we have today.

One such collision involved Earth and a protoplanet roughly the size of Mars, known as Theia. The force of the collision destroyed Theia, but because the blow was glancing, the impact caused a significant portion of Earth's mantle to be ejected into space, along with most of Theia's mantle. Earth's massive gravity held this matter in orbit, however, and about half of it eventually fell back down. The rest coalesced to form the Moon.

Evidence strongly supporting this hypothesis was gathered on the Moon by the Apollo 11 astronauts. The rocks that they brought back turned out to be nearly identical in chemical composition to Earth rocks, except for two key differences: The Moon rocks had no iron, and they had no water.

The lack of iron was perfectly consistent with the Theia hypothesis (also known as the big splash) because neither Earth's mantle nor Theia's would have had much iron in it at the time of the collision. (Upon impact, Theia's iron core simply sank into Earth's core.) The lack of water was similarly predictable. Rocks on Earth have large amounts of water locked away in their crystalline structures, but the cinderlike rocks from the Moon had none. This is because the collision between Earth and Theia would have generated a great deal of heat, enough to reliquefy Earth's crust and therefore certainly enough to have evaporated any water that might have existed in the ejected matter.

Apollo 11 astronaut Edwin E. "Buzz" Aldrin, Jr., conducts scientific experiments on the Moon, which included the gathering of Moon rocks.

About thirty million years after its formation, Earth collided with the protoplanet Theia. The resulting impact ejected a great deal of matter, which became the Moon.

VI. THE DECLARATION OF RIGHTS

FOLLOWING THE TENNIS COURT OATH of June 20, 1789, Louis XVI and the National Assembly found themselves stalemated, each refusing to recognize the legitimacy of the other. In nearby Paris, where reports from Versailles were arriving daily, the population strongly supported the National Assembly. This made the king nervous, and in early July he ordered his army to encircle the city. His goal was to isolate the National Assembly from its Parisian base, but what he accomplished was merely a spike in the political temperature. Shopkeepers, tradesmen, and workers began frantically searching for weapons with which to defend themselves; and on July 14, a mob stormed the Bastille, once a formidable prison but now primarily an armory. The battle that followed ended with the beheading of the fortress commander and a parade of captured soldiers through the streets. This was the moment when the king could have ordered a suppression of the rioting populace, but he never did, perhaps because he didn't have the stomach for all the blood that would have been spilled.

The storming of the Bastille.

Meanwhile, in the countryside, a panic called the Great Fear took hold. Put on edge by the disorder and strife in Versailles and Paris, peasant communities were further alarmed by the widespread rumor that vagrants and bandits were planning to steal their crops. Transforming fear into aggression, many peasants reacted by raiding the homes of local nobles and burning documents authorizing the collection of seigneurial dues.

Worried that these raids might escalate into a peasant revolt, the renamed National Constituent Assembly (which now included deputies from other estates) met on August 4 to take up the issue of seigneurial dues. At the end of a long day, a vote was taken, and feudalism was abolished in France. Although characterized by one observer as "a moment of drunkenness," these August Decrees, which outlawed centuries-old privileges, laid the groundwork for the Declaration of the Rights of Man, which the Assembly adopted on August 26.

Caught up in the headiness of the time and propelled by forces beyond their control, the members of the Assembly created in the Declaration of Rights the most important statement of democratic principles in modern history. Using universalist language, they declared that all men were "born and remain free and equal in rights." The Declaration of Rights further asserted that sovereignty, far from residing in the person of an absolute monarch, belonged exclusively to the nation itself.

The Great Fear *motivated the National Constituent Assembly to take up the issue of economic fairness, out of which the Declaration of Rights quickly developed.*

VI. **THE CRISIS PASSES**

THE CUMULATIVE RESPONSE to the energy crisis brought on by the 1973 Arab oil embargo produced a number of effects that contradicted the pessimistic predictions of energy skeptics and environmental naysayers. Working in combination, conservation, efficiency, and a few new technology programs changed consumer behavior and succeeded in reducing the rate of demand growth. During the early 1980s, however, as petroleum prices stabilized and even declined, the sense of crisis passed, and the United States fell back into its complacent, pre-embargo ways.

Beginning in February 1982 (and with the brief exception of a three-month period during the run-up to the 1991 Gulf War), the cost of unleaded regular gasoline remained at or well below $1.33 per gallon until February 2000. During those eighteen years, low oil prices reshaped the energy environment yet again, raising the cost of alternative technologies relative to fossil fuels and undermining the commercial viability of most new alternative energy projects. (Ironically, the reduction in demand growth brought about in part by 1970s conservation measures contributed to a condition of electricity oversupply during the early 1980s. This further damaged the economic competitiveness of renewable technologies.)

As a result, the alternative energy industry entered a rather lean period. Research funding lagged, direct investment dried up, and alternative projects already on the grid struggled to remain competitive. Technologies considered vital to the national interest just a few years earlier became marginalized as the mantra of *cheap and plentiful above all else* strongly reasserted itself. Even those energy companies that still believed alternative technologies were the future of the industry couldn't afford to fund research and development because, with petroleum prices low, so were their profits. Some companies were pressured by investors to slash their funding of alternative energy research, and others were forced to sell off their alternative ventures entirely.

For the most part, the only alternative energy players left standing were the companies dedicated to the development of specific alternative technologies. Their goals, not surprisingly, were cost reduction and scalability (the ability of a technology to function efficiently in small-, medium-, and large-scale applications). Wind power proved to be the most viable in this regard, but biomass, geothermal, and solar applications also advanced, with technological improvements gradually reducing power-generation costs and improving competitiveness. Even so, none of these alternatives could compete head-to-head with large-scale, conventionally generated electricity during this period.

The return to *cheap and plentiful petroleum during the 1980s and 1990s ended most alternative energy investment and left just a few dedicated players in the game.*

VI. BUDDHISM'S FIRST FIVE HUNDRED YEARS

DURING THE LAST FORTY-FIVE YEARS OF HIS LIFE, the Buddha offered many teachings elaborating on different aspects of the Four Noble Truths, including lessons on the precise nature of ignorance and the wisdom that was its antidote. Finally, at the age of eighty (ca. 480 BCE), having exhausted the last remnants of the karma that impelled his existence, the Buddha passed into "final *nirvāṇa*," instructing the *sangha* to rely on his teachings in guiding one another.

The death of the Buddha in an eighteenth-century painting.

To further this goal, the Buddha instructed his monks to convene a council after his death, at which his teachings were to be recited from memory. (At the time, Indian culture was largely oral.) The Buddha's intention was to avoid a schism of the sort that had recently affected the Jain community, but his plan wasn't entirely successful. At the end of this First Council, a contingent of tardy monks refused to accept the consensus reached prior to their arrival, citing a number of unique teachings they claimed to have received directly from the Buddha.

About a century later, the *sangha* convened a Second Council, which produced another, more formal schism relating to monastic vows (rather than divergent teachings). At one point, the Buddha had instructed his monks that they could dispense with some of the more minor regulations concerning possessions, but he never identified which vows were superfluous, so all were initially retained. Sometime after his death, however, a group of monks began permitting leniencies, which angered the more traditional members of the *sangha*, causing the schism.

In 327 BCE, Alexander the Great invaded India, leaving behind garrisons. In the process of ejecting these garrisons following the death of Alexander, the first Indian empire was formed under Chandragupta Maurya. About 270 BCE, Aśoka, the third emperor of the Mauryan dynasty, ascended to the throne. During his highly successful thirty-seven-year reign, Aśoka significantly expanded the empire and also converted to Buddhism, beginning a golden age of royal patronage. He paid for the construction of monasteries and sent missionaries west and east along the Silk Road, which began on the Mediterranean and passed through central Asia before terminating in China.

Unfortunately, all this royal patronage attracted numerous charlatans, who knew little and cared less about Buddhist thought and practice. To deal with this problem, Aśoka convened a Third Council, which purged the *sangha* of non-Buddhists. About the same time, literate monks began setting down the oral tradition in scriptural texts known as *sūtras*.

After the Buddha's death, *efforts were made to preserve his teachings, at first through an oral tradition and later in written texts known as* sūtras.

VII. THE DIVINITY SCHOOL ADDRESS

IF EMERSON'S "American Scholar" address was a challenge to Harvard's Unitarian intelligentsia, then his July 15, 1838, speech to the graduating class at the Harvard Divinity School was more like an insult. At least, that was how it was perceived.

Christianity, Emerson bluntly told the six graduating students, had lost its redemptive power. Dogma and doctrine had replaced intuition and insight, leaving the church lifeless. "Jesus Christ," Emerson said, "belonged to the true race of prophets....He saw that God incarnates himself in man, and evermore goes forth anew to take possession of his world. He said, in this jubilee of sublime emotion, 'I am divine. Through me, God acts; through me, speaks. Would you see God, see me; or, see thee, when thou also thinkest as I now think.' But what a distortion did his doctrine and memory suffer in the same, in the next, and the following ages!"

According to Emerson, Jesus' great insight was that truth came not from received wisdom but from intuition—an argument similar to the one Emerson made in "The American Scholar," only now applied to religion. Ignoring this insight, the Christian churches had taken Jesus' words and ossified them. "The idioms of his language, and the figures of his rhetoric," Emerson said, "have usurped the place of his truth; and churches are not built on his principles, but on his tropes."

The older Christian clergy, Emerson went on, preached sermons laden with prefabricated concepts and phrases because they had nothing spontaneous or intuitive to offer. Meanwhile, younger ministers were having their individuality destroyed by oppressive institutionalized conformity. Only by finding their own personal connection to the divine in the natural world could such young clergymen speak new truths for a new generation. "Speak the very truth, as your life and conscience teach it," Emerson urged the graduating class, "and cheer the waiting, fainting hearts of men with new hope and new revelations."

The students appreciated his speech, but the numerous faculty and Unitarian elders in the hall were appalled. Invitations for Emerson to preach guest sermons at Unitarian churches nearly disappeared, and Harvard ostracized him for thirty years. On the other hand, the courage that he showed in delivering such a speech before such an audience spread Emerson's fame and attracted many new members to the Transcendental Club.

Emerson's home in Concord, Massachusetts.

In his 1838 Harvard Divinity School address, *Emerson castigated the Unitarian church for replacing Jesus' intuition and insight with dogma and doctrine.*

VII. THE SEASONS

ANOTHER IMPORTANT CONSEQUENCE of Earth's collision with Theia was the tilt the impact imparted. Before the collision, Earth rotated on an axis perpendicular to its own orbit. The impact with Theia, however, shifted this angle by roughly twenty-three degrees. Such a tilt may not seem like much, but it explains why Earth has changing seasons.

Earth's axis tilts in relation to its orbit. This tilt causes the seasons.

Imagine yourself standing at the center of an elliptical rug. You are the Sun. Now imagine a navel orange on the edge of the rug directly in front of you, with its navel pointing toward you at a twenty-three-degree tilt. The orange is Earth, and its navel is Earth's geographic North Pole. At this particular moment, the scene represents Earth's orientation relative to the Sun at the height of summer in the Northern Hemisphere (the summer solstice).

Continuing this thought experiment, imagine rotating the orange on its axis. The navel always remains visible to you, just as the Sun never sets on the North Pole during the Arctic summer. This also explains why the days are longer and warmer in the North during the summer months: Much more of the hemisphere is exposed to solar radiation while the North Pole remains tilted toward the Sun.

Now imagine you and the orange moving a quarter turn counterclockwise around the outer edge of the rug. Do not, however, change the orientation of the navel, which should now be tilted toward your left. In this position, which represents the Northern Hemisphere's autumnal equinox, Earth's rotational axis sits perpendicular to the Sun, therefore its rotation produces days and nights of equal length.

Another quarter turn with no change in navel orientation creates a position that represents the winter solstice in the Northern Hemisphere—which is, of course, the summer solstice in the Southern Hemisphere. This should be obvious because, as the orange rotates on its axis, you can't see the navel North Pole at all, while the opposite South Pole remains always visible. This explains why, during the winter solstice in the North, the extreme northern latitudes experience twenty-four hours of darkness, while the extreme southern latitudes enjoy twenty-four hours of sunshine.

A final quarter turn brings you to the position representing the Northern Hemisphere's vernal equinox, which is also the Southern Hemisphere's autumnal equinox. Once again, days and nights are momentarily equalized all over the planet before the cycle repeats.

Another consequence *of the collision between Earth and Theia was the tilting of Earth's rotational axis, producing the seasons.*

VII. **THE CONSTITUTION OF 1791**

DURING THE FALL OF 1789, the French political landscape shifted from Versailles to Paris. Following the king's refusal to accept the August Decrees, an armed mob of

Parisian men and women traveled to Versailles, where they rousted Louis XVI from the Sun King's palace and forced him to return with them to Paris. The National Constituent Assembly soon followed, and Paris once again became the French capital.

While Louis XVI stewed in the Tuileries (his Parisian palace), the Assembly began work on the constitution it had sworn to draft. Moderates wanted the new government to take the form of a constitutional monarchy based on individual rights and the rule of law. Although this vision satisfied neither the royalists nor the more radical Parisians, a constitution drawn up along these lines was nevertheless negotiated, and it took effect in September 1791.

A cleric, aristocrat, and commoner rescue the Constitution of 1791.

The Constitution of 1791 created a new Legislative Assembly, whose members were to be elected every two years. The monarchy, meanwhile, was reduced to a weak executive branch. The king could appoint his own ministers and supervise the implementation of laws, but he couldn't propose new legislation, and his veto power was only temporary: After two years, laws that he had vetoed became nevertheless enforceable. Economically, the new constitution provided for taxes to be assessed more equitably, for guild monopolies to be dissolved, and for a free-market economy to replace the current protectionism. The Constitution of 1791 even reorganized the country, discarding the provinces and replacing them with departments (which were divided into districts, and the districts into communes).

With regard to elections, new property qualifications limited suffrage to about one-third of the white male population, and even those people couldn't vote for the national legislature directly. They merely chose forty-three thousand electors from an even wealthier stratum of society, and those electors chose the legislature. Thus, the Constitution of 1791 reflected strongly the elite, enlightened views of the bourgeois who wrote it. But the new Legislative Assembly contained many more left-leaning deputies than the National Constituent Assembly had, and these men harshly criticized the constitution's restrictions on suffrage. No less angry but substantially more sinister was the reaction of the nobility who made up the country's officer corps. Many of these nobles quietly emigrated to Austria and Prussia, where they began plotting counterrevolution—specifically, the overthrow of the new regime and the restoration of the old French monarchy.

The Constitution of 1791 *created a new regime: a constitutional monarchy dedicated to the bourgeois values of private property, free markets, and democratic elections.*

VII. **THE CHANGING CLIMATE**

WITH THE 1982–2000 run of cheap petroleum now behind us, today's energy climate feels much more like the 1970s than it does the 1990s. Petroleum prices are rising sharply; political instability, especially in the Middle East, has led to renewed calls for energy independence; and conservation is again in vogue. Yet this time around, there is an important new factor to consider: global warming.

The challenge posed by global warming has made alternative energy technologies relevant on a massive, world-saving scale. According to the current scientific consensus, climate change is being driven by the release of carbon dioxide and other greenhouse gases into the atmosphere. Because the burning of fossil fuels is by far the leading source of these emissions, conventional energy lies at the heart of the global warming debate. The implications are as profound as the use of fossil fuels is widespread, bringing into question the ways in which the developed world travels, manufactures and ships its goods, lights and heats its homes, and even produces and distributes its food. The high standard of living in developed countries is inextricably tied to the cheap, plentiful energy they enjoy.

An important symbolic step was taken in December 1997, when many leaders of the industrialized world agreed in Kyoto, Japan, to impose limits on carbon emissions. The developed nations that signed the Kyoto Protocol were required to meet individual targets set at least 5 percent below each country's 1990 emissions level. To meet such a goal, a nation could begin by reducing demand and improving energy efficiency, but these strategies alone wouldn't be sufficient, No developed country could meet its Kyoto target, the experts believed, without replacing some conventionally generated energy with clean, renewable alternatives.

With the possible exception of the current interest in green utility programs and hybrid cars, the changes wrought by Kyoto haven't yet reached the consumer level. Within the energy industry, however, corporations are now on notice that they ignore their carbon profiles at their own peril. Recalculating once more, the leading energy companies have found that the numbers again favor investment in alternative technologies. Government tax incentives have, of course, helped this process along, but the threat to energy company profits posed by hard emissions caps is real enough that several additional strategies are being developed beyond alternative energy investment. These include carbon-trading markets, where clean companies can sell emissions "credits" to dirtier ones, and carbon sequestration, an innovative but expensive technique for burying carbon dioxide emissions in caverns underground.

The need to reduce *carbon emissions because of global warming has revitalized the alternative energy sector, with government and industry again initiating investment.*

VII. THE SPREAD OF BUDDHISM

FOR FIFTEEN HUNDRED YEARS after the reign of Aśoka (that is, until about 1200 CE), the teachings of the Buddha spread and flourished throughout Asia: from Persia to China, Japan, and Indonesia; from Śrī Laṅka to Tibet and the northern Silk Road; and across all points in between.

The period from the fourth century CE to the seventh century CE saw particular growth in the influence of the *saṅgha*. Since the time of the Buddha, there had been centers of study where Buddhist monks and nuns could gather. But during the middle centuries of the first millennium CE, royal patronage expanded the scope of these institutions, giving rise to large interdisciplinary universities staffed by the leading scholars of the day. Renowned for their excellence, these universities drew students from all over the Buddhist world, encouraging tolerance, diversity, and interreligious dialogue.

Perhaps because of this atmosphere of diversity, several new traditions emerged that would have transformative effects on Buddhist philosophy. The first involved a *siddha* named Nāgārjuna. *Siddhas* were highly accomplished monks with special abilities, such as the ability to travel to different realms of existence. Near the end of the second century CE, according to tradition, Nāgārjuna traveled to the realm of the Nāgas (semiphysical serpentlike beings), where he retrieved texts that recorded teachings on the perfection of wisdom, which the Buddha had given the Nāgas. Nāgārjuna's dissemination of these texts inspired a new movement within Buddhism of monks and nuns who aspired to follow the Buddha's example beyond simply following his teachings. They called their chosen path, based on the Perfection of Wisdom *sūtras* and related texts, the Mahāyāna, or Great Vehicle.

A twelfth-century CE text of the Perfection of Wisdom *sūtras*.

Another important Buddhist tradition that emerged during the first millennium concerned the *tantras*, which were texts that purportedly contained highly esoteric teachings given personally by the Buddha to a few select disciples. Reputedly, they were passed down in secret from master to disciple for eleven centuries until they became semipublic around the seventh century CE. Thereafter, the *tantras* and the many commentaries written on them by university scholars dominated intellectual life in India until the brutal Muslim invasions of the early thirteenth century. Buddhist scholars bore the brunt of the violence, with Islamic sources recording the execution of entire university populations. As the remnants of these great universities fled into the Himalayas and Tibet, Buddhism disappeared in India.

During the first millennium CE, *Buddhism spread across India and central Asia as universities developed, fostering new traditions such as the Mahāyāna and the tantric.*

VIII. THE DIAL

FROM 1836 ON, the members of the Transcendental Club often discussed how desirable it would be to have a literary magazine of their own, one that could publish their "new ideas" and attract likeminded intellectuals to their circle. Especially after Emerson's Divinity School speech, most American literary periodicals wanted nothing to do with the controversial transcendentalists, but it wasn't until the fall of 1839 that the decision was made to go ahead with Margaret Fuller as editor. (Emerson was the natural choice, but he declined, being already too busy.)

Margaret Fuller

Fuller (1810–50) was a teacher and social activist who, according to Susan B. Anthony and Elizabeth Cady Stanton in their *History of Woman Suffrage* (1881), "possessed more influence on the thought of American women than any woman previous to her time." She had become well known in and around Boston for the "conversations" she held at a popular Boston bookstore. The participants in these meetings were female intellectuals, many of them wives of prominent transcendentalists, who had little opportunity to make use of their educations and express themselves.

The club's publication was christened the *Dial* (as in *sundial*) because, according to George Ripley's prospectus for the magazine, it "will endeavor to occupy a station on which the light may fall; which is open to the rising sun; and from which it may correctly report the progress of the hour and the day." The first issue appeared in July 1840, and the magazine was published quarterly thereafter. It contained articles, essays, and poems written by members of Emerson's wide and growing circle of transcendentalist friends.

The reviews were mixed. In and around Boston, where the ideas of the transcendentalists were familiar and accepted, the *Dial* was greeted favorably. But elsewhere, newspapers and other magazines either ignored the *Dial* or dismissed it as ridiculous. "Who reads the *Dial*," asked one Yale minister, "for any other purpose than to laugh at its baby poetry, or at the solemn fooleries of its misty prose?"

The *Dial*'s three hundred subscriptions produced enough income to pay for the printing of the magazine but left nothing over to compensate the contributors or the editor. After two years, Fuller resigned to write a book, at which point Emerson replaced her as editor, calling his acceptance of the job an act of "petty literary patriotism." The *Dial* struggled for another two years before ceasing publication in April 1844.

The *Dial* *was the organ of the Transcendental Club, publishing articles, essays, and poems written by club members and their friends on a quarterly basis.*

VIII. PLATE TECTONICS

SPARED FURTHER PLANET-SIZED IMPACTS, Earth finally began to settle down and cool. As it did, its layers became more and more distinct. At the planet's center there formed a solid ball of iron and nickel about 750 miles in radius. This was the inner core, where the temperature was easily hot enough to melt any metal but the pressure generated by the weight of the planet was even greater, forcing the iron and nickel to solidify. Around the inner core, an outer core of iron and nickel developed, about 1,400 miles thick. Because the outer core was subjected to much less pressure, it remained in a liquid state.

Earth's outermost layer, known as the crust, solidified quickly but only to a depth of at most 60 miles. (In some places, the crust is just a few miles thick.) The rest of the planet, about 1,800 miles of thickness, became the rocky region known as the mantle. Most of the mantle also solidified, but higher temperatures kept a narrow band of the upper mantle in a molasses-like state, so that it flowed but only very slowly.

According to the modern theory of plate tectonics, however, it is more accurate to say that Earth has two outermost layers. The top one is the lithosphere, made up of the crust and the rigid uppermost layer of mantle. The lower one is the asthenosphere, that part of the upper mantle where the rock is partially molten and thus flows like a liquid on geological time scales. The lithosphere, however, is not one piece; rather, it's broken up into seven major (and many minor) pieces once called continents but now called plates.

Moving slowly in relation to one another, these plates come together along lines called boundaries. Plates moving away from one another meet along divergent boundaries; plates moving toward one another meet along convergent boundaries. Divergent boundaries create deep gashes in the crust that are subsequently filled by matter bubbling up from the mantle. Convergent boundaries produce either subduction zones or crumple zones.

When a heavier plate smashes into a lighter plate, a subduction zone is formed. The lighter plate rides over the heavier plate, forcing the heavier plate down into the mantle, where its leading edge melts. When plates of equal density meet, however, the result is much more violent, and crumple zones form. (Think of pressing with equal force on both ends of an aluminum can until the surface buckles.) The Himalaya Mountains, which sit on the boundary between the Indian and Eurasian plates, were formed by this sort of crumpling.

As solid and stationary *as Earth's surface may appear, it's actually slowly on the move.*

VIII. THE WAR WITH AUSTRIA AND PRUSSIA

IN JUNE 1791, Louis XVI, disguised as a valet, attempted to flee France with his wife, Marie Antoinette. En route to Austria, where Marie's brother was emperor, they were captured in the small town of Varennes and returned to the Tuileries, where the king lived neither as a prisoner nor as a free man. Following his flight, the antiroyalist radicals in the Legislative Assembly (known as Jacobins) treated him as a traitor, accusing him of treachery and characterizing his vetoes of key legislative acts as deliberate attempts to undermine the Revolution. There was much truth in these charges, but the moderates who still controlled the Legislative Assembly (known as Feuillants) were so invested in the idea of a constitutional monarchy that they refused to give it up on Louis XVI's account.

Meanwhile, saber rattling from Austria and Prussia contributed to the volatile atmosphere. Neither had to start a war, however, because on April 20, 1792, the Legislative Assembly declared war first. Its motivation was complicated, and different deputies had different reasons, but the primary Feuillant rationale was that a war with external enemies would shift attention away from domestic problems and rally the country behind the tottering government.

Although the king wanted France to lose, because an Austro-Prussian victory would mean the end of the Revolution and his own return to power, it's not clear that he actively conspired with the enemy. Initially, the Austrians and Prussians didn't seem to need his help. The emigration of so many nobles had decimated the French officer corps, and the loyalty of those who remained in the regular army was often suspect. Patriotic fervor inspired many militiamen to join the army of volunteers that was raised, but these men possessed few military skills, and their effectiveness was limited.

A 1792 cartoon of Louis XVI toasting the nation.

In August 1792, a Parisian mob, angry about the country's early losses in the war and suspicious of the king's role in them, stormed the Tuileries. Six hundred royal guards were killed, but Louis XVI escaped, fleeing across the street to the chambers of the Legislative Assembly. At this point, the Jacobins finally gained ascendance over the Feuillants, persuading the rest of the deputies that maintaining the charade of the constitutional monarchy was now pointless. Quickly, the Legislative Assembly suspended the Constitution of 1791, authorized elections for a National Convention to write a new republican constitution, and put the king on trial for treason.

The Feuillants *acceded to war because they thought it would shift attention away from the country's domestic troubles, but early losses only strengthened the Jacobins.*

VIII. THE SECOND ALTERNATIVE ENERGY BOOM

VENTURE CAPITALISTS looking for new investment opportunities in the wake of the dot-com bubble were the first group to target alternative energy as a promising sector. At the time, about 2002, alternative energy was indeed a woefully undercapitalized industry with large upside potential, but it didn't remain that way long.

Large multinational petroleum corporations, acutely conscious of their poor public image as energy profiteers and environmental villains, quickly began investing in renewable technologies themselves, especially as global warming became more of a public concern. These investments were made, no doubt, to improve the investing company's corporate image, but they also reflected a growing consensus among energy companies that the alternative sector had the strongest potential for growth in an otherwise slow global energy market. Adopting as its new "brand" the slogan *Beyond Petroleum*, the multinational oil company BP aggressively pursued solar-cell research and distribution. Meanwhile, its rival Shell created a renewable energy unit that soon became one of the world's largest producers of wind energy. Chevron, another former petroleum stalwart, accomplished much the same in the field of geothermal energy.

These developments encouraged smaller energy companies, especially those in the business of constructing energy infrastructure, to develop alternative energy expertise in expectation of future work. The anticipation even spread to Wall Street, where investment banks began thinking about entering the alternative energy business themselves. The plan was to fund the construction of low-emission power plants, use these plants to accumulate green energy credits (if such a system were ever enacted), and then sell the amassed credits in the carbon-trading marketplace.

In 2005, total global investment in the alternative energy sector reached eighty billion dollars. A year later, that figure jumped 25 percent to one hundred billion dollars. Among developed countries, solar, wind, and biofuels were the top investment draws. In the developing world, the most notable investments were made in Chinese solar power, Indian wind power, and Brazilian biofuels. Overall, the investment boom of 2002–6 increased the annual growth rate of alternative energy production from an average of 2.2 percent during the period 1970–2000 to about 8 percent in 2006. During that same period, alternative energy more than doubled its market share, reaching 2 percent of the total global energy market in 2006 as it began to compete directly with conventionally produced energy in some electricity markets.

Around 2002, *money began flowing back into alternative energy from venture capitalists and from energy companies looking to improve their image and growth potential.*

VIII. THE BUDDHIST CANONS

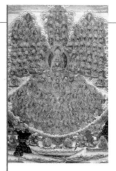

As Buddhist thought spread between 250 BCE and 1200 CE, so did Buddhist texts, but they typically traveled individually rather than as a complete canon. Even though the *sangha* began committing the Buddha's teachings to written form within three hundred years of his death, it took another five or six hundred years before the first formal canon, or compilation of *sūtras*, appeared in India during the fourth century CE. This canon, which was itself hardly complete, divided the texts it contained into three categories based on the three stages of the Eightfold Path.

The Buddha among monks in a Tibetan scroll-painting.

After several hundred more years, Buddhists in other countries began putting together their own canons. The first step in the redaction process was the gathering together of all known translated texts. Then local scholars weeded out duplicates, eliminated dubious texts, and edited those that remained for consistent vocabulary. Finally, the texts were grouped together by theme or subject and arranged into sequences based on length and, when known, chronology. Typically, the canons also included commentaries, some by Indian authors and others by indigenous translators.

In Laṅka (now Śrī Laṅka), Theravāda scholars perpetuated a version of the fourth-century Indian canon, which excluded Mahāyāna and tantric texts. Written in the Pāli language (and hence known as the Pāli canon), it underwent several changes in later years, such as the purging of mystical elements, before being shared with other Theravādan countries, including Burma and Thailand.

In China, another major canon developed that, like all the others, reflected the philosophical interests of its translators. The Chinese canon, compiled from texts that had traveled east along the Silk Road, also included commentaries heavily influenced by the Mahāyāna tradition. This canon was then exported to Korea and Japan.

In Tibet, a third major canon developed that was markedly different from the other two, both in content and in organization. Aided by its proximity to India, the Tibetan *sangha* accumulated far more material than any other Buddhist group—especially Mahāyāna and tantric texts. During the twelfth century CE, when the Tibetan canon was first redacted, it was organized into two sections: one containing "translated words" (Kangyur) of the Buddha and the other containing translated Indian commentaries (Tengyur). The Kangyur included monastic disciplines, *sūtras*, and *tantras*, while the Tengyur covered not only Buddhist philosophy and scripture but also Buddhist presentations of the wider Indian systems of knowledge, from grammar and poetics to medicine and political theory.

As Buddhism spread *through Asia, different collections of* sūtras *and commentaries were redacted in different countries into three principal canons.*

IX. BROOK FARM

OF ALL THE TRANSCENDENTALISTS, George Ripley was perhaps the most interested in social reform. He considered the United States "vicious in its foundations" and became so dissatisfied with the Unitarian Church as a vehicle for social activism that he left the pulpit in 1840. With his wife, Sophia, he spent the summer of 1840 on a dairy farm nine miles outside of Boston owned by Charles and Maria Ellis. The beauty of the natural landscape was such that Ripley thought it would make a perfect home for an experimental community based on transcendentalist principles.

Announcing his intentions at an October 1840 meeting of the Transcendental Club, he wrote a letter to Emerson a few weeks later, outlining his plan in greater detail: "Our objects, as you know, are to insure a more natural union between intellectual and manual labor than now exists; to combine the thinker and the worker, as far as possible, in the same individual;…and thus to prepare a society of liberal, intelligent, and cultivated persons, whose relations with each other would permit a more simple and wholesome life, than can be led amidst the pressure of our competitive institutions."

In April 1841, the Ripleys and fifteen others, including Nathaniel Hawthorne, moved to the Ellis farm in West Roxbury. Forming a joint-stock company, they purchased the property in October and renamed it Brook Farm. The two principle activities were farming and teaching, with the latter accounting for most of the community's operating income (in the form of tuition payments from nonmembers). As the number of residents increased, however, eventually reaching 120, the economy of the farm diversified. Industries, such as shoemaking, were launched, and the domestic chores of cooking and cleaning became full-time pursuits.

Yet Brook Farm never stabilized and, from the beginning, struggled to stay afloat financially. Initially, all labor was voluntary, then a quota system was imposed (requiring ten hours of labor a day during the growing season), and finally timekeeping was instituted to police the slackers. Such rigidity, of course, undermined Brook Farm's purpose of facilitating moral growth through proximity to nature.

Ripley tried saving the community by reorganizing it in 1844 along lines suggested by French social reformer Charles Fourier, who believed that humanity's natural goodness was being perverted by faulty social organization. Nevertheless, Brook Farm continued to struggle, and when a March 1846 fire destroyed an expensive new building, the community's financial position became untenable, and it collapsed.

Brook Farm *was an experiment in transcendentalist living founded by George Ripley in 1841. It never stabilized, however, and struggled financially until its collapse.*

IX. **THE OCEANS**

LITTLE IS KNOWN FOR CERTAIN about the origin of Earth's oceans, but there are currently two main hypotheses: One is that the water was always here; the other is that it came from somewhere else. The first of these hypotheses stems from the simple observation that, among all the gases released by the Hawaiian volcanoes, steam (water vapor) is the most prevalent. Thus it could be that simple volcanic outgassing of water trapped within Earth's rocky mantle produced the planet's oceans.

Comets may have provided some of the water for Earth's oceans.

The premise of the second hypothesis, that the source of Earth's water is extraterrestrial, seems unlikely at first glance because, at least in our solar system, liquid water is quite rare. In the solid form of ice, however, water in actually quite abundant. Comets, for instance, are made of ice mixed with other debris. Specialists believe that large comets may contain fifty or more cubic kilometers of water in the form of ice. Although 10 of these comets, if they collided with Earth and melted, would provide enough water to fill Lake Erie, another 240 would be needed to fill Lake Superior, and about 7 million would be necessary to fill the Atlantic Ocean. That so many millions of large comets would have impacted Earth seems not very likely, but comets may well have been the source of a great deal of the water on Earth.

Another potential source of extraterrestrial water is the asteroid belt between Mars and Jupiter. Occasionally, the gravitational field of Jupiter shifts one of these asteroids into a new orbit that now crosses the orbit of Earth. Given enough time, this asteroid and Earth will occupy the same intersection point at the same time, resulting in a collision. It has been estimated that forty thousand tons of matter rains down on Earth every year as a result of this process. Examination of these meteorites has shown that the rock in their cores is often infused with a high concentration of water molecules. (A meteorite is the portion of an asteroid that survives its passage through the atmosphere and impact with the ground without being vaporized.)

Although neither the from-here nor the from-elsewhere hypothesis is particularly compelling, both are plausible, and perhaps both are true. It seems most likely that several processes were at work over hundreds of millions of years to make Earth the only planet known to be covered with liquid water.

Scientists disagree about the source of the water that fills Earth's oceans. Some believe that it came from the mantle, while others look to extraterrestrial sources.

IX. REGICIDE AND RADICALIZATION

BECAUSE THE JACOBINS insisted on universal male suffrage, most adult males were allowed to vote in the September 1792 elections for the National Convention. The result was that younger and more radical deputies were elected—many, but not all of them, Jacobins. Soon, a republic was proclaimed, and while the work of drafting the new constitution went forward, the members of the Convention turned their attention to judging the king. After a monthlong trial, Louis XVI was found guilty

Louis XVI at the guillotine.

of treason on January 15, 1793. Although the vote to convict was unanimous, the vote to impose the death penalty was much narrower. On January 18, a motion to grant the king a reprieve was defeated, and on January 21, he was beheaded by guillotine before a cheering crowd in what is now the Place de la Concorde.

The death of the king meant that there was no turning back. It deeply disturbed Europe's other monarchies and brought Britain, Spain, the Netherlands, Russia, and a host of others into the war against the regicidal French. Before the proclamation of the French republic, there had been only a few small and inconsequential republics in Europe; but France was one of the richest and most powerful nations on the Continent, and republicanism there represented a political threat of an entirely different order.

Meanwhile, a serious split developed among the Jacobins who controlled the new republic. The more moderate Girondins wanted greater public order; the radical Montagnards, on the other hand, were willing to countenance unruly street behavior if the result was greater popular democracy. For example, when Parisians entered the city's prisons in September 1792, murdering as many as fourteen hundred suspected counterrevolutionaries, the Girondins recoiled in horror, but the Montagnards joined forces with the mob—to manage its violence, perhaps, but also to gain its political support.

To the Montagnards, the ideal revolutionary was one who didn't merely *vote* for revolution but *acted* for it. The Girondins worked as best they could to prevent the radicalization of the National Convention, but on May 31, 1793, the Montagnard leader Maximilien Robespierre exhorted the Parisian mob to invade the Convention and expel the "corrupt deputies." The Girondin leaders were soon arrested, and the National Convention passed into Montagnard control. An impressive array of new democratic laws followed, including acts that established public education, created public welfare programs, and granted women (considered the property of their husbands under the ancien régime) the right to divorce.

Following the king's execution, *the radical Montagnards gradually overcame the resistance of the moderate Girondins to seize control of the National Convention.*

IX. SOLAR ENERGY

THE POTENTIAL OF SOLAR ENERGY is nearly limitless. In a single day, the total energy reaching the earth from the Sun is more than the global population consumes in a decade. Yet the story of solar energy thus far has been one of unrealized potential. Although progress has been made in developing solar technology, current solar energy production meets less than 0.1 percent of world demand.

The main reason is cost. Depending on the scale of the installation, solar energy still costs from three to six times as much as conventional energy. On the other hand, since the mid-1990s, the cost of solar energy has been steadily declining at a rate of about 4 percent per year, and this trend is expected to continue. The savings have come primarily from improvements in the efficiency of the power conversion and economies of scale in manufacturing. Meanwhile, on the demand side, the market for solar energy has grown significantly since the 1980s, reaching annual growth rates of 25 percent in recent years.

There are two main conversion technologies: photovoltaic (PV) cell and solar thermal. Photovoltaic cell technology uses semiconductors to convert the radiant energy of the Sun into electricity. When sunlight falls on the boundary between two semiconductors, a voltage (defined as a difference in electric potential) is created. This voltage causes electrons to flow, generating an electric current. Although single PV cells generate tiny amounts of electricity (roughly half a volt's worth, or 0.1–0.4 amps, depending on the cell's efficiency), thousands of cells ganged together in arrays can produce electricity on a utility-sized scale. (The term *utility scale* refers to projects that produce enough power to supply long-term utility contracts.)

Solar thermal technology generates electricity by converting sunlight into heat and using that heat to drive a steam generator. The process begins with collectors that focus sunlight onto receivers, usually fluid-filled tubes, which absorb the sunlight and convert it into heat. The simplest collector is the parabolic dish. By virtue of its shape, all of the sunlight striking the mirrored dish is reflected to a single point, called the focus, where the receiver is mounted.

Photovoltaic cell panels at a Sacramento substation.

A variation, the parabolic trough, focuses the sunlight along a focal line rather than at a focal point. Still other systems employ tracking mirrors called heliostats. Swiveling assemblies pivot these mirrors so that they follow the sun, always reflecting its light to a central receiver mounted on a tower.

The main solar technologies, *photovoltaic cell and solar thermal, have recently enjoyed high growth rates, but they still meet less than 0.1 percent of total global demand.*

IX. SELFLESSNESSS

SEVERAL KEY IDEAS at the root of Buddhism differentiated it from other Indian religions—the most important being selflessness. While the Vedic tradition (and the Hinduism it begat) spoke of an eternal self (*ātman*), the Buddha taught a doctrine of "no-self" (*anātman*), which denied the existence of a personal essence. According to the Buddha, a person was merely the coming together of parts, both physical and mental, which changed from moment to moment and eventually dispersed. Although one often speaks of a "self" that experiences things, this was merely a rhetorical convenience, the Buddha said, and shouldn't be confused with an actual permanent self, which didn't exist.

The Buddha considered the acceptance of selflessness a key factor in overcoming suffering. The reason was that belief in this illusory self understandably produces a desire to benefit and protect one's self—which, in turn, leads to anger and suffering as these efforts are thwarted, which they often are. The belief in a permanent self also allows the Three Poisons of ignorance, desire, and hatred to feed upon one another, clouding one's mind and inspiring further actions harmful to oneself and others. For most non-Mahāyāna schools of Buddhism, the realization of the ultimate truth of selflessness constitutes *nirvāṇa*, a state of existence outside the endless cycles of death and rebirth in which suffering is eliminated.

Interwoven with the Buddha's concept of selflessness was his doctrine of the impermanence of all things. Just as people are made up of discrete parts that change from moment to moment, so are things impermanent because they, too, are composed of ever-changing parts. To the extent that such things are coveted (and thus considered permanent), they also give rise to suffering.

Within the Mahāyāna tradition, the status of all phenomena with regard to permanence became the central focus in defining the precise nature of reality. Because all matter and consciousness changes from moment to moment, there can be no permanent identity. Furthermore, the same changeability applies to the component parts of matter and consciousness, so these must also be empty of permanent identity. Realization of these ultimate truths, according to the Mahāyāna schools, produces the state of Buddhahood.

This belief suggests the possibility of multiple Buddhas, which the infinite nature of the universe would also seem to imply. In fact, different Buddhist scriptures speak of many prior Buddhas in this world-system, Śākyamuni Buddha being only the most recent.

Among the key ideas *that differentiated Buddhism from other Indian systems of thought was the concept of selflessness and its corollary, the impermanence of all things.*

X. SELF-RELIANCE

Emerson in middle age.

IN 1841, Emerson published his second book, *Essays*. His aunt Mary Moody Emerson called it a "strange medley of atheism and false independence," but favorable reviews in London and Paris laid the foundation for his international fame. The most talked-about essay in the collection, "Self-Reliance," emphasized a familiar Emersonian theme: the need to look inward for knowledge and guidance.

Like "The American Scholar," "Self-Reliance" begins with a discussion of the importance of thinking for oneself rather than blindly accepting the ideas of others. In Emerson's view, individual intuition matters much more than secondhand knowledge gained from books, especially with regard to morality. The difference between right and wrong, according to Emerson, is to be learned not from society but from the feelings within an individual's own heart.

"Trust thyself: every heart vibrates to that iron string," Emerson wrote. "Accept the place the divine providence has found for you, the society of your contemporaries, the connection of events. Great men have always done so, and confided themselves childlike to the genius of their age, betraying [revealing] their perception that the absolutely trustworthy was seated at their heart, working through their hands, predominating in all their being. And we are now men, and must accept in the highest mind the same transcendent destiny; and not minors and invalids in a protected corner, not cowards fleeing before a revolution, but guides, redeemers and benefactors, obeying the Almighty effort and advancing on Chaos and the Dark."

In urging his readers to "confide themselves childlike to the genius of their age," Emerson was borrowing an analogy from Wordsworth. According to the poet, adults who reconnect with nature become childlike in their newfound spontaneity and innocence. Self-reliant people, according to Emerson, similarly resemble children in that they are neither hesitant nor hypocritical. Also like children, who are not yet fully under the yoke of social conformity, they apply their own moral standards to what they see and make judgments accordingly.

The opposite of self-reliance in Emerson's scheme is conformity, which must be avoided. "Whoso would be a man must be a nonconformist," Emerson wrote. This may seem contradictory, given that Emerson is advocating the acceptance of his own ideas by the reader. Yet the paradox is easily resolved: As the reader develops more self-reliance, he will look past what Emerson has written to develop ideas of his own. This, Emerson believed, is how society regenerates itself.

In "Self-Reliance," *Emerson emphasized the importance of thinking and acting according to one's intuition rather than conforming to the moral judgments of society.*

X. THE FIRST LIFE

IN 1953, chemists Stanley L. Miller and Harold C. Urey conducted a famous experiment in a laboratory at the University of Chicago. Into a closed system, they introduced methane, ammonia, hydrogen, and water vapor—a mixture of gases thought to represent Earth's early atmosphere. Miller and Urey then sent an electrical current through the gases, creating sparks. These sparks represented the lightning that would have been produced by static electricity in the early atmosphere. After a week of continuous operation, the investigators noticed that a brown slime had formed. When Miller and Urey analyzed the slime, they found that it contained amino acids, which are the building blocks of the proteins found in every living cell.

Soon other researchers began exploring different ways in which organic compounds could be synthesized from the inorganic matter thought to be present on the early Earth. In 1961, Spanish biochemist Joan Oró discovered that he could produce amino acids using a solution of hydrogen cyanide, ammonia, and water. Even more importantly, he found that his experiment also produced the organic compound adenine, one of the basic components of nucleic acids such as RNA (ribonucleic acid) and DNA (deoxyribonucleic acid).

Still other researchers, following a different approach, investigated whether organic compounds could have been deposited on Earth by asteroids and comets (both of which have been found to contain many such compounds). To test this hypothesis, experimenters re-created the conditions of impact by placing a solution of amino acids in a metal capsule and subjecting it to the temperature and pressure of a five-thousand-mile-per-hour collision. The result was creation rather than destruction, as some of the amino acids were transformed into peptide chains. Linked together, peptide chains form proteins.

Exactly how and when these organic compounds became living things, we do not know. But we do know that all life on Earth is based on a universal genetic code, which ensures that all living things perform the same basic operations in exactly the same way. To explain why this would be, biologists have proposed the concept of LUCA, the last universal common ancestor. According to this hypothesis, all life on Earth is descended from a single organism and thus shares its basic genetic code.

The organic compounds *necessary for life could have been created in Earth's early atmosphere, but they also could have been deposited by comets and asteroids.*

X. **THE TERROR**

WHILE THE DRAMATIC EXPANSION of democratic rights enacted by the Montagnards greatly pleased their Parisian constituency, it cost them whatever little support they had in the rest of the country. In the towns of the south that had been Girondist strongholds, armed resistance arose; and in the west, peasants rebelled against the government's new conscription laws. Therefore, in the fall of 1793, as several different foreign armies prepared to invade the country, the government in Paris faced the prospect of civil war as well. The Revolution was entering its darkest hour.

On September 5, a delegation of Parisians appeared before the Convention to demand that it "make terror the order of the day." The word *terror* was not idly chosen but used to evoke the depth of the crisis. It referred specifically to the imposition of martial law but later came to describe more generally the harsh rule of the Montagnards from the fall of 1793 through the summer of 1794. The justification for the Terror was the saving of the republic from collapse; yet even as it protected France, the Terror tainted the Revolution with a legacy of extremism and ideological violence that could never be expunged.

Suspending the new Constitution of 1793, the Montagnards transferred the sovereign power of the Convention to a legislative committee known as the Committee of Public Safety. Dominated by Maximilien Robespierre, the twelve-member Committee curtailed individual liberties and expropriated private property for the war effort. Anyone who disagreed with its policies was accused of corruption, arrested, and summarily executed—even women and children. The regime's most vocal critics were thus silenced, while others fled or retreated into a sullen obedience.

The Committee of Public Safety in a ca. 1794 engraving.

Such methods, though heinous, were for a time effective; and by the spring of 1794, a better-equipped French army was pushing back against the foreign invaders while quashing civil rebellions at home. Even after the immediate crisis passed, however, the killings continued and even expanded. Realizing that their own turn would inevitably come, the members of the Convention acted on July 27, 1794, to disband the Committee. Robespierre and several of his colleagues were arrested and sent to the guillotine the next day. With their deaths, the Terror ended, but not the retribution. For many years thereafter, those who had implemented the Terror locally still felt the murderous wrath of their vengeful fellow citizens.

The Terror *began as an expedient response to the internal and external threats faced by the Montagnard government. It escalated, however, into an ideological bloodbath.*

X. WIND ENERGY

FOR CENTURIES, windmills were used to harness wind power for the grinding of grain. Although the technology has improved in recent years, the basics of wind power remain unchanged. Modern wind turbines still utilize the same basic components found in windmills: vertical blades, a horizontal rotor, and a machine to be turned (in this case, an electric generator).

Modern turbine blades have an airfoil shape (curved on the top, flat on the bottom) similar to that used for airplane wings, and they function according to the same principle. Both aircraft wings and turbine blades generate a force that aerodynamic engineers call lift. In aircraft applications, lift causes the wing to rise up in the air. In wind turbines, however, the movement of the blade is constrained by the horizontal rotor to which it is attached. Therefore, instead of rising, it spins the rotor, powering the generator. The faster the rotor spins, the more power is produced.

A line of wind turbines at Tehachapi Pass, California.

The most critical factor is wind speed. Because power generation is proportional to the cube of the wind speed, even slight variations in wind speed can have a dramatic effect. (Doubling the wind speed, for example, increases the power output eightfold.) For this reason, developers of wind farms locate their projects only where long-term meteorological data have shown the wind to be strong and reliable.

The biggest economic problem with wind turbines is their low efficiency. Even in the windiest places, the wind never blows consistently strong. Therefore, for much of the day, expensive wind turbines turn slowly and produce little electricity. On average, the typical wind turbine produces only about 30 percent of its rated capacity. (In comparison, conventional energy plants operate at 80 to 95 percent of capacity.) To ameliorate this problem, newer wind turbines are equipped with longer blades that capture more wind energy, dramatically improving turbine efficiency and also extending turbine life because of reduced wear and tear on its machinery.

With these advances, wind power has become increasingly competitive, even before government tax subsidies are factored in. Like solar, it has grown steadily in recent years, averaging about 25 percent per year. To date, most wind projects have been located on land, but the new frontier seems to lie offshore, where wind conditions are generally more favorable and larger facilities can be built with less impact on local communities.

The critical issue in wind power is turbine design. Because power varies with the cube of the wind speed, turbine blades need to capture wind as efficiently as possible.

X. THE FOUR FOUNDATIONS OF MINDFULNESS

TEXTS IN THE non-Mahāyāna Laṅkan canon record meditative practices prescribed by the Buddha as antidotes to the Three Poisons of desire, hatred, and ignorance of the true nature of reality. These practices, known as the Four Foundations of Mindfulness, encourage mindfulness with regard to particular aspects of reality. By analyzing these aspects of reality in a meditative state, a practitioner can overcome ignorance and realize the ultimate truth of selflessness.

The first of these meditations is directed at desire, especially at desire that manifests itself as an attachment to possessions or as an attachment to one's sense of self. Using this meditation, a practitioner becomes mindful of the composition of the human body, its many flaws, and its inevitable disintegration following death. Awareness of these realities helps one overcome the fantasy that a permanent self exists—which is at the root of all desire.

The second meditation targets feelings of hatred by helping practitioners become mindful of their feelings. Although feelings of hatred appear to arise spontaneously in response to external stimuli, they are actually, according to Buddhist thought, more usefully seen as a part of one's internal mental makeup. Analyzing the causes that give rise to these feelings allows the practitioner to reflect on other possible emotional responses. Because Buddhists define the mind simply as the capacity for knowing (rather than an object in itself), nothing can limit its possible responses to stimuli. Therefore, by cultivating loving and compassionate responses to negative stimuli, hatred can be overcome.

The third meditation focuses on becoming mindful of one's mind. Intended as antidote to ignorance, it makes use of the single most common meditative technique: contemplating one's own breath.

Buddhists believe that through proper application of these three "antidote" meditations, one can achieve the state of calm abiding necessary for the fourth meditation, when the practitioner searches for his supposed "self." He looks everywhere in his body and in his mind until he realizes, finally, that no self can be found because none exists.

When performed correctly (so that the end result is a realization of selflessness), the Four Foundations of Mindfulness bring the practitioner to a state of *nirvāṇa*—that is, liberation from death and rebirth and also relief from suffering. An individual who attains this state through the Four Foundations of Mindfulness is known as an *arhat*, meaning "one worthy of veneration."

The Four Foundations of Mindfulness *are non-Mahāyāna meditative practices that counteract the Three Poisons and bring the practitioner to a state of* nirvāṇa.

XI. THE POET

IN 1844, six months after the demise of the *Dial*, Emerson published a second collection of essays, known as the *Second Series*, which included "The Poet." This lead essay described poets as heroic artists capable of regenerating society because their intuitive vision allows them to speak new words about original experiences.

The study in Emerson's Concord home.

Emerson's description of the ideal poet, of course, sounded much like his descriptions of the ideal intellectual (in "The American Scholar") and the ideal minister (in the Divinity School address).

Emerson's goal was to foster ingenuity in American poetry—which, he lamented, suffered from a familiar ailment: imitation. In mid-nineteenth-century America, poets were typically considered "rhymesters," whose verse followed classical (meaning European) forms but lacked intellectuality. Even more important to Emerson was American poetry's lack of vision. "The breadth of the problem is great," Emerson wrote, "for the poet is representative. He stands among partial men for the complete man, and apprises us not of his wealth, but of the commonwealth."

It would be wrong, however, to believe that Emerson considered the ideal poet a superior person. Emerson was too democratic for that. Rather, he conceived of the ideal poet as the people's ultimate representative, seeing the world anew for them and naming what he saw, no matter the form. "For it is not metres," Emerson wrote, "but a metre-making argument, that makes a poem,—a thought so passionate and alive, that, like the spirit of a plant or an animal, it has an architecture of its own, and adorns nature with a new thing. The thought and the form are equal in the order of time, but in the order of genesis the thought is prior to the form. The poet has a new thought: he has a whole new experience to unfold; he will tell us how it was with him, and all men will be the richer in his fortune. For, the experience of each new age requires a new confession."

Because Emerson believed in American exceptionalism and considered the United States a land of possibility, he yearned for a national literature that challenged the frontiers of poetry just as the pioneers were challenging the frontier of the West. Even so, near the close of "The Poet," Emerson was forced to admit, "I look in vain for the poet whom I describe."

The ideal poet, *in Emerson's view, possesses the vision necessary to see the world anew and then speak what he sees, regardless of form, for the benefit of the entire community.*

XI. CHEMOSYNTHESIS AND PHOTOSYNTHESIS

IT TOOK SEVERAL HUNDRED MILLION YEARS to clean up the large mess left over from planet building, and during this time, Earth endured a heavy bombardment of debris. Some estimates suggest that asteroids as large as the one that wiped out the dinosaurs collided with Earth about once every month. So whenever and wherever life began, it couldn't have spread very far under such dangerous conditions.

There was no life on land yet, and organisms living near the surface of the oceans probably could not have survived all the asteroid impacts. Yet organisms living in out-of-the-way places deep beneath the surface could have survived, producing the energy that they needed through chemosynthesis. This is the process by which energy stored in the chemical bonds of inorganic compounds is liberated for use by living things.

There are places on Earth still where life depends on chemosynthesis. Volcanic vents in the deep ocean floor, for example, teem with bacteria able to withstand the tremendous pressure, seven-hundred-degree Fahrenheit temperatures, and complete darkness. Extracting their energy from hydrogen sulfide gas that bubbles up through the vents, these bacteria not only thrive but also form the base of a complex food web that supports many other species.

Once the debris thinned and the period of heavy Earth bombardment ended, it became possible for organisms to survive near the surface. Some indeed took up residence there and began utilizing a different source of energy: sunlight. Much more abundant and accessible than the energy stored in inorganic compounds, sunlight proved to be an enormous boon to these new organisms, which harvested its energy through a process called photosynthesis.

In its most basic form, photosynthesis proceeds this way: Sunlight strikes a green pigment in the organism (chlorophyll), exciting some of its electrons—that is, transferring enough energy to the electrons so that they can escape the gravitational pull of the nucleus they have been orbiting and become free. Following a series of chemical pathways, these electrons eventually find a home in the energy-rich bonds of the sugar glucose. Because glucose is a highly stable molecule, it can store this excess energy until the organism needs it. Meanwhile, the organism harvests new electrons (to replace those stored in the glucose) from water molecules, which are split to form hydrogen ions and oxygen gas.

The earliest life *obtained the energy it needed through chemosynthesis. Later organisms, living closer to the surface of the oceans, began using photosynthesis instead.*

XI. THE SANSCULOTTES

THE ONLY THING about the French Revolution more remarkable than its breathless pace was the degree of power it accorded "the people." The Constitution of 1793, for example, gave French citizens the power to overthrow the government if it violated their rights. Taking these words to heart, Parisians began protesting in the streets and sometimes even in the National Convention chamber, demanding political change and routinely getting it. Never before had ordinary people exercised so much influence over those who governed them.

Who were the members of these often menacing crowds? In Paris, many were artisans who worked in shops rather than in factories and whose trades prior to 1789 had been tightly controlled by monopolistic guilds. They were usually educated and, before the Revolution, often had a little money as well. Along with clerks, journalists, and low-level civil servants, they became civic leaders and joined forces with the

A sansculotte in revolutionary garb ca. 1794.

poorest Parisians, including day laborers and the unemployed, to push for price controls and other populist policies. Collectively, these people—the artisan leaders and the day-laborer followers—were known as sansculottes, because they often wore the trousers of workingmen rather than the fancier breeches known as *culottes*.

The Terror was their proudest moment. During its yearlong reign, many sansculottes were appointed to positions of power in towns and villages, where their job was to ensure local obedience to the Committee of Public Safety. Others joined revolutionary militias that went sent out into the countryside to impose the government's will on the rebellious peasantry. Even their appearance became fashionable, prompting numerous Frenchmen to give up their powdered wigs and waistcoats as remnants of a bygone aristocratic age. Women's dresses and hairstyles also became much less elaborate, and Parisians began addressing one another using the informal pronoun *tu* rather than the more formal *vous*, which was a term reserved for one's superiors.

These and other changes promoting sansculotte egalitarianism resulted from a determined propaganda campaign designed to support the Revolution in its new and more radical course. The names of streets were changed. The kings, queens, and knaves were replaced in decks of playing cards with figures symbolizing liberty, equality, and fraternity. A new revolutionary calendar was introduced with renamed months and five new holidays celebrating civic values. With the death of Robespierre, of course, the influence of the sansculottes quickly waned, but the new calendar did remain in effect well into Napoleon's reign.

The influence of the sansculottes, *although short-lived, inspired an extreme egalitarianism that affected many different aspects of French society.*

XI. BIOMASS ENERGY

BIOMASS, the world's oldest conversion technology, releases the energy stored in biological matter such as plant material and animal waste. The original source of this energy is the solar radiation that plants capture during the process of photosynthesis. Using carbon dioxide, water, and the energy of the sun, plant cells produce energy-rich carbohydrates, releasing oxygen as a by-product. Burning these carbohydrates (which, in chemical terms, means applying oxygen) reverses the process and releases the energy.

Virtually anything that can be burned can be used as a biomass fuel: wood chips, sawdust, animal dung, and even industrial products made from plant and animal material such as rubber tires and leather goods. Because it's so versatile, biomass is in use, in one form or another, everywhere in the world and accounts for fifteen times the energy produced by solar and wind technologies combined. Sometimes, as in the case of a woodstove, its application is small, and heat energy is the only end product. In larger applications, however, the heat generated is typically used to generate electricity.

Utility-scale biomass facilities are very similar to conventional electricity plants, except that they burn nonfossil fuels to generate heat for conversion into electricity. Wood and paper products are among the most common biomass fuels, and many wood and paper product manufacturers have constructed biomass plants on site to convert their waste into useful electricity. Solid waste (that is, garbage) is another common biomass fuel. The facilities that burn garbage are called waste-to-energy plants. Although they are more expensive to run than coal-fired plants (because garbage is a much less efficient fuel), waste-to-energy plants provide the additional benefit of disposing of the waste, which would otherwise clog landfills.

A second garbage-related biomass technology focuses on the methane gas produced by decomposing organic matter such as yard waste and food scraps. Often situated next to large landfills, these facilities capture the methane being generated within the landfill and burn it in conventional generators to produce electricity. Large dairy and pig farms, which produce huge amounts of manure, also take advantage of these methane-powered plants.

Because so many enterprises, large and small, produce burnable waste, the applicability of biomass is widespread. Easily scalable and highly adaptive, it can be used to reduce the pressure on landfills while producing energy that would otherwise be derived from fossil fuels. Although no cleaner to burn than fossil fuels, biomass fuels are, for the most part, renewable.

Highly adaptive *biomass facilities use the same basic equipment as conventional power plants, except that they burn biological waste instead of fossil fuels.*

XI. BODHISATTVAS

THE PERFECTION OF WISDOM *SŪTRAS*, which form the basis of the Mahāyāna tradition, describe the Buddha's path to enlightenment. These and other *sūtras* record incidents from the Buddha's past in which he cultivated specific virtues— including generosity, patience, ethics, effort, concentration, and wisdom. Once the Buddha achieved perfection in all of these virtues, he became enlightened, and his suffering ceased. Until then, however, for many cycles of death and rebirth, the Buddha was a *bodhisattva*—that is, a being whose goal is enlightenment (*bodhi*).

In constrast with Nāgārjuna, who commented only on the philosophical doctrines implicit in the Perfection of Wisdom *sūtras*, the fourth-century CE monk Asaṅga offered commentaries on the Buddha's path to enlightment, which these *sūtras* explicitly described. After meditating for twelve years in a cave without result, Asaṅga emerged one day to find a wounded dog. Attempting to help the dog, he generated compassion, at which point the *bodhisattva* Maitreya appeared

A tenth-century Chinese painting of a *bodhisattva*.

before him. Maitreya took Asaṅga back to the plane of existence where Maitreya abided (waiting to be reborn as the fifth Buddha of this world-system) and gave Asaṅga a number of teachings. After returning to earth, Asaṅga wrote down these teachings, along with his own commentaries on them. Together, these texts explained the details of the path to enlightenment for *bodhisattvas*.

Unlike the followers of non-Mahāyāna traditions, who pursue the goal of becoming an *arhat*, Mahāyāna adherents take the greater state of Buddhahood as their ultimate goal. The difference between the two goals has to do with motivation. For all Buddhists, the motivation for practice is the wish to be free from suffering. Within the Mahāyāna tradition, however, there is an additional dimension: compassion, or the wish for others also to be free from suffering.

All beings experience suffering and seek liberation, but a *bodhisattva* feels such great compassion for others that putting an end to their suffering becomes his foremost concern, even above ending his own suffering. At all times, the mind of the *bodhisattva* is focused on achieving enlightenment for the sake of helping others. When this selfless altruism is combined with meditations on the impermanent nature of matter and consciousnesss, the results are, according to the Mahāyāna tradition, enlightenment and Buddhahood.

Within the *Mahāyāna tradition,* bodhisattvas *aspire to achieve enlightenment for the sake of alleviating the suffering of others.*

XII. THE EMERSONIAN POET: WALT WHITMAN

IT HAS OFTEN BEEN SUGGESTED that, if "The Poet" was Emerson's wish, then Walt Whitman (1819–92) was that wish's fulfillment. In his essay on the ideal poet, Emerson had written, "Our logrolling, our stumps and their politics, our fisheries, our Negroes, and Indians,…the northern trade, the southern planting, the western clearing, Oregon and Texas, are yet unsung. Yet America is a poem in our eyes; its ample geography dazzles the imagination, and it will not wait long for metres."

Eleven years later, Whitman produced those meters in *Leaves of Grass*. Echoing Emerson's words, Whitman wrote in the expansive preface to that collection, "The United States themselves are essentially the greatest poem. In the history of the earth hitherto the largest and most stirring appear tame and orderly to their ampler largeness and stir."

Before self-publishing *Leaves of Grass* in 1855, the thirty-six-year-old Whitman had worked as a journeyman printer and journalist in and around Brooklyn, New York. As editor of the daily *Aurora* (1842–44) and the *Brooklyn Daily Eagle* (1846–48), he had read a great deal of contemporary literature, ostensibly for the purpose of writing reviews. Recalling the effect that Emerson's work had on his own budding poetic aspirations, Whitman later said, "My ideas were simmering and simmering, and Emerson brought them to a boil."

Inspired directly by "The Poet," Whitman's sprawling free verse was unlike anything seen before in America or Europe. Disregarding conventional form, it saw the world anew and communicated that sight to the wider community. At once personal and yet linked to the community by the act of expression, Whitman's "I" claimed nothing for itself but channeled the divine energy of nature into open sentences and flowing words that were intended to elevate the common man to the level of the divine. In "Song of Myself," for example, Whitman effused, "I celebrate myself, / And what I assume you shall assume, / For every atom belonging to me as good belongs to you."

Something of a self-promoter, Whitman sent a copy of *Leaves of Grass* to Emerson in Concord, and the great man, amazed by what he read, responded immediately. "I am not blind to the worth of the wonderful gift of 'Leaves of Grass,'" Emerson wrote, "I find it the most extraordinary piece of wit and wisdom that America has yet contributed."

Walt Whitman fulfilled *the wish expressed by Emerson in "The Poet" for the emergence of an American bard who would sing of the nation's transcendent self.*

Walt Whitman circa 1854.

XII. THE OXYGEN CATASTROPHE

BEFORE THE EVOLUTION of photosynthetic life about 3.5 billion years ago, there was no gaseous oxygen on Earth. Instead, the atmosphere, formed by the vaporization of volatile compounds during Earth's molten stage, was full of carbon dioxide, methane, nitrogen, and steam—a combination of gases that gave the early atmosphere a reddish tint.

The first photosynthetic life was a form of blue-green algae called cyanobacteria. Because these bacteria thrived in the oceans, they began to produce, as a by-product of their photosynthesis, a lot of oxygen gas. Before this oxygen could begin to accumulate in the atmosphere, however, it first had to escape the oceans, which took about 1.1 billion years.

The reason this took so long was that the oceans were rich in iron, ejected from the mantle as the result of undersea volcanic activity. Although the oxygen gas created by the cyanobacteria bubbled upward, it rarely reached the surface because, along the way, it reacted with dissolved iron in the seawater to produce iron oxide. This relatively heavy compound, in turn, precipitated out of the seawater and fell to the ocean floor, where it was compressed by sedimentation into rich iron ore. (Chemically, the process by which oxygen reacts with other elements is called oxidation; more commonly, however, it's known simply as rust.)

Finally, about 2.4 billion years ago, the last of the dissolved iron was oxidized, and the oxygen gas being produced by the cyanobacteria began to escape into the atmosphere in very large quantities. This was the Oxygen Catastrophe, and it transformed the conditions under which future life evolved.

As oxygen accumulated in the atmosphere, it took different forms. The most common form, molecular oxygen, consists of two oxygen atoms bonded together to create a single molecule (O_2). Sometimes, however, under conditions of intense ultraviolet radiation, three oxygen atoms can bind together to form an even larger molecule (O_3). This alternative form, ozone, is found almost exclusively in the stratosphere, where the Sun's ultraviolet radiation splits molecular oxygen into two single oxygen atoms that collide with molecular oxygen to form ozone.

One of ozone's most interesting chemical properties is its ability to absorb ultraviolet radiation. Without protection from the Sun's ultraviolet rays, most life on Earth wouldn't be able to survive. Therefore, it wasn't until the formation of the ozone layer in Earth's atmosphere that more complicated forms of life, especially land-based life, could evolve.

The first photosynthetic life, *cyanobacteria, produced large quantities of oxygen that changed the composition of the atmosphere.*

XII. WOMEN AND THE REVOLUTION

Parisian fishwives join the Revolution in a 1794 etching.

DURING THE ANCIEN RÉGIME, women in France had no legal standing. They were considered the property of their families and had no ability to seek relief, in court or otherwise, from the dictates of their fathers and husbands. Some high-ranking women, especially the mistresses of kings, were able to exercise considerable political power, but they did so (like the king) through private patronage rather than public authority. Widows alone had a modicum of status: As heads of households, they could run businesses and participate in local governmental meetings.

The Revolution transformed the role of women in French society but in very mixed ways. Although women initially gained legal rights on a par with those accorded men, these rights were gradually repealed until women finally found themselves in worse shape than ever before. During the ancien régime, a wife or a mistress who was well connected could exercise a great deal of influence. After the Revolution, however, patronage as a means to power was abolished, and the public institutions that replaced it were not nearly as receptive to women.

Among the legal privileges that French women gained, if only temporarily, were the right to divorce, the right to own property, and the right to petition courts on their own behalf. Taking advantage of these and other aspects of the new egalitarianism, many women became politically active. Marching on Versailles in October 1789, they played a key role in forcing the king to move his household to Paris; they also formed political clubs, published pamphlets, and petitioned the legislature. The most radical joined the Society of Revolutionary Republican Women, whose members dressed like—and armed themselves like—sansculottes.

This sort of open political participation was viewed rather nervously, however, and when women became noticeably more aggressive in their demands during 1792 and 1793, a backlash took place. Men, especially male legislators, wanted women to remain in the domestic sphere, so they began using the tools of state to end female participation in public life. In 1793, the Convention outlawed all women's political clubs, and not long afterward the Committee of Public Safety began sending the most prominent female activists to the guillotine. Under Napoleon, women were banned from attending legislative debates, and they finally lost the rights that the fickle Revolution had given them: to plead in court, to file for divorce, and to own property without their husband's consent.

The French Revolution *gave women many important new rights, only to repeal them later and return women to their pre-1789 status.*

XII. **BIOFUELS**

BIOFUELS ARE fuels made from biological material. Therefore, they are technically a subset of biomass technology, but they aren't treated that way, because they represent an entirely different approach to generating energy. Burning biological material directly, it turns out, is one of the least efficient ways to release its stored energy. Too much is wasted. A more efficient approach is to "gasify" the material first, which happens naturally in methane-producing landfills, or to liquefy it in biofuel plants.

Biofuel plants turn "energy crops" such as corn and sugarcane into liquid fuels such as ethanol and biodiesel. Biofuel projects are not scalable, however. Most are huge, capital-intensive ventures that require the construction of large, sophisticated refineries. In addition, biofuel production affects agricultural demand. Because energy crops aren't waste materials but are grown specifically for conversion into biofuels, they compete for agricultural resources and thus drive up the cost of food crops.

Ethanol, the most widely available biofuel, is manufactured in much the same way as beer: The sugars and starches found in corn, sugarcane, or even yard clippings are fermented and then distilled. The world's leading ethanol producers are currently the United States and Brazil.

4 CYL. MODEL T
FORD, 1908

Henry Ford's 1908 Model T automobile ran on ethanol as well as gasoline.

Industrially produced ethanol is nothing new. It became available during the 1840s, when it was used primarily as a lighting fuel. Later it was picked up by the early automobile manufacturers. Henry Ford, for example, designed his 1908 Model T to run either on gasoline or on ethanol. A century later, virtually all of the gasoline sold in the United States has a 10 percent ethanol content. Brazil's biofuel program is even more extensive. About 85 percent of Brazilian cars have "flex-fuel" engines—which means that, like the Model T, they can run either on gasoline or on ethanol.

Biodiesel is a particularly interesting form of biofuel because it isn't made from dedicated crops. Instead, it recycles used cooking oils and restaurant grease to produce a less-refined fuel that can be used in unmodified diesel engines, making it very viable commercially. The Department of Energy wants biofuels to replace 30 percent of all US gasoline and diesel use by 2025. It remains unclear, however, what effect this will have on carbon emissions, because the inputs and outputs are so difficult to measure. There is also evidence indicating that current biofuel production consumes more total energy than it creates.

Converting crops into biofuels is an efficient way to release the energy stored inside them, but the process is expensive and requires a huge upfront investment.

XII. BUDDHIST EPISTEMOLOGY

AS BUDDHIST CENTERS of learning grew in size and stature during the first millennium CE, they began participating in intercollegiate debates, which were an important Indian tradition. The stakes were high—winners earned not only patronage but also control of the losing institution—so Buddhist scholars had to prepare themselves well. A critical tool they gained was the epistemology (theory of knowledge) developed by Dignāga during the fifth century and refined by Dharmakīrti a century later. (Both were Mahāyāna monks in the lineage of Asaṅga, which means that they received teachings through a master–disciple chain leading back to Asaṅga himself.)

While their Hindu opponents asserted an epistemology based on the Vedas, Dignāga and Dharmakīrti rejected the idea that scripture could serve as a valid basis for knowledge. In their view, no external source, not even the Buddha himself, was ultimately authoritative. The only way to obtain true knowledge was through unmistaken personal experience supplemented by logical reasoning.

According to the Hindus, the identities that we give to things (calling an object a "table" or a "chariot") are real. According to Dignāga and Dharmakīrti, however, these identities are yet another form of grasping at self-identity (the opposite of selflessness). "Table," in other words, is a learned concept, not a transcendent reality.

Although conceptual categories such as "table" and "chariot" may seem useful in everyday life, they are, according to Dignāga and Dharmakīrti, fundamentally misleading. Only sense perception is free from the taint of conceptual categories, which the mind imposes to make sensory experience seem more understandable.

Touching a hot iron, for example, can be described as two successive moments of consciousness: a moment of tactile sense consciousness (finger touching iron) followed by a moment of a conceptual consciousness (the mind imputing the identity *hot* to the sensory experience). In this way, the mind superimposes an identity onto the experience in order to label it and give it a greater sense of realness than it actually possesses.

Similarly, a person looking at a blue wall would first perceive its shape and color and then impute to it the identity *blue wall*. This distinction (between actual experience and artificial identity) is relatively easy to grasp, but it begs the question *Where does the artificiality break down and reality begin?* Is the blueness of the wall's paint real or merely a conceptual imputation? Are the molecules of paint real or an imputation? The answer to this question is found in Asaṅga's mind-only school of philosophy.

The epistemology *developed by Dignāga and Dharmakīrti privileged sense perception over other forms of knowledge because it was the only one free from conceptual taint.*

XIII. THE EMERSONIAN POET: EMILY DICKINSON

OUTWARDLY, Emily Dickinson (1830–86) lived a life of quiet isolation. She never married and rarely traveled, confining herself entirely after the late 1860s to the boundaries of her family's property in Amherst, Massachusetts. Inwardly,

A daguerreotype of Emily Dickinson taken ca. 1847.

however, she was passionately alive, writing 1,775 poems in an epigrammatic style—similar to Emerson's—that used vivid imagery and unusual syntax to shock readers into discovery.

Dickinson began writing verse about 1850, apparently inspired by her reading of Emerson's poems. In contrast with Whitman's seemingly uninhibited free verse, Dickinson typically composed her poems in the form of English hymns—that is, in quatrains (four-line stanzas) composed of six-syllable lines with an alternating *abab* rhyme scheme. Yet Dickinson never felt bound to this form, any more than she felt bound to Congregationalist doctrine, and she often toyed with it, adding twists and complexity to suit the pattern of her thought.

Always in Dickinson's best poems, there exists a beneficial tension between the conventionality of her form and the nonconformity of her self-reliant ideas. The first stanza of her poem 324, for example, is reminiscent of Emerson's *Nature*: "Some keep the Sabbath going to Church— / I keep it, staying at Home— / With a Bobolink for a Chorister— / And an Orchard, for a Dome." Dickinson's "I" worships not in the social institution of the church, but in nature, where birds serve as the choir and an orchard as the church.

In the poem's second stanza, Dickinson's language becomes even more metaphoric: "Some keep the Sabbath in Surplice— / I just wear my Wings— / And instead of tolling the Bell, for Church, / Our little Sexton—sings." Finally, in the third and last stanza, the speaker, sufficiently suffused with nature, experiences God directly: "God preaches, a noted Clergyman— / And the sermon is never long, / So instead of getting to Heaven, at last— / I'm going, all along."

Publishing only seven poems during her lifetime, Dickinson never provided the heroic leadership that Emerson sought in his ideal poet. But she certainly understood what Emerson meant by the need for a personal relationship with nature. Her "I" has no use for organized religion or the Calvinist salvation that comes "at last" because it understands that a person can become conversant with the divine outside of church and thus experience heaven "all along."

Emily Dickinson was *another important American poet of the mid-nineteenth century whose work proceeded from a fundamentally transcendentalist viewpoint.*

XIII. ICE AGES

ICE AGE IS ONE OF THE MOST CONFUSING terms used in the study of Earth history. In its most technical sense, it refers to any period when ice accumulates on the planet's surface. According this definition, we are currently living in an ice age that began about forty million years ago. Less scientifically, however, the term is often used to describe periods of recent Earth history marked by a substantial expansion of the polar ice caps and mountain glaciers. The most recent of these periods, called glacials, ended about ten thousand years ago, when ice that had overspread much of the North American and Eurasian continents finally receded. The contrast between these especially chilly intervals and the world we experience today may seem dramatic, but on a geological time scale such fluctuations are relatively minor and not properly termed ice ages.

The scientific definition of *ice age* is important because glaciers and polar ice are not the permanent features one might think them to be. In fact, there have been at least five periods in Earth's past, each 100 to 200 million years long, when the planet was entirely ice-free. The first ice age for which substantial physical evidence exists began about 2.7 billion years ago. During a subsequent ice age that began about 850 million years ago, glacial ice penetrated Earth's tropical regions and nearly reached the equator.

It isn't known for certain why ice ages begin and end, but many theories have been proposed. One focuses on the changing location of the continental plates over time. Because Earth's oceans are largely responsible for the movement of heat around the planet, especially its transfer from the equator to the poles, patterns of ocean flow strongly affect climate. When warm water from the equator flows without obstruction to the poles, ice cannot form there. However, when a continental plate sits on top of a pole (as is currently the case with Antarctica), or when continental plates block the flow of warm water to a polar ocean (as is currently the case with the Arctic Ocean), the polar regions get colder, and the accumulation of ice becomes possible. Other important contributing factors are thought to be atmospheric composition (especially the concentration of "greenhouse" gases), variations in Earth's orbit around the Sun, and variations in the Sun's energy output.

Ice age is a loosely used term. *According to its proper scientific definition, we are currently living in an ice age that began about forty million years ago.*

XIII. SLAVERY AND THE REVOLUTION

ONE OF THE GREAT PARADOXES of the French Revolution (as of the American) was its treatment of slaves. While the rights and freedoms of so many citizens were greatly expanded, those of the slaves were decidedly not.

Although no slaves were held in France itself, the French empire included several colonies with highly prosperous slave economies. The Caribbean colony of Saint Domingue (now Haiti), for instance, thrived on a lucrative sugar industry built on the backs of half a million imported African slaves. These laborers created the value that allowed a handful of white planters to live at the pinnacle of wealth. Also residing on the island were some free people of color, who owned slaves and were allowed to intermarry with whites but couldn't hold public office and were barred from a few key professions.

During the early years of the Revolution, slavery was hardly an issue. Most French citizens had never seen a slave, and they believed that the property rights of slaveholders trumped whatever rights an individual slave might have. Fearful that granting rights even to free people of color might lead to dangerous unrest and destruction of property, the National Constituent Assembly sided with the white colonial lobby and left conditions in the colonies just as they were.

As the French revolutionaries learned, however, democratic ideals can be difficult to restrain. Already, the events of 1789 had raised expectations in Saint Domingue's tinderbox society, and in May 1791 the free colored community took up arms against the colonial administration. Although this insurgency was quickly suppressed, the much larger slave revolt that followed in August proved more difficult to handle. Alarmed by the violence, the Legislative Assembly decided in April 1792 to take the half step of granting full rights of citizenship to free people of color, but it continued to balk at emancipating the slaves.

Once Britain and Spain joined the war against France in 1793, however, the French attitude changed. Because both the British and the Spanish coveted Saint Domingue, they began courting Toussaint L'Ouverture, the former slave who had

led the August 1791 uprising. With this pressure (and because Toussaint was gaining control of the colony, thus achieving a de facto liberation of the slaves), the National Convention voted in February 1794 to accept the fait accompli, formally abolishing slavery in the colonies. Although reluctant, the Convention's emancipation nevertheless reflected the power exerted by democratic ideals in even the most dire circumstances.

Toussaint meets
with the British.

One can see *in the fitful history of abolitionism during the Revolution what happens when idealism meets the forces of racism and avarice.*

XIII. GEOTHERMAL ENERGY

THE WEIGHT OF THE PLANET, pressing down on the earth's core, creates an immense amount of heat. This heat is so intense that, after traveling all the way through the mantle and most of the crust, it still boils ground water and even melts rock. The point of geothermal technology is to tap this energy by making use of the hot water and steam (hydrothermal fluids) generated by the heat at or close to the earth's surface.

The Nesjavellir geothermal power plant near Pingvellir, Iceland.

In geothermally active areas, where hydrothermal fluids develop especially close to the surface, the most common application is simply to pump the steam or hot water into a building and use it for the purpose of heating that building. Nearly every structure in volcanic Iceland, for example, is heated this way. Geothermal generating plants, however, operate differently, depending on the kind of hydrothermal fluid being used.

There are three types of geothermal generating plants. Dry steam plants pump steam containing very little condensed water directly from an underground geothermal reservoir into an aboveground generator, which spins to produce electricity. Flash plants make use of a different type of hydrothermal fluid, superheated water, which must be at least 360°F to be effective. (In the language of engineering, *superheated* means water that has been heated above its boiling point but remains in a liquid state because of the high pressures underground.) As with other hydrothermal fluids, the superheated water is pumped to the surface, where—because of the lower pressure—it instantly "flashes" into steam. This steam is then used to spins a generator, just as it in a dry steam plant.

When the temperature of the superheated water in the geothermal reservoir is less than optimal for flash plant operation, a binary, or two-stage, process is used. Binary plants pump the hydrothermal fluid through a heat exchanger, which transfers some of the energy from the water to a secondary liquid with a much lower boiling point. This secondary liquid then flashes (vaporizes), driving the generator.

Currently, flash plants are the most common geothermal installation, but that will certainly change as more geothermal plants are built. With most of the best sites already taken, new plants will have to make use of reservoirs containing superheated water below 360°F, which means they will have to be built as binaries.

Where geothermal activity *is near the surface, hot water and steam are used for heating. Elsewhere, geothermal plants use these hydrothermal fluids to produce electricity.*

XIII. MIND-ONLY PHILOSOPHY

WHILE TEACHING Asaṅga about the various stages along a *bodhisattva*'s path to enlightenment, Maitreya also passed on to the monk a new way of interpreting the Perfection of Wisdom *sūtras* that accorded with other Mahāyāna texts. This new way emphasized what is experienced during meditation.

Maitreya taught Asaṅga that every being possesses in embryonic form the enlightened qualities of a Buddha. Therefore, another way to think about the process of achieving enlightenment is to see it as the removal of obscurations from the mind that block its natural state—specifically the mind's capacity for compassion, generosity, and the other "perfections."

From Maitreya's teaching, Asaṅga developed what became known as the mind-only school of Mahāyāna philosophy. Its central doctrine was that only consciousness is real. In other words, nothing exists outside the mind. External objects are not real, Asaṅga reasoned, because they have no existence separate from the consciousness perceiving them. Instead, both the moment of perception and the object being perceived arise inseparably from the same "karmic seed," or cause.

Following this reasoning, the mind-only school defines ignorance of the true nature of reality as habitual belief in the existence of an independent external world—that is, the belief that objects exist independently of the consciousnesses perceiving them. The common belief that external objects have such an independent existence is a misconception removable through meditative practice (*yoga*). Such meditation helps the practitioner reach the calm, focused state necessary to realize that the external world is a dreamlike illusion.

In this illustrated text, a *bodhisattva*, probably Maitreya, sits with his hands held in the traditional teaching posture.

When the Buddha speaks in the Perfection of Wisdom *sūtras* about selflessness extending beyond people to objects, he means that objects lack an independent state of existence separate from the mind perceiving them—or at least that was the interpretation that Asaṅga gave to these passages. In Asaṅga's view, this emptiness of self-identity—that is, objects lacking existence external to the mind—is the ultimate truth of Mahāyāna Buddhism, and its realization constitutes enlightenment in the mind-only school.

One of two major *Mahāyāna philosophies, the mind-only school denies the existence of an independent external world and holds that only consciousness is real.*

XIV. THE DISCIPLE: HENRY DAVID THOREAU

ALTHOUGH HENRY DAVID THOREAU (1817–62) was graduated from Harvard College with the Class of 1837, he apparently left Cambridge soon after commencement, because he wasn't in attendance the next day when Emerson delivered his "American Scholar" address. Thoreau's absence seems ironic now because of all the disciples of Emerson, Thoreau probably came closest to meeting the "American Scholar" ideal.

Henry David Thoreau in 1856.

Returning to his hometown of Concord, Thoreau worked for several years as a grammar school teacher and also in his father's pencil-making business. Over that time, he became friendly with his neighbor Emerson, who in April 1841 invited Thoreau to join his household. During the next two years, Thoreau worked as a handyman for the Emersons but was treated more like a family member than a servant. With Emerson's encouragement, he began writing for the *Dial* and even helped Emerson with the editing.

In early 1845, Emerson offered Thoreau the use of a woodlot he owned on nearby Walden Pond. In late March, Thoreau began building a small cabin there, which he occupied for the next two years. "I wanted to live deep and suck out all the marrow of life," he later wrote. Because Walden Pond was located so close to Concord, Thoreau couldn't have expected a wilderness experience, but that wasn't what he was seeking. Instead, he was looking for "wildness," a sense of nature that would help him better understand society. He wanted to find a middle ground between nature and society where the two could coexist in balance. Although Thoreau still performed odd jobs and took the occasional hot meal in town, he grew his own vegetables and attempted quite consciously to escape the materialism that Emerson had so decried in *Nature*.

In July 1846, Thoreau spent a night in the Concord jail after being arrested for refusing to pay some delinquent taxes. His refusal was based on his objection to the Mexican War, which he believed was being fought to extend slavery westward. Although Thoreau was released the next day after his aunt (over his objections) paid the taxes for him, the experience proved memorable and served as the basis for his 1849 essay "On Civil Disobedience," in which Thoreau asserted the moral right of an individual to protest government actions that he deems unjust. In proper transcendentalist fashion, Thoreau grounded this right in the individual's ability to intuit morality for himself, whatever the government (or the church) might say.

Henry David Thoreau, *Emerson's neighbor and most important protégé, echoed his mentor's individualism, disdain for conformity, and aversion to materialist pursuits.*

XIV. THE CAMBRIAN EXPLOSION

ANIMALS ARE MULTICELLULAR HETEROTROPHS, which means that they have multiple cells and lack the ability to make their own food. Therefore, in order to ingest the energy they need to survive, they eat other organisms. Possible foodstuffs include other animals as well as plants, which make their own food (glucose) through photosynthesis.

During photosynthesis, the energy present in sunlight is used to transform carbon dioxide and water into energy-rich glucose and oxygen. When animals eat, this process is reversed. Animals breathe in oxygen, which reacts with (or burns) glucose to retrieve the energy stored in its chemical bonds. (The waste products are carbon dioxide and water.) Therefore, oxygen had to be present in Earth's atmosphere before animal life could evolve.

This evolution finally took place about 700 million years ago, leading up to a period known as the Cambrian Explosion (which began about 540 million years ago). For the prior 3 billion or so years, the only life on Earth was unicellular organisms. With the arrival of multicellular organisms, however, the evolutionary possibilities expanded exponentially.

The pioneer of this field of research, paleontologist Charles D. Walcott, was hiking in British Columbia one day in 1909 when he came upon some unusual fossils that would change the way he (and the rest of the world) thought about

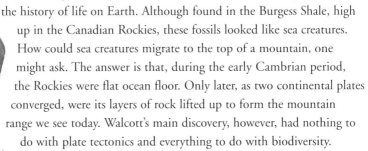

the history of life on Earth. Although found in the Burgess Shale, high up in the Canadian Rockies, these fossils looked like sea creatures. How could sea creatures migrate to the top of a mountain, one might ask. The answer is that, during the early Cambrian period, the Rockies were flat ocean floor. Only later, as two continental plates converged, were its layers of rock lifted up to form the mountain range we see today. Walcott's main discovery, however, had nothing to do with plate tectonics and everything to do with biodiversity.

A fossil of a trilobite.

What Walcott realized was that the fossils he continued to collect in the Burgess Shale dated back to a time early in the Cambrian period when animal life went from simple to exotic in the span of just 30 to 50 million years. Along with the more common trilobites and spiny worms, he found a shocking number of freakish evolutionary oddities, such as one bizarre creature with five eyes and a mouth located on the end of a long hoselike projection. The word *explosion* was later chosen to describe this period because the diversification occurred so suddenly, so rapidly, and so extensively.

Only unicellular life *existed until about seven hundred million years ago. At that point, the first animals appeared, triggering an explosion of evolutionary diversity.*

XIV. RELIGION AND THE REVOLUTION

OF ALL THE INSTITUTIONS of the ancien régime, probably none affected the average man or woman more than the Roman Catholic Church. Most French citizens were Catholics, and the parish church was the center of French communal life. It registered births and marriages; recorded deaths; and, until the Revolution, ran all the primary and secondary schools. The church was also the largest landowner in France, and it enjoyed legal privileges commensurate with its wealth.

When the Revolution replaced the divine right of kings with popular sovereignty, it shifted the primary allegiance of each French citizen from the king to the nation. While the king had openly favored Catholicism and persecuted those with different beliefs, the Declaration of the Rights of Man reversed this policy and embraced freedom of religion for all. The church, of course, opposed this kind of political reform, and it made its position clear: French Catholics would have to choose between their country and their faith. This was perhaps the most difficult choice that any French citizen had to make during the Revolution.

Between 1789 and 1792, the church lost a good deal of its standing as successive revolutionary governments stripped it of privileges and enacted reforms that many pro-Revolution Catholics found offensive. Church land was confiscated, marriage became a civil function, and the state took control of all public education. In 1790, the government insisted that priests swear an oath of loyalty, pledging to serve the state above the pope. (About half the clergy refused.) Just as horrifying to the laity was the introduction of popular elections for parish priest in which all citizens, even non-Catholics, were allowed to vote. It was this issue, along with conscription, that fueled the armed uprisings in western France during the summer of 1793.

During the Terror that followed, those clergy who had refused to take the oath were exiled or imprisoned. Meanwhile, sansculottes pursuing a policy of dechristianization attacked the remaining clergy, pillaged churches, and stripped graveyards of their religious symbols. In Paris, all the religious trappings were removed from Notre Dame so that the cathedral could be transformed into a "temple of reason." About the same time, the Convention approved the new revolutionary calendar, which replaced the old religious holidays with new secular ones. Although the worst violence ended before the close of the Terror, the French government continued to keep the church at arm's length until the Concordat of 1801, which marked Napoleon's reconciliation with Rome.

The choice *between citizenship and faith forced on the people by a succession of governments sharply divided revolutionary France.*

XIV. TIDAL ENERGY

TIDAL ENERGY is hydropower that uses ocean tides to generate electricity. It comes in two basic forms: kinetic and potential. Tides create kinetic energy when they cause seawater to flow; they create potential energy when they cause the sea level to rise.

From a strictly theoretical standpoint, tapping the kinetic energy created by tides is simple. You install an underwater turbine in an area of concentrated seawater flow and let the ocean do the rest. Of course, installing a turbine underwater is an engineering feat that has yet to be mastered. The few demonstration projects that currently exist use devices similar to wind turbines. Seawater, however, is about eight hundred times more dense than air, which means that a single tidal turbine can produce much more power than a single wind turbine. The key, as with wind power, is finding the right location. The sites that work best are narrow channels, such as straits, where constriction of the tidal current makes the seawater flow faster.

Harnessing the potential energy created by tides is a bit more cumbersome and much more expensive. The basic strategy is to build a special kind of dam, called a barrage, across the mouth of a bay or estuary. During incoming tides, water passes into the tidal basin through sluice gates in the barrage's caissons, slowly turning turbines (also built into the caissons). At high tide,the sluice gates close, and the main action begins. As the tide ebbs, the difference in height between the basin level and the sea level (called the head) grows, creating enormous potential energy. When the sluice gates finally open and the seawater pours out, the water's potential energy is transformed into kinetic energy, which the turbines then convert into electricity. For a barrage to be economically viable, the head it creates must be at least ten feet. At the Annapolis plant on Canada's funnel-shaped Bay of Fundy, the head approaches fifty feet.

The Annapolis tidal power plant on the Bay of Fundy.

Although tidal energy is classified as clean and renewable, it does have some environmental impact issues. Barrages, in particular, can harm tidal ecosystems—altering seawater distribution in the intertidal zone, impeding the movement of fish, and contributing to coastal erosion. Tidal turbines, on the other hand, are thought to have much less environmental impact. About a dozen tidal turbine projects have been proposed worldwide, but none has yet been built on a utility scale.

Tidal energy *refers both to the kinetic energy present in seawater flow and to the potential energy developed when sea levels rise.*

XIV. MIDDLE WAY PHILOSOPHY

THE OTHER MAJOR BRANCH of Mahāyāna philosophy, which Nāgārjuna began during the late second century CE and Candrakīrti developed four hundred years later, came to be known as the middle way school because it represented a "middle way" between the extremes of existence and nonexistence. However, this was more a rhetorical victory than a doctrinal distinction, because all of Buddhism advocates a middle way.

Unlike mind-only philosophy, the middle way school accepted the reality of the external world but considered it relative (as in *not absolute*). Instead of one reality (that is, the mind), Nāgārjuna stated that there were two levels of reality. On the level of conventional reality, the various objects that one sees can indeed be said to exist. They appear to function and seem to have an identity. When analyzed logically, however, this identity disappears. To make his case, Nāgārjuna offered a variety of analytical meditations concerning different objects. In each case, he showed that the belief that a word or concept corresponded to an object leads to absurd contradictions.

Following Nāgārjuna's lead, Candrakīrti applied this rigorous logic to the example of a chariot, arguing that no specific object corresponded to the word *chariot*. If one removes the wheels, for example, is a chariot still a chariot? Obviously not, which would imply that its chariotlike nature, or "chariotness," resides in its wheels. But this is also not the case. Perhaps its chariotness resides in all its component parts—the wood, nails, and so forth that make it up—but if this were the case, then a pile of unassembled or broken parts would also be a chariot. If one ultimately concludes that what makes a chariot a chariot is the form and arrangement of the parts, then *chariot* ceases to exist as a real physical thing and becomes merely an idea. This "disappearance" of identity, according to Candrakīrti, is precisely what the Buddha meant by selflessness, and the meditative realization of this truth of "emptiness" constitutes enlightenment within the middle way school.

Unlike the mind-only school, *which considers the external world inseparable from the mind perceiving it, the middle way school considers the external world independently real but not absolute.*

XV. **WALDEN**

AT EMERSON'S SUGGESTION, Henry David Thoreau had been keeping a journal since 1837, and while living on Walden Pond he made numerous entries recording his ideas, experiences, and observations. These entries later became the basis of his masterful *Walden; or, Life in the Woods* (1854).

Walden Pond at the turn of the twentieth century.

In many respects, *Walden* can be read as Thoreau's attempt to apply transcendentalist principles to daily life, especially the idea that God is thoroughly embedded in nature. (George Ripley often complained that Thoreau was a pantheist who believed God *was* nature.) "I went to the woods," Thoreau wrote, "because I wished to live deliberately, to front only the essential facts of life, and see if I could not learn what it had to teach, and not, when I came to die, discover that I had not lived."

A key theme of the book is how best to manage the material aspects of life: "Simplicity, simplicity, simplicity I say, let your affairs be as two or three, and not a hundred or a thousand; instead of a million count half a dozen, and keep your accounts on your thumb nail." Through simplicity, Thoreau believed, individuals could resist the temptations of materialism that would cut them off from spiritual insight. Contrasting his austere life in the woods with the materialist lives of the people of Concord village, Thoreau celebrated his surroundings as the "perfect forest mirror," turning nature into the hero of the work, a metaphor for the hope and promise that arises when human beings follow their natural instincts.

This extreme emphasis on nature—at times humorous, at times exaggerated—led some to consider Thoreau a crank or an eccentric. For example, this passage fueled speculation that he ate raw animal flesh: "As I came home through the woods with my string of fish, trailing my pole, it being now quite dark, I caught a glimpse of a woodchuck stealing across my path, and felt a strange thrill of savage delight, and was strongly tempted to seize and devour him raw; not that I was hungry then, except for that wildness which he represented." In fact, Thoreau was neither a crank nor an eccentric but an artist who rewrote *Walden* seven times over seven years to creating just the right juxtapositions that would provoke his readers into thought and help them see the world anew through his eyes.

Thoreau's *Walden* *applies transcendentalist ideas to daily life in an exaggerated and puzzling style designed to provoke thought and jolt readers into self-awareness.*

XV. MASS EXTINCTION

THE CREATURES THAT EVOLVED during the Cambrian Explosion were mostly invertebrates—that is, animals lacking backbones. For the next 290 million years or so, comprising the entire Paleozoic era, they had the run of the planet while various vertebrate species struggled up the evolutionary ladder. The first fish didn't appear until the Ordovician period, and the first terrestrial plants and animals aren't found until the Silurian. Later—during the Devonian, Carboniferous, and Permian periods—insects came into being, huge forests of ferns overspread the landscape, and the first reptiles appeared. Then, quite suddenly, the marine invertebrates that had dominated for so long disappeared. By the end of the Permian period about 250 million years ago, they were gone. What happened to them?

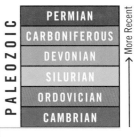

The periods of the Paleozoic era.

One current hypothesis is that a massive comet struck the Earth at the end of the Permian period, causing global temperatures to rise and creating other conditions quite hostile to living things, especially marine life. Other hypotheses relate to climatic instability and the collision of several lithospheric plates, wiping out a great deal of shallow marine environment. Whatever occurred, the fossil record suggests that as many as 90 percent of the species alive at that time perished. Although a tragedy for the invertebrate species involved, this mass extinction nevertheless cleared away a good deal of evolutionary underbrush so that the vertebrate species that did survive could flourish.

Into this breach stepped the reptiles. While one group branched off, creating a lineage that would eventually produce the first mammals, another evolved into the dinosaurs, which quickly became the dominant life-form on Earth. For this reason, the Mesozoic era (encompassing the Triassic, Jurassic, and Cretaceous periods) is known as the Age of the Dinosaurs.

For tens of millions of years, while these titanic reptiles roamed the planet, the early mammals bided their time, remaining small (none larger than a modern-day rat) and hidden in forgotten corners of the landscape. Then, about 65 million years ago, another remarkable evolutionary opportunity presented itself. An asteroid the size of Mount Everest is believed to have collided with Earth near the Gulf of Mexico, radically altering the climate and causing another mass extinction. All of the dinosaurs were wiped out, but some mammals managed to survive, and with their chief competition removed, they soon became the new masters of the planet.

The fossil record shows *two mass extinctions, one ending the Paleozoic era and another ending the Mesozoic. Both may have been caused by objects colliding with Earth.*

XV. THE DIRECTORY

WITH THE FALL OF ROBESPIERRE, the members of the National Convention retreated from radicalism and focused instead on stability. After dismantling the legal architecture of the Terror, they set about writing a new, more conservative constitution. The new document, unlike the suspended Constitution of 1793, reimposed property qualifications for suffrage and restricted the field of legislative candidates to the thirty thousand most wealthy Frenchmen (as determined by property taxes). Furthermore, in order to prevent the abuse of authority that had characterized the Terror, the Constitution of 1795 divided power in the new government, which was called the Directory. In addition to an executive committee with limited powers, there would be a new bicameral legislature. The lower house would have the power to write laws (but not enact them), while the upper house had the power to enact laws (but not to propose or alter them).

The result was a weak government that lacked the strength to manage the affairs of a country still at war and still sharply divided between radicalism and counterrevolution. Even as the Constitution of 1795 was being drafted, noble émigrés invaded Brittany in a failed attempt to overturn the republic. Meanwhile, fears of leftist insurrection were reinforced by the exposure of a plot, conceived by former Montagnard Gracchus Babeuf, to impose egalitarianism through state dictatorship. Babeuf's reliance on a small revolutionary vanguard—that is, a few conspirators working to seize power without the consent of, but in the name of, the people—marked the first time in history that the tools of political conspiracy were used for the purpose of promoting such revolutionary change. This quite modern, altogether paradoxical idea would later appeal very strongly to Vladimir Lenin.

The one area in which the Directory enjoyed unqualified success was warfare. Bolstered by conscription and improving with experience, the French army moved from defense to offense, and by 1799 it had conquered Belgium, the Netherlands, Switzerland, several of the German states, and all of Italy. As it moved farther south and east, however, and began resupplying itself through plunder, the army became increasingly independent of the Paris government. Its leaders—especially young, brave, decisive generals like Napoleon Bonaparte—contrasted sharply with the stodgy, vacillating leadership of the Directory. Thus, when the elections of 1799 brought more leftists into the government and the Directory's fearful executive committee asked the army to intercede, Bonaparte welcomed the opportunity to intimidate the legislators into ending the republic and declaring a new provisional government.

When the Directory *proved too weak to govern a still-divided France, the resurgent French army stepped in and, under Napoleon, took control of the country.*

XV. FUEL CELLS

FUEL CELLS produce energy through a chemical reaction that usually involves just hydrogen, oxygen, and water. As an alternative energy source, they have compelling advantages: scalability, portability, and zero carbon emissions. However, they also have an important drawback, high cost, which has kept them out of wide commercial use.

What makes fuel cells so attractive to energy profressionals is that they promise to excel where most alternative technologies fail—that is, at providing reliable energy that can be tapped on a limited basis at any time. For this reason, fuel cells, though expensive, are already in use as backup generators at emergency response facilities, where power interruptions can be calamitous (and cost is thus secondary).

The basic components of a fuel cell are two electrodes (an anode and a cathode), a catalyst, and an electrolyte. Electrodes are conductors that collect (anode) or emit (cathode) electrons, catalysts are substances (platinum in the case of most fuel cells) that trigger chemical reactions, and electrolytes are nonmetallic conductors that permit the passage of positively charged ions but not negatively charged electrons. In fuel cells, the electrolyte acts as a selective barrier between the anode and the cathode.

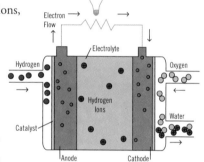

Hydrogen atoms enter the fuel cell on the anode side, where the catalyst strips them of their electrons, creating positively charged hydrogen ions (essentially single protons). The electrolyte allows these ions to pass through to the cathode side of the cell, but it blocks the negatively charged electrons. Instead, these stripped electrons are collected by the anode and forced to travel through an external circuit to the cathode, where a second reaction takes place. Again in the presence of a catalyst, the electrons and the hydrogen ions recombine with oxygen from the air to form water. Forcing the stripped electrons to travel through an external circuit, of course, is how the fuel cell produces electricity.

The fact that fuel cells weigh less than most batteries, operate silently, and produce energy indefinitely (as long as their hydrogen fuel supply lasts) has suggested a number of military applications, yet these represent only a small part of fuel cell research. Much work is being done on the development of fuel cells capable of powering automobiles, and "micro" applications, including the installation of fuel cells in electronic devices, are also being pursued.

Because fuel cells *produce electricity using chemical reactions, they can operate at any time, in any place, and on any scale, but they are also expensive.*

XV. THE PATH OF RAPID PROGRESS

ATTAINING ENLIGHTENMENT has always seemed a rather staggering task. According to the Mahāyāna tradition, the Buddha himself had to endure numerous lifetimes as a *bodhisattva* before reaching this goal. For obvious reasons, many Buddhists over the centuries have sought a more rapid path to enlightenment.

The Buddha, it was said, taught such a method to a few select disciples, who passed it on secretly in texts known as *tantras*. The *tantras* were kept secret because

A disciple receives instruction from his master.

they were considered very powerful and dangerous if misused. Eventually, they became semipublic around the seventh century CE.

While nontantric Buddhist practice recognized only the destructive nature of the Three Poisons (desire, hatred, and ignorance), the tantric system took a different view: Although still considered harmful in and of themselves, the Three Poisons were nevertheless valued for the highly focused state of mind that they created in individuals.

A mind filled with desire, for example, contemplated nothing but the object of that desire. If this powerful state of mind could be redirected to a virtuous end, such as selflessness, then it could speed one's progress along the path toward enlightenment.

All traditions of Buddhism teach compassion toward other beings. The Mahāyāna tradition, however, teaches the special form of compassion associated with the *bodhisattva*, which puts concern for the suffering of others above concern for oneself. This Mahāyāna intent to attain Buddhahood in order to help others played an important role in the development of the tantric system, because it provided motivation for risking the dangers of the Three Poisons. A *bodhisattva*, it was believed, finding the suffering of others unbearable, could embark on the tantric path in order to achieve enlightenment as quickly as possible for the sake of others.

As the *tantras* gained wider circulation after the seventh century CE, commentaries bearing the names of familiar Mahāyāna scholars, such as Nāgārjuna and Candrakīrti, also began to appear. These texts contained instructions on how to generate the powerful states of mind associated with the Three Poisons, but the instructions were often couched in cryptic terms, whose meaning was discernible only to students who had received personal instruction from a master. Although numerous students over the centuries have committed these supplementary spoken instructions to writing, it has always been maintained that they are no substitute for direct instruction.

Tantrism makes *use of the potentially dangerous but highly focused states of mind associated with the Three Poisons to quicken one's progress along the path to Buddhahood.*

XVI. EMERSON AND SLAVERY

IN THE SAME WAY that ripples in a pond reveal the tossing in of a stone, individualism is revealed in society, according to Emerson, by the disruption of social conventions. Within the context of Emerson's life, however, this point remained mostly abstract. While some transcendentalists—Thoreau, in particular— relished political protest, Emerson remained aloof for philosophical reasons. As he pointed out in "Self-Reliance," society reforms from within through the perfection of the individual, not from without through political pressure.

When "Self-Reliance" appeared in 1841, the issues of territorial expansion and slavery were already threatening civil war, yet Emerson refused to look outward, even though he must have realized how unfeeling this brand of nonconformity made him appear. "I am ashamed to think how easily we capitulate to badges and names," Emerson wrote in "Self-Reliance. "If an angry bigot assumes this bountiful cause of Abolition, and comes to me with his last news from Barbadoes, why should I not say to him, 'Go love thy infant; love thy wood-chopper: be good-natured and modest: have that grace; and never varnish your hard, uncharitable ambition with this incredible tenderness for black folk a thousand miles off. Thy love afar is spite at home.' Rough and graceless would be such greeting, but truth is handsomer than the affectation of love."

Yet as time passed and the political situation worsened, Emerson's position began to shift. The transition from a buoyant, optimistic world of ideas to a harsh world of cold political reality certainly couldn't have been easy for Emerson, but he managed it with the encouragement of several close abolitionist friends. The turning point came in 1850, when Congress passed the Fugitive Slave Law, which required northerners to return escaped southern slaves. Like many of his neighbors, Emerson hid runaways and also began speaking out more forcefully against Negro bondage. "All I have and all I can do shall be given and done in opposition to the execution of the law," Emerson wrote in a July 1851 journal entry.

Meanwhile, as he became more deeply involved with abolitionism during the 1850s, Emerson couldn't help noticing the strange usage of the word *liberty* in the political debate. Both sides claimed it as their raison d'être: Abolitionists wanted liberty for the slaves; southerners wanted liberty to conduct their own affairs as they saw fit. Ironically, all were reading the cultural text of America—specifically, the Constitution—with innovative eyes.

Changes in the American political situation, *especially the growth of abolitionism, helped move Emerson from the world of literary ideas into the world of social action.*

A slave displays the scars of his captivity.

XVI. THE FOSSIL RECORD

EVERYTHING THAT WE KNOW about early life on the planet comes to us through fossils preserved in rocks. To understand the fossil record better, it helps to know something about how these rocks were created.

Rocks form in several different ways. For instance, when volcanic lava cools, it forms igneous rock. Although igneous rocks are quite hard, they still are subject to environmental stress and erosion. Cracks develop in them, into which water seeps. When the water freezes, it expands, widening the cracks. Over time, these processes break down igneous rock gradually into sand and silt.

Running water slowly carries this sediment from hillsides to river, lake, and ocean bottoms, where it accumulates in layers. Over time, the weight of new layers compresses the older layers into sedimentary rock. Should an animal die under the right conditions, its body will become encapsulated in this sediment, and, if the conditions remain favorable, its bones will be replaced gradually by minerals, creating a sedimentary rock formation with features identical to those of the original skeleton.

All sediments are capable of producing fossils, but the best fossils come from the finest sediments, such as clay. Fossils produced from clay preserve in exquisite detail the bones, shell, and other rigid parts of an animal's body. Some even preserve the outlines of its soft tissue.

Understanding how sedimentary rock forms also helps in the dating of fossils. Although sediments are constantly being created and deposited, their amounts can vary, depending on environmental conditions. Some years produce much more sediment than others because of lower temperatures or higher rainfall. Volcanic activity can also be a determining factor. Massive eruptions can spread thick layers of volcanic ash over the entire planet, eventually producing very useful layers of sedimentary rock. Employed as reference points, these layers can aid in the dating of other layers in different locations around the world. A fossil's age, of course, corresponds directly to the age of the sedimentary layer in which it was found.

Although a great many fossils have already been found, it is important to remember that the history of Earth is an enormous book whose pages we have been reading for a very short time. How many fossils still remain to be discovered? How many were destroyed before we even knew to look for them? It is impossible to say, except that both numbers must be quite large.

The fossilized skull of a protoceratops.

Created as a by-product *of sedimentation, fossils have preserved a great deal of unique information about early life on the planet.*

XVI. THE NAPOLEONIC ERA

Jacques-Louis David's 1800 portrait of Napoleon.

THE GOVERNMENT CREATED by Napoleon and his supporters after the overthrow of the Directory was called the Consulate. It succeeded because it gave France stability and the trappings of democracy without any of the burdens that the past few years had made obvious. Although the government's three-member executive ostensibly took direction from an elected legislature, the real power in the Consulate was reserved for Napoleon. As First Consul, he issued edicts and appointed not only government ministers but also departmental administrators (prefects), who strengthened the authority of the central government throughout the country, especially in the regions outside Paris. To help the prefects in this work, Napoleon established France's first national police force, which he charged with investigating critics of the regime and suppressing political dissent. Within a few years, hundreds of political clubs, salons, and newspapers were shut down.

In 1802, a national referendum (with widespread ballot fraud to ensure the proper result) confirmed Napoleon as First Consul for life. In 1804, following a similar referendum, Napoleon dispensed with even the appearance of public participation and declared himself emperor. Henceforth, he ruled by decree as France's absolute monarchs had. Another similarity was the stratified society he encouraged, in which an elite of nobles and bourgeois enjoyed vast benefits. Expatriate nobles willing to accept his reign were permitted to return to France, while wealthy bourgeois (who had previously been considered commoners) were elevated to the noble ranks. Even the former revolutionary Emmanuel Sieyès was made a count, and he began appearing at Napoleon's court decked out in fine imperial regalia. "Have you seen Sieyès at court?" one wag wrote. "What *is* the third estate?"

Even so, the Napoleonic empire was by no means a return to the ancien régime. The lands confiscated from noble families when they emigrated remained beyond their reach, and none of the legal privileges that they had so long enjoyed were reinstated. To the contrary, Napoleon retained the legal equality established by the Revolution and reinforced it with the Civil Code of 1804. This set of laws, based on the Revolution's fundamental principle of individual liberty, guaranteed freedom of religion, the right to private property, and the right to free trade. On the other hand, it did favor wealthy men at the expense of other social classes and women.

Napoleon initially provided *the trappings of democracy without any of the burdens. The empire he later established had a strong central state and a small, wealthy elite.*

XVI. **THE LIMITS OF ALTERNATIVE ENERGY**

THE CONCERNS ABOUT ENERGY security, high petroleum prices, and global warming that launched the current alternative energy boom haven't abated. In fact, they've deepened, and there is more concern than ever about the world's dependence on fossil fuels. Many now look to alternative technologies for near-term solutions

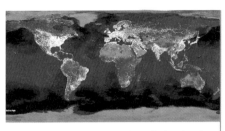

to these problems, but there is a fundamental error in this strategy: The world simply consumes too much energy.

World demand is so enormous that alternative technologies, as they exist today, can't possibly replace the energy being extracted from fossil fuels. Too much is required in too

This composite orbital image shows the location of permanent nighttime lights on the earth's surface.

many different applications. Even working in combination, alternative technologies can't replace a single fossil fuel—coal, petroleum, or natural gas. The consensus among energy experts is that fossil fuels, along with nuclear energy, will continue to fulfill our basic energy needs for decades to come. Inventions may occur suddenly, but commercialization and infrastructure development take time. Even if a technological breakthrough occurred tomorrow, it would take at least two decades to implement. After all, it took a century to create today's fossil fuel infrastructure.

Consider the transportation sector. The disadvantages of burning gasoline are well known, but global dependence on gas-burning internal combustion engines seems unlikely to change anytime soon. To begin with, the cost of replacing the current infrastructure seems prohibitive. The introduction of a new automotive fuel, for example, would require the replacement of hundreds of millions of engines, the refitting of hundreds of thousands of filling stations, and the reconstruction (or new construction) of hundreds of new refineries.

Energy economists are particularly concerned about what will happen when the populations of developing giants such as China and India—accounting for 2.5 billion people, or nearly 40 percent of the world population—begin to buy cars in large numbers as well. China already has serious air pollution problems, and in 2006 it overtook the United States as the world's leading emitter of carbon dioxide. Its citizens will hardly be able to afford the extra cost of buying "green" cars, and even if they could, the capacity to produce so much green transportation simply doesn't exist, at least not yet.

Fossil fuels *will probably dominate the energy market for decades to come because alternative technologies can't yet meet world demand.*

XVI. BUDDHISM IN SRI LANKA AND SOUTH ASIA

ALTHOUGH THE BUDDHA was said to have visited the southern Indian island of Laṅka (now Śrī Laṅka), monastic Buddhism didn't take root there until the reign of the Indian emperor Aśoka during the third century BCE. For several hundred years thereafter, while Indian Buddhism underwent a number of transformations, the Laṅkan Buddhists held to the teachings of Aśoka's missionaries, known as "the elders." Because the word for "elders" in the local language Pāli was *thera*, the Laṅka tradition became known as Theravāda ("doctrine of the elders"). With the arrival of the Mahāyāna tradition during the third century CE and tantrism after that, some diversity appeared within the island's monastic community. But the Theravādan tradition continued to dominate, and the doctrines it promulgated (especially the goal of becoming an *arhat*) were soon codified into the Laṅkan canon, composed during the fourth and fifth centuries CE.

During the eleventh century, Laṅka was invaded by Hindu Tamils from the Indian mainland, who suppressed Buddhism on the island. The Mahāyāna and tantric traditions were eliminated, and though the Theravāda tradition survived, many of its lineages were broken. (These were the lengthy master–disciple chains through which a tradition's teachings were passed on.) When the Tamils were finally deposed a few decades later, the Theravāda tradition was reinstated with the help of Burmese monks who likewise traced their roots to the missionaries sent by Aśoka.

Between the ejection of the Tamils and the arrival of Portuguese colonizers during the sixteenth century, Laṅkan Buddhists conducted a series of purges that rid the Theravāda canon of its more mystical elements. References to supernatural abilities and travel to nonearthly realms were deleted, and tales of the Buddha's former lives were recast as literary allegory (rather than literal truth).

Under the colonial rule of the Portuguese, the Dutch, and ultimately the British, the island's Buddhist traditions were again suppressed. However, as an ironic consequence of the colonial enterprise, some British officials became interested in Laṅkan books on the history and doctrines of Buddhism, and they published English translations of these works, which became influential throughout the Western world and inspired a great deal of interest in Buddhism. The Theravāda tradition, now thoroughly purged of mysticism, held a particular appeal for Protestants, who appreciated its rationalism. At the present time, the Theravāda tradition still flourishes in Śrī Laṅka, Burma, Thailand, Cambodia, and Laos.

The Theravāda tradition, *which dates to the third century BCE, follows a conservative view of the Buddha's teachings, devoid of many later Mahāyāna and tantric elements.*

XVII. SUN AND SHADOW: EMERSON AND MELVILLE

AS THE 1850S began and the United States entered an age of political crisis, the American literary landscape flickered with light and shadow. Emerson and the transcendentalists, not surprisingly, held to their sunny, optimistic worldview: Humanity was innately good. Utilizing intuition and free will, some people would establish relationships with nature and connect with the divine. These people would then share their spiritual gains with the rest of society, curing its ills. Of course, not all of America's literati shared this opinion. Where Emerson saw sunlight, for example, Herman Melville (1819–91) saw shadow.

Herman Melville

By 1850, the year that he wrote most of *Moby-Dick*, Melville was a well-established author, having published five popular seafaring romances. Because of his attacks on conformity, defense of self-reliance, and occasional use of Emersonian symbolism, critics associated him with the transcendentalists, and Melville didn't object. *Moby-Dick*, however, marked a turning point in his career and also in his philosophy. An important influence at the time was his friend Nathaniel Hawthorne.

During the summer of 1850, Melville, his wife, and their infant son left New York City to spend several months at a farmhouse near Pittsfield, Massachusetts. There, he was introduced to Hawthorne, who had already become a full-time Berkshires resident. Immediately, the two men struck up a friendship, and Melville soon decided, somewhat impulsively, to relocate to the area himself. As their letters make clear, Hawthorne provided Melville with an important literary sounding board—a debt that Melville repaid by dedicating *Moby-Dick* to Hawthorne.

Like Melville, Hawthorne was beginning to rebel against transcendentalism's relentless optimism. "You may be witched by his sunlight," Melville wrote of Hawthorne, "transported by the bright gildings in the skies he builds over you;—but there is the blackness of darkness beyond; and even his bright gildings but fringe, and play upon the edges of thunder-clouds." From this point of view, it becomes much easier to read *Moby-Dick* as Melville's application of transcendental idealism to tragic drama.

Emerson thought of nature as beautiful, and Melville would certainly have agreed, but nature in *Moby-Dick* is also alien and dangerous. Despite his evident heroism, Ahab is doomed—an entirely untranscendental fate—because nature, symbolized by the white whale, has overwhelmed him. Humanity can't see truth in nature, according to Melville, because nature is inscrutable.

Like his friend Hawthorne, *Melville began his literary career as a transcendentalist, but he later rejected Emerson's optimistic viewpoint, especially with regard to nature.*

XVII. RADIOCARBON DATING

RADIOMETRIC DATING using isotopes with long half-lives works very well for extremely old rocks. When analyzing a sample that's billions of years old, it helps to have a durable tool like uranium-238, whose half-life is 4.5 billion years. However, just as one wouldn't use a jackhammer to crack open a walnut, isotopes with long half-lives aren't suitable for analyzing more recent artifacts, such as wooden tool handles or human bones. For these organic objects, one needs an isotope with a relatively short half-life. The most useful has proven to be carbon-14, with a half-life of 5,730 years.

Among the cosmic particles that regularly enter Earth's upper atmosphere are high-speed neutrons, which sometimes react with atmospheric nitrogen in an unusual manner. The nucleus of a nitrogen atom has seven protons and seven neutrons. When impacted by a speeding neutron, however, it absorbs the neutron while ejecting a proton. The resulting atom, now containing just six protons, becomes the element carbon, though an unstable form because it has eight neutrons instead of the usual six.

Immediately, the new carbon-14 atom bonds with molecular oxygen to form radioactive carbon dioxide. Over time, this gas diffuses through the atmosphere and dissolves in the oceans, producing a constant background level of carbon-14 in the air and the water. Plants ingest the radioactive carbon dioxide for use in photosynthesis, and when animals ingest these plants, they also take in some carbon-14. As a result, plants and animals come to have the same ratio of carbon-14 to carbon-12 in their bodies as exists in the environment as a whole.

At death, however, an organism's intake of carbon-14 ceases. Therefore, from that moment on, because radioactive decay continues, the ratio of carbon-14 to carbon-12 in its body drops. The more time that passes, the lower this ratio falls when compared with the constant background level. Radiocarbon dating (a form of radiometric dating) uses the difference between these two ratios to calculate the time that has passed since the death of the organism that produced the sample.

Because carbon-14's half-life is so short, it becomes an ineffective tool after eighty thousand years or so, making it useless for dating seventy-million-year-old dinosaur bones. On the other hand, its short half-life make it an accurate tool for dating recent artifacts such as lumps of charcoal from a Neandertal fire pit or a mummy unearthed from a northern European bog.

Radioactive carbon-14 *enters the food chain through photosynthesis. Because its rate of decay is known, it can be used to date recent organic remains.*

XVII. THE SPREAD OF REVOLUTIONARY VALUES

IRONICALLY, the determination of France's neighbors to suppress the Revolution led directly to the spread of its egalitarian values across the face of Europe. Although the war that began in 1792 threatened the survival of the Revolution for a time, it eventually produced a succession of French military victories that spread the Revolution from the Atlantic Ocean to the steppes of Russia.

The National Convention and later the Directory justified the occupations that began in 1794 as a means of helping oppressed commoners in other countries "recover their liberty." Accordingly, French generals reshaped foreign governments along democratic lines. In the Netherlands, Switzerland, and several of the Italian states—now France's "sister republics"—royal governments were replaced with written constitutions and elected legislatures. Popular participation was encouraged by the establishment of a free press and the development of local political clubs.

Soon enough, however, France began exploiting these "freed" countries, expropriating war indemnities and replacing locally elected leaders with French officials. With the advent of Napoleon, the treatment grew even worse, and the sister republics were transformed into kingdoms with the emperor's siblings as monarchs.

Between 1805 and 1809, Napoleon subdued Austria, Prussia, Spain, and Portugal. The glory associated with these victories stoked French pride and strongly reinforced the emperor's hold on power. By 1812, in fact, he thought that his power was limitless. Thus, when Russia backed out of the continental system of trade he had established in 1806, Napoleon decided to make an example of his erstwhile ally. In June 1812, he invaded Russia with more than half a million men. In November of that year, he retreated into Poland with fewer than fifty thousand left.

Emboldened by the success of Russian resistance to Napoleon, more nations joined the British-led coalition against France, and the numerical superiority of their combined armies proved irresistible. Subsequent defeats forced Napoleon to abdicate in April 1814. Meanwhile, Louis XVI's younger brother returned to Paris and became France's new constitutional monarch, reigning until his death in 1824 (interrupted only by Napoleon's brief return to power in 1815). Although some still hoped for a return to the ancien régime, the new monarchy never gained ascendancy over the legislature, nor did the nobility recover its lost lands and privileges.

Although France's record as a conquering power was mixed, its occupation of foreign territory during the 1790s spread the values of the Revolution throughout Europe.

France as a monster, with one foot on Switzerland, threatens Great Britain in this 1798 cartoon.

XVII. SHORT-TERM STRATEGIES

ALTHOUGH ALTERNATIVE ENERGY won't be replacing conventional resources anytime soon, it can still play a role in addressing the global warming crisis. Already, on a small scale in some regional markets, alternative technologies have begun to make inroads into commercial electricity production. These beachheads include wind in the United States, Denmark, the United Kingdom, and Spain; ethanol in Brazil and the United States; biomass in Europe, Asia, and the developing world; and photovoltaic solar in the American Southwest. All will surely expand over time and begin to make a cumulative difference, perhaps in twenty years. Meanwhile, energy companies are working to apply other new technologies to conventional energy so that fossil fuels can be burned more cleanly and efficiently.

The incentives for change—such as government tax credits, international climate agreements, and depletion of conventional resources—are already strong and are likely to grow stronger as carbon-emission caps become a reality. The first steps will be gradual—for instance, a nuclear renaissance and cleaner coal technology. A number of national governments are already talking about financial guarantees for next-generation nuclear plants, and some progress has been made on a new technology for pulverizing coal so that it burns more cleanly.

Next may be an expansion of the market for cleaner-burning natural gas. Although most natural gas reserves are located in the Middle East—far from consumers in the United States, Asia, and Europe—a technology developed during the 1960s and improved since then can condense natural gas at temperatures approaching -275°F for distribution in cryogenic tankers. Although the process is expensive and requires the construction of new terminals to handle the liquefied natural gas (LNG), it has become price-competitive as the price of petroleum soars.

New technologies are also being applied to the demand side of the equation, decreasing the need for—or at least the growth of the need for—fossil fuel energy. Recent developments range from energy-saving home appliances to sophisticated software programs that help industrial processes run more efficiently. At the same time, consumers are becoming ever more mindful of their energy use, and their behavior is changing. New metering technologies will allow consumers to monitor their energy use more closely. As a result, thermostats will be lowered, lights will be dimmed, and other conservation measures will be adopted, if only to offset the expected rise in utility rates. Soon enough, other "smart" technologies will allow homeowners to control every energy system in their house, promoting even greater conservation and efficiency.

The most promising *short-term strategies include building on gains made in biofuels, wind, and solar; cleaning up conventional energy; and reducing the growth of demand.*

XVII. BUDDHISM IN CHINA, KOREA, AND JAPAN

THE TRANSLATION OF Buddhist *sūtras* into Chinese began during the first century CE and continued through the eighth century, with the majority of the work being done by Parthian, Kuchean, and Chinese translators. Reflecting the diverse religious traditions of these Silk Road peoples, the Chinese Buddhist tradition featured an assortment of texts and philosophies, including elements of the Laṅkan canon as well as many Mahāyāna *sūtras* and commentaries. Mixed in with these were indigenous Taoist traditions and even some Confucian mores, making the Chinese tradition the most syncretic form of Buddhism.

The primary reason Buddhism developed this way in China was that Chinese society wasn't very receptive to the monasticism at the heart of the Buddhist faith. The idea of sons and daughters leaving their homes and parents to seek enlightenment threatened the strong family orientation of Chinese culture, especially the emphasis that the Chinese placed on filial piety (the doctrine of extreme respect for the institution of the family). As a result, Buddhist missionaries in China presented the faith with its monastic aspects intentionally downplayed. They substituted instead the concept of the lay *bodhisattva*—that is, a *bodhisattva* who is not necessarily a monk or nun.

Another differentiating aspect of Chinese Buddhism was its focus on meditation to the exclusion of other practices. Like the Mahāyāna philosophy of the middle way, the Chinese tradition taught that enlightenment existed "beyond words and letters." In the Chinese system, this state of existence could be reached through the practice of meditation known as Ch'an-na—a transliteration of *dhyana*, the Sanskrit word for "meditation."

Usually called Ch'an for short, this Chinese practice traced its roots back to the Indian monk Bodhidharma, whose arrival in China during the early sixth century CE established the lineage through which the meditative teaching was transmitted. In this way, Bodhidharma functioned as a crucial link between the Indian masters who had inherited the meditative teaching from the Buddha and the Chinese "patriarchs" through whom it was later passed down.

Chinese meditative practice subsequently spread to Korea, where it became Son, and to Japan, where it became Zen. With the immigration of many Chinese and Japanese Buddhists to California during the nineteenth and twentieth centuries, Ch'an/Zen Buddhism spread to America as well, first becoming widely popular during the cultural experimentation of the 1950s and 1960s.

Strongly reflecting *China's indigenous, family-oriented culture, Chinese Buddhism stressed the practice of meditation—which became known as Ch'an in China.*

XVIII. THE TRANSCENDENTALIST LEGACY

IN ITS TIME, as a popular movement, transcendentalism never got very far. Books by transcendentalists didn't sell very well, and with the coming of the Civil War, the movement ended. Among the northern intellectual elites, transcendentalism caused more of a stir, often dividing readers into pros and antis, but much of this debate was forgiven and forgotten after the war, when social realism replaced romanticism as the Next Big Thing.

Yet Emerson's attempt to liberate New England from its theocratic roots hardly went for naught. "Every one has heard the story," Thoreau wrote in the final chapter of *Walden*, "of a strong and beautiful bug which came out of the dry leaf of an old table of apple-tree wood, which had stood in a farmer's kitchen for sixty years, first in Connecticut, and afterward in Massachusetts,—from an egg deposited in the living tree many years earlier still, as appeared by counting the annual layers beyond it; which was heard gnawing out for several weeks, hatched perchance by the heat of an urn." The transcendentalists planted such eggs themselves, which have since hatched.

Where self makes an assertion against society, where intuition triumphs over dogma, where innovation moves ahead of tradition, transcendentalism can be found, because the movement brought forth these forces in American society. Within literature, it helped Whitman and Dickinson lay the foundation for a new, uniquely American poetry, practiced in years to come by poets such as Wallace Stevens, Marianne Moore, John Ashbery, and Allen Ginsberg. The transcendentalist influence can also be seen in novels such as *The Adventures of Huckleberry Finn*—whose buoyant optimism, even in the face of despair, helped forge America's national literature.

Within civil society, transcendentalism also grew stronger with age. Emerson's philosophy proved especially attractive to social reformers of the twentieth century, who appreciated its emphasis on intuitive (rather than learned) morality. Meanwhile, Thoreau's thoughts on civil disobedience inspired Mohandas K. Gandhi and Martin Luther King, Jr., among many others.

For these reasons, scholars today tend to view transcendentalism as an intellectual expression of American democracy itself. In the transcendentalist world, all Americans, regardless of their social status, have an equal opportunity to experience nature and communicate with the divine. All have the same chance, as Emerson told the Harvard Divinity School Class of 1838, to "cheer the waiting, fainting hearts of men with new hope and new revelations."

A daguerreotype of Emerson.

Although the transcendentalist movement *ended with the coming of the Civil War, its influence continues to be felt in American literature and culture.*

XVIII. HUMAN TIME AND GEOLOGICAL TIME

ALTHOUGH IT MAY SEEM to us that Earth has finally arrived at its ultimate state, this is an illusion based on the egotism of humanity and our inability to comprehend the full dimension of geological time. To put it plainly, humanity has not been an important factor in Earth history. Compared with the age of the planet (about 4.5 billion years), the age of the species *Homo sapiens* (about 150,000 years) is but the blink of an eye. In quantitative terms, humans have been around for only 0.003 percent of Earth's history, or less than eighteen minutes over the course of a year.

We may understand this intellectually but not intuitively. Because planetary change takes place so slowly, we don't notice it and tend to think it's not happening. Nevertheless, most of the processes that have defined Earth's history, such as plate tectonics, seem to function as they always have. The lithospheric plates, for instance, continue to move at roughly the same rate they have over the last three billion years. At just centimeters per year, this movement is difficult to perceive, but it's nonetheless significant.

According to plate tectonics, the continental plates have in the past, and will again, come together to form supercontinents. For example, about 225 million years ago, all of the extant continents joined together to form a single landmass known as Pangaea, fitting together like the pieces of an enormous jigsaw puzzle. This supercontinent, one of many that have formed over the course of Earth's history, took tens of millions of years to come together through multiple collisions and tens of millions of more years to break apart through a process called rifting. Geologists believe that unitary supercontinents form about every 250 million years, which is roughly the same amount of time that it takes our solar system to complete a single orbit around the center of the galaxy. Some geologists have suspected a connection, but none has yet been demonstrated.

Could some past cataclysmic events on this planet have resulted from Earth's passing through a particularly dangerous region of space? That is certainly a possibility, and if so, such events will likely happen again—but not quickly.

Because the human time frame *is so short, we tend to ignore processes like plate tectonics that take place on a geological time scale.*

XVIII. THE LEGACY OF THE FRENCH REVOLUTION

VIEWING THE FRENCH REVOLUTION from the perspective of the early nineteenth century, one might conclude that the Revolution had little lasting effect. France's development of a modern centralized state, though accelerated by Napoleon, was an inevitability of the modern age. So was the rise of the French bourgeois. In those areas where the Revolution did break new ground, such as the granting of equal rights to women, the momentum couldn't be sustained, and the gains vanished. Universal male suffrage, for example, didn't return to France until the 1880s.

Rioters burn some of the king's carriages during the 1848 uprising.

Yet historical appearances can be deceiving, because the events that took place in France between 1789 and 1815 reworked the way that the French and other Europeans thought about politics and society. The interminable legislative debates, the violence in the streets, the euphoria, and the propaganda all contributed to a new sense of what it meant to be a citizen. Before the Revolution, subjects of Louis XVI would identify themselves simply as peasants from Brittany or Parisian bourgeois. Afterward, they saw themselves more importantly as citizens of the French nation, a status that entitled them to equal treatment under the law and certain civil rights. Emerging from the Revolution, this sense of national identity quickly spread across Europe, sparking nationalist movements in the politically balkanized states of Germany, Italy, Hungary, and Greece.

The social and political energies unleashed by these ideas made life in Europe both terrifying and exhilarating. The principles enunciated in the Declaration of Rights, for example, inspired popular uprisings in 1830, 1848, and 1871 in Paris alone. Meanwhile, the debate over equal rights for women and other minorities led to widespread campaigns for women's suffrage and the abolition of slavery.

Others found different lessons in the Revolution, seeing in its dictatorial years a blueprint for political action. Lenin, for example, was influenced by Babeuf's use of political conspiracy when he created his own revolutionary vanguard in exile. The Revolution also left a dark legacy with regard to ideological violence. These contradictions, particularly the use of authoritarianism in the name of democracy, are what make the French Revolution such a fascinating period in history. In 1789, the French people became the first to wrestle with these issues. Since then, the problems that they encountered have become the challenge of the modern world.

The French Revolution *changed the way that people thought about politics and society, bringing to light certain contradictions that still challenge the modern world.*

XVIII. THE GLOBAL ENERGY FUTURE

BY THE END OF THE TWENTY-FIRST CENTURY, the global energy picture will be entirely transformed. This has to happen because there simply isn't enough fossil fuel left in the world for today's conventional energy to remain conventional. As global petroleum reserves decline, oil and gas will become more and more expensive. Eventually, economics, if not global warming, will force a change. Petroleum experts anticipate that global oil production will peak between 2025 and 2050, with supplies running out entirely between 2075 and 2125. By then, one or more replacement technologies will have to be in place. What form these will take is impossible to say, but they probably won't rely on any device currently in development.

For the time being, research into alternative energy will proceed in two directions simultaneously: upward to greater economies of scale and downward to decentralization (which means the placement of smaller applications closer to the sources of energy need). Alternative technologies that can be applied to utility-scale projects no doubt will be, taking advantage of new capital and new machinery to produce competitive power. At the same time, technologies better suited to site-specific applications will likely prosper at the other end of the size spectrum. Wind and solar thermal will probably find application on the large scale—wind farms in the short term and perhaps space-based solar power stations in the long. On the small scale, fuel cells and photovoltaic cells are both troubled by cost and efficiency problems, but if these can be overcome, both technologies have the potential to become truly ubiquitous energy sources, powering a wide range of large and small mechanical and electronic devices.

Biotechnology and nanotechnology also offer interesting possibilities for the future. The developing nanotech capability to manipulate matter at the atomic level may help biotech engineers solve the most serious problem with biofuels: that manufacturing them seems to consume more energy than it creates. One day, it may be possible for bioengineers to produce plant and animal organisms that function just like miniature fuel cells, using chemical processes to take the energy created by photosynthesis and convert it into a more usable form. If this can be accomplished, then humanity could return to its original fuel source, biomass, without having to burn the material in order to access its stored energy.

With oil supplies expected to *run out between 2075 and 2125, fossil fuels cannot be the future of conventional energy. What will replace them is a matter of speculation.*

XVIII. BUDDHISM IN TIBET

The Samye monastery, the first Buddhist monastery in Tibet.

THE TRANSMISSION OF BUDDHISM from India to Tibet began during the seventh century CE as part of a political campaign undertaken by the Tibetan king, who wanted to unify his new empire through the imposition of a single religion and a common language. His effort included the recruitment of Indian monks and the translation of Buddhist texts. In the 780s, the Indian scholar Padmasambhava introduced tantrism to Tibet about the time the first Buddhist monastery was established there. With the collapse of the Tibetan empire in 842, the growth of Tibetan Buddhism stalled; but in the mid-tenth century, royal patronage resumed, and Indian monks were once again brought to Tibet.

When invading Muslim armies began destroying Buddhist institutions in India during the early thirteenth century, many survivors fled to Tibet. Yet after this influx, Tibet found itself cut off, because India had been its link to the non-Buddhist world. As a result, the Tibetan tradition subsequently developed along its own lines. Over time, it flourished and came to dominate the intellectual life of central Asia.

Although the full range of Buddhism was present in Tibet, the tantric tradition was particularly strong. In time, several different tantric lineages came to compete with one another, dividing up the country into sectarian camps. Scholar-yogis associated with each camp vied for disciples and royal patronage by taking part in contests that tested their academic abilities and levels of spiritual attainment. After the Mongols invaded during the thirteenth century, this patronage continued to flow from Tibet's Mongolian overlords, who left the Buddhist monastics in charge.

Of the four major Tibetan Buddhist sects, the last to emerge was the Geluk (also spelled Gelug). Founded during the early fifteenth century by Tsong-kha-pa, the Geluk sect emphasized monasticism and celibacy. During the early sixteenth century, the Mongols began patronizing the Geluk above other sects. As a result, the Geluk sect gained political ascendancy and a century later established a central government headed by the fifth member of a line of reincarnated monks known as the Dalai Lamas.

From then onward, Tibet maintained a complex relationship with Mongolia and later with China, which invaded the country in 1950. In 1959, after a failed revolt, the government of the fourteenth Dalai Lama and thousands of refugees fled into exile. As a result of this diaspora, Tibetan Buddhism is now the fastest-growing Buddhist tradition among Americans and Europeans.

The Muslim invasion *of India benefited Buddhism in Tibet because many Indian scholars fled there; but the invasion also cut Tibet off from the non-Buddhist world.*

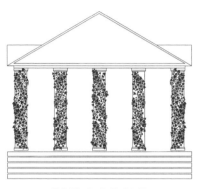

SYLLABUS

III

I. WHAT IS ROCKET SCIENCE?

PEOPLE COMMONLY USE THE PHRASE *rocket science* when they're speaking generally of an activity that requires great intelligence or technical skill. (Think of the quip "He's no rocket scientist.") Beyond this jocular use, however, most people don't really understand what *rocket science* means.

Most space missions have three distinct phases: getting the vehicle off the ground, maneuvering it in space, and returning it to a planetary surface. While this sequence of events may seem quite straightforward, it's important to remember that the rocket science involved in each phase exists at the very edge of human understanding. Merely to launch a space vehicle, a rocket scientist needs to have at least a graduate-level understanding of propulsion engineering, fluid mechanics, flight dynamics, atmospheric dynamics, the mechanics of materials, control engineering, and avionics—not to mention the math and computer skills necessary to make effective use of this knowledge. That's quite an extensive list for an event lasting only ten minutes.

If the objective of the mission requires only Earth orbit, then a rocket scientist can get by with expertise merely in orbital mechanics, ionospheric dynamics, and low-temperature plasma dynamics; if the mission required the space vehicle to leave orbit, however, the rocket scientist will also need astrodynamics. If the vehicle is supposed to carry human astronauts, add aerospace physiology; and if it's going to reenter Earth's atmosphere, add aerothermochemistry, high-temperature plasma dynamics, aeroacoustics, and aeroelasticity.

Because mastering all of these disciplines would take several lifetimes, rocket scientists work in teams. Each member of the team oversees a particular aspect of the mission related to his or her expertise. In general, most rocket scientists master only one discipline, but they must have a profound working knowledge of all the others in order to communicate well and work effectively with the other members of their team. Weakness in any one member can lead to disastrous results. That's why, considering all the difficulties involved, it may well take someone as smart and skilled as a rocket scientist to build and operate a spacecraft.

The work of a rocket scientist *requires expertise that is as varied as it is cutting edge. Mastery of one discipline is insufficient; he or she must possess a profound working knowledge of them all.*

The 1966 launch of a Titan rocket.

I. THE PERIODIZATION OF MARX'S LIFE AND WORKS

KARL MARX WAS BORN IN 1818 in Trier, a city on the Moselle River in what was then Prussia. He died nearly penniless in London sixty-five years later. In between, he wrote and published thousands of pages of social, economic, and political analysis. These writings describe a path to social change that revolutionized the world.

Karl Marx in 1875.

Scholars typically group Marx's writings into two categories: those composed before 1848 (when many European countries experienced political turmoil and uprisings) and those composed afterward. Such a distinction, however, is overdrawn, because one of the most remarkable characteristics of Marx's thought is its consistency. Therefore, rather than place so much emphasis on 1848, it's more helpful to divide Marx's adult life in four less sharply defined phases.

The most important aspect of the first phase (1835–45) was Marx's association with the Young Hegelians, whom he met while attending university in Prussia. In 1843, after completing his dissertation on ancient Greek philosophies of nature, Marx moved to Paris, where he began a lifelong collaborating with another Young Hegelian, Friedrich Engels (1820–95). Marx's years in Paris with Engels would be among the most productive of his life. The culmination of this second phase (1845–49) was their writing of the famous *Communist Manifesto*, published in February 1848.

The next year, Marx moved his family to London, beginning the third phase of his career (1849–63), during which he systematically deconstructed capitalism as a social, political, and economic form. The result was his magnum opus, *Capital*, only portions of which were published during his lifetime. Remaining in London for the rest of his life, Marx had no regular income. Instead, he and his family subsisted entirely on his sporadic earnings as a journalist; small remittances from his wife's family; and money from Engels, the scion of prominent and wealthy Prussian capitalists.

While in London, Marx remained active in politics, helping to found the International Workingmen's Association in the early 1860s (known as the First International). During this final phase of his life (1863–83), he became more optimistic about the prospects for revolutionary change; however, by the time of his death, the First International had fallen apart, his wife had already died, and so had four of his seven children. Stateless and largely alone, Marx passed away on March 14, 1883, with fewer than a dozen people in attendance at his funeral.

Marx worked out a set of ideas *over four phases of his life: his Young Hegelian days, his years in Paris, the writing of* Capital, *and his work with the First International.*

I. THE PARISIAN ART WORLD

FOR YOUNG ARTISTS during the nineteenth century, Paris was an attractive place to make a career. The city was quickly becoming a capital of the international art world, and there was a great deal of government patronage to be had. However, along with the government support came regimentation.

The key institution was the government-sponsored Académie des Beaux-Arts. Its members were older, established artists who, not surprisingly, favored older, established methods of painting. In general, they liked history paintings more than portraits and portraits more than landscapes.

What the members of the Académie liked meant a great deal because these men dominated the Parisian art world. They sat on the juries that awarded the best prizes; advised the government on official purchases; and, even more importantly, decided which artists would be permitted to exhibit at the annual government-sponsored Salons. Beyond the professional acceptance that inclusion in a Salon conveyed, it also brought an artist's work before the most important patrons and collectors under the most favorable of circumstances. When the government established the Académie, its intention was merely to honor France's great artists. Over time, however, the system that developed went much farther, bestowing upon the members of the Académie the power to make or break an artist's career. Essentially, the Académie rewarded those artists who followed its lead and censored (primarily through Salon rejection) those who did not.

The Académie even determined, for the most part, how the craft of painting was taught. Many members served on the faculty of the government-sponsored École des Beaux-Arts, which was the most important art school in France because so many Académie members served on its faculty. The training at the École, which had rigorous entrance exams, was highly formalized and oriented toward studio painting. First, students drew from printed sources; then, from plaster casts of antique sculptures; and finally, when judged sufficiently proficient, from live nude models.

Above all, the École emphasized the importance of line, as seen in Alexandre Cabanel's 1863 painting *The Birth of Venus*. (In painting, *line* refers to the distinct edges that define a particular shape.) Mastery of the human form, in particular, was considered the most important measure of artistry, but nearly as important was the technical virtuosity demonstrated by invisible brushwork and a smooth finish.

Alexandre Cabanel, *Birth of Venus* (1863)

Until the late nineteenth century, *art in France was dominated by the Académie, which decided how painting would be taught and whose works would be exhibited.*

I. WHAT MAKES US HUMAN?

STUDYING THE HUMAN SPECIES poses unique problems, because the researchers are also the subjects of the research. As a result, human attempts at self-examination have historically been lacking in objectivity. For example, the ancient Greek philosopher Aristotle believed that all life was organized in a fixed hierarchical order. Not surprisingly, Aristotle placed humans at the top of this order. Even so, in spite of its difficulties, the quest for human self-appraisal—the search to understand who we are and where we came from—is indeed a worthwhile pursuit.

What makes us human and other primates not? Very little, actually. Judging by the genetic code found in our DNA, humans and chimpanzees (our closest living relatives) are more than 98 percent identical. Nevertheless, it's not difficult to tell the two species apart, suggesting the existence of some physical traits that are definitively human. For example, we humans have very large brains for our body size, a trait that has been linked to our high intelligence relative to human ancestors and other primates. Also, humans stand and walk on two legs, a behavior known as bipedalism. Chimpanzees, on the other hand, typically perform a specialized form of quadrupedal movement known as knuckle-walking.

Taking a different approach, some theorists have argued that humanity is best defined by the extraordinary cognitive skills we possess, such as our ability to make and use tools and the facility with symbolic representation that has made art, music, and language possible. However, these high-level cognitive skills may not be as uniquely human as they appear.

The skull of *Paranthropus boisei*, an early human ancestor.

Chimpanzees, for example, have been known to manufacture and use simple tools. Researchers have seen them using rocks to crack open nuts and using leaves as sponges to drink from shallow pools of water. Studies involving the teaching of American Sign Language to apes in captivity have also suggested, somewhat controversially, that nonhuman primates can learn a symbolic language.

Aristotle's interpretation notwithstanding, humans clearly belong to a large biological spectrum, the nature of which makes it difficult for researchers to separate out particular species. Yet the difficulties involved don't stop them from trying. Many professionals—especially paleoanthropologists, geneticists, and archaeologists—have dedicated their careers to finding an answer to the question *What makes us human?* Most begin their search by looking back into our evolutionary past.

Humans belong to a biological continuum, *making it difficult to isolate one species from another, yet researchers continue to search for traits that define us as human.*

I. DEFINING THE HOLOCAUST

THE TERM *Holocaust* refers to the mid-twentieth-century attempt by Nazi Germany to round up and eliminate the Jews of Europe. (Some people also include in their definition of the Holocaust the Nazis' efforts to rid Europe of other groups, including the physically and mentally handicapped, Gypsies, homosexuals, and Jehovah's Witnesses.) During World War II (1939–45), the word *holocaust* was used at times to describe the suspected fate of Europe's Jews, but it didn't become widely used as a proper noun until the late 1970s, when a television documentary titled *Holocaust* fixed the name in people's minds.

Among Jews, the Hebrew term *Shoah* (meaning "upheaval") and the Yiddish term *Khurbn* (meaning "catastrophe") are also used. The Nazis themselves called the Holocaust the Final Solution, because they thought this euphemism would hide their true intentions.

Although the Holocaust remains the most significant effort ever made by a national entity to destroy an entire people, its scope wasn't immediately apparent. During World War II, those few people who tried to call attention to what was happening were typically ignored or dismissed because the crime seemed so unbelievable and the world's attention was focused on the battlefield. After the war, however, as the evidence of what had taken place emerged, people finally

A 1942 roundup of Polish Jews.

began to understand the enormity of the crime. The exact number of Jews killed by the Nazis can never be known, in part because of the cloak of secrecy under which the Nazis operated and in part because of the chaos that reigned during the final frantic months of the war; but most historians agree that the best estimate is approximately six million.

The incredible scale of the Final Solution challenged the Nazis' ability to carry it out. New techniques had to be developed if millions of people were to be identified, gathered together, and exterminated. The innovative methods that the Nazis developed included propaganda campaigns to turn local populations against their Jewish neighbors; the establishment of walled-off urban ghettos, in which Jewish populations were concentrated; and the construction of death camps, in which Jewish prisoners were put to death as efficiently as possible. The Nazis believed that by murdering Jews (and other people deemed "undesirable"), they could cleanse the European gene pool and create a master race that would rule Europe and perhaps the world for the next thousand years.

During the Holocaust, *the Nazi government in Germany murdered six million Jews in an effort to cleanse the European gene pool of "undesirable" elements.*

II. SOME FUNDAMENTAL PHYSICAL CONCEPTS

BECAUSE MANY TERMS in rocketry have much looser meanings in everyday life, a few technical definitions are in order. In physics, for example, *force* refers to an energy brought to bear on an object. This energy can be either a "push" (repulsion) or a "pull" (attraction). If not opposed by an equal and opposite force, it will cause acceleration, which is a change in the velocity (speed) of an object. In order to hold a baseball still in your palm, your palm must exert a force on the baseball equal and opposite to the force of gravity. If you remove your palm, then the unopposed force of gravity will cause the baseball to accelerate to the ground.

Thrust in physics refers to the force caused by a mechanical reaction. *Mechanical* in this sense means that the force is created by physical contact. *Reaction* means that the force causing movement in one direction is created by the expulsion of a reaction mass in the opposite direction. A rocket sitting on its launchpad is stationary because the force of gravity pulling it down is opposed by the force of the ground pushing it up. That rocket will remain stationary until another force is applied. When its engines ignite, the burning of its fuel will cause gaseous exhaust to be expelled. This is the reaction mass that creates the thrust that accelerates the rocket off the launchpad (as long as the force of the thrust exceeds the force of gravity).

In scientific terminology, *mass* describes the amount of matter in a given object. In other words, it measures the atomic particles themselves. *Weight*, on the other hand, is the force that gravity exerts on a particular mass. On the Moon, your mass would be the same as it is on Earth, but your weight would be less because the Moon's gravitational pull is less.

Momentum, defined as an object's mass multiplied by its velocity, can be either linear (if the object is moving in a straight line) or angular (if the object is spinning). Momentum measures how difficult it is to start or stop a moving object. One of the most powerful laws in all of physics is the conservation of momentum, which states that momentum in a closed system can neither be created nor destroyed. Therefore, when a rocket's engines ignite and begin to expel reaction mass, conservation of momentum requires that the rest of the rocket be subject to an equal force in the opposite direction.

Rockets lift off *the ground when their engines expel enough reaction mass to create sufficient thrust to overcome the attractive force of gravity.*

II. THE HEGELIAN DIALECTIC

THE PHILOSOPHY OF HISTORY developed by G. W. F. Hegel (1770–1831) is best known for the powerful new concept it introduced: the dialectic. This idea, which Marx adopted and then modified to suit his own purposes, is among the more

G. W. F. Hegel

difficult concepts in philosophy. However, like most great ideas, it's also fundamentally simple. Consider this old joke about Block Island, a Rhode Island vacation resort famous for its strong and constant sea breezes. The joke went something like this: "Did you hear the wind stopped blowing on Block Island and all the houses fell down?"

This joke points out what Hegel had recognized and incorporated into his theory of the dialectic: A lot can be learned by analyzing the oppositions embedded in a thing and

how those oppositions ultimately break it apart. In Hegel's view, things are never fully understood until they are "negated." Furthermore, once this negation takes place—that is, once the antithesis inherent in the thesis is exposed—an opportunity for the development of a new and better understanding arises. This is the synthesis— or the rebuilding the houses, if you will. The synthesis then becomes the new thesis, itself subject to negation, and the cycle continues. (Although thesis–antithesis– synthesis is a handy way of thinking about the dialectical process, Hegel himself moved beyond the three-part concept because he found it too mechanical.)

Hegel wrote most of his philosophy during the late Enlightenment, when scientific thought was in ascendance. Like many philosophers of the period, he was particularly interested in relating these new scientific views to previous ways of thinking, especially as they related to religion. European politics was changing, too, and Hegel, a Prussian, watched the French Revolution and the rise of Napoleon closely. In fact, it has been suggested that Hegel developed his dialectical method as a way to explain the events he was witnessing, specifically the shifts from religion toward science and monarchy toward democracy.

Hegel defined human history as a succession of social schemes, each reflecting a new stage in the working out of God's plan for humanity. With each of these stages came new growth in human understanding made possible by the negation of the previous stage. Hegel used the term *geist* (meaning "spirit") to describe this understanding. Eventually, Hegel believed, the *geist* would reach completeness, at which point God's purpose in creating humanity would be fulfilled.

Hegel believed *that ideas can't be fully understood until they are negated. His notion of the dialectic explains how negated ideas become the basis for new understanding.*

II. THE RISE OF LANDSCAPE PAINTING

BEFORE THE 1830S, most French artists, following the dictates of the Académie, disregarded landscape painting. They didn't paint much scenery, and when they did, it was usually as idealized backdrops for history paintings, not actual views. By the 1820s, however, with the rise of romanticism, landscape became more acceptable as a subject. At the Salon of 1824, several landscapes exhibited by English artists John Constable and J. M. W. Turner caused quite a stir with their natural light effects and use of color. These paintings inspired a group of French artists to focus on landscapes as their primary subject matter. Because most of these young painters had trained privately (that is, outside the École des Beaux-Arts), the Académie insistence on formal composition had little hold on them, and they felt free to experiment, as Constable had, with the poetic effects of natural light and atmosphere.

Théodore Rousseau, *The Forest in Winter at Sunset* (1845–67)

The most influential of these artists was Jean-Baptiste-Camille Corot (1796–1875). Other notable members of the group included Narcisse Diaz de la Peña, Jules Dupré, Constant Troyon, Charles-François Daubigny, and Théodore Rousseau. Because they preferred to paint rugged, unspoiled countryside, they began making annual trips to the forest of Fontainebleau, forty miles southeast of Paris. During these trips, most of the group lodged in Barbizon, a village on the edge of the forest, and by the 1840s, many were living there full time, further distancing themselves from the Parisian art establishment.

Rather than creating formally arranged panoramic scenes, the Barbizon painters sought to capture smaller slices of nature. Although the availability of paint in metal tubes after 1841 allowed them to work en plein air (that is, outdoors), they typically revised and repainted these canvases in their studios before considering them finished works. Overall, the work of the Barbizon School was realistic rather than allegorical, showing actual nature as opposed to imagined natural scenes. Yet the artist's emotional response to nature was also highly valued. According to the Barbizon aesthetic, an artist needed to interpret a scene emotionally, not simply paint it as it was.

Their removal from Paris notwithstanding, the Barbizon artists were not the complete outsiders they sometimes seemed to be. They continued to submit their work to the Paris Salon, and by the 1850s, Barbizon landscapes pervaded these annual exhibitions. With Académie acceptance came critical acclaim and also the recognition by a new generation of artists that landscapes might indeed be a fit subject for painting.

During the 1830s and 1840s, *the painters of the Barbizon School stepped outside the French mainstream to focus on landscape paintings and the effects of natural light.*

II. METHODS FOR STUDYING HUMAN ORIGINS

THE SPECIES TO WHICH HUMANS BELONG, *Homo sapiens*, is believed to have emerged between 100,000 and 200,000 years ago. Because this time period predates all written records, researchers have had to rely on other sources of information to unlock the secrets of our evolutionary past. The most useful have been fossil remains, the archaeological record, and genetic analysis.

Fossils are the preserved remains of once living organisms, and they provide the best direct evidence of evolution. They can take a range of forms, because fossilization is an ongoing process. Some recent fossils, especially bones, may contain organic matter that was once part of a living organism. As time passes, however, minerals in the soil (such as calcium phosphate) replace the organic content of fossils, preserving their shape but not their genetic information.

Paleoanthropologists specialize in tracing human evolution through the fossil record. From close observation of fossilized remains, they infer as much as possible about our ancestors' anatomy, ecology, diet, means of locomotion, and social behavior. In addition, paleoanthropologists work with geologists to estimate the age of remains using a variety of techniques.

Archaeology, a subfield of anthropology, focuses on the material culture that past human and prehuman populations have left behind. About 2.6 Ma (million years ago), stone tools began appearing in East Africa—a development that marks the beginning of the archaeological record. Using these tools and later artifacts, archaeologists have been able to infer a great deal about the cognitive capabilities and behavioral patterns of the people who made them.

Geneticists, meanwhile, have been making their own inferences about human origins based on modern DNA research. In 1967, for example, Vincent Sarich and Allan Wilson developed a way to use current genetic data to determine the approximate date when two different groups of organisms last shared a common ancestor. Their work was based on an idea called the molecular clock, which held that genetic differences accumulate at a known rate over time. Using Sarich and Wilson's technique, geneticists have been able to determine that humans and chimpanzees share an approximately 6-million-year-old common ancestor.

However, before we can understand the ways in which these different methods provide clues to human origins, we must first establish a theoretical framework in which to place these clues. Without such a framework, the fossil, archaeological, and genetic evidence that has been developed would be meaningless—simply facts in search of an explanation.

Different types of researchers *rely on different methods to reconstruct our evolutionary past—including the examination of fossils, material culture, and modern genetic data.*

II. A BRIEF HISTORY OF ANTI-SEMITISM IN EUROPE

IN DEVELOPING AND CARRYING OUT the Final Solution, the Nazis drew on a long tradition of anti-Jewish hatred in Europe based primarily on the idea that Jews had been responsible for the death of Jesus Christ. The guilt for this crime, it was believed, extended down through the generations. During the Middle Ages and the early modern era, Jews in Europe were routinely accused of conspiring with the devil, working to undermine Christianity, and even murdering Christian children for use in diabolical religious ceremonies. Periodically, European Jews were forced to convert to Christianity during brutal attacks known as pogroms (originally a Russian term), and discriminatory laws were commonplace. Some countries, such as England in 1290 and Spain in 1492, expelled their Jewish populations entirely.

During the eighteenth century, however, with the rise of the Enlightenment, religious tensions in Europe eased, and a new spirit of tolerance took hold. Influential philosophers such as Voltaire and Jean-Jacques Rousseau argued that societies needed to accommodate religious differences because there were no greater crimes than those committed in the name of God. As a result, Jews began receiving much more favorable treatment in European host countries, and they were slowly accepted as citizens.

By the late nineteenth century, most Jews in western and central Europe enjoyed equal treatment under the law, and many had integrated themselves into their host societies—attending universities, joining professions, and beginning to see themselves as citizens of the nations in which they lived. At the same time, however, the severe political, economic, and cultural changes accompanying industrialization provoked new suspicions. The national allegiance of Jews was often called into question, and new ideas about race led some to conclude that Jews were inherently foreign and thus a biological threat. In 1879, one such eugenicist, Wilhelm Marr, founded the first German organization devoted specifically to meeting this alleged threat. Marr called his group the Anti-Semitic League, and the word *anti-Semitism* soon became a new name for anti-Jewish hatred.

At the turn of the twentieth century, two arrests took place that seemed to reinforce doubts about Jewish loyalty. The first involved Capt. Alfred Dreyfus, a French officer of Jewish descent accused of passing military secrets to the Germans. The second involved a Russian Jew named Menahem Mendel Beilis, who was charged with ritually murdering a Christian boy. Although both men were shown to be innocent, their trials polarized Europe and returned the Jewish Question to the fore.

Alfred Dreyfus with his family.

Although the Enlightenment *eased anti-Jewish hatred, new doubts about Jewish loyalty emerged during the late nineteenth century as industrialization stirred up Europe.*

III. NEWTONIAN MOTION

WITHOUT THE PHYSICAL LAWS discovered and defined by Isaac Newton (1643–1727), there could be no rocket science. While an undergraduate at Cambridge University from 1661 to 1665, Newton studied the works of modern mathematical philosophers and astronomers such as Descartes, Galileo, Copernicus, and Kepler. Between 1665 and 1667, while the university was closed due to the Great Plague sweeping the country, he lived at his mother's home to Woolsthorpe, where he worked on several of his own ideas concerning gravitation, motion, and what would become differential calculus. When Newton returned to Cambridge in 1667, however, he set aside these pursuits and became involved in other research projects.

Two decades later, in 1684, Edmond Halley, Christopher Wren, and Robert Hooke had a conversation at the Royal Society (England's national science academy) about planetary motion. Hooke claimed to have proven that the orbits of planets had to be elliptical, but Wren disbelieved him, offering Hooke forty shillings for a proof produced within two weeks. Hooke never collected the money, but Halley remained interested in the problem and mentioned it during a subsequent visit with Newton, now the Lucasian Professor of Mathematics at Cambridge. Newton replied that he had worked out the proof years before but would have to look for the papers. Resurrecting his work from the plague years, Newton recreated the proof and sent it to Halley, who urged him to publish the manuscript and even paid the attendant costs. Three years later, Newton's classic *Philosophiæ Naturalis Principia Mathematica* appeared, including the orbital proof as well as Newton's theory of universal gravitation and his three laws of motion.

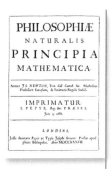

Newton's *Principia*

Newton's first law of motion concerned inertia, which is the tendency of a mass to continue moving at a constant speed (including a speed of zero) until acted upon by a force. It states that zero net force yields zero net acceleration. Newton's second law stated that, for any given object, the force applied and the resulting acceleration are proportional. This law was expressed in Newton's famous equation $F = ma$, where F is force, m is mass, and a is acceleration. (It may be helpful to think of acceleration in this sense as the change in momentum caused by the force.) Newton's third law, also known as the law of reciprocal actions, stated that for every action, there is an equal and opposite reaction. It is from this third law that the conservation of momentum is derived.

Newton's three laws of motion, *especially his third law of reciprocal actions, provide the scientific basis for all rocket science.*

III. THE YOUNG HEGELIANS

THE YOUNG HEGELIANS were philosophers influenced by the work of Hegel but born a generation later. The most famous Young Hegelians were Bruno Bauer, Ludwig Feuerbach, and Marx himself. Bauer (1809–82) and Feuerbach (1804–72) accepted the logic of Hegel's dialectic but rejected his notion that the endpoint of history (the fulfillment of the *geist*) was already present, if not fully understood, in Christian doctrine. In Bauer and Feuerbach's view, Christian doctrine was not a universal truth but the embodiment of the limited understanding of a particular historical age.

According to Bauer, Christian principles mirrored ideas commonly held by non-Christian thinkers of the first century, such as Seneca the Stoic. Viewed in this way, Christianity became for Bauer merely the vestige of a more general consciousness, which corresponded to the state of human understanding at that time. Feuerbach, on the other hand, conceived of the problem somewhat differently. He thought that Christianity represented a projection of human characteristics onto an abstract entity and that, in giving up those characteristics to God, Christian believers deceived themselves and were consequently diminished. In clinging to such outdated ideas as Christianity, Feuerbach argued, humans were losing the opportunity to learn from Christianity's negation—that is, to learn how religion had taken elements of their self-understanding and attributed them to a distant, mystical godhead. Feuerbach used the term *alienation* to describe this process of taking aspects of oneself and placing them outside and above the individual.

The work of Bauer and Feuerbach transformed Christian doctrine from the endpoint it had been in Hegel's scheme into merely an intermediate stage in the ongoing development of human understanding. Like all other intermediate stages, Christianity was therefore destined, by Hegel's own logic, to be negated and overcome. Although this perspective appealed strongly to many young socialists, it also earned the Young Hegelians the reputation of being anti-Christian and antisocial (in the sense of threatening the established social order).

In his own work, Marx built on the advances made by Bauer and Feuerbach, but he rejected their thinking (inherited from Hegel) about how new ideas were formed. Marx argued that new ideas arose not from old ideas but from the ways in which people organize themselves to satisfy their material needs. In other words, rather than seeing forms of social organization as reflections of current ideas, Marx saw current ideas as reflections of forms of social organization. In this way, Marx said, he "turned Hegel on his head."

The Young Hegelians *separated Hegel's dialectic from its original Christian context, arguing that all ideas reflect the historical moments in which they appear.*

III. THE SEEDS OF ARTISTIC REVOLUTION

GUSTAVE COURBET (1819–77) grew up in the French countryside amid bourgeois farmers and vintners. He wanted to be an artist, however, and so moved in 1839 to Paris, where he honed his skills copying the works of Old Masters at the Louvre. Courbet also painted at the Académie Suisse—not a school per se, but a studio where young artists could pay a fee to draw and paint live models.

Courbet's artistic awakening came in 1848, when a severe economic crisis in France led to widespread political unrest. In February 1848, King Louis-Philippe was forced to abdicate, and the Second Republic was declared. The radical leadership of the new provisional government established universal male suffrage, abolished slavery, and created National Workshops to provide state jobs for the legions of unemployed. In April 1848, however, voters elected a new, more moderate government, which closed the National Workshops because of their high cost. This action sparked the June Days Uprising in Paris, which was harshly suppressed.

Caught up himself in the politics of the revolt, Courbet came to believe that art should have social import, and he began painting scenes of contemporary bourgeois life—which was a revolution in itself. In *The Burial at Ornans* (1849–50), for instance, Courbet depicted a bourgeois funeral in his rural hometown. The extremely large scale of this canvas, usually reserved for grand works of history, aggrandized the event and ennobled its everyday participants. Meanwhile, Courbet employed a new style of painting that pointedly emphasized coarse brushwork over the fine line and smooth finish required by the Académie. Some Académie members dismissed Courbet's new paintings as "unfinished" because of their rough appearance, but many young artists paid this criticism no mind. They knew that Courbet was striving to paint the world as he saw it, and they wanted to do the same thing.

Gustave Courbet, *The Burial at Ornans* (1849–50)

Courbet's rebellion peaked in 1855, when three of his canvases were rejected for the French exhibit at the 1855 Exposition Universelle on the grounds that they were vulgar and unfinished. Insulted but undeterred, Courbet financed his own Pavilion of Realism at the exposition, displaying forty of his paintings and distributing a manifesto that explained his social realism as "living art." Although a financial failure, Courbet's pavilion made the important point that paintings rejected by the Académie could still reach a large audience.

Gustave Courbet's choice *of subject matter and combative independence posed serious challenges to the authority of the Académie during the 1850s.*

III. THE THEORY OF EVOLUTION

EVOLUTION REFERS TO the genetic transformation of populations over time. In this sense, a *population* is a group of living things that mate randomly with one another. A *species* is a group of populations whose members can interbreed. If two populations of the same species are separated, they can grow genetically apart and lose their ability to produce fertile offspring together. At this point, they become different species.

Before the development of evolutionary theory, the prevailing view in Europe, based on religious doctrine, was that species were unchanging. Beginning with the Renaissance, however, scientists began to observe nature from a less biased point of view. Gradually, they collected evidence proving that species indeed changed over time. Among the most important early theorists of evolution were French naturalists Georges-Louis Leclerc, comte de Buffon (1707–88), and Jean-Baptiste Lamarck (1744-1829).

Charles Darwin in 1855.

It was Charles Darwin (1809–82), however, who developed the theory of evolution by natural selection that is still supported today. While conducting field research, Darwin had noticed that traits sometimes varied among the members of a population. Contemplating this observation, he realized that some of the variations must be more useful for survival than others. That is, individuals with a favorable variation (based on the environment the population inhabits) would be more likely to reproduce and pass on the trait to offspring, thereby increasing its prevalence in the population. For example, a recent long-term study of Galapagos finches showed that their average beak size increased significantly over several generations of drought. The reason was that finches with large beaks are better adapted to breaking open large seeds, which are the only food source available to them during long periods of drought. Finches possessing this variation were thus more likely to survive and more likely to pass on the variation to the next generation.

The next major development in evolutionary thought occurred at the turn of the twentieth century, when the work of Austrian monk Gregor Mendel (1822–84) was rediscovered. Experimenting with pea plants, Mendel had developed a set of laws explaining how traits were passed on from one generation to the next. Mendel's work on heredity strengthened Darwin's theory, which hadn't included a specific mechanism for trait inheritance. Building on Mendel's work, later evolutionary theorists identified the gene as the basic unit of heredity, and this discovery led to the modern definition of evolution as change in the genetic composition of a population over time.

Charles Darwin is considered *the founder of modern evolutionary theory, but his theory was built on the work of earlier scholars and has been improved upon since.*

III. JEWISH LIFE ON THE EVE OF DESTRUCTION

WHO WERE THE JEWS OF EUROPE when the Nazis came to power? Although viewed as a monolith by contemporary anti-Semites, the Jews of Europe were actually quite diverse. They lived in every country and numbered about 9.5 million people. Germany had about five hundred thousand Jewish citizens, amounting to less than 1 percent of the total population, while Poland had the highest concentration. Its 3.3 million Jews represented about 10 percent of the total population.

For the most part, European Jews were highly urbanized, with more than 75 percent living in cities and towns; but the degree to which they integrated themselves into the social fabric of the countries in which they lived varied widely.

Some Jews became highly acculturated, considering themselves proud patriots first and Jews second. These people generally spoke and wrote in the language of their host country, served in its military, and ceased to follow religious customs and practices. They became prominent lawyers, doctors, professors, and authors. Some—including Léon Blum, who served as prime minister of France twice during the late 1930s—rose to the very pinnacle of European society.

Other Jews were much less integrated. Continuing to practice the religious ways of their ancestors, these Jews tended to speak in the Yiddish and Hebrew languages (which were foreign to most non-Jews), and they lived according to strict traditional laws in relatively closed communities. Their contact with non-Jews was limited, and they considered the modern secular world a threat to their way of life. Because they were easily identifiable as Jews, given their distinctive style of dress and speech, they often bore the brunt of anti-Semitic discrimination and hatred, which they saw as a test of their faith.

Still other Jews, uninterested in the religious ways of their ancestors yet unwilling to give up their unique Jewish national identity, took part in widespread secular movements designed to bring about a Jewish renaissance. Most of these people sought to eliminate the stain of exile from the Holy Land by either cultural or political means. For some, this meant a return to Hebrew as a spoken language; for others, such as the Zionists, it meant a return to political sovereignty in Israel. All of these movements, however, shared the fundamental belief that Jewish life was stunted by powerlessness and that Jews needed to return to a time when they could determine the course of their own development.

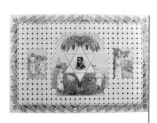

A pro-Zionist print from 1925.

Some Jews lived in Europe as patriots, *deeply invested in their host countries; others, in religious communities; and still others joined secular movements for a Jewish rebirth.*

IV. ORBITAL MOTION

CONSIDER TWO ASTRONAUTS standing on an airless moon. Each drops a baseball from the same height at the same time. Both balls hit the ground simultaneously, which should be no surprise. Next, they repeat the experiment, except that now one of the astronauts throws the ball forward, parallel to the ground. Again, both baseballs hit the ground simultaneously. This is because the only downward force acting on them is gravity, which causes both of them to accelerate downward at the same rate.

If the astronaut tossing the baseball forward throws it harder, it will land a little while after the ball that is merely dropped. Careful measurement will show that it also falls farther because of the moon's curvature. That is, as the moon's surface curves away, the thrown ball has a greater distance to fall before hitting it.

Finally, our astronauts decide to throw their balls forward very fast. At a certain speed of release, they notice that the thrown baseballs fall at the same rate that the moon's surface curves away. This is called the moon's orbital velocity, and balls thrown at this speed will enter a circular orbit. If the balls are thrown a little faster, they'll remain in orbit but climb a little higher on the far side of the moon, creating an elliptical orbit. If the balls are thrown faster still, they'll eventually reach the moon's escape velocity and leave its orbit entirely.

There's one problem, though, and it has to do with Newton's second law ($F = ma$), which states that an unopposed force on an object should cause it to accelerate indefinitely. If this is so, then why don't the orbiting baseballs continue to accelerate until they reach escape velocity?

The answer has to do with vectors. A vector is a quantity that describes both magnitude and direction. For example, if you describe a car as moving at forty miles per hour, you are noting merely the magnitude of its velocity. But if you describe that same car as moving *north* at forty miles per hour, you are giving its velocity vector.

In relation to $F = ma$, both force and acceleration are vector quantities, with acceleration defined as a change in velocity (also a vector quantity). Therefore, as the baseballs orbit the moon, their velocities indeed vary in accordance with Newton's second law—changing not in magnitude, but in direction.

Orbital velocity is the speed required *for a launched object to attain orbit of an astronomical body. Escape velocity is the speed required to escape that body's gravitational pull.*

IV. HISTORICAL MATERIALISM

DURING THE EARLY 1840S, when Marx was still in his early twenties, he developed a philosophy of history that later became known as historical materialism. This theory was based on the concept, adopted from Bauer and Feuerbach, that ideas reflect the historical moment in which they are produced.

Many different philosophies have been labeled *materialist*. With regard to Marx, however, the term invokes the philosophical tradition begun by the Scottish political economists of the eighteenth century, notably David Hume (1711–76). Hume was among the first modern philosophers to seek explanations for things in the observable physical (material) world rather than in divine forces or reason alone. For Hume, this empirical approach meant that information derived from the senses was a privileged form of knowledge. Human understanding (or reason) was secondary, Hume believed, and played but a small role in the shaping of human history.

In Marx's view, the key to unraveling human history lay in recognizing the relationship between human understanding and the material state of the world. In order for human beings to survive, Marx explained, they organize themselves collectively to wrest food and shelter from the natural world. Of course, the ways in which they organize themselves change over time. According to Marx, each new way defines a new historical era and, more importantly, conditions the manner in which people of in that era think about themselves and the world around them.

Marx's historical materialism thus combined the Young Hegelian principle that ideas reflect historical contexts with Hume's preference for material-based knowledge over pure thought. At its root, historical materialism is the idea that the way in which humans collectively produce the means for their day-to-day survival determines how they think and the social institutions they create.

As Marx pointed out, however, every past system of production has generated material conditions that eventually rendered it obsolete (or negated). In a limited sense, this is true today of global warming, which has revealed one of the contradictions inherent in our own system of production: The industry that benefits us also harms us. Overcoming such negations requires the creation of new forms of social organization. Most of the time, this process takes place gradually; but sometimes, when the fundamental organization of society is at stake, the shift comes suddenly and dramatically. Marx called these transitions from one historical stage to the next "revolutions."

According to historical materialism, *new systems of production don't arise from improved human understanding. Rather, they create the new understanding.*

IV. THE PAINTER OF MODERN LIFE

BORN INTO THE Parisian *haute bourgeoisie*, Édouard Manet (1832–83) entered the studio of Thomas Couture in 1850. Couture was an academician who specialized in historical painting, and during the six years that Manet studied with him, this genre experienced something of a resurgence. Critics began writing about art and history, and the Old Masters became popular again through a series of new exhibitions.

Manet became particularly interested in the writings of Charles Baudelaire, who penned a series of articles for *Le Figaro* collectively titled "The Painter of Modern Life." In these essays, Baudelaire urged artists to become detached observers of modern life. He argued that if art was to be relevant, it would have to take on modern subject matter and come to terms with the constant flux and change that defined modern city life. In Baudelaire's view, modern art should be contingent, fleeting, and sketchy, mirroring the conditions of the urban environment. Manet was convinced but not quite ready to jettison all tradition, so he tried to integrate the two perspectives.

Édouard Manet, *Le Déjeuner sur l'herbe (Luncheon on the Grass)* (1863)

With his 1863 canvas *Luncheon on the Grass*, Manet showed how he could be both new and old at the same time. An educated Parisian would have quickly recognized that the painting borrowed its central composition from Raphael and Raimondi's *Water Nymph and the River God*, a standard Renaissance source, so this was something old. The new elements included not only the contemporary urban setting but also the faces in the painting, which were *recognizable*—that is, they belonged to well-known modern Parisians, whom the typical Salon-goer could be expected to recognize. In combining these elements, Manet also blurred the lines between academic genres.

Manet's juxtaposition of modernity with tradition—not to mention his juxtaposition of a nude woman with clothed men in a contemporary setting— showed his willingness to challenge the rigidity of the academic establishment, and it attracted to his studio a number of talented young artists, some of whom would later become associated with impressionism. These young artists also appreciated Manet's unwillingness to build readable narratives into his paintings. Before the age of abstraction in art, viewers were trained to "read" symbols and other clues in paintings to reveal their historical or moral meanings. For Manet, however, a painting was simply a painting—no underlying allegory, just paint on canvas.

Édouard Manet *responded to Charles Baudelaire's call for a new, more modern style of painting by blurring the lines between the existing academic genres.*

IV. OUR CLOSEST RELATIVES

THE SYSTEM THAT biologists use to classify organisms is named for Carolus Linnaeus (1707–78), a Swedish naturalist who devoted his life to classifying living things. According to the Linnaean system, humans are members of the kingdom Animalia, the phylum Chordata (vertebrates), the class Mammalia, and the order Primates.

Like all mammals, primates are homeothermic (warm-blooded), and primate females possess mammary glands, which they use to feed their newborns. However, primates are placental mammals, which means that their fetuses develop fully within their mother's body, nourished by food and oxygen provided by the mother's placenta. (Marsupials, on the other hand, are nonplacental mammals that give birth to partially developed fetuses, which finish their development within their mother's pouch.)

Compared with other mammals, primates also show an increased dependence on vision and a decreased reliance on smell. Their cerebral cortex (the part of the brain associated with learning and intelligence) is larger and more complex, and their hands and feet (which have nails rather than claws) can grasp, enabling primates to manipulate objects and move around in trees. In addition, primates tend to reach maturity more slowly than other mammals, allowing time for complex social behaviors to be learned. Learning these behaviors is important, because primates tend to live in large groups with complicated rules governing relationships.

Species within the primate order are divided into two suborders: moist-nosed strepsirhines and dry-nosed haplorhines. The more primitive strepsirhines, which include lemurs and lorises, tend to be small, solitary, and nocturnal. The haplorhines include both tarsiers and the anthropoids (monkeys, apes, and humans). However, in an argument typical of Linnaean controversies, some researchers want to group the tarsiers with lemurs and lorises based on certain shared primitive characteristics, while others defend the current classification because tarsiers share a number of cranial and dental features with anthropoids.

Anthropoids include Old World monkeys, New World monkeys, and hominoids (apes and humans). Among the hominoids are the lesser apes (gibbons and siamangs), the great apes (orangutans, gorillas, chimpanzees, and bonobos), and humans. Together, the great apes and humans make up the family Hominidae.

Genetic analysis shows that humans are most closely related to the African apes, especially chimpanzees and bonobos. For this reason, researchers sometimes study the behavior of living African apes in order to infer how early human ancestors may have behaved. Such work supplements but can't replace the fossil record, which remains the only direct evidence of our evolutionary past.

The human species *belongs to the order Primates, which differs from other mammalian orders in its larger cerebral cortex and long period of maturation.*

IV. WORLD WAR I AND THE COLLAPSE OF GERMANY

WITH THE OUTBREAK OF WORLD WAR I IN 1914, jubilant crowds of men in many European countries hurried to enlist in what promised to be a short, triumphant campaign. It soon became apparent, however, that victory for neither side was imminent and that the fighting would be more terrible than anyone could have imagined. Nowhere was the despair felt more keenly than in Germany—where, by 1916, the citizenry wanted to know why their mighty country was faring so poorly.

German soldiers during World War I.

Although there was a simple explanation—that the Central Powers were not as strong as they perceived themselves to be—the German general staff began suggesting that the reason for their failures might be Jewish soldiers shirking their duty and harming the war effort from within. The generals even ordered a census to determine whether German Jews were fulfilling their military obligations. The results, covered up until after the war, showed that the number of Jews serving in the German military was proportionally much higher than their presence in the overall population. Nevertheless, it became a widely accepted myth that German Jews had stabbed the country in the back and bore the responsibility for its defeat.

The harsh 1919 Treaty of Versailles did little to restore calm and order. To the contrary, the reparations payments it imposed threatened the German economy, and its "war guilt" clause, placing the blame for the conflict fully on the German people, humiliated them, contributing to a highly unstable postwar situation.

Because Germany's new parliamentary government convened initially in the city of Weimar (Berlin being too conflict-ridden), the period of Germany history from the end of the Great War to the Nazi seizure of power in 1933 is known as the Weimar Republic. From the outset, however, Weimar Germany was paralyzed by political extremism, with left-wing Red Guards and right-wing Freikorps fighting each other in the streets. Over the next fourteen years, there were terrible periods of political violence and hyperinflation; and yet the country also enjoyed a remarkably rich cultural life, with Berlin becoming home to many new artistic, intellectual, and sexual movements. Strongly attracted by what was happening in Berlin, Jews from all over Europe migrated there, and the city quickly became a center of Jewish cultural activity. Meanwhile, the success of many prominent German Jewish businessmen and politicians became fodder for a growing ultranationalist movement that sought to restore Germany's imperial pride.

The myth that disloyalty *among Jewish soldiers had caused Germany's defeat in World War I was picked up by ultranationalist groups angered by Weimar Germany's woes.*

V. **WHAT IS A ROCKET?**

AS DEFINED EARLIER, the reaction mass of a rocket is the matter that's ejected out the back end in order to make the rest of the rocket move forward. This technology works because of the conservation of momentum. The expulsion of the reaction mass creates a downward momentum (the mass of the exhaust multiplied by its velocity). If momentum is to be conserved, the rocket must move upward with a momentum equal to that of the expelled gases.

Here's another way of thinking about reaction mass: Imagine a hunter strapped to a sled in the middle of a frozen lake. The surface of the lake is so

The space shuttle is rolled out to its launchpad.

smooth that the hunter can't stand without slipping and falling. How can he reach the shore? He merely has to fire his rifle away from the shore. As the bullet leaves the rifle at a high rate of speed, it creates a kick that travels through the hunter's body to the sled, pushing the sled in the opposite direction of the bullet (that is, toward the shore). In this thought experiment, which illustrates the conservation of momentum, the bullet is the reaction mass. The more bullets the hunter fires, the faster his sled will travel.

Some people believe mistakenly that all rockets are massive, complicated space-age wonders—perhaps because many of them are. The Space Transportation System (STS), for example, more commonly known as the space shuttle, is a massive vehicle that weighs approximately 4.5 million pounds when fueled. In about eight minutes, it performs an intricately choreographed ascent, shedding two solid rocket boosters, an external fuel tank, and about 95 percent of its mass to achieve a low Earth orbit. With more than a million parts, it's arguably the most complicated flying machine ever built.

Yet, according to its scientific definition, a rocket is actually quite humble. It's simply a motor that uses an internally stored reaction mass to create a high-speed exhaust jet, which in turn produces thrust. Using this definition, one can even call the hunter's rifle in the above example a rocket. Another simple form of rocket is an inflated balloon. The pressurized air inside the balloon is its reaction mass. When the stem is released, the air rushes out, creating a high-speed exhaust jet that causes the balloon to whiz around the room. Because the exhaust is room temperature, the balloon is classified as a cold-gas rocket.

A rocket is *a motor that uses an internally stored reaction mass to create a high-speed exhaust jet, which produces thrust.*

V. FRIEDRICH ENGELS AND THE WORKING CLASS

IN 1842, a year after receiving his doctorate, Marx was working for the *Rheinische Zeitung*, a leftist newspaper in Cologne, when he met Moses Hess. A well-connected socialist organizer and theorist, Hess introduced Marx to the local workers' groups that became the focus of Marx's reporting. When Prussian authorities shut down the *Rheinische Zeitung* for political reasons in 1843, Marx moved to Paris. There he began collaborating with Arnold Ruge, another expatriate Prussian socialist, on a new radical periodical.

Friedrich Engels in 1856.

In August 1844, Marx and Engels met in Paris to discuss a book that Engels was writing on the working class in England. Although Engels belonged to a family of prominent Prussian industrialists, he had taken an early interest in socialism, much to the dismay of his Christian conservative father. In order to discourage this interest, Engels's father forced his son to abandon his university studies and accept a job as an office clerk in Manchester, England, where the family shared ownership of a spinning factory. On his way to Manchester in 1842, the twenty-two-year-old Engels met Marx in Cologne, and the two began corresponding.

While working in Manchester, Engels became interested in how industrialization had transformed that once small country town. The research that he conducted eventually became the basis for his first book, *The Condition of the Working Class in England*. Engels's description of the conditions under which English textile workers labored was horrifying. More important, though, was his explanation of how that situation had come to be: The English working class (proletariat) had literally been "called into existence by the introduction of [industrial] machinery," he wrote.

From the start, Marx embraced Engels's analysis, which neatly matched his own materialist view of history. For example, Engels's opinion that the working class had arisen from the manufacturing process itself echoed Marx's thoughts about dialectical progress. Furthermore, Engels's recognition of the need for social change (and the class politics it implied) supported the socialist politics Marx had adopted from Hess and Ruge.

Engels stayed on in Paris for a short time to help Marx with the work on Ruge's journal. Shortly after the publication of its first issue, however, the journal was shut down by the French authorities, and Marx moved on to Brussels, where Engels joined him in April 1845. There, the two of them began organizing the city's large population of German expatriate workers.

Marx's early work in Paris *was aided by Engels's explanation for the rise of the working class in England: that industrialization itself had "called" the proletariat into existence.*

V. THE SALON DES REFUSÉS

TODAY, impressionism is seen primarily as a style of painting. During the early 1860s, however, when impressionism emerged, it was less a stylistic movement than a visceral reaction to the strictures imposed by the Parisian art establishment. Talented young artists such as Pierre-Auguste Renoir and Claude Monet wanted to take painting in new and progressive directions; the Académie and the Salon did not.

Claude Monet, *Women in the Garden* (1867)

Of course, artists had been complaining about the Salon system since the 1830s, and Courbet had publicly defied it in 1855 with his Pavilion of Realism; yet the Salon seemed as impregnable as ever until 1863, when Louis-Napoleon (also known as Napoleon III) decided to indulge himself. Having become emperor in 1852 (when the Second Empire supplanted the Second Republic), he had authority over both the Salon and the Académie, and he thought it might be amusing (and perhaps charitable) to hold a separate exhibition of works rejected by the Salon in 1863, so that their creators might receive a little exposure.

The paintings exhibited at this government-sponsored Salon des Refusés (Salon of the Refused) were supposed to be second-rate—after all, that was the entire point of the jury system—but such was not the case. The reason, of course, was that Salon juries didn't simply separate good craft from bad; they also rejected work that was transgressive of Académie protocols. Certainly, the Salon des Refusés contained some poor canvases, but it also included more than a few excellent, if transgressive, works such as Manet's *Luncheon on the Grass*. The presence of so many scandalous but undeniably great paintings turned what should have been a minor show into a huge popular success, which threatened the authority of the Académie.

In 1867, many of the artists who had exhibited at the first Salon des Refusés petitioned the emperor for a second. Louis-Napoleon, having learned his lesson, turned them down; but by this time, a fraternity of sorts had formed around Frédéric Bazille. Its members gathered regularly at Bazille's large studio to paint together, and many even lived there when short of cash. Eventually, in response to their continued rejection by the Salon (which threatened their ability to make a living), they organized themselves into a group known as the Société Anonyme.

During the 1860s, the artists who would later become known as impressionists began to find common ground in their shared dissatisfaction with the Salon system.

V. THE EVOLUTIONARY TIME SCALE

GEOLOGISTS HAVE DEVELOPED a time scale that covers all of earth history. Like the Linnaean system of taxonomy, the geological time scale is hierarchical: It breaks down earth history into eons, eras, periods, and epochs. The two eons are the Precambrian, which began with the formation of the earth 4.5 billion years ago, and the Phanerozoic, which began about 543 million years ago (Ma) and continues until the present day. The Phanerozoic eon is itself divided into three eras. From oldest to most recent, these are the Paleozoic, the Mesozoic, and the Cenozoic. During the Paleozoic era, the first fish, amphibians, and reptiles emerged. During the Mesozoic era, the first mammals joined them. The first primates didn't appear until the Cenozoic era, which began about 65 Ma. The oldest members of the human lineage arose much more recently, about 6 Ma.

When a paleoanthropologist discovers a new fossil or an archaeologist uncovers a new remain, the first thing he or she does is attempt to determine its age. Dating techniques fall into two categories: relative dating and absolute dating. Relative dating techniques determine whether one object is older or more recent than another object. One of the basic principles underlying relative dating is stratigraphic superimposition. This is the idea that objects found in deep rock layers are typically older that objects found in layers closer to the surface.

Absolute dating uses radiometric techniques to calculate the age of an object in years. Developed during the mid-twentieth century, radiometric dating relies on the known rates at which certain radioactive isotopes decay into more stable forms. Initially, the radioactive isotope carbon-14 was used to date organic remains. Because its half-life (the time it takes for half of a sample to decay radioactively) is relatively short, however, the usefulness of the technique was limited to objects less than 40,000 years old. A subsequent radiometric technique, based on the isotope potassium-40 (which has a much longer half-life than carbon-14), enabled scientists to date some of the oldest human-lineage fossils found in East Africa. First, using potassium-40 dating, researchers determined the absolute ages of the stratigraphic layers in the area. Then they used relative dating to establish the approximate age of each fossil based on its position relative to these stratigraphic layers.

Researchers use a combination of *relative dating (based on stratigraphic superimposition) and absolute dating (based on radiometric analysis) to determine the age of fossils and artifacts.*

V. THE MAKING OF A MASS MURDERER

BORN IN 1889 in the Austrian town of Braunau am Inn, Adolf Hitler was baptized a Catholic. His father, Alois, worked as a customs agent. His mother, Klara, was his father's third wife. Adolf himself proved to be a poor student, and twice he was forced to repeat a year in school. Although he wanted to become an artist, his father insisted that he prepare for a career in the civil service. Upon his father's death, Hitler applied to the Vienna Academy of Arts but failed the entrance exam. Nevertheless, he moved to Vienna in 1908 and spent the next five years struggling, often unsuccessfully, to make a living as an artist. Meanwhile, he fell under the influence of both the growing pan-German nationalist movement and the virulent anti-Semitism of Vienna mayor Karl Lüger, who blamed the Jews for Europe's economic ills and especially its socialist unrest.

Hitler was a part of what historian Robert Wohl has called the Generation of 1914. The rapid pace of social change that characterized the years before the Great War (largely the result of industrialization) made it difficult for younger Europeans to accept and be satisfied by the attachment to formality and imperial ritual that had sustained their parents' generation. According to Wohl, the members of the Generation of 1914 found the worldview of their parents stultifying and oppressive; they were bored with their lives and wanted something momentous and exciting to occur. While they waited, they became obsessed with ideas of heroism, sacrifice, uniqueness, vitality, and nationalism. The Great War, when it finally did come, gave meaning to their lives and presented them with the perfect opportunity to demonstrate their personal valor.

In the spring of 1913, Hitler moved to Munich, Germany, in order to avoid arrest for evasion of Austrian military service. (Before the fighting began, the Generation of 1914 considered military service ceremonial rather than valorous.) With the outbreak of war, he joined the German army and, by all accounts, served bravely. In October 1918, he was temporarily blinded in a mustard gas attack, and a month later he was convalescing when Germany surrendered. The news unsettled Hitler deeply because, like so many other Europeans, he had been indoctrinated into believing that his country was invincible. Accepting the falsity of this view was unbearable; so he, like many other German nationalists, became convinced that the only reasonable explanation for Germany's defeat was betrayal from within.

Adolf Hitler ca. 1928.

As a member of the Generation of 1914, *Adolf Hitler sought to prove his valor as German soldier during World War I. Germany's defeat, however, deeply unsettled him.*

VI. THE EARLIEST ROCKETS

THE EARLIEST ROCKET in recorded history was built by the Greek mathematician Archytas around 400 BCE. Archytas's invention, which he called the Pigeon, was a bird-shaped device propelled along a wire by a jet of steam. The operator would heat water stored inside the Pigeon's belly until the escaping steam produced enough thrust for the bird to move. The apparatus thus met all the criteria of a rocket: It used an internally stored reaction mass (the water in the Pigeon's belly) to create a high-speed exhaust jet (the steam), which in turn provided the thrust.

The first recorded use of the rocket principle in a machine that performed work dates to about 50 CE, when Hero of Alexandria built a type of steam engine known as an aeolipile. This gadget, named for the Greek god of the wind, consisted of a basin of water attached to a hollow ball mounted on a bearing. On each side of the ball was a protruding nozzle, bent in such a way that steam—generated in the basin and exiting through the nozzles—would cause the ball to spin. When attached to pulleys and gears, the aeolipile could be used to perform simple mechanical tasks, such as opening temple doors. However, because the rocket principle behind Heron's invention wouldn't be understood for another sixteen hundred years, it remained largely a curiosity.

Chinese using rockets in 1232.

The next important advance in rocket science came during the ninth century CE, when Chinese Taoist monks, searching for the elixir of immortality, discovered gunpowder. For hundreds of years, the new propellant was used mainly in fireworks; but during the early thirteenth century, as invading Mongol armies threatened China, it found its first military application. As early as 1232, Chinese soldiers were using gunpowder-fueled rockets on the battlefield, and by 1260 the use of rockets was widespread.

To the victors belong the spoils, and so it was with the Mongols. Despite the rockets deployed against them, they nevertheless conquered much of northern China and learned how to make gunpowder themselves. Later, as the Mongols moved westward into eastern and central Europe, they took the technology of gunpowder rockets with them, and before long all of Europe had learned the secret. Over time, advances in metallurgy led to the development of firearms— at which point rocketry took a backseat to cannon, muskets, and pistols, although it was never entirely abandoned.

The first rockets *were novelties whose principle of operation was little understood. With the advent of gunpowder, however, rocketry began to have military applications.*

VI. MARX AND SOCIALISM

DURING HIS YEARS IN PARIS AND BRUSSELS, Marx read the writings of, argued with, and borrowed from many other radical political intellectuals. One of the most important of these was Pierre-Joseph Proudhon, whom Marx engaged on the issue of private property, eventually publishing *The Poverty of Philosophy* (1847) in response to Proudhon's *The Philosophy of Poverty* (1846).

Like other French socialists of this period, Proudhon sought to address long-standing disparities of wealth in the French countryside, made even worse by a post-Napoleonic government seeking to lower food prices (and thus farm income) in order to encourage industrialization. Peasants were powerless to resist this trend because they didn't own the land they farmed. Instead, the land was owned by aristocratic landlords who contributed nothing to production yet benefited from the peasants' labor. Such an arrangement makes sense only if one believes that landowners have a moral right to the property they've inherited, and Proudhon didn't. Rather, he was angered by the inequity of the system and proposed doing away with private ownership of farmland altogether. He wanted instead to grant usufruct to the farmers who worked the land. (Usufruct is the legal right to use and enjoy the benefits of property without the right to lease, sell, or pass it down to one's heirs.)

Marx was intrigued by Proudhon's views on private property. Like Proudhon, he recognized that the systems of private property created and sustained uneven distributions of wealth and that the state was complicit in the process. However, he considered Proudhon's analysis simplistic and naive and his proposed remedy excessively moralistic and utopian. Pleas for justice and fairness were inadequate, Marx believed; scientific solutions based on the laws of political economy were more what he had in mind.

According to Marx, there was no need to seek the abolition of private property, because the dialectical movement of history would force change of its own accord. The steadily increasing impoverishment and disaffection of the working class, driven by the exploitative system of private property, would eventually cripple production and threaten humanity's very existence. Only then would a new system of production be forced on society—one in which the needs of working people were taken into account. Appeals to social conscience were pointless, Marx believed. Only productive crises led to meaningful change—a conclusion that strongly differentiated his views from those of his socialist contemporaries.

A key difference between *Marx and his colleagues was that socialists such as Proudhon thought change had to be made, while Marx thought it would come of its own accord.*

VI. WHAT IS IMPRESSIONISM?

THE ARTISTS ASSOCIATED WITH IMPRESSIONISM had highly disparate styles and aesthetic goals, yet they did share some commonalities, especially when it came to influences, core values, and their shared rejection of the Salon system. For example, all looked to the same predecessors for inspiration—the Barbizon painters Corot and Rousseau, as well as Courbet and Manet. In his 1867 canvas *Women in the Garden*, Claude Monet shows the clear influence of the Barbizon School in his use of natural light.

During the summer of 1869, Monet and Pierre-Auguste Renoir painted together at a popular bathing spot on the Seine known as La Grenouillère (the Frog Pond). Working in tandem, they "finalized" the key stylistic traits that would come to define impressionism (to the extent that impressionism could be defined). These traits were plein air painting; small, rapid brushstrokes; a bright palette; and a preference for color and light over line and form. On the other hand, the obvious differences between the canvases produced by Monet and Renoir that summer indicate how very different impressionist styles could be. For example, Monet was very interested in the effects of light on water, whereas Renoir was much more taken with social relationships. As Courbet had preached, a good artist paints the world as he sees it.

In 1874, the Société Anonyme finally mounted their own exhibition, which they held in an empty studio on the Boulevard des Capucines. Thirty artists participated—among them Monet, who exhibited his now famous *Impression, Sunrise* (1872). The painting represented the artist's impression of the harbor at Le Havre as the sun came up. Critics were understandably perplexed by the work they saw and seized on the word *impression* to describe it. One wrote that the paintings were "impressionist...in the sense that they render not the landscape but the sensation produced by the landscape." It wasn't until 1876, however, that the artists involved accepted the term as a convenient means of describing of their aesthetic aims. Its connotation of a quick, unmediated, and personal response to fleeting sensation was especially appropriate because fleeting sensation was what the impressionists wished to convey on canvas (as opposed to the studied artfulness of academic studio paintings). Their credo was to paint not what the mind knows but what the eye sees.

Claude Monet, *Impression, Sunrise* (1872)

The term **impressionism** *loosely identifies a group of very different artists. All, however, used visible brushwork and color, rather than line, to model forms on canvas.*

VI. THE HOMININ LINEAGE

AS DISCUSSED PREVIOUSLY, humans and great apes are currently grouped together in the family Hominidae, but this hasn't always been the case. Until a few generations ago, the great apes were excluded on the grounds that they lacked certain traits, such as bipedalism. However, once DNA studies showed the close genetic relationship between humans and African apes, the great apes were reclassified as hominids.

Within the reclassified family Hominidae, humans and great apes are divided into tribes. Chimpanzees, for example, belong to the tribe Panini, while humans (along with our extinct ancestors) belong to the tribe Hominini. Therefore, paleoanthropologists currently refer to members of the human lineage as hominins. (Although one still finds some authors using the term *hominid* to describe the human lineage exclusively, this use is outdated because great apes are now also considered hominids.)

When dealing with million-year-old skeletal remains, it's often difficult to distinguish among the various hominid tribes. How do paleoanthropologists know that a particular bone belongs to a hominin species? They can't run genetic tests, because DNA deteriorates after 130,000 years, so they have to rely on anatomical clues to puzzle out proper attributions. An important indicator is bipedalism, which seems to have evolved early in hominin development. Anatomical indicators of bipedalism include the shape of the spine, the pelvis, the knee joint, the foot, and even the base of the skull (which changed so that the head could rest comfortably atop an upright body).

Another important indicator is dentition, or tooth morphology. (The term *morphology* refers to the structural characteristics of plant and animal anatomy.) Fossilized teeth are generally well preserved because the enamel that covers the crown of each tooth is composed primarily of inorganic minerals that are resistant to decay. This allows for close examination of the characteristics that distinguish ape teeth from those of the early hominins. Apes typically have large upper canines that are sharpened by lower premolars. (Paleoanthropologists call this arrangement a canine/premolar honing complex.) Modern humans have smaller canines and no honing complex. Early hominins, as one might expect, fall somewhere in between, with intermediate-sized canines and a reduced honing complex.

Most of the early hominin fossils that have been found come from the Great Rift Valley of East Africa. Some researchers have argued that a major cooling and drying trend took place in Africa between 8 and 5 Ma, altering the environment and driving the evolution of these early hominin traits.

Humans and our extinct ancestors *are grouped together in the tribe Hominini, fossils of which are identified by various anatomical adaptations to bipedalism.*

VI. **THE RISE OF THE NAZI PARTY**

KNOWN IN GERMAN as the Nationalsozialistische Deutsche Arbeiterpartei (National Socialist German Workers Party), the Nazi party was one of many groups in Weimar Germany whose strong authoritarianism appealed to people like Hitler—disaffected soldiers and social misfits who were angry at the outcome of the war and unable to find a place for themselves in the postwar world. One of the most important early Nazis was Capt. Ernst Röhm, a decorated soldier who believed that the party could restore Germany's pride. Through his many influential contacts, Röhm was able arrange for the diversion of military funds to the party, which allowed the Nazis to purchase a newspaper: the *Völkisher Beobachter*.

Hitler joined the party in 1920, attracted by its position that Germany had lost the war because of Jewish and Communist disloyalty. Throwing himself into organizational work, he moved quickly up the ranks, earning a reputation as a strong speaker and propagandist. Several other Nazi leaders, threatened by Hitler's growing prestige, attempted to purge him in during the summer of 1921. Their failure, however, allowed Hitler to consolidate his power, and in July 1921 he began referring to himself as the Führer (meaning "leader").

Nazi leaders at a 1933 party rally in Nuremberg.

Ultimately, Hitler wanted to seize control of the state, and he pursued this goal in two different ways. The first was through political violence. He created a Nazi paramilitary, the Sturmabteilung (SA), and used it to battle Communist paramilitaries in the streets. As the strength of the Nazis grew, so did Hitler's ambitions, and in November 1923 he attempted a coup d'état known as the Beer Hall Putsch. Although unsuccessful, this affair transformed Hitler into a national figure, and he made use of his brief stay in prison to compose a highly compelling, popular, and embellished autobiography titled *Mein Kampf* (*My Struggle*), in which he laid out his political ideology and his views concerning "the Jewish peril."

By the time of his pardon and release in December 1924, Hitler had gathered around him many of the people who would later become key figures in the Holocaust—including Rudolf Hess, to whom he dictated the text of *Mein Kampf*; Hermann Göring, who became his second in command; and Heinrich Himmler, whom he placed in charge of the Schutzstaffel (SS). Like the "storm troopers" of the SA, this "protective squadron" was a paramilitary force but more tightly organized. It served as Hitler's personal guard and also carried out his most violent policies.

After joining the Nazi party in 1920, *Hitler moved up quickly in the ranks, becoming Führer in 1921. In 1923, he attempted to seize power in the Beer Hall Putsch.*

VII. THE FOUNDING FATHERS OF ROCKETRY

AS ROCKET SCIENCE MOVED from fireworks to moon shots during the twentieth century, many people contributed to its growth, but the work of three men, in particular, stands out. As an adolescent, Konstantin Tsiolkovsky (1857–1935), the father of Russian astronautics, read and was fascinated by Jules Verne's science-fiction classic *From the Earth to the Moon* (1865). Yet Tsiolkovsky was perplexed: His calculations showed that passengers aboard Verne's spaceship would be crushed by the force of its acceleration, so he built a centrifuge to test his theory on chickens. Thus began Tsiolkovsky's celebrated career. In 1903, the year that the Wright brothers made the first powered airplane flight, Tsiolkovsky published his most famous work, "Exploration of the Universe with Reaction Machines." This article, considered the first scientifically sound proposal for spaceflight, included a mathematical description of a rocket motor fueled by liquid oxygen and liquid hydrogen (the same fuels that the space shuttle burns today).

Hermann Oberth (1894–1989) also became enamored of spaceflight at an early age by reading Jules Verne. After serving as a medic in World War I, he studied physics at the University of Heidelberg, where his 1922 doctoral dissertation, "By Rocket into Planetary Space," was rejected because the university considered it too speculative and outlandish. Undeterred, Oberth published a brief description of his ideas in 1923 and, as they caught on, a full-length account in 1929. During World War II, he worked on Germany's V-2 rocket program and after the war wrote about space-based telescopes, space stations, and electric rocket propulsion. Named for him, the Oberth effect describes the final speed that results from a rocket burn when the rocket is in orbit around a gravitational body (the closer the rocket's burn is to the body on a descending pass, the faster the rocket's final speed will be).

Unlike Tsiolkovsky and Oberth, both of whom preferred Verne, Robert Goddard (1882–1945) became fascinated with spaceflight after reading H. G. Wells's *The War of the Worlds* (1898). Among Goddard's many achievements in rocketry, his

most remarkable was the invention of the first practical liquid-fueled rocket. In March 1926, he launched a prototype, nicknamed Nell, which flew for 2.5 seconds, attaining an altitude of forty-one feet. All of the early rocket pioneers had realized the advantages of a liquid-fueled rocket (the specifics of which will be discussed later), but none before Goddard had been able to overcome the technical problems involved.

Robert Goddard at the March 1926 launch.

The founding fathers of twentieth-century rocketry—*Tsiolkovsky, Oberth, and Goddard—all drew inspiration from the science-fiction novels they read as young men.*

VII. THE COMMUNIST MANIFESTO

IN 1836, a group of German expatriates living in Paris founded a secret society called the League of the Just. The goal of the league was to establish a utopian socialist republic in the German states. Three years later, after taking part in a Paris worker uprising, the group was banned by the French government. Some members returned to the German states; others relocated to London, Brussels, and Switzerland. In June 1847, members of the league met in London with Engels, who was acting for the Communist Correspondence Committee of Brussels, which he and Marx had founded in early 1846. An agreement was reached to merge the two organizations, after which Marx and Engels were charged with writing a manifesto for the new Communist League.

The term *communism* was relatively new, entering the political lexicon when French socialists began using it to describe the doctrine that workers should own the factories in which they worked. Although the system of wage labor has by now become so well ingrained that it seems almost natural to modern workers, those of the early industrial age saw quite clearly the degree to which their labor was making industrialization possible. Therefore, many believed, they had a legitimate claim on factory ownership.

The Communist Manifesto, which Marx and Engels published in February 1848, laid out a clear path to political revolution. Yet the twenty-four-page booklet was more than simply a call to arms, because it also included a sophisticated analysis of the historical situation, a thorough explication of the current political climate, and a vision of the communist future that was to come. All of these elements, though blended somewhat uneasily in *The Communist Manifesto*, were consistent themes of Marx's writing throughout his entire life.

The *Manifesto* began by reaching out to other communist groups in Europe and thus internationalizing the struggle. The second section placed the conflict between workers and factory owners in deep historical perspective, referencing similar conflicts in the past between "freeman and slave, patrician and plebian, lord and serf, guild-master and journeyman, in a word, oppressor and oppressed." The closing sections urged worker participation in party politics and described the salient differences between communism and socialism—especially the differences between the communist political program, which advocated nationalization of factories and worker control of the state, and the socialist program, which sought through democratic means to pass legislation improving working conditions and promoting the redistribution of wealth.

In *The Communist Manifesto, Marx and Engels described the historical situation, the current political conditions, and the communist future to come.*

VII. HIGH IMPRESSIONISM

THE FIRST IMPRESSIONIST SHOW in 1874 was such a success that more followed. The core group participating in the 1876, 1877, and 1879 exhibitions included Monet, Renoir, Camille Pissarro, Edgar Degas, Alfred Sisley, Berthe Morisot, and Paul Cézanne.

As noted previously, impressionists tended to paint in highly individualized styles that were difficult to fit within a single rubric. Degas, for example, worked primarily in the studio, crafting pictures that used quick brushwork but also fine line to create both texture and clarity. On the other hand, Monet, Pissarro, Sisley, and Morisot used loose brushwork, natural light effects, and an overall palette of high-keyed (bright and luminous) color that Degas would hardly have found acceptable in his own work.

Berthe Morisot, *Summer's Day* (1879)

Even so, the decade of the 1870s is known as the period of "high impressionism" because the stylistic unity among impressionist artists, though not great, was never greater. Except for the anomalous interest that Degas and Renoir showed in figures, landscapes predominated. Also, all of the artists grounded their work not in what their minds knew but what their eyes saw. In other words, intellectual concepts, such as those derived from literary or historical sources, were thought to be unnecessary. Instead, visual experiences—the physical sensations caused by light striking the optic nerve—were believed to be more than sufficient subjects for paintings.

Another interesting feature of this period was the fascination many impressionists had with Japanese prints, which were finally becoming available in Europe now that Japan had opened to the West. Their subject matter (seasonal effects, intimate scenes, snapshots of everyday life) was, from a Western point of view, highly unconventional, and so were the compositional devices (radical cropping, asymmetry, oblique perspective) that they used.

Impressionist paintings of this period typically portrayed various aspects of life in Paris and its suburbs. Most often, the impressionists painted scenes of leisure, but they also favored subjects relating to Paris's transformation into a modern city. With impressionism, however, there is always an exception, and in this case it was Pissarro, who preferred to paint the countryside.

The 1870s was *the decade of "high impressionism," when the stylistic traits and aesthetic interests of the artists involved were as unified as they ever would be.*

VII. EARLY HOMININS

ACCORDING TO THE MOLECULAR-CLOCK METHODOLOGY developed by Sarich and Wilson, the human lineage split off from the last of the other hominids about 6 Ma. It's likely that this date will ultimately prove to be correct, but there is not yet any direct evidence confirming it. Although some recently discovered fossils from 6 Ma may belong to the first hominins, this identification hasn't been established; and until it is, the oldest conclusively identified hominin remains date back only to 4 Ma.

The earliest hominins are called australopiths, after the genus *Australopithecus* ("southern ape") to which they belong. Australopiths were apelike creatures with small brains and small bodies that moved bipedally. Historically, australopiths were divided into two categories, gracile and robust, depending on differences in their skull morphology related to chewing. Now, many researchers prefer to classify robust australopiths as a genus (*Paranthropus*) unto themselves.

The first gracile australopith fossils were identified by Raymond Dart in 1925. They were the remains of a child discovered at Taung in South Africa. The Taung Child was determined to have been a member of the species *Australopithecus africanus*. Thus far found only in South Africa, *A. africanus* lived between 3 Ma and 2 Ma. Subsequent discoveries have shown that a slightly more primitive australopith, *A. afarensis*, lived in East Africa between 4 Ma and 3 Ma. The most famous *A. afarensis* specimen, nicknamed Lucy, represents 40 percent of an adult female skeleton. In 1995, Meave Leakey and colleagues discovered the remains of an even older (4.2 to 3.9 Ma) East African australopith, which they named *A. anamensis*. Based on its primitive jaw morphology and bipedal traits, *A. anamensis* is most likely a direct ancestor of *A. afarensis*.

Australopithecus africanus

Three species of robust australopiths have also been identified. The oldest is *Paranthropus aethiopicus*, which lived from about 2.8 Ma to 2.2 Ma and is believed to have been ancestral to the other two *Paranthropus* species. *Paranthropus boisei*, which lived from approximately 2.3 Ma to 1.4 Ma in East Africa, had a significantly larger brain than *P. aethiopicus*. *Paranthropus robustus*, which lived from 1.8 Ma to 1.5 Ma in South Africa, is morphologically similar to its East African relative. There is no evidence that the robust australopiths left any descendants.

Although genetic evidence shows *that hominins likely diverged from other hominids about 6 Ma, the first conclusively identified hominin fossils date back only to 4 Ma.*

VII. THE NAZI SEIZURE OF POWER

IN ADDITION TO HIS USE of political violence, Hitler also sought power through the ballot box. After the Beer Hall Putsch, the Nazis began running candidates in regional elections, and in 1928 they won a large number of seats in the Reichstag (the German parliament). Four years later, Hitler ran for the German presidency; and though he lost to incumbent Paul von Hindenburg, the Nazis won more seats than any other party in the July 1932 and November 1932 Reichstag elections. With no faction holding a clear majority, the aging, enfeebled Hindenburg faced a political crisis. In exchange for their cooperation, the Nazis insisted that Hitler be appointed chancellor (prime minister), and in January 1933 Hindenburg finally capitulated.

Less than a month later, a fire destroyed the Reichstag. Because the arsonist was found to have been a Communist, Hitler used the incident as an excuse to crack

SA members outside a Jewish shop in Berlin on April 1, 1933.

down on his political rivals. He ordered the arrest of large numbers of Communists and leftists and, during the chaos that followed, pressured the Reichstag into passing the Enabling Act. This legislation, passed on March 23, gave him sweeping powers to suspend civil liberties and govern by decree. Henceforth, Hitler ruled Germany as a dictator.

On April 1, 1933, Hitler began a propaganda campaign (supported by intimidation and violence) aimed at encouraging non-Jews to stop patronizing Jewish businesses. The SA painted Stars of David on the windows of Jewish shops that day and stood outside them with signs that read, "Germans, defend yourselves, don't buy from Jews!" But the boycott failed because most Germans weren't yet ready to single out the Jews for discrimination.

In the weeks and months that followed, however, Jews were banned from the civil service, forbidden to attend public cultural gatherings, and prohibited from working as journalists. The decidedly more racist Nuremberg Laws, enacted during 1935, stripped Jews of their citizenship and forbid them from marrying or having sexual relations with Germans (so that German blood might remain pure).

The Jewish response was varied. Some Jews clung to their patriotism and struggled to prove their loyalty. Others saw the repression as an opportunity to renew their commitment to their faith and ethnicity. (In a famous April 1933 editorial, newspaper editor Robert Weltsch encouraged his readers to "wear the yellow badge with pride.") Many Jews, however, began thinking about leaving the country.

Immediately after the Reichstag granted him dictatorial power in March 1933, Hitler began using the power of the state to marginalize Germany's Jewish population.

VIII. SPECIFIC IMPULSE

ROCKET ENGINES come in many different designs, some of which convert fuel into thrust more efficiently than others. One type of rocket might require one hundred kilograms of propellant to increase its velocity by one hundred meters per second, while another might require two hundred kilograms to achieve the same result. Trade-offs are inevitable, and less efficient rockets may have other advantages, such as being safer to operate or cheaper to build; but motor efficiency remains one of the most important factors in designing a rocket, because it dictates the amount of propellant a rocket will have to carry to accomplish a particular mission.

Efficiency is particularly important at launch time, when rocket motors have to increase vehicle speed from zero to orbital velocity. This, in turn, requires a considerable change in momentum (the rocket's mass multiplied by its velocity). In rocket science, a change in momentum is called impulse.

When working with impulse, time is not the crucial factor. Whether a rocket's motor applies a large amount of thrust over a short period of time or a small amount of thrust over a long period of time, the resulting impulse will be the same. Much more important for rocket designers is the amount of propellant required to produce a particular impulse.

Specific impulse (usually written as I_{sp}) measures the amount of impulse produced by a given amount of propellant. After all the math is done and units of measure cancel each other out (a process known as dimensional analysis), what's left is a speed, often called the effective exhaust velocity. Calculated another way, I_{sp} can also express the ratio of a rocket's impulse to its change in mass (as its propellant is ejected). If, following the current convention, units of mass are replaced by units of weight, then I_{sp} can be conveniently measured in seconds.

As a measurement of rocket performance, I_{sp} is analogous to the miles-per-gallon standard used to judge automobiles. The higher the I_{sp}, the less propellant is needed to change the rocket's velocity. A drawback, though, is that I_{sp} doesn't indicate how energy-efficient a rocket engine is. For example, many high-I_{sp} propulsion systems require elaborate, heavy, and often dangerous onboard machinery to achieve their high propellant efficiencies. Therefore, these systems are impractical despite their high I_{sp}.

Specific impulse *is the change in momentum produced by a given amount of propellant. As a measurement of rocket performance, it's analogous to the miles-per-gallon standard used for cars.*

VIII. THE EVENTS OF 1848

"A SPECTRE IS HAUNTING EUROPE," Marx and Engels had written in *The Communist Manifesto*; and the same month that the *Manifesto* appeared (February 1848), political crisis indeed struck. The epicenter was France, where the republican gains of the French Revolution had been slowly whittled away and King Louis-Philippe now ruled as constitutional monarch. A crop failure in 1846 had begun a downward economic spiral; and by 1848, a severe depression gripped the country, undermining middle-class stability and throwing large numbers of Parisian proletariat out of work. Because the few labor laws that existed proved too weak to be of much help, the political radicalism of Proudhon and other socialists began to catch on. Meanwhile, in the countryside, where the rural economy had ossified, the situation was no better, and the government was equally unpopular.

In February 1848, after the French government responded to rioting with violence of its own, Prime Minister François Guizot resigned and fled the country along with the king, who abdicated in favor of his nine-year-old grandson (who was quickly deposed). Shortly thereafter, the residents of Paris forced reluctant members of the Chamber of Deputies to declare the creation of the Second Republic. The new provisional government included such a wide range of interests, however, that it became impossible to agree on a single direction. Although the threatening Paris mob initially forced the new government to proclaim universal male suffrage and establish a "right to work" through the creation of National Workshops that guaranteed state jobs for the unemployed, bourgeois interests soon reasserted themselves. In national elections held that April, voters sided with the conservatives, electing a new legislature that immediately closed the hugely expensive National Workshops. The response among workers in Paris was the June Days Uprising, during which more than fifteen hundred protesters were killed when army troops stormed several barricaded sections of Paris. With the suppression of the Parisian workers' movement, class conflict quickly gave way to political maneuvering; and in December, Louis-Napoleon Bonaparte, the emperor's grandson, became president of France.

At first, Marx and his fellow communists expressed great enthusiasm for the developments in Paris; but as the emotion of the moment subsided, Marx quickly recognized that the sort of sweeping change he had imagined in *The Communist Manifesto* was not, in fact, imminent. Because of the nature of class politics in France, Marx concluded, the "revolution" of 1848 was more likely to fulfill bourgeois than worker aims.

The 1848 overthrow of *France's constitutional monarchy led some radicals to believe that the working class was finally gaining control.*

VIII. LEISURE AND THE MODERN CITY

BEFORE 1852, when Louis-Napoleon became emperor, Paris was a medieval city of narrow, winding streets. During the Second Empire, however, the city was redesigned under the auspices of Georges-Eugène Haussmann into the modern metropolis we know today. Most importantly for the impressionists, Haussmann gave Paris the grand boulevards, spacious squares, and graceful parks that allowed a new, elegant street life to develop. Impressionists were especially drawn to those aspects of Paris that made the city beautiful and cosmopolitan, such as its theaters and cafés. (Unlike Courbet, the impressionists avoided the more blunt aspects of life, such as the recent Franco-Prussian War, choosing instead to depict how quickly France had recovered.)

Cosmopolitan Paris provided the perfect backdrop for the "slice of life" subjects that impressionists favored because, during the 1870s and 1880s, the city's streets were teeming with life. Paintings such as Renoir's *Pont Neuf, Paris* (1872) and *Moulin de la Galette* (1876) exemplify the way in which impressionists caught moments of modern life on canvas. They painted fleeting glimpses of anonymous people who were subsequently reabsorbed into the bustling crowd. This approach, of course, was totally at odds with the academic preference for narrative and allegorical subject matter based on historical or mythological sources. On the other hand, it was completely in accord with Baudelaire's thinking, which Manet had successfully followed.

Many different features of modern Paris suited the impressionists' purposes, but none more so than a relatively new aspect of Parisian bourgeois life—leisure. By the 1870s, the professional and merchant classes were finding that they had not only the time but also the means to enjoy themselves in the city's new parks and also to leave Paris for recreational trips to the suburbs and outlying countryside. Places such as Argenteuil, Asnières, Bougival, and Croissy Island

Pierre-Auguste Renoir, *Pont Neuf, Paris* (1872)

in the Seine became popular destinations for leisure activities such as sailing and bathing, which the impressionists captured on countless canvases.

One of the most popular bathing places was La Grenouillère, where Monet and Renoir painted together during the summer of 1869. Louis-Napoleon's brief visit to this Croissy Island locale, also in 1869, made the place highly fashionable for a time and ensured a steady stream of elegantly dressed Parisians for the impressionists to witness and observe.

Following Baudelaire and Manet's lead, *the impressionists were "painters of modern life," who took as their primary subject the life they found in Paris and its environs.*

VIII. NEW DISCOVERIES

NEW FOSSILS ARE CONSTANTLY BEING DISCOVERED. Sometimes, the evidence they contain reinforces existing interpretations of human evolution. At other times, the new material sparks controversy and causes paleoanthropologists to rethink the classifications they have made. Often, the discovery of new remains leads to the proposal (though not necessarily the acceptance) of new hominin species.

Kenyanthropus platyops

In 2002, researchers working in Chad discovered some fossils dating back approximately 7 million years. Based on their analysis of a nearly complete cranium, they identified the fossils as a new species of hominin, which they named *Sahelanthropus tchadensis*. The cranium was identified as that of a hominin because it had small canine teeth and its shape indicated bipedality. However, because the skull's condition is poor, these conclusions are speculative, and *Sahelanthropus* may not be a hominin at all.

Other early hominin species that have been proposed include *Orrorin tugenensis*, *Ardipithecus kadabba*, and *Ardipithecus ramidus*. The *Orrorin* fossils— a few teeth and several femoral bone fragments—are approximately 6 million years old. Some researchers believe that features of the bones suggest bipedality, as does an isolated toe bone of *Ardipithecus kadabba*, which lived from about 5.8 Ma to 5.2 Ma. But the classification of these species as hominins is contested, with *Ardipithecus ramidus* (living about 4.4 Ma) being the least disputed of the three.

Fossils from more recent periods are also subject to controversy. In 2001, Meave Leakey and colleagues announced their discovery in Kenya of 3.5-million-year-old remains that they attributed to a new hominin species, *Kenyanthropus platyops*. This classification was based mainly on a relatively complete but highly distorted cranium, which other paleoanthropologists insist is much too distorted to support such a conclusion. In 1995, researchers in Chad announced their discovery of hominin fossils dating back between 3.5 and 3.0 million years. The Chad team declared that these fossils belonged to a new species, which they named *Australopithecus bahrelghazali*; other paleoanthropologists, however, believe that the Chad fossils are merely an additional specimen of *Australopithecus afarensis*.

The recent identification of some 2.5-million-year-old remains as a new species of australopith (*A. garhi*) has attracted interest for an altogether different reason. The *A. garhi* fossils were found close to mammalian bones bearing cut marks, indicating the use of stone tools for meat acquisition. It isn't clear, however, whether the proximity of the fossils to the marked bones is meaningful or merely coincidental.

The discovery of new fossils *sometimes reinforces and sometimes challenges the classifications paleoanthropologists have made of our prehuman ancestors.*

VIII. LIFE UNWORTHY OF LIFE

AS PART OF ITS COMMITMENT to "racial hygiene," the Nazi government targeted not only Jews but also Germans with physical and mental disabilities. Such people were considered a diseased element threatening the health of the German national body, and in July 1933 legislation was passed to prevent the spread of the problem. The Law for the Prevention of Hereditarily Diseased Offspring mandated that all Germans diagnosed with hereditary diseases such as schizophrenia, manic depression, and epilepsy be sterilized. Over the twelve-year span of Nazi rule, Genetic Health Courts forced the sterilization of more than four hundred thousand Germans.

By late 1938, however, the Nazis had moved on to more radical methods, adopting a plan for the euthanasia, or "mercy killing," of children designated Lebensunwertes Leben ("life unworthy of life"). Although no law was passed, a Reich Committee for the Scientific Registration of Serious Hereditarily and Congenitally Based Illnesses was established to carry out the new policy. Doctors and midwives were required to report all disabled children three years of age or younger, and beginning in the spring of 1939 five thousand such children were put to death in asylums across the country. "If people say that human beings have no right to kill them [the ill and handicapped]," an SS journal proclaimed, "then one must reply that humans have a hundred times less right…to keep something alive that was not born to live."

The "success" of the juvenile euthanasia program led to its expansion, and during the summer of 1939 Hitler ordered the creation of a secret euthanasia program for adults. The new operation was given the code name T4, because it was headquartered at Tiergartenstrasse 4, Berlin. Although some victims were given injections of phenol (carbonic acid), death was more commonly administered by carbon monoxide poisoning using a small, improvised chamber. Families of victims were typically sent letters explaining that their relatives had fallen ill while under hospital or asylum care and that their bodies had been cremated.

T4 was eventually halted in August 1941, when an accumulation of mistakes threatened to expose the program to the public. Some families had become suspicious, for example, when they were told that relatives who had previously undergone appendectomies had died of appendicitis. During its two years of operation, however, the T4 program put to death more than seventy thousand Germans, laying the groundwork for the mass exterminations still to come.

The first victims of Nazi mass murder *weren't Jews but the physically and mentally handicapped, tens of thousands of whom were secretly put to death to preserve German "racial superiority."*

IX. THE IDEAL ROCKET EQUATION

GENERALLY CREDITED TO KONSTANTIN TSIOLKOVSKY (although independently derived by others from Newton's second law as early as 1813), the ideal rocket equation expresses the relationship, during a burn, among a rocket's changing mass (as it expels propellant), the speed of its exhaust gases, and the resulting change in rocket velocity. The equation is written mathematically as

$$\Delta v = v_e \ln (m_f / m_e)$$

where Δv is the change in the rocket's velocity, v_e is the velocity of the exhaust gases, and m_f / m_e is the ratio of the mass of the rocket when fully fueled to the mass of the rocket once all the fuel has been consumed. (The operator ln indicates the natural logarithm.)

Mission planners commonly use the ideal rocket equation to calculate the amount of propellant needed to perform a particular maneuver. Its beauty is that, even without knowledge of the motor's design, you can still estimate the propellant needs with great accuracy. For example, let's say you want to send a satellite at rest on the launchpad into an orbit that requires a change in velocity (Δv) of 9.5 km/s (kilometers per second). Let's also assume that the rocket carrying the satellite has an engine exhaust velocity (v_e) of 4.5 km/s. Given these values, the mass ratio must be 8.3. In other words, the rocket will weigh 8.3 times more when fully fueled than when empty. Therefore, about seven-eighths of its initial mass—88 percent, to be precise—will have to be propellant, leaving only 12 percent for the rocket's engines, its fuel tanks, and the satellite itself.

The ideal rocket equation does have a few drawbacks, however. As the word *ideal* indicates, the equation assumes that rockets convert all their propellant into thrust without any energy loss. This doesn't happen in the real world, where a great deal of energy is lost in the form of heat that can't be recovered. The equation also doesn't factor in the power of the engine, which must be strong enough (especially in launch situations) to overcome opposing forces (such as gravity).

By relating changes *in a rocket's velocity to changes in its mass (which decreases as propellant is expelled), the ideal rocket equation helps mission planners compute accurate estimates of propellant needs.*

IX. POLITICAL ECONOMY

FEARFUL OF THE RADICALISM then on display in Paris, the Belgian government expelled Marx in March 1848. First, Marx moved his wife and children to Paris; then, he and Engels returned to Cologne, where revolution also seemed to be under way. With Engels's financing, they revived the *Rheinische Zeitung* newspaper (renaming it the *Neue Rheinische Zeitung*) and published its first issue on May 31. Later that summer, Marx traveled to Vienna and Berlin, where popular uprisings were also taking place. In November, however, counterrevolutionary forces reasserted

Marx with his wife, Jenny.

their control over the Prussian government; and in February 1849, Marx was put on trial for sedition. Although he was acquitted, he was ordered to leave the country in May. At first, Marx traveled to Paris, where he lived for three months with his family before being deported again. Finally, on August 26, he arrived in London, where his family joined him three weeks later.

Once settled in London, Marx began a comprehensive rethinking of the classic texts of political economy, which he had initially read while in Paris during the early 1840s. The end result of this decades-long project was *Capital*, the first volume of which was published in 1867. The second and third volumes, edited by Engels, appeared posthumously—in 1885 and 1894, respectively—while a fourth volume, compiled from Marx's notes on surplus value, wasn't published until 1905–10 (when it appeared piecemeal). Although these four volumes added up to thousands of pages of writing, *Capital* represented merely one chapter in Marx's monumental *Grundrisse der Kritik der Politischen Ökonomie* (*Outline of the Critique of Political Economy*), which he prepared between 1857 and 1861 as a plan for his future work. Like so much of Marx's writing, the eight-hundred-page *Grundrisse* remained unpublished until the twentieth century.

With *Capital*, Marx sought to understand better the relationship between class politics and capitalist economics. His basic answer to the question of how capitalism sustained itself was that capitalists paid workers only enough to enable them to return to work the next day. In this way, capitalists remained capitalists, and workers remained workers. But this simple answer begged a number of additional questions: How did such a system come into existence? What are its long-term consequences? Shouldn't competition among firms help workers earn higher wages? Ultimately, Marx's work answered these and other questions as well.

After being deported from Belgium, *Prussia, and France, Marx settled in London, where he began work on the critique of political economy that produced* Capital.

IX. PIERRE-AUGUSTE RENOIR

THE ONLY IMPRESSIONIST born into the working class, Pierre-Auguste Renoir (1841–1919) began his artistic career as an apprentice porcelain painter. At the age of nineteen, he entered the atelier (studio) of Charles Gleyre, an academic painter associated with the École des Beaux-Arts who also took private students. At Gleyre's studio, Renoir met Monet, Sisley, and Bazille, and through them Pissarro and Cézanne. In this way, the core of the impressionist group was formed.

Unlike his friends, Renoir was primarily a figure painter who specialized in depicting beautiful women and the *joie de vivre* of modern urban life. His most famous urban leisure scenes are *Moulin de la Galette* (1876), for which he used friends as models, and *Luncheon of the Boating Party* (1881). These earned him the sobriquet "the new Watteau" because they reminded critics of the early-eighteenth-century artist Jean-Antoine Watteau, who became famous for his paintings of courtiers enjoying themselves in lush outdoor settings (a subgenre known as *fêtes galantes*). Renoir was also influenced by several Rococo painters of the late eighteenth century, especially François Boucher and Jean-Honoré Fragonard, who celebrated the elegance and fineries of the French court in a manner that was later considered excessive but also featured a loose, brushy style that Renoir and other impressionists later adopted.

Renoir was particularly interested in the effects of ambient light on color and shadow. Instead of painting what his mind knew to be the correct color, he painted what his eye saw. For example, grass in bright light is not always green, and skin in shadow often looks purplish in tone. (This effect is called ambient color or coloristic shadow.)

Renoir chose not to exhibit with the impressionists at their 1879, 1880, and 1881 shows because during those years he experienced a change in style. Influenced by the Old Masters, he began to move away from impressionism toward more solid form and stable composition. He became more meticulous in his brushwork and replaced the hot colors he had previously used with a much cooler palette. During the 1890s, however, Renoir returned to his loose, brushy style and hot palette of the 1870s, particularly to paint large figural studies of nudes out of doors.

Renoir specialized in depicting *the* joie de vivre *of modern urban life. He became known as "the new Watteau" because his paintings resembled Watteau's* fêtes galantes.

Pierre-Auguste Renoir, *Luncheon of the Boating Party* (1881)

IX. EARLY HOMO

APPROXIMATELY 2.4 MA, not long after *Paranthropus* came onto the scene, the first members of the genus *Homo* began appearing in Africa. The timing of these two events may not have been coincidental. Some paleoanthropologists believe that it's likely these two groups represent different adaptive strategies to the same climatic shift. (About this time, the African climate became drier and cooler.) *Paranthropus* probably relied on chewing adaptations to exploit tough, fibrous food material, while early *Homo* species may have begun using tool technology to obtain meat. By evolving in these different ways, *Paranthropus* and *Homo* would have benefited by avoiding feeding competition with each other.

Early *Homo* can be identified by their larger brain sizes and smaller teeth relative to australopiths. The species *Homo habilis*, which lived from 2.4 Ma to 1.5 Ma, was first described by Louis Leakey and colleagues in 1964. Leakey based his identification on specimens discovered at Olduvai Gorge, Tanzania. Koobi Fora, another productive site in East Africa, has also yielded a diversity of early *Homo* crania. The most famous of these, KNM-ER 1470 (known by its Kenya National Museum acquisition number), displays a larger cranial capacity and larger teeth than the *H. habilis* specimens found at Olduvai Gorge. Although some paleoanthropologists believe that these larger Koobi Fora skulls make up a distinct species (*Homo rudolfensis*), most researchers group them with the smaller Koobi Fora and Olduvai Gorge skulls, classifying them all as *Homo habilis*.

About 1.8 Ma, the species *Homo erectus* arose in Africa. Paleoanthropologists initially believed *H. erectus* descended directly from *H. habilis*, but recent evidence has shown that *H. habilis* and *H. erectus* coexisted for nearly half a million years. Although coexistence doesn't preclude an ancestral–descendant relationship, it does make one more difficult to infer. (It's much easier to recognize an ancestral–descendant relationship when one species appears to supersede another, as is the case with *Australopithecus anamensis* and *A. afarensis*.)

Homo erectus became the first hominin species to leave Africa when it began migrating into Southeast Asia about 1.7 Ma. It had a bigger brain and larger body than *H. habilis*, as well as limb proportions more typical of modern humans, which allowed it to move around more efficiently. Because populations of *H. erectus* remained extant until approximately 100,000 years ago, some paleoanthropologists prefer to split the species into early African forms (1.8 to 1.5 Ma), which they call *H. ergaster*, and later forms, which they call *H. erectus*.

Early *Homo* specimens *are generally classified either as* H. habilis *or as* H. erectus, *but some researchers think otherwise and recognize additional species.*

IX. WORLD WAR II

THE ECONOMIC AND POLITICAL RESURGENCE over which Hitler presided soon brought Germany into conflict with its European neighbors. Because Hitler and the Nazis despised the Treaty of Versailles, they repeatedly (and flagrantly) violated its terms,

A newspaper hawker in London.

most notably by rearming their country. Attempts during the late 1930s to appease Hitler only emboldened him to act more aggressively. European leaders such as British prime minister Neville Chamberlain worked assiduously to achieve "peace in our time," but their efforts proved illusory. War was inevitable, and it finally came on September 1, 1939, when Germany invaded Poland. Hitler's justification for this act was the Nazi idea of Lebensraum ("living space"), which entitled the German master race to seize whatever territory it deemed necessary for national existence or economic self-sufficiency.

Countries such as France and Great Britain that had signed mutual defense agreements with Poland, hoping that such alliances would contain German ambitions, immediately declared war on Germany and began mobilizing their forces. But no troops were sent to Poland, and the ill-prepared Polish army was quickly overrun. The unexpected appearance of Soviet troops in eastern Poland on September 17 offered a gleam of hope, until it became apparent that the Soviets were acting in concert with the Germans. (A nonaggression pact signed by Germany and the Soviet Union during the summer of 1939 had included a secret protocol dividing up Poland between the two nations.) Thus, within three weeks of the German invasion, Poland ceased to exist as an independent nation.

In seizing western Poland, the Germans gained control over one of the largest population of Jews in Europe. Of the approximately 3.3 million Jews living in Poland at the time, about 2 million came under Nazi hegemony during September 1939. Very quickly, the region became what historian Raul Hilberg has called "an area of experimentation." Most Polish Jews were rounded up and imprisoned in urban ghettos that isolated them from the rest of the population, but some were simply murdered in place by mobile SS killing units known as Einsatzgruppen.

Following its success in Poland, the German military conquered Denmark, Norway, Belgium, the Netherlands, and France. These victories brought even more Jews under Nazi domination so that by the fall of 1940, more than four million (or about half of the entire European population) were subject to Hitler's will.

Between the September 1939 invasion *of Poland and the June 1940 fall of France, more than four millions Jews, or half the European population, fell under Nazi control.*

X. THE PARTS OF A ROCKET ENGINE

A SIMPLE CHEMICAL ROCKET ENGINE has three primary components: a combustion chamber, where propellant is burned to produce hot gases; a throat, which constricts the outward flow of the gases; and a nozzle, through which the gases leave the rocket.

These hot gases are the rocket's reaction mass. The amount of mass that leaves the rocket divided by the time it takes for that mass to leave is the mass flow rate. This rate is important to rocket designers because it determines engine thrust. Increasing the amount and velocity of the exhaust gases increases their momentum and thereby produces more thrust. So, the higher the mass flow rate, the greater the thrust.

The engine's narrow throat paired with its widening, bell-shaped nozzle creates what engineers call a convergent–divergent design. As the hot gases move toward the throat, they converge, causing the pressure to increase. Then, as they move through the throat into the divergent nozzle, they expand and accelerate, reaching supersonic speeds. The nozzle accomplishes this by converting the gases' thermal energy (heat) into kinetic energy (motion).

Nozzles are designed to flare in such a way that by the time the hot gases move from the throat to the nozzle exit, the pressure has been reduced to match the atmospheric pressure outside. This reduction in pressure can be accomplished either by lengthening the nozzle or by widening its exit area. When the pressure at the nozzle exit exactly matches the ambient pressure, the nozzle is said to be adapted, meaning that the expansion of the exhaust gases has been optimized.

If the nozzle exit pressure is less than the local atmospheric pressure, then the nozzle is said to be overexpanded. If this is the case, engine thrust is dampened because the outside air presses in on the exhaust gases, hampering their flow. On the other hand, if the nozzle exit pressure is greater than the local atmospheric pressure, then the nozzle is underexpanded. In this case, energy is wasted, because some of the gas will move sideways (into the surrounding low-pressure area) rather than downward, again decreasing thrust.

Because the shape of a particular nozzle isn't changeable, rocket engines can be optimized for only one altitude. A rocket designed for launch at sea level usually employs nozzles designed for ideal expansion two-thirds of the way up into orbit. This configuration offers better overall performance than nozzles optimized for sea level.

The convergent–divergent design *of rocket engines dramatically accelerates the exhaust gases to supersonic speeds, efficiently creating a great deal of thrust.*

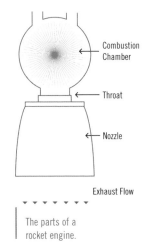

Combustion Chamber

Throat

Nozzle

Exhaust Flow

The parts of a rocket engine.

X. THE LABOR THEORY OF VALUE

FROM THE HEGELIAN PERSPECTIVE that he had never abandoned, Marx saw capitalism as a once revolutionary movement that had swept aside the misconceptions of a previous age (feudalism) to reveal "facts" about human society that couldn't have been known until the previous age was negated.

Although the process of rendering goods for sale interchangeably and in cash was nothing new, the commoditization that characterized capitalism was different because it was virtually universal. Under feudalism, rents had often been paid in kind, and guilds had set the rates at which their members were compensated; however, under capitalism, rents and wages became payable in cash at market rates.

Relationships—such as membership in the same community, religion, or family—that had once regulated the economic dealings between people now came to be seen as impediments to the free flow of trade. In a market economy, such as the one that capitalism established, the overriding factor in any exchange is price. It doesn't matter who the sellers are, or how they are related to the buyers; the market sets the price.

The most important aspect of this change, Marx thought, was that labor became a commodity, which could be bought and sold without reference to social connections between buyer and seller and without the implication of any future relationship, moral or otherwise. By transforming labor into a commodity, like a bushel of wheat or a pair of shoes, capitalism had revealed something important about the nature of labor: its value. Until labor became a commodity, no one had thought to inquire into its value. Under capitalism, however, the question became both central and, for the first time, answerable.

To define the value of labor, Marx drew on the labor theory of value developed by the British political economist David Ricardo (1772–1823). According to Ricardo, the value of any commodity was the total amount of labor required to produce it. The value of a ton of coal, for example, was equal to the labor required to dig it out of the ground—including not only the miners' labor, but also the labor required to make the tools they used. Applying this logic to labor itself, Marx reasoned that the value of labor was the total amount of labor needed to produce a worker capable of working a full day—in other words, the cost (in labor) of food, shelter, clothing, and the other necessities of life.

The labor theory of value *holds that the value of a commodity is equal to the total amount of labor required to produce it—expended both by the producer and by the makers of his tools.*

X. CLAUDE MONET

Claude Monet, *Haystack at the Sunset Near Giverny* (1891)

ALTHOUGH BORN IN PARIS, Claude Monet (1840–1926) spent most of his well-off childhood at Le Havre in Normandy. As a teenager, he met the artist Eugène Boudin, who encouraged him to paint landscapes en plein air. In 1859, a wealthy aunt financed his return to Paris. He wanted to pursue a career as an artist there but had little interest in the academic training available at the École des Beaux-Arts. Already critical of the Salon system, Monet had an independent streak that often put him at odds with his family, who wanted him attend the École. Instead, Monet painted for a time at the Académie Suisse (where he met Pissarro and Cézanne) before entering in 1862 the atelier of Charles Gleyre (where he met Renoir and Sisley). Monet's close association with these artists, especially Renoir, led to the creation of the impressionist style and the organization of the first impressionist shows.

During the bloody Franco-Prussian War of 1870–71, Monet decamped to England, returning to France after the fighting was over to settle in the Parisian suburb of Argenteuil, where he painted frequently in the company of Renoir and Manet. Although Monet had experimented with figure painting during the 1860s, in Argenteuil he focused on landscapes and gradually found his métier in the study of the transformative effects of natural light. He thought a great deal about what the eye sees at any given moment and how that changes at different times of the day and year. Because of his quick brushstrokes, his paintings look unrehearsed, as though they were painted swiftly "in the moment." In reality, of course, Monet's compositions were thoroughly planned and his subjects carefully chosen. During the 1880s and 1890s, for instance, he began creating series of paintings focusing on a single subject, such as his famous haystacks. The point was to explore the variety of natural light by showing how a common subject appeared at different times of the day and during different seasons of the year.

Unlike his friend Renoir, who found success with American collectors relatively early in his career, Monet didn't become popular until the 1880s. About this time, he moved to Giverny, which soon became an artistic center, in no small part because of his presence there.

Whereas other impressionists *found their subject matter in Paris's rich urban life, Monet preferred to paint the transformative effects of natural light on suburban scenery.*

X. THE MUDDLE IN THE MIDDLE

THE PLEISTOCENE EPOCH (the sixth of the Cenozoic era) began 1.8 Ma, about the time that *H. erectus* appeared. The stage known as the Middle Pleistocene began about 900,000 years ago. By that time, *H. erectus* had spread throughout Africa and Asia. The Middle Pleistocene ended about 127,000 years ago, by which time *H. sapiens* had already emerged (or was just about to). Many fossils dating from the Mid-Pleistocene are transitional, displaying some characteristics associated with primitive *H. erectus* and others associated with modern *H. sapiens*. Not surprisingly, paleoanthropologists have had a great deal of trouble classifying these remains.

Historically, Mid-Pleistocene *Homo* specimens have been collectively labeled "archaic *Homo sapiens*," but this description implies ancestral–descendant relationships that don't necessarily exist.

According to one view, all Mid-Pleistocene *Homo* belong to the same species, *H. heidelbergensis*—European members of which gave rise to *H. neanderthalensis* (the Neandertals), while African populations gave rise to *H. sapiens* (modern humans).

A Mid-Pleistocene *Homo*.

An alternative hypothesis is that the European and African populations represent separate lineages belonging to different species, *H. heidelbergensis* (for the European ancestors of the Neandertals) and *H. rhodesiensis* (for the African ancestors of modern humans).

The discovery of 780,000-year-old remains at the Gran Dolina site in Spain has recently added a new twist to the story. Reportedly, these remains provide the earliest evidence for the presence in Europe of hominins more advanced than *Homo erectus*. Researchers working on the Gran Dolina fossils insist that they belong to a new species, *H. antecessor*, that may have been ancestral to later Mid-Pleistocene *Homo*, Neandertals, and modern humans.

Another enigmatic discovery was made in 2004, when researchers unearthed an 18,000-year-old skull and partial skeleton at Liang Bua on the Indonesian island of Flores. Referred to as Liang Bua 1 (LB1), these remains belong to a small-bodied hominin similar in size to *Australopithecus afarensis* with a very small brain. Researchers originally proposed that the fossils belonged to a dwarfed species they named *Homo floresiensis*. They believed that *H. floresiensis* descended from a population of larger-bodied *H. erectus* isolated on the island for a long time. Others, however, have argued that LB1 is simply modern human who suffered from microcephaly (abnormal smallness of the head). The status of *H. floresiensis* remains a hotly debated topic in paleoanthropological circles and requires much more research.

Paleoanthropologists are still not sure *how to classify Mid-Pleistocene fossils that show traits of both primitive* Homo erectus *and modern* Homo sapiens.

X. THE GHETTOIZATION OF POLAND

AT THE OUTSET OF THE WAR, the treatment of Polish Jews, despite the Nazis' later reputation for planning and efficiency, was rather haphazard. The reason for this seems to have been that, prior to the invasion, the Germans didn't give much thought to the matter. Afterward, some Nazis argued for the enslavement of the Polish Jews; others thought they should simply be deported. During the spring of 1940, a plan was circulated to relocate all of the Jews to Madagascar, but this idea went nowhere. Instead, the German army moved ahead with ghettoization, or the imprisonment of Jews in walled-off neighborhoods established in Poland's major cities. Some of these ghettos were small, but others were massive, such as those in Cracow and Vilna. The largest of all was the Warsaw ghetto, which housed 450,000 Jews at its peak.

Ghettoization was imposed for a variety of reasons. The most important was that it concentrated Jews in locations where their slave labor could be accessed easily by the German military. The unsanitary, overcrowded conditions in the ghettos also encouraged the spread of disease, which killed off many Jews.

To administer the ghettos, the Nazis appointed Jewish councils known as Judenräte. Members of the Judenräte oversaw municipal services, such as the distribution of food, and maintained order through the creation of Jewish police forces. Some Jews joined or served the Judenräte because they feared Nazi reprisals if they refused. Others took part because they hoped that their involvement would mitigate the suffering of fellow Jews. Still others were motivated by the fruitless hope that collaboration might save themselves and their families.

The most difficult task forced on the Judenräte was the preparation of lists of Jews to be transferred out of the ghettos. The Nazis told the Judenräte that the deportees were being sent to work camps in the east, but by late 1942 it had become clear (through the loose talk of guards and the reports of Polish partisans) that the deportees were actually being sent to death camps.

The building of a wall across a street in Warsaw to enclose the ghetto there.

In nearly every ghetto, Jews organized resistance groups and armed themselves with weapons smuggled in by sympathetic or mercenary Poles. In January 1943, such a group in the Warsaw ghetto used armed force to stop the deportations, but only temporarily. On April 19, the SS began clearing out the entire ghetto, and by May 16 it was no more.

After a period of indecision, *the Nazis moved ahead with the ghettoization of Poland's Jews. Those not suitable for slave labor were gradually deported to death camps in the east.*

XI. ROCKET STAGING

WHEN YOU LOOK at a rocket sitting on a launch pad, most of what you see is propellant tankage. Having to haul these tanks into orbit requires a great deal of fuel. Much less fuel would be required if the extra weight were simply jettisoned once it was no longer needed. This is the idea behind rocket staging.

A multistage rocket, such as the Saturn V used in the Apollo missions, employs two or more independent stages to reach orbit. Each stage contains its

The first stage of the Saturn V rocket.

own engines and its own propellant. As a stage burns out, its machinery is discarded, and the next stage (if there is one) ignites.

Although there are many different ways to stage a rocket, the most common schemes are serial and parallel staging. In serial staging, the motors are stacked one on top of the other, as in the Saturn V, and they burn sequentially. This gives engineers the opportunity to design different nozzles for different stages, so that each is adapted for the atmospheric pressures in which it will be operating. In parallel staging, main and auxiliary rockets burn simultaneously. This is the staging system used in the space shuttle, which employs two solid rocket boosters (SRBs) to augment the thrust of its main engine.

How much does staging help? Consider the example of a 500-kilogram payload sitting atop a rocket restricted to 7,000 kilograms of total mass while on the launchpad. A single-stage rocket built under these constraints using current technology would accelerate the payload to 6.6 km/s, which is well below orbital velocity. In contrast, a two-stage rocket using a serial design would accelerate the payload to 7.9 km/s, which is enough to place the satellite in orbit.

Yet staging is not without its disadvantages. Serial staging requires the lifting off the ground of heavy motors that are not initially in use. Also, staging adds to the complexity of a rocket, thereby increasing both the cost of its construction and the chance of malfunction. An even more important consequence of complexity is the small army of technicians required to launch and support the vehicle. It's this high labor factor that has been driving up the cost of spaceflight to the point at which multistage rockets are becoming prohibitively expensive. In the near future, single-stage-to-orbit (SSTO) rockets may be the only economically viable way to launch payloads. Unfortunately, with current technology, SSTO rockets are not yet powerful enough to do the job.

Without multiple stages *(which can burn either serially or in parallel), rockets constructed today using current technology couldn't launch payloads into Earth orbit.*

XI. SURPLUS VALUE

IF THE VALUE OF A WORKER'S DAY is merely the labor required to keep the worker alive for that day, then workers are clearly capable of creating what Marx called surplus value. This is the difference between the value of a worker's labor and the value of the commodities he or she produces with that labor. The amount of surplus value that an individual worker creates varies greatly depending on a multitude of factors including the worker's diligence, the effectiveness of his or her tools, and even the availability of housing (which wouldn't affect the value of the commodities produced but would affect the value of the worker's labor).

Surplus value, however, is not the same as profit, just as labor value is not the same as wages. In a capitalist economy, prices are based not on value (which is theoretical), but on market conditions. If the wages paid workers fall below the value of their labor (in the Ricardian sense), then the society will fail, because workers will be unable to survive for another day of work. Short of this, however, capitalists seek to pay their workers as little as possible, regardless of the theoretical value of their labor.

Like labor value, surplus value is also theoretical, but profits are real. They represent the difference between the costs of production and the market price realized. Under capitalism, employers seek to maximize profit by either reducing their costs (such as by cutting wages) or increasing their revenue (such as by improving production efficiency). Without surplus value, however, there could be no profit.

For Marx, the most important thing about surplus value was the struggle for its control being carried on between employers and workers. Employers wanted it for themselves in order to maximize their profit, while workers also wanted a share so that they could earn more money than it simply took to survive. Marx used the term *relations of production* to describe the relationships among people (especially social structures such as laws) that determined how surplus value would be allocated in a particular society.

Under capitalism, employers controlled what Marx called the means of production—that is, the natural resources, machinery, and so on necessary for the production of goods. This gave them the leverage they needed to purchase the labor of workers on the own terms. The workers, Marx pointed out, had no choice but to sell.

Surplus value is the difference *between the value of a worker's labor and the value of the commodities that he or she produces with that labor. It is related to, but not the same as, profit.*

XI. CAMILLE PISSARRO

BORN ON THE WEST INDIES ISLAND OF St. Thomas, Camille Pissarro (1830–1903) was the son of a merchant, and he initially pursued a business career before moving to Paris in 1855 to study art. For three years, he painted at the Académie Suisse and in 1859 had his first work accepted at the Salon. As with most impressionists, however, Pissarro's relationship with the Salon system was bittersweet. During the early 1860s, he became friendly with Monet and Cézanne, who were also painting at the Académie Suisse, and shared their disgruntlement at repeated Salon rejection. In 1863, Pissarro exhibited at the Salon des Refusés, and during the early 1870s he helped lead the effort to organize the impressionist exhibitions. In fact, he was the only artist to participate in all eight impressionist shows (1874, 1876–77, 1879–82, 1886).

Like Monet, Pissarro was primarily a landscape painter. His earliest influences were the Barbizon painters, especially Corot. By the late 1860s, however, he had begun shifting Barbizon realism to an impressionist style characterized by loose brushwork and his experimentation with the effects of color and light. Like Monet (but unlike Frédéric Bazille, who died in the fighting), Pissarro spent the ten-month Franco-Prussian War living safely in England. While there, he was able to view firsthand numerous landscapes by Constable and Turner, whose explorations of light and color became significant influences on Pissarro's work. During the 1870s, he and Cézanne painted together in Pontoise, the inexpensive but pretty Parisian suburb where Pissarro had settled after his return from England. During this time, Pissarro's mature impressionist style emerged.

Camille Pissarro, *Hoarfrost* (1873)

Always a very experimental artist, Pissarro began making prints during the late 1870s and early 1880s, usually in the company of Edgar Degas and Mary Cassatt. As was often the case with Pissarro, these technical explorations brought about stylistic developments in his painting, especially with regard to the composition of his landscapes. Like the Japanese prints that he was emulating, Pissarro began using trees, flowers, and fences to "screen off" parts of the landscape that he was painting, thus preventing the viewer from seeing the entire subject unobscured.

Pissarro was a highly *experimental artist who was principally interested in color and light. He was also the only artist to exhibit in all eight impressionist shows.*

XI. WHO WERE THE NEANDERTALS?

BECAUSE NEANDERTALS LIVED relatively recently, from 130,000 to 24,000 years ago, researchers know more about them, especially their anatomy and material culture, than they do about other archaic hominins. Furthermore, because DNA can survive up to 130,000 years, scientists have even been able to study their genetic makeup as well.

The first Neandertal fossils were discovered in the Feldhofer Cave in Germany's Neander Valley in 1856. Since then, many more Neandertal fossils have been recovered at sites all over Europe and western Asia—the most famous of which being La Chapelle-aux-Saints and La Ferrassie in France, Shanidar in Iraq, and Amud and Kebara in Israel. Although the anatomical, cultural, and genetic differences between Neandertals and modern humans have been closely studied, paleoanthropologists still debate whether Neandertals interbred with early modern humans and thus belong to the same species (*Homo sapiens*), or whether they should be placed in a species of their own (*Homo neanderthalensis*).

Neandertal remains display a combination of primitive and derived skeletal features. Primitive features, or those that resemble the traits of a species' ancestors, include a long and low cranium, a projecting face, and a mandible (jawbone) that lacks a chin. (Chins, which are bony protuberances on the midline of the mandible, are found only in modern humans.) Derived features, or those that have evolved away from the ancestral condition, include a large brain (actually larger than the modern human brain) and a bulge at the back of the cranium called an occipital bun.

The Neandertal skeleton was robust, meaning that it had thick bones. It also had relatively short limbs, suggesting that it was cold-adapted and constructed to conserve body heat. Archaeological and bone-collagen analyses have also indicated that Neandertals were adept hunters whose diets relied heavily on meat. Most likely, they were capable of hunting big game.

Neandertals are known to have used complex Mousterian tools. This technology required much greater planning and cognitive abilities than previous tool-production techniques. A few of the later Neandertal sites in Europe even contain examples of a more advanced blade-based technology known as Châtelperronian industry. To make these blades (thin flakes of stone that were twice as long as they were wide), Neandertals couldn't simply strike two rocks together. Rather, they had to use a hammerstone and a chisel-like piece of bone to apply the precise force necessary to remove the prepared flake.

Researchers know more about *Neandertals than about other early hominins, yet they still argue about whether Neandertals belong to the same species as modern humans.*

XI. THE EINSATZGRUPPEN

ON JUNE 22, 1941, having secured nearly all of Western Europe, Germany broke its nonaggression pact with the Soviet Union and launched a surprise attack code-named

Einsatzgruppen in Ukraine, 1942.

Operation Barbarossa. Although Hitler's campaign ultimately failed, over the next three years it brought several million more Polish and Russian Jews under his sway. By this time, German officials were thinking more carefully about the form the Final Solution would take. No longer was there much talk about quarantines or deportations. The general understanding was that the Jews of Europe would be killed.

With regard to those Jews living in the newly conquered territories of the Soviet Union, the extermination took place in two phases. The first was carried out by four battalions of Einsatzgruppen created under the supervision of Reinhard Heydrich, chief of the Reich Security Main Office. The task of the Einsatzgruppen was to conduct "cleanup" operations, which meant killing Jews wherever they were found during the early stages of the invasion. As these battalions of Einsatzgruppen moved from one location to the next, they separated the Jews from the general population, gathered them together, and murdered them, usually by marching them into burial pits and then shooting them. Afterward, the homes, shops, and synagogues of the victims were usually burned. The scale of killing was extreme, with thousands put to death in a single action.

To improve the efficiency of the work, German technicians developed "gas vans." These were large trucks reconfigured so that the carbon monoxide produced by their engines could be piped into hermetically sealed rear compartments. Jews were loaded into the rear compartments and driven to a burial site. By the time they arrived, they were dead. With these and other technological aids, the Einsatzgruppen were able to exterminate more than one million Jews.

At times, local populations aided the Einsatzgruppen in their work. Many of the Poles and Russians living in the western Soviet Union were longtime anti-Semites; and, knowing the German opinion of the Jews, they felt free, once the Germans arrived, to act upon their long-standing hatred. In several communities, Jews were attacked and even murdered by their non-Jewish neighbors. Among the most shocking incidents took place in the Polish town of Jedwabne, where members of the non-Jewish community herded the town's Jewish residents into a barn and set it on fire, killing them all.

Hitler's June 1941 invasion *of the Soviet Union brought several million more Jews under his control. More than a million were promptly murdered by Einsatzgruppen.*

XII. SOLID-FUELED ROCKET MOTORS

THERMODYNAMIC PROPULSION produces thrust by converting chemical energy into thermal energy. The most common thermodynamic motor, and the only one currently capable of launching payloads into space, is the chemical rocket, in which two or more chemicals react to produce hot gases.

Chemical rockets come in two varieties: solid-fueled and liquid-fueled. In solid-fueled rockets, the propellant and the oxidizer (which allows the propellant to burn in the absence of atmospheric oxygen) are blended together to form a single solid mass. The space shuttle's solid rocket boosters (SRBs) are solid-fueled motors that use ammonium perchlorate as an oxidizer, aluminum as a propellant, and iron oxide as a catalyst (to speed

A space shuttle SRB.

the oxidation reaction). All of these chemicals are bound together by hydroxyl-terminated polybutadiene, a rubbery substance that functions as a glue. If you held a small piece of SRB fuel in your hand, you'd think it was a gritty pencil eraser.

The thrust produced by a solid-fueled motor depends on the burn rate of the fuel block, which in turn depends on the amount of surface area being burned. If more of the fuel block's surface is exposed to the combustion reaction, then the burn rate will increase, more reaction mass will be expelled, and more thrust will be generated.

This thrust is usually controlled by the design of the fuel block, which can be either end burning or internal burning. In end-burning motors, the combustion reaction travels up from the nozzle end to the top of the casing in much the same way that a cigarette burns from the tip to the filter. This design produces a constant thrust throughout the burn. Internal-burning motors are more common, however, because they allow for variation in thrust. In these, the reaction takes place along a central channel whose geometry controls the burn rate and thus the thrust. The shuttle's SRBs, for example, use a star-shaped channel to control the amount of fuel block surface area being exposed to combustion.

The primary advantage of solid-fueled motors is their simplicity. Being little more than rubber-filled tubes, they have few moving parts, are highly reliable, and produce a tremendous amount of thrust for their weight. On the other hand, they have a much lower specific impulse than liquid-fueled motors and are thus much less efficient. Also, once ignited, they can't be turned off, meaning that there's no way to abort a mission while the rocket is still on the ground.

In solid-fueled rocket motors, *the fuel block consists of all the chemicals necessary for combustion, combined into a solid mass.*

XII. COMMODITY FETISHISM

AS DISCUSSED EARLIER, in commoditizing labor, capitalism stripped away past ideas about how people were connected to one another (as master and slave or lord and vassal). This represented progress in dialectical terms, because the ideas capitalism stripped away were illusions designed to perpetuate old relations of production. In doing away with these ideas, however, capitalism didn't replace them with truth. Instead, a more subtle illusion was installed: commodity fetishism.

According to Marx, in order for an object to be a commodity, it has to be useful to someone other than the producer/owner. This mutual utility provides the basis for commodity exchange, in which one set of goods is traded for another (or for money, which serves as a mechanism for delayed exchange). In pursuing exchange, producers demonstrate to one another (and themselves) the broad mutual interdependence characteristic of all human societies.

This intent to exchange raises certain important economic questions. For instance, what price should be charged? Ideally, the price of an object should reflect the amount of labor that went into producing it. However, in a market economy, price is set by the market, which responds to factors unrelated to labor (such as supply and demand). Therefore, Marx pointed out, price is a poor indicator of the value of goods bought and sold in the marketplace.

The upshot is that, under capitalism, people exchange goods not as the producers of useful things, but as owners of commodities (for which money acts as a handy substitute). Therefore, instead of connecting people as the makers of useful things so that they can trade with one another, markets isolate people, permitting them to interact only as the holders of money. There is no acknowledgment of the intense interdependence people actually have with one another in their collective struggle to wrest food and shelter from the natural world. Instead, there is only the alienating illusion that personal relationships are determined by distant and independent market forces, rather than by people themselves.

According to Marx, this false belief that market forces determine human relationships is a form of fetishism, because it attributes creative power (an intrinsic aspect of human beings) to inanimate commodities. Under capitalism, commodity fetishism dominates people's perception of themselves because it hides from them the underlying truth that human beings really are related to one another as producers of useful things that contribute to their collective survival.

Commodity fetishism is the false *belief promoted by capitalism that people are related to one another only as buyers and sellers in a marketplace ruled by forces beyond their control.*

XII. ALFRED SISLEY

ALFRED SISLEY (1839–99) was born in Paris to wealthy British parents, who sent him to London in 1857 to prepare him for a career in business. While in London, however, Sisley developed an intense interest in art, and in 1862 he returned to Paris, where he entered the studio of Charles Gleyre. Sisley specialized in landscapes, and his earliest pictures emulated the Barbizon School—that is, they used dark, muted colors and thick, rough brushstrokes. He exhibited a few paintings at the Salon during the 1860s, which was the heyday of the Barbizon painters, but the Franco-Prussian War brought his career to a temporary halt. Sisley wasn't involved in the fighting, but the war bankrupted his father, who died soon thereafter. This left Sisley without financial support and meant that he would have to earn a living from painting.

Sisley's mature style developed during the early 1870s, when he was working in close collaboration with Renoir and Monet. Because Sisley was most interested in the seasonal qualities of light and atmosphere, the objects in his paintings—buildings, bodies of water, foliage—became mere receptors and reflectors of light, absorbing it and taking from it their color and character. Above all, though, Sisley's work was known for its remarkable consistency. All of his landscapes show a high degree of compositional similarity, and his interest in

Alfred Sisley, *The Bridge at Villeneuve-la-Garenne* (1872)

presenting wide views never faltered. Unlike Monet and Pissarro, who usually focused on a single aspect of the landscape they were painting, Sisley liked to present broad horizons, using a river or a road receding into the background to emphasize the depth of the perspective. In general, Sisley preferred neither city nor country subjects but the suburban spaces in between, where many of the impressionists lived because housing was cheap and, despite the occasional factory, the scenery was pretty.

During the 1880s, Sisley's work did undergo a few stylistic shifts. His color became more pronounced and his subjects less serene, more emotionally intense. But he resisted the subjectivity that was beginning to show up in his friend Monet's paintings and remained true to painting what he saw—which was, after all, the founding ideal of impressionism.

During his life, *Sisley was one of the least-known impressionists, but he was also the most consistent and remained dedicated throughout his career to painting what he saw.*

XII. HOMO SAPIENS

NO ISSUE IN THE STUDY OF HUMAN ORIGINS is more important than the question of what defines *Homo sapiens* as a species. Without an answer to this question, there would be no way for paleoanthropologists to determine the timing and location of our species' emergence.

Making use of the fossil record, researchers have been able to identify several anatomical traits that seem to define *Homo sapiens* as a species. In addition to possessing chins, modern humans have large brains encased in high crania (which means that the human skull is relatively long top to bottom and relatively short front to back). The human cranium also has an inflated frontal region to make room for the increased size of the human frontal lobe (the part of the brain related to cognition and planning). On the other hand, the human skull generally lacks the robustness found in archaic species, and its teeth are relatively small.

Indications of modernity are also found in the archaeological record. These include toolmaking, a rapid pace of technological development, and the appearance of personal ornaments and complex art forms (such as engravings, sculptures, and cave paintings). There is some disagreement, however, over the origin, time frame, and spread of these behaviors. One group of researchers has pointed out that a dramatic change in behavior seems to have taken place in Europe and the eastern Mediterranean between 50,000 and 40,000 years ago. Before this time, the archaeological record shows practically no evidence of personal ornaments, art, or blade-based technologies. Afterward, the evidence for these behaviors is abundant. The reasons for this abrupt shift aren't known, but similarly modern behaviors do seem to have arisen sporadically in Africa 30,000 to 40,000 years earlier.

The occurrence of modern behavioral traits at an earlier stage in Africa has led some researchers to propose that *Homo sapiens* originated in Africa—an interpretation supported by a great deal of fossil evidence. Fossils between 160,000 and 154,000 years old displaying intermediate traits have been found in several African sites, such as Herto in Ethiopia; and other fossils, found at the Klasies River Mouth and Border Cave sites in South Africa, are believed to be the earliest known humans. These latter fossils are about 120,000 years old.

Using anatomical and behavioral traits *to define what makes us human, researchers have been able to develop well-supported theories about the timing and location of human emergence.*

XII. THE DEATH CAMPS

WHILE THE EINSATZGRUPPEN carried out the first wave of Final Solution killings, plans were under way for a second wave, during which Jews from all over occupied Europe would be shipped to death camps. These differed from concentration camps (also called labor camps) because most of the prisoners in death camps weren't expected to live for more than a day.

A notable step forward took place on January 20, 1942, when senior Nazi officials from a wide variety of ministries met in Wannsee, an upscale suburb of Berlin, to discuss how the killings should be coordinated. Chaired by Heydrich, the meeting reviewed a document—prepared by Heydrich's secretary, Adolf Eichmann— listing country-by-country figures for the number of Jews to be exterminated. The statistical work seemed meticulous. It covered not only the larger Jewish populations, such as the 850,000 living in France, but also such seemingly insignificant groups as the 200 Jews thought to be residing in Albania. Eichmann's grand total was eleven million, but this figure was as much a product of his imagination as of his research.

Although the minutes of the Wannsee Conference make no explicit reference to mass murder, German Foreign Office documents seized after the war and presented at Eichmann's 1961 trial demonstrate that the participants indeed discussed openly the best methods for killing so many millions of Jews. The meeting concluded with the agreement of all present that each ministry should coordinate its efforts through Heydrich's office.

Cremation ovens at Buchenwald.

The first extermination camp, constructed on the grounds of a dilapidated castle in the Polish town of Chelmno, was already up and running. Using a methodology that would later become standard, Jewish victims were transported to Chelmno by rail. Upon their arrival, they were divided into groups of 50 to 70 and led into the castle basement under the pretext that they were being allowed to shower. Instead, they were herded into gas vans and driven to mass graves approximately 2.5 miles away. With three trucks working simultaneously, the Chelmno camp was able to kill about a thousand Jews a day. By the end of 1942, the cumulative total reached 145,000.

The major death camps were constructed in German-incorporated Poland, because of its high number of Jews and also because of its relative remoteness. Along with Chelmno, the most notorious camps were Auschwitz, Belżec, Majdanek, Sobibór, and Treblinka. In all, about 2.5 million Jews were killed in these places.

At the Wannsee Conference, *senior Nazi bureaucrats coordinated plans for the next phase of the Final Solution, which would take place in the new Polish death camps.*

XIII. LIQUID-FUELED ROCKET MOTORS

THE SIMPLEST FORM of liquid-fueled rocket uses a single liquid, or monopropellant, to produce thrust. The monopropellant hydrazine, for example, reacts in the presence of an iridium catalyst to produce a large volume of extremely hot hydrogen and nitrogen gas. When this reaction mass is expelled through a nozzle, thrust is created. Monopropellant motors are especially useful in applications that require simplicity and high reliability, such as maneuvering thrusters. They are not, however, high performing, and most monopropellants are highly toxic.

Bipropellant motors use two liquids, one of which is an oxidizer, to create thrust. Smaller models typically employ a pressurized neutral gas (such as helium) to feed the fuels into the combustion chamber. Larger models use turbopumps to generate much higher rates of fuel flow. Each of the six turbopumps that feed the space shuttle's main engine (SSME) can fill an average swimming pool in about twenty seconds.

Some bipropellant systems, the SSME among them, require spark plugs (similar to those found in automobile engines) to start the combustion process. Just prior to SSME ignition, a shower of sparks can seen on the shuttle launchpad as the flow of propellant and oxidizer begins. Once combustion is under way, however, the sparks are no longer necessary. In other bipropellant systems, the liquids react upon contact with each other. Reactions that take place in this way—that is, without an external aid such as a spark—are called hypergolic. The Messerschmitt Me 163 Komet, a rocket-powered fighter developed in Germany during World War II, was powered by the hypergolic reaction between hydrazine hydrate and methanol.

An SSME test firing.

The advantages that liquid-fueled motors have over other chemical rockets are many. For one, they produce much higher effective exhaust velocities, which means that they have higher specific impulses (about 363 seconds, compared with the 285 seconds produced by the average solid-fueled system). For another, liquid-fueled rockets have controllable thrust (i.e., throttle capability), which allows them to be stopped and restarted during a launch, making aborts safer and increasing operational flexibility. A significant disadvantage, however, is that most liquid fuels need to be stored cryogenically—that is, at extremely low temperatures. (Otherwise, they would expand into gases.) This is difficult to do for long periods of time, especially in space. Therefore, liquid-fueled motors are usually used only for launch purposes.

Monopropellant motors *are highly reliable for simple liquid-fueled applications, but they can't produce the thrust generated by large bipropellant systems.*

XIII. MODES OF PRODUCTION

MARX WAS VERY AWARE that labor and surplus value had not always been treated the way they were under capitalism. In medieval Europe, for instance, churches collected tithes, which were contributions made for the support of the church. To pay these tithes, congregants turned over a portion of the surplus value they created, even though the recipients of the tithes (the clergy) had played little or no role in creating that value. The church members parted with the surplus value not to survive in a market economy but out of a sense of religious obligation.

Marx observed that the level of surplus value also changed greatly over time. As the efficiency of production improved, less labor was required to keep workers alive. This reduced the labor value that went into production, thereby raising the amount of surplus value created. Consider, for example, food production: When John Deere invented the self-scouring steel plow in 1837, he helped farmers increase the amount of food they could produce per hour of labor. This development lowered the cost of the food necessary to keep workers alive and thus raised the amount of surplus value they created. The same logic also applied to advances in shelter, health care, transportation, and other technologies that allowed workers to use their labor more efficiently and effectively.

In any given age, Marx wrote, all of these factors and more combine to produce a social system characteristic of that age—comprising not only economic relationships and technologies (the means of production) but also ideas and rules about production, distribution, and exchange (the relations of production). He called these systems modes of production. Each was a historically specific configuration that combined a particular productive technology with a comprehensive set of ideas about how society should organize labor and distribute the products of that labor. In feudalism, for instance, religion played an important role in coaxing surplus value from the populace; under capitalism, on the other hand, workers gave up their claims to surplus value when they agreed to accept a wage.

Although Marx identified and discussed several different modes of production, he was particularly interested in three: feudalism, capitalism, and communism. Because modes of production are self-contained and self-reproducing, they don't evolve. Therefore, Marx explained, transitions from one mode to the next are never gradual. Instead, dialectical tensions build until, finally, a revolution takes place, society breaks with the past, and a new mode of production emerges.

Modes of production *are self-sustaining social systems characterized by historically specific means of production and relations of production.*

XIII. BERTHE MORISOT

BERTHE MORISOT (1841–95) had an interesting artistic lineage. She was the daughter of a high-ranking Parisian civil servant but, more to the point, also the grandniece of Rococo master Jean-Honoré Fragonard. Morisot began taking painting lessons in her teens and during the early 1860s studied with Corot, who taught her how to paint in a manner that would appeal to Salon tastes. As a result, Morisot enjoyed a good deal of academic acceptance early in her career. But during the late 1860s, she rebelled against the smooth Salon style. The change took place around 1868, when she began spending a lot of time with Édouard Manet. After meeting one day at the Louvre, the two artists became friends and fell into a long personal and professional relationship that included Morisot's 1874 marriage to Manet's younger brother, Eugène.

Through Manet, Morisot met the other impressionists but, limited by social custom, couldn't socialize with them in their studios or in the cafés that they frequented. Instead, she and Eugène held regular social gatherings in their home

Berthe Morisot, *Hide and Seek* (1873)

(known as salons), which the leading lights of the Parisian avant-garde attended. Because new artistic ideas were often discussed and debated at these salons, Morisot became an important link in the definition and promotion of the impressionist aesthetic.

Beyond limiting her social life, Morisot's gender also restricted the way she could paint. For example, she couldn't set up an easel in public as her male colleagues did, because this would have been socially unacceptable for a woman of the upper middle class. So Morisot painted mostly domestic scenes: mothers with their children, women in gardens, families on outings, and so on.

Although Morisot's early paintings were heavily influenced, first by Corot and then by Manet, she gradually moved away from her mentors' styles toward a much looser brushwork that, by the late 1870s, could verge on abstraction. Combined with her existing tendency to dissolve form and her preference for a high-keyed palette of greens, blues, and yellows, this new style of brushwork prompted contemporary critic Paul Mantz to declare Morisot's work the epitome of the impressionist style.

As a woman, *Morisot was limited not only in how she socialized but also in how she could paint. Even so, her work was thought to epitomize the impressionist style.*

XIII. THE DEBATE OVER MODERN HUMAN ORIGINS

THERE ARE CURRENTLY two main factions in the debate over modern human origins. One side supports the out-of-Africa model (also known as the replacement hypothesis), while the other defends multiregional evolution (also known as the regional continuity hypothesis). The out-of-Africa model proposes that modern humans first evolved in Africa about one hundred thousand years ago and then dispersed throughout the world. According to this view, archaic hominins already in Europe and Asia were replaced by migrating African *H. sapiens* with little or no hybridization (interbreeding) between modern and archaic populations.

In contrast, paleoanthropologists such as Milford Wolpoff advocate multiregional evolution, which holds that modern humans arose in several different regions simultaneously. Multiregionalists believe that both genetic continuity (the passing on of traits from one generation to the next) and gene flow (the movement of genes across populations through interbreeding) were responsible for the emergence of modern humans from several different populations of archaic ancestors.

Lately, however, the growing consensus that anatomically modern humans first appeared in Africa has led some researchers to formulate intermediate hypotheses, which accept an African origin (based on the fossil record) but also allow for varying amounts of hybridization between modern and archaic populations. (The boundaries between species can sometimes become messy, allowing for a measure of interbreeding.) In fact, the modern human debate now largely focuses on how much hybridization occurred between dispersing African *H. sapiens* and local archaic populations. The key question is whether or not archaic European and Asian hominins contributed to the modern human gene pool.

The most contentious arguments concern a group of European fossils dating back about thirty-five thousand years. These specimens, the earliest modern human remains discovered in Europe, display a combination of primitive and derived traits that some researchers believe indicates the presence of hybridization between modern humans and Neandertals. Others suggest that the features in question, such as robust skeletons and large molars, are simply primitive African traits or adaptations made by African *H. sapiens* to the colder European climate.

Most of the genetic studies that have been performed on human and Neandertal DNA support the out-of-Africa hypothesis, suggesting that no significant hybridization took place. However, opponents have offered valid critiques that leave the door open for some sort of multiregional evolution.

Most evidence currently supports *the out-of-Africa model for modern human origins, but the potential for modern human–Neandertal hybridization cannot be excluded.*

XIII. AUSCHWITZ

OF ALL THE PLACES ASSOCIATED WITH THE HOLOCAUST, Auschwitz was by far the most notorious. During the four years that it operated, 1.1 million Jews were killed

Jewish men disembarking at Auschwitz.

there, along with more than 100,000 Poles (mostly political prisoners) and 20,000 Roma and Sinti (Gypsies). Located outside the Polish town of Oswiecim, Auschwitz (as the Germans called Oswiecim) was actually three camps in one. Auschwitz I served as the administrative hub and housed male inmates. Auschwitz II, also known as Birkenau, contained the women's barracks, the four main gas chambers, and the crematoria. Auschwitz III, also known as Monowitz, was a labor camp run by the I. G. Farben conglomerate. Its factories attempted to produce synthetic oil and rubber for the German war effort.

As at Chelmno, Jews from all over Europe were brought to Auschwitz in cattle cars. Those not healthy enough to work were put to death. The rest were forced to live and toil in unbearable conditions. Prisoners were shaved of all their hair, given meager rations, and forced to sleep in overcrowded barracks that lacked adequate sanitation facilities. Disease and vermin were rampant.

Order was maintained primarily through violence. In addition to the camp guards, Jewish prisoners also had to contend with block leaders and Kapos. These were non-Jews who had been sent to Auschwitz as punishment for a variety of crimes. Block leaders maintained order in the barracks, while Kapos oversaw the work gangs. Regular "selections" were held to sort out healthy from unhealthy inmates. Those deemed no longer fit for work were immediately executed.

One of the most disturbing aspects of Auschwitz was the way in which the Germans made prisoners complicit in the killing of other prisoners. For example, special groups of prisoners called Sonderkommanden (Special Units) were charged with emptying the gas chambers, stripping the corpses of their possessions, and burning the remains. In exchange for this grisly work, the Sonderkommanden enjoyed special privileges and perhaps the opportunity to live a little longer. Former Auschwitz inmate Primo Levi has called the morally difficult situation in which these prisoners found themselves "the gray zone." Levi's term refers to any prisoner who, by force or choice, compromised his own moral values in order to stay alive. Such cases blur the seemingly rigid distinction between victims and perpetrators of the Holocaust.

Of the death camps, *Auschwitz was the most notorious, not only for the magnitude of the killing that went on there but also for the complicity forced on many inmates.*

XIV. **EXOTIC ROCKET MOTORS**

SEVERAL NEW ENGINE TECHNOLOGIES are currently being developed for use in space. Because most produce only a few pounds of thrust, the vehicle containing them must first reach orbit by other means before putting these systems to use.

The arc-jet motor produces thrust by passing liquid propellant through an electric arc (a stream of electricity that completes a circuit by jumping the gap between two electrodes). The energy in the arc converts the propellant (usually liquid hydrogen) into a very hot gas, which is then ejected out a nozzle to produce thrust. While the specific impulse of an arc-jet motor is high (about 2,500 seconds), the thrust it produces is low (only a few pounds). Also, the electrical equipment required to produce the arc is heavy and tends to burn out quickly.

A resisto-jet motor operates in much the same way as an arc-jet, except that it uses an electric filament (like the heating element in a toaster oven) to heat the propellant. Resisto-jets have much longer operational lives than arc-jets but are no more powerful and have a lower specific impulse (only 300 to 900 seconds).

Ion motors generate thrust by ionizing propellant—that is, stripping away electrons to create charged particles—and then accelerating those charged particles (ions) through an electrical field. This process is exceptionally efficient, yielding a specific impulse between 5,000 and 10,000 seconds, but the power requirements (first to ionize the propellant and then to accelerate it) are high.

The test firing of an ion motor.

Plasma motors use a powerful electric arc to convert propellant into plasma, which is then accelerated through a strong magnetic field. (Plasma is superheated gas that, unlike normal gas, consists of positively and negatively charged atomic particles and thus responds to a magnetic field.) Plasma motors are highly efficient (their I_{sp} is about 5,000 seconds), and they can produce several hundred pounds of thrust, but they're also dangerous, because the plasma can interact with the motor casing to cause a catastrophic failure.

The nuclear thermal engine, by far the most powerful of these exotic rocket motors, produces up to 10,000 pounds of thrust using a small fission reactor to heat a liquid propellant such as liquid hydrogen. The specific impulse of nuclear thermal motors is fairly high (about 1,000 seconds), but the extensive shielding required to protect the payload and/or crew from harmful radiation creates a low thrust-to-weight ratio, limiting their usefulness.

Most of the exotic *motors currently in development have high specific impulses but produce only a few pounds of thrust, limiting their usefulness to vehicles already in space.*

XIV. FROM FEUDALISM TO CAPITALISM

FEUDALISM, according to Marx, was the mode of production that immediately preceded capitalism. In other words, the capitalist revolution resolved, in a dialectical sense, the contradictions that had built up over time in feudalist society.

The feudalist mode of production, Marx explained, was dominated by agriculture. Aristocratic and religious elites held the land, providing little in the way of labor, while peasants worked to make the land productive. The elites maintained their land monopoly primarily by force and extracted surplus value from the peasantry through a combination of tradition and patronage (such as the sponsoring of feast days). The peasants, for their part, were ostensibly free, but their economic opportunities were sharply limited. There was little they could do beyond renting land from a lord and paying for it with surplus crops.

Working under such a system, peasants could see clearly how much of their labor went into their own households and how much was diverted to the lord of the manor. Indeed, the expropriation of surplus value was so apparent under feudalism that only the palpable threat of force prevented most peasants from revolting. When one adds to this situation the constant pressure to increase production to meet rising rents, the tension within the system becomes obvious, and so do the contradictions. When rents rise too high, for example, peasants and their equipment break down from overuse, leading to economic decline and social disruption. During the Middle Ages, for example, outbreaks of plague coincided with periods of high rent, because of the poverty and dislocation that high rents caused.

In the end, feudalism could produce only so much from the land, so early capitalists began seeking new opportunities in the growing commodity markets. In Great Britain especially, landowners saw in the new textile factories an opportunity to transition their lands from tenant farming to wool production, which required much less labor. As this took place, peasants were forced off the land and into factories, where more and more employment was becoming available. In time, two new classes emerged: the bourgeoisie, who owned the factories, and the proletariat, who worked in them. Although this revolutionary change (the replacement of one mode of production with another) took place in Britain without a clash of arms, such was not the case in Mexico, for example, where the transition to capitalism was violent indeed.

The tensions and contradictions *within feudalism created the opportunity for a new mode of production, capitalism, to resolve feudalism's contradictions and supplant it.*

XIV. EDGAR DEGAS

BECAUSE EDGAR DEGAS (1834–1917) exhibited in seven of the eight impressionist shows and was instrumental in organizing many of them, he is frequently classified as an impressionist. Nevertheless, Degas was not a follower of the impressionist aesthetic. He studied at the École des Beaux Arts under Jean Auguste Dominique Ingres, a lion of the academic establishment, and never disdained his formal training. His approach to composition was controlled; his draftsmanship, exquisite. What Degas *didn't* care about was natural light and painting en plein air, which set him apart from the impressionist mainstream. Renoir and Monet were about surface; Degas was about structure.

Edgar Degas, *The Place de la Concorde* (1875)

What Degas appreciated most about the impressionist movement was the creative opportunities it offered. Even though he had the skills and connections to be successful within the Salon system, he still resented its rigidity and the limitations that it placed on new artistic ideas. Degas may have found it easy to be so open-minded because he was himself an innovator, both in subject matter and in compositional technique. Although one may legitimately question whether his style was impressionist, certainly it was equally modern.

Degas specialized in figure painting, but his canvases looked more like genre scenes than portraits. (Genre scenes depict the common daily activities of middle-class life, such as men playing chess or women reading.) Critic Louis-Edmond Duranty called this approach, also perfected by Degas's friend Manet, the "modern portrait." Degas closely observed his subjects, and his many studies of dancers demonstrate his ability to capture them in the sort of natural and spontaneous poses that one associates with photography.

Also, like Pissarro, Degas was heavily influenced by Japanese prints, which led him to experiment with asymmetrical compositions and radical cropping. Instead of presenting a full view of his subject, Degas would give the viewer just a part— a body without legs, legs without a body, the front half of a person entering the frame, the back half of a person leaving it. His many studies of women bathing, brushing their hair, or dressing were also derived from Japanese prints.

Although Edgar Degas's *emphasis on figure and composition was far from the impressionist mainstream, he was no less innovative than the other impressionists.*

XIV. THE MIGRATION OF MODERN HUMANS

ACCORDING TO THE GENERALLY ACCEPTED molecular-clock evidence, modern humans emerged between 200,000 and 100,000 years ago. According to the fossil evidence, this emergence took place in Africa. But there seems to have been a rather long gap between the appearance of *H. sapiens* and its spread to other parts of the world. Beyond some fossil remains recovered at the Israeli sites Qafzeh and Skhūl, there seems to be no evidence that *H. sapiens* migrated out of Africa prior to 60,000 years ago (and even the Israeli remains don't seem to indicate a major dispersal event).

Anatomically modern humans began to appear in Asia about 60,000 years ago, as demonstrated by fossil evidence from sites such as Wadjak in Indonesia. The earliest archaeological evidence of modern humans in Europe are 40,000-year-old tools that reflect an advanced technology known as Aurignacian industry, which has been found only in association with modern humans. The earliest fossil evidence of modern humans in Europe, unearthed at sites such as Peştera cu Oase in Romania and Mladeč in the Czech Republic, is even more recent, dating back no more than 35,000 years. The famous Cro-Magnon fossils discovered in the Dordogne region of France date back only 27,000 years.

Initially, modern humans occupied merely those parts of the world that archaic hominins had already exploited. As time went on, however, they migrated farther, colonizing regions into which archaic populations had never ventured. For example, it seems that modern humans were the first hominins to reach Australia. This particular migration represents, according to some researchers, a key development in modern human behavior, because it required the use of watercraft. The earliest remains of modern humans in Australia, discovered at Lake Mungo, date to around 40,000 years ago. In contrast, modern humans didn't arrive in the Americas until about 13,000 years ago, and colonization of the Pacific islands didn't take place until between 3,500 and 1,500 years ago.

Although tens of thousands *of years passed between the emergence of* H. sapiens *in Africa and its migration to other continents, once that migration began, it proceeded quickly and extensively.*

XIV. **THE JEWISH REACTION**

THE MOST COMMON JEWISH REACTION to the anti-Semitism of the Nazis was flight. Of Germany's five hundred thousand Jews, as many as half left the country before 1939. Once the Nazis invaded Poland, many other Jews in Western Europe tried to join the exodus, but the outbreak of war made travel very difficult, and few countries were willing to open their borders to refuges, especially large number of Jewish refugees.

One reason that more Jews didn't leave Europe (and that more countries weren't willing to take them in) was that, during the early 1940s, the concept of genocide remained largely unimaginable. By the time that most Jews realized the magnitude of what was happening—often not until their arrival at a death camp—it was too late for them to save themselves. The veil of secrecy that the Nazis wrapped around the Final Solution served well to keep most Jews unaware of their ultimate fate.

Jews trapped in the Nazi zone of control managed as best as they could. Some hid themselves or their children with sympathetic non-Jewish friends; others tried to pass themselves off as non-Jews. Those who were captured and imprisoned in ghettos tried to maintain as normal a life as possible. Under the most dire of circumstances, they organized a wide range of self-help and mutual aid societies, including schools, food banks, theater groups, and political clubs, often in violation of Nazi regulations. Within the Vilna ghetto, a group of scholars created the Oyneg Shabes archive to preserve the records that they began keeping of every facet of ghetto life. (These were buried underground in the hope that they would survive the war.)

Even in the death camps, where prisoners were forced to compete with one another for scarce resources under brutal conditions, a few found companionship and allies. In her autobiography *Smoke over Birkenau*, Italian journalist Liana Millu describes the deep friendships she formed while an inmate in the camp.

In several ghettos and camps, Jews went a step farther, forming resistance groups to fight the Nazis. Famous instances include the Warsaw Ghetto Uprising of April–May 1943—in which the Jewish Fighting

During the Warsaw Ghetto Uprising, April 1943.

Organization, led by twenty-three-year-old Mordecai Anielewicz, organized more than seven hundred ghetto members to fight off the Nazis for nearly a month. Similarly, in October 1944, an uprising of Sonderkommanden in Birkenau destroyed one of the camp's crematoria and temporarily slowed down the gassing of Jews.

Many Jews simply fled the Nazis. *The millions who didn't or weren't able to managed as best they could—whether in hiding, in the ghettos, or in the labor and death camps.*

XV. THE SPACE ENVIRONMENT

A shuttle astronaut performs an EVA (extravehicular activity).

WHERE DOES EARTH END and space begin? The answer isn't as simple as it may seem. The US government awards wings to astronauts who have flown in a powered vehicle to a height of 50 nautical miles (about 80 km) above Earth's surface. The rest of the world recognizes a spaceflight boundary of 100 kilometers; but even at this altitude, a spacecraft can circle Earth only a few times before its orbit decays due to atmospheric drag. To maintain orbit for a day or longer, a spacecraft must attain an altitude of at least 80 nautical miles (about 130 km). This may sound high up, but if Earth were a peach, then this altitude would be right at the top of its fuzz.

Even at an altitude of 300 kilometers, there's more than enough atmosphere to make knowledge of its effects essential. Beyond the drag it causes on spacecraft, the atmosphere at that height has a different composition than the air at sea level. Significantly, it contains a much higher percentage of atomic oxygen. Unlike molecular oxygen, which consists of two oxygen atoms bonded together, atomic oxygen is highly reactive and will attack spacecraft components susceptible to oxidation (rust), weakening and eroding them.

In the deep space beyond Earth's atmosphere, a near-perfect vacuum exists, but this type of environment can cause problems as well, such as outgassing (the emission of gases from within a spacecraft) and off-gassing (the emission of gases from the surface of a spacecraft). Both of these conditions can cloud sensors and interfere with instrument readings. The near-perfect vacuum of space can also cause cold-welding, which is a fusing together that occurs when parts manufactured from similar metals come into contact in a vacuum.

Gravity can be another confusing aspect of the space environment. The idea that vehicles in Earth orbit operate in zero gravity is a common misconception. Let's say that you could build a tower as tall as the typical low Earth orbit (about 300 km). Standing at the top of the tower, you would experience a gravitational pull equal to about 91 percent of Earth's gravitational force at sea level. The reason that astronauts in orbit float around is not that they're weightless; the reason is that they're in free fall. Like all objects in orbit, astronauts are falling all the time, but they don't hit the ground because the ground is always curving away from them.

Although most people think *of space as a zero-atmosphere, zero-gravity environment, vehicles in low Earth orbit do experience the effects of both atmosphere and gravity.*

XV. THE FIRST INTERNATIONAL

WHILE WORKING TO IDENTIFY and analyze the different modes of production that had preceded capitalism, Marx also labored to bring about its replacement. In September 1864, he played a leading role in a meeting held at St. Martin's Hall in London, where a group of leftist leaders from different countries founded the International Workingmen's Association (the First International).

The purpose of the First International was to coordinate the activities of workers' groups throughout Europe—from Britain, France, and Belgium to the Italian state, the German states, Russia, and beyond. Not only geographically diverse but philosophically inclusive as well, the First International included Marxists, Proudhonians, anarchists, utopian socialists, and many other labor organizers and activists. Marx handled most of the group's policy statements and pamphleteering.

Given the many doctrinal differences that existed, maintaining order and amity within the First International was a constant struggle. Often, those (like Marx) who believed that workers needed to seize control of the state battled with others (like anarchist Mikhail Bakunin) who saw little role for the state and wanted to seize the factories instead. This division eventually produced an irreconcilable split in the organization, leading to Bakunin's expulsion in September 1872 and the disbanding of the First International four years later. At its height, however, the organization had several million members.

No external event affected the First International more than the Franco-Prussian War of 1870–71. The defeat of the French army at Sedan in September 1870 sparked an immediate popular uprising in Paris. Louis-Napoleon (who had declared himself emperor in 1852) was deposed, the Third Republic was proclaimed, and a government of the proletariat known as the Paris Commune was established. Marx and Engels gave advice to the Communards and, on behalf of the First International, organized international workers on their behalf. However, as in 1848, violent suppression soon followed, and hopes for the imminent overthrow of capitalism faded.

While Bakunin blamed the failure of the Commune on a lack of leadership, Marx lamented that the revolutionaries hadn't finished off the federal army when they had the opportunity. Instead, the forces of reaction were allowed to regroup and retake the city. For Marx, the most important lesson of the Paris Commune was that workers needed not only to seize power when they had the chance but also to eliminate all forces that might oppose them.

Through his work with the First International (1864–76), *Marx tried to prepare the European left for communist revolution when it came.*

XV. MARY CASSATT

MARY CASSATT (1844–1926) was the only American associated with the French impressionists. She was born in Pittsburgh, Pennsylvania, where her well-to-do father was a financier and stockbroker. In 1855, the family moved to Philadelphia, where Cassatt later enrolled in the Pennsylvania Academy of Fine Arts. After four years of classes there, the eighteen-year-old Cassatt left Philadelphia to study painting in Europe. With the exception of a few brief visits home (such as during the Franco-Prussian War), Cassatt lived the rest of her life on the Continent, mostly in Paris.

During her early years in Paris, Cassatt won some attention for her portraiture and genre scenes, and in 1868 she began exhibiting at the Salon. In 1877, she met Degas. Because their work had much in common, he invited her to exhibit with the impressionists, which she did in 1879. Like Degas, Cassatt favored a very structured compositional approach, but her style during the late 1870s and 1880s remained in keeping with impressionist practice: cosmopolitan subjects painted in brushy strokes using high-keyed color.

Like Morisot, Cassatt was limited in her career by nineteenth-century gender roles and concepts of social propriety. Because she was a respectable woman, there

Mary Cassatt, *Lady at the Tea Table* (1883)

were places she couldn't go and subjects she couldn't paint, such as the Parisian street scenes that were often the subject of her colleagues' work. She did, however paint subjects that she knew from her own experience, such as women attending the theater, which she often did in the company of her sister Lydia. Other subjects that Cassatt painted, which were appropriate to her status as an upper-class woman, included domestic interiors, garden scenes, and portraits of mothers with children.

Important changes in Cassatt's style arose from the printmaking experiments she conducted with Degas and Pissarro. Cassatt, too, was influenced by the flat perspective and broad swaths of color found in the Japanese originals. By the 1890s, these qualities had so transformed her work that it seemed less impressionist and more in keeping with post-impressionism.

Cassatt was the only American *and one of the few women associated with impressionism. She worked closely with Degas and was highly influenced by Japanese prints.*

XV. TOOLS

THE FIRST STONE TOOLS, known to archaeologists as lithics, began to appear about 2.6 Ma. These mark the start of the Stone Age, which archaeologists have divided into three periods: the Paleolithic, Mesolithic, and Neolithic. The Paleolithic, the oldest of these periods, has been further subdivided into Early, Middle, and Late stages.

The Early Paleolithic began 2.6 Ma with the rise of the first toolmaking technology, known as Oldowan (after Olduvai Gorge). Oldowan toolmakers started with a hammerstone and a core (the stone blank that became a tool). Using the hammerstone, the toolmaker knocked flakes from the core. The prepared core was then used for cracking open the bones of hunted or scavenged animals, while the sharper flakes were used for cutting. Some evidence suggests that *H. habilis* made the first Oldowan tools, but it's difficult to associate this toolmaking with only one species of hominin because Oldowan tools appeared at a time when *Australopithecus* and *Paranthropus* were also present. (*A. garhi*, for example, may have been the originator of Oldowan tools, because remains of this species have been found near bones marked by stone tools.)

A drawing of an Acheulean hand ax.

Acheulean technology improved on Oldowan techniques and enabled *H. erectus* to begin making bifacial tools, such as teardrop-shaped hand axes, about 1.4 Ma. (Bifacial means that flakes were removed from both sides of the core.) Acheulean artifacts are also much more uniform in appearance than their Oldowan predecessors, suggesting that *H. erectus* and the other Mid-Pleistocene *Homo* who used this technology had a clear mental image of what their tools should look like.

The tools of the Middle Paleolithic, which began 200,000 years ago, reflect increased technological sophistication as well as further cognitive development. The best-known Middle Paleolithic assemblages are the Mousterian tools associated with the Neandertals. Also, the first clear evidence of the controlled use of fire dates to the Middle Paleolithic.

Beginning 50,000 years ago, the Late Paleolithic saw the appearance of blades and microliths (small stone flakes hafted onto wooden or bone handles). These tools, mainly associated with modern humans, show increased variation in the use of materials such as bone and antler. Researchers have also noticed a much quicker pace of technological change during the Late Paleolithic and greater standardization of tool types. Tools from this period include fishhooks, harpoons, and needles.

The earliest stone tools *appeared about 2.6 Ma, at the start of the Early Paleolithic. The first toolmaking technology was perhaps invented by* H. habilis—*but perhaps not.*

XV. OTHER VICTIMS OF NAZISM

IN ADDITION TO JEWS and the mentally and physically handicapped, the Nazis targeted several other groups for elimination. These included the Roma and the Sinti (Gypsies); homosexual men; and, to a lesser extent, Jehovah's Witnesses, The reason for their persecution was that, in one way or another, all of these groups threatened the purity of the German master race.

The Nazis' treatment of the Roma and Sinti in many ways mirrored their treatment of the Jews: Gypsies were considered racially inferior and targeted for genocide. A special camp was set up for them within Birkenau, where families were permitted to stay together until they were exterminated together. In the meantime, Dr. Josef Mengele performed brutal pseudoscientific experiments on many of the inmates. The Roma word for the Holocaust is *Porajmos*, meaning "the devouring."

With regard to gays, the Nazis were able to take advantage of the same sort of long-standing hatred and prejudice that many Germans felt toward Jews. In 1871, the year of Germany's unification, Paragraph 175 was added to the Criminal Code, stating, "Unnatural fornication, whether between persons of the male sex or of

These Gypsy children were sent to Auschwitz.

humans with beasts, is to be punished by imprisonment." During the sexually liberated Weimar period, an active campaign was undertaken to remove Paragraph 175 from the Criminal Code, but the effort failed. Thus, when the Nazis came to power in 1933, they didn't have to enact new laws to imprison homosexual men; they merely had to enforce the law already on the books.

Nazis prosecuted homosexual activity because they thought it weakened Germany, contributing to the country's moral decay, declining birthrate, and overall insecurity. During the twelve years of Nazi rule, as many as fifty thousand men were prosecuted under Paragraph 175. Some were jailed briefly, and others forced to join the military. The worst offenders, numbering about fifteen thousand, were placed in "protective custody" and sent to concentration camps, where they were forced to wear pink triangles on their prison uniforms. Lesbian activity, on the other hand, existed in an official limbo, neither condoned nor criminalized. As historian Claudia Schoppmann has noted, because not many women moved in Nazi circles of power, "it was considered superfluous to criminalize lesbians."

Because Jehovah's Witnesses weren't considered racially inferior, they weren't targeted for destruction. Yet, because their faith prohibited them from swearing oaths to Germany, they were persecuted; imprisoned; tortured; and, at times, executed.

Beyond Jews and the disabled, *the Nazis also victimized Gypsies, homosexual men, and Jehovah's Witnesses—all of whom were considered threats to German racial purity.*

XVI. DESIGNING FOR THE SPACE ENVIRONMENT

WHEN DESIGNING VEHICLES for Earth orbit, the most important force to take into account is gravity, which causes both linear acceleration and rotational torque. For example, unless the space shuttle orbiter fires its maneuvering thrusters, gravity will inevitably turn the orbiter so that its nose is pointing down and one wing is pointing in the direction of travel. Building spacecraft to be durable means carrying extra weight into orbit, which is expensive, but the alternative—building a light, flimsy vehicle—is dangerous, because gravity could easily deform it.

Spacecraft designers also have to take into account harmful solar radiation. The Sun produces both electromagnetic radiation (EMR) and penetrating charged particles (PCPs). Earth's atmosphere protects life on the surface from the harmful effects of high-energy EMR, just as the planet's magnetic field shields surface life from dangerous PCPs; but in low Earth orbit, where the atmosphere is thin and the magnetic field is weak, these defenses are inadequate.

EMR travels through substances as well as empty space in waves of energy that move at the speed of light. Light is itself a form of EMR, which is generated by the vibration of charged particles. Radio waves and microwaves are relatively benign forms of low-energy EMR. On the other hand, at the high-energy end of the electromagnetic spectrum (above the range of visible light), EMR becomes ionizing, which means that it can alter the structure of molecules, including molecules of human DNA. Ultraviolet (UV) light and X-rays are examples of high-energy EMR against which astronauts and electronic equipment need to be protected.

The high energy of PCPs is also troublesome. Along with producing their own ionizing radiation, PCPs often crash computer systems by flipping polarities in their magnetic memory. All computers store information in bits of binary code, with 1 corresponding to "on" and 0 corresponding to "off." When high-energy PCPs penetrate computers, they can change "off" bits to "on," for example turning the eight-bit byte 10101010 into 11111111. Laptops left on in the space shuttle orbiter overnight typically lock up and need to be rebooted the next morning.

Engineers have not yet developed a way to protect spacecraft or astronauts from PCPs, some of which are energetic enough to pass through six feet of lead shielding. The only countermeasure currently available is to build in enough computer redundancy so that spacecraft can operate safely. Astronauts, meanwhile, can absorb the equivalent of two to three chest X-rays during each day they spend in space.

Spacecraft designers must take into account the ways in which the space environment differs from Earth, where the planet's atmosphere and magnetic field protect life from harmful EMR and PCPs.

XVI. THE ROLE OF THE STATE

THE DEFEAT OF FRANCE by the Prussian army in 1870 accelerated the formation of a new pan-German empire, known as the Second Reich. Many German workers, feeling confident in their numbers and strength, believed that they could exert a great deal of influence over the new imperial parliament through the use of electoral politics. At a congress held in Gotha in May 1875, some of Marx's followers agreed to merge their efforts with those of Ferdinand Lassalle, who believed that a united socialist front would have the wherewithal to win electoral control of the state. The result was the formation of the Socialist Workers' Party of Germany.

Marx, however, strongly objected to Lassalle's premise. In his view, contained in his *Critique of the Gotha Programme*, the ruling class in countries with strong state-oriented traditions would never give up power without violence. Therefore, Marx wrote, in nations such as Germany and France, the "lever of our revolution must be force."

For Marx, having witnessed several European wars and as many bloody suppressions of worker-based revolutionary moments, control over the state and the military seemed necessary, indeed unavoidable, if large-scale social change was to be accomplished. Yet, how that power was to be gained and managed remained unclear, even to Marx. After 1871, he seems to have envisioned a moment when workers would take up government positions even as they retained their status as workers. As he wrote in the *Critique of the Gotha Programme*, "Between capitalist and communist society, there lies the period of the revolutionary transformation of the one into the other. Corresponding to this is also a political transition period, in which the state can be nothing but the revolutionary dictatorship of the proletariat."

Party political activity such as that contemplated at Gotha threatened to delay the revolution, Marx believed, because it allowed national governments to co-opt or buy off worker movements with promises of electoral participation. Indeed, Marx's criticism of Gotha included the pointed charge that socialists demanded only incremental changes, such as the reduction of the workday from ten hours to nine hours, and not the radical break that was actually required. Marx, however, never did explain specifically how such a radical break was going to come about.

Marx believed *that the implementation of communist revolution required a temporary dictatorship of the proletariat, which could not be achieved through electoral means.*

XVI. PAUL CÉZANNE

UNLIKE THE MANY Paris-born impressionists, Paul Cézanne (1839–1906) came from southern France, specifically the town of Aix-en-Provence. To satisfy the wishes of his father, who was a successful banker, Cézanne studied law at the University of Aix and began his adult life as a stockbroker. But his desire to study painting soon proved irresistible, and it brought him to Paris in 1861. Bypassing the École des Beaux-Arts, Cézanne went directly to the Académie Suisse, where he met Pissarro.

Most of Cézanne's early paintings were portraits and still lifes, created with large but controlled brushstrokes that applied the paint thickly to the canvas. Sometimes, Cézanne even used a palette knife instead of a brush—a style that many critics found crude. Like most of the artists associated with impressionism, Cézanne consistently sought Salon acceptance throughout the 1860s but was just as consistently rejected.

In 1872, perhaps eager for a change in genre, Cézanne joined his friend Pissarro in Pontoise and began painting landscapes en plein air. The experience transformed Cézanne's style. Embracing the fundamental impressionist goal of painting what the eye sees, he gave up the broad, heavy brushstrokes that had characterized his earlier work and began applying paint in smaller touches of varying tones and hue. The result was luminous, atmospheric color.

Cézanne participated in the first (1874) and third (1877) impressionist exhibitions but stopped showing with the group thereafter. Part of the reason was that he could be quite cantankerous. He also didn't see himself as an impressionist. Working with Pissarro had been a revelation, but his brushstrokes were never rapid, never spontaneous, and he wasn't the least bit interested in the dissolution of form toward which Monet, Morisot, and Pissarro were striving. Instead, Cézanne was interested in solidity, in the physical presence of objects. His primary concern was how to represent three-dimensional objects within the two-dimensional space of the canvas. His later work, which foreshadowed cubism, emphasized the underlying structure of objects, rather than the objects themselves. Such paintings as his multiple views of Mont Sainte-Victoire and his large and powerful *Bathers* (1904–6) were important steps in resolving this compositional problem.

Cézanne was one of the most *individualistic artists associated with impressionism, and his work had a strong influence on early-twentieth-century experimentation.*

Paul Cézanne, *Bathers* (1904–6)

XVI. SYMBOLIC REPRESENTATION

SYMBOLIC REPRESENTATION lies at the heart of modern civilization. It refers to the attachment of abstract meanings to things—the process that makes language, art, and religion possible. The key to recognizing symbolic behavior is that it typically has no utilitarian function. For instance, the Egyptian practice of burying a pharaoh with his worldly goods had no practical purpose, but it did have great symbolic significance in relation to Egyptian religion. The earliest uncontested archaeological evidence of symbolic behavior dates to around forty thousand years ago, when modern humans began wearing personal ornamentation. About the same time (the Late Paleolithic), evidence also begins to appear of cave painting, rock carving, and ritual burial of the dead.

Cave paintings have been discovered in Africa and Australia, but the most famous are those found in Europe at sites such as the Lascaux Cave in France. No one knows why early humans painted images on the walls of caves, but archaeologists agree that the paintings must have had some symbolic value. Rock carvings have also been found that date to the Late Paleolithic. Some of these—such as Venus figurines, which display exaggerated female breasts and hips—are believed by some to be fertility symbols,

The issue of whether Neandertals practiced symbolic behavior is hotly contested. The case for personal ornamentation (found at some later European sites) is fairly strong, but the claim that Neandertals buried their dead ritually is much more speculative. At Teshik Tash in Uzbekistan, the skeleton of a nine-year-old child was found apparently surrounded by upright goat horns. At Shanidar in Iraq, an older corpse was discovered covered with wildflowers. Yet there is no evidence that mourners placed

A twenty-five-thousand-year-old Venus figurine.

these items where they were found. Other Neandertal sites have produced such well-preserved skeletons that burials have been inferred. Even so, it's not known whether these bodies were buried for reasons of hygiene or for symbolic purposes.

Unlike the Neandertals, humans of the Late Paleolithic left behind clear evidence of their ritualistic practices, such as the beads and pendants with which they decorated the bodies of their dead. Often, the pendants were made from the teeth of animals not hunted as a food source, indicating that the killing of these animals likely fulfilled a nonutilitarian purpose. Also, producing the beads and pendants took a great deal of time, from which one can also infer the great importance of symbolic behavior to Late Paleolithic humans.

Evidence for symbolic behavior *among human populations of the Late Paleolithic includes cave paintings, rock carvings, and ritual burial of the dead.*

XVI. ANNE FRANK

TEENAGER ANNE FRANK is probably the most famous victim of the Holocaust. Her fame derives from the remarkable diary she kept while hiding out from the Nazis during the German occupation of the Netherlands. Born in 1929, she left Germany with her family in 1933 to escape Nazi rule, only to have the Nazis occupy her new home, Amsterdam, seven years later. The Franks lived openly for a time, but when Anne's older sister, Margot, learned during the summer of 1942 that she would soon be sent to a work camp, the family went into hiding. Their refuge was a secret annex of rooms above and to the rear of Otto Frank's office. Joining the Franks in hiding were four family friends.

Anne's diary tells the story of the two years she and the others spent in the cramped secret annex. The basic needs of the Franks and their friends were met by four former employees of Otto Frank, who brought them food, passed on news of the outside world, and guarded their secret closely. Anne wrote about the tensions that ebbed and flowed in the annex, as well as of her complicated feelings for Peter van Pels, the only young man in the group and increasingly the focus of her romantic attention.

It isn't known who ultimately informed the authorities, but in August 1944 the police stormed the secret annex and arrested the inhabitants. All eight were sent to the Westerbork transit camp, and from there to Auschwitz. In October 1944, Anne and her sister, Margot, were transferred again to Bergen-Belsen, where both died of disease in March 1945, just a few weeks before the camp was liberated.

Anne's diary, meanwhile, was recovered by friends following the police raid and kept safe until after the war, when it was returned to Otto Frank, the only member of the family to survive the camps. He arranged for its publication in 1947.

In 2005, a file containing eighty pages of documents relating to Otto Frank's efforts to secure entry for his family into the United States was discovered in the archives of the YIVO Institute for Jewish Research in New York City. The paperwork tells the compelling story of Frank's desperate but ultimately futile attempt during the second half of 1941 to overcome the bureaucratic obstacles blocking so many Jews trying to escape the war.

Anne Frank is remembered *today because the diary that she kept during her two years in hiding in Amsterdam personalized the horrors of the Holocaust.*

XVII. INTRAGALACTIC SPACE TRAVEL

GIVEN THE SPEED OF TECHNICAL INNOVATION, it's not difficult to imagine humans in the not-so-distant future traveling in rocket ships to other star systems. When this happens, however, it won't be accomplished with any current propulsion technology, nor even with a technology now on the horizon.

To understand the magnitude of the difficulty, consider that the fastest speed ever attained by a spacecraft is just over one hundred thousand miles per hour. Even at this speed, it would take more than forty-four thousand years to reach the Sun's nearest stellar neighbor, Proxima Centauri, about 4.2 light-years away. Furthermore, an intragalactic spacecraft would first have to climb out of the Sun's powerful gravity well by running its motor constantly. This would, of course, use up a great deal of propellant. In order to reach Proxima Centauri in less than a thousand years, a chemical rocket would have to use more atoms of propellant than there are atoms of matter in the universe.

During the 1950s, some thought was put into propelling spacecraft with nuclear bombs. The idea was to drop a bomb out the back end of a spacecraft and then detonate it, the force of the resulting explosion driving the vehicle forward. Theoretically, such a system would have a specific impulse of about five thousand seconds, or ten times the efficiency of a chemical rocket. Yet storage of the nuclear devices posed something of a problem. Considering that a supertanker holds about four hundred thousand tons of crude oil, a spacecraft would need about a billion supertankers traveling alongside it to carry all the "propellant" bombs needed for a trip to Proxima Centauri.

Even if an intragalactic spacecraft's engines were to use the most powerful force known to humans—the explosive reaction that takes place when matter comes into contact with antimatter—there would still be fuel storage problems. Take, for example, one antimatter motor design, in which positrons (antielectrons) are sprayed onto the surface of a nozzle to create thrust. Such a motor would have a specific impulse of perhaps fifty thousand seconds, but the spacecraft would still need a storage tank the size of ten space shuttle external tanks to hold enough propellant to reach Proxima Centauri.

Travel between star systems isn't possible *using current technology, and even theoretically feasible systems like matter–antimatter drives can't really do the job in a practical way.*

XVII. THE CONTRADICTIONS OF CAPITALISM

AT THE CORE OF MARXISM is the dialectical idea that modes of production such as capitalism sow the seeds of their own destruction. In fact, Marx's views concerning historical inevitability are what distinguish his thought from that of classical economists like Ricardo and contemporary socialists like Proudhon. Marx saw his argument as neither moral nor psychological nor philosophical but ultimately scientific. It wasn't that people would simply come to see capitalism as a bad idea. Rather, the day-to-day workings of capitalism would, sooner or later, render that mode of production, like its predecessors, incapable of reproducing itself.

According to Marx, the economic ups and downs of the capitalist system were more than mere "business cycles," as most economists described them. Over time, Marx believed, the highs would grow higher and the lows would grow lower until a tipping point was reached, when a cascading failure of the system would usher in a new mode of production.

This pattern, Marx went on, applied to individuals as well. Caught up in the capitalist system, individuals would move back and forth psychologically between adherence to the capitalist ideology and recognition of the personal costs of participation in the system. Stripping away past ideologies of religion, race, and family, capitalism made clear the dependence of workers on one another, yet it also left those workers isolated, alienated, and living as though they were subject to the impersonal forces of the market. Like the system itself, people living under capitalism would lurch back and forth in ever-deepening crises.

Marx in London, 1861.

The power and attraction of Marx's thought has always been its complex interweaving of this economic analysis with his practical politics, utopian vision, and loyalty to the fate of the working class. Specialists in each of these areas have lamented Marx's inclusion of the others—that is, Marxist economists prefer to study only Marx's views on economics, but they find it difficult to disentangle his economic analyses from his pronouncements on politics and the coming revolution. Marx himself resisted such tendencies to separate out the different aspects of his work. In the last of his *Theses on Feuerbach* (1845), he stated, "The philosophers have only interpreted the world in various ways; the point is to change it." This famous dictum, which guided his career from the start, ultimately became his epitaph.

According to Marx, *the contradictions inherent in capitalism would produce increasingly wild swings between prosperity and depression until a tipping point was reached.*

XVII. **THE CRISIS OF IMPRESSIONISM**

SOME ART HISTORIANS have characterized the early 1880s as the "crisis of impressionism" because the artists associated with the movement, never all that cohesive, began to go their separate ways. Previously, they had set aside stylistic and aesthetic differences in order to pool their resources so they could mount exhibitions independent of the Salon (whose acceptance they continued to crave). But even this loose alliance proved increasingly difficult to maintain as Renoir and Pissarro began to consider impressionism merely a phase in their artistic development and Degas and Cézanne, never comfortable with the *impressionist* label, looked in other directions as well.

The shift can be detected as early as 1880–81, when some of the core artists—including Renoir, Monet, and Sisley—stopped participating in the impressionist exhibitions. Each had his own reason—Renoir, for example, wanted to try his hand exclusively with the Salon—but there were common difficulties as well. On a stylistic level, many impressionists felt that they could no longer ignore their differences, and on a personal level, they resented the control that Degas was exerting, especially the large number of friends he was insisting be included in the shows.

Camille Pissarro, *Peasants Resting* (1881)

The defection of these founding members communicated a sense of disarray and greatly complicated the task of defining what it meant to be an impressionist. The situation changed briefly in 1882, when Renoir, Monet, and Sisley returned for the seventh impressionist exhibition, having seemingly resolved their differences with Degas and others. Partly because of their reintegration and partly because a number of innovative new works were on display (such as Pissarro's 1881 canvas *Peasants Resting*), the 1882 show seemed to reaffirm the experimental fervor that had long characterized the impressionist movement. Sadly, this was an illusion, because impressionism was essentially at an end.

Just twelve years separated the first impressionist show in 1874 and the last in 1886, yet so many important ideas were established in this time: the idea of painting slices of modern life, the idea of exploring natural light and color, the idea of working outside the Salon system, and the idea of capturing momentary visual impressions on canvas—that is, painting what the eye saw. These ideas were transgressive, they were revolutionary, and they would change the course of Western art.

By the mid-1880s, *the center of impressionism could no longer hold, and the artists, split by factionalism, dispersed to follow their own stylistic paths.*

XVII. THE ORIGIN OF LANGUAGE

THE USE OF LANGUAGE is one of the key characteristics that distinguish *Homo sapiens* from other primates. Because no direct evidence of language exists in the fossil record, researchers have had a difficult time inferring its development. Fortunately, the evolutionary history of the human brain and throat offers some insight.

The human brain plays a vital role in the production and comprehension of language; therefore, the emergence of language capabilities should be reflected somehow in changes to the brain's structure. If this is true, the fossil record can help. Although brain tissue doesn't fossilize, surviving crania can be used to make endocasts, which reveal the shape of the brain that the cranium being cast once held. Because studies of modern human brains have identified the areas where speech production and language comprehension take place, researchers using endocasts can trace the development of these areas over time.

Differences observed in the throat anatomies of modern humans and primates have also aided researches in making inferences about the development of language capabilities. The larynx, for example, occupies a lower position in the human throat than it does in the throats of other primates. This arrangement makes possible the large human pharynx, which produces the relatively wide variety of sounds used in human speech. There is, however, a strong disadvantage to this arrangement: a greatly increased risk of choking while eating or drinking. Therefore, language must have been a strongly advantageous trait; otherwise, the increased incidence of choking would have ensured its elimination through the process of natural selection.

Another important indicator is the hyoid, a small throat bone only rarely preserved in the fossil record. The discovery of a Neandertal hyoid bone at Kebara in Israel has led some researchers to conclude, because of its humanlike appearance, that Neandertals were capable of human speech. However, even if this were so, the capacity to produce humanlike sounds doesn't necessarily imply the ability to communicate symbolically.

Although the origin of language will always be debatable because the evidence is scarce, most researchers agree that by the Late Paleolithic, humans likely possessed a full range of language capabilities. (The explosion of symbolic behavior found in the archaeological record demonstrates the existence of symbolic communication at this time.) However, some forms of communication must have existed previously. Otherwise, early humans wouldn't have been able to pass on the complex knowledge required to make their increasingly sophisticated tools.

Symbolic language is one of the key characteristics that distinguish humans from other primates, yet its development is difficult to study because of the lack of direct evidence.

XVII. **THE WORLD REACTS**

DURING THE SPRING OF 1938, journalist Dorothy Thompson wrote an article for *Foreign Affairs* magazine about the growing refugee crisis in Europe. According to Thompson, millions were wandering the world, looking for safe havens, and not all of them were German Jews. Some were Polish and Romanian Jews, also fleeing

Jews seeking exit permits line up in Vienna in 1938.

anti-Semitism; others were Spaniards uprooted by the recent civil war; and many were anti-Nazi Austrians escaping the Anschluss (the German annexation of Austria in March 1938). "To close one's eyes to [the crisis] would be 'ostrichism' in an acute form," Thompson wrote.

During the summer of 1938, representatives from thirty-two countries attended a nine-day conference on the refugee problem held in Evian, France. Although the delegates expressed their unanimous desire to help the Jewish refugees, only the Dominican Republic pledged to take any in. This offer was itself something of a ruse on the part of the Dominican leader, a dictator who wanted to deflect criticism from his own poor human rights record. Few Jews learned of the offer, even fewer were able to obtain passage, and only 650 ended up relocating there.

The United States, the country with perhaps the greatest capacity to absorb refugees, remained highly reluctant to relax its tight immigration quotas, which reflected a strong xenophobic strain in American society. In addition to their fundamentally racist dislike of immigrants, many Americans objected to the potential competition for jobs and the possibility that some among the refugees would be spies. Pres. Franklin Roosevelt and other US officials sympathized with the refugees but were unwilling to expend much political capital on their behalf.

As conditions in Germany worsened, activists worked with Congress to expand the immigration quota allotted to Germany. The Wagner-Rogers bill would have allowed the admission of an additional twenty thousand German children, both Jews and non-Jews. Private agencies secured housing and funding for all twenty thousand, but the bill never made it out of committee. Once the war began, the number of refugees increased dramatically, while borders tightened further. A second refugee conference, held in Bermuda in April 1943, brought no tangible results.

Jews did find refuge in some unexpected places. On the eve of the war, Britain accepted ten thousand in the famous Kindertransport; Shanghai, China, took in twenty thousand more; and several thousand others made their way to Bolivia.

As the world moved closer to war, *many countries expressed their sympathy for Jewish refugees, but nearly all, like the United States, failed to offer tangible help.*

XVIII. **THE REACTIONLESS DRIVE**

AS RECENTLY AS A FEW DECADES AGO, it didn't seem possible that a spacecraft could travel between star systems within a single human lifetime. However, our understanding of physics isn't what it used to be, and it continues to evolve.

Using new, more powerful instruments like the Hubble Space Telescope and the Chandra X-Ray Observatory, astronomers have measured the movements of distant galaxies and found that some of them are traveling away from each other in ways that are inconsistent with our understanding of gravity. Physicists model gravity as an attractive force (a pull), but something is clearly *pushing* these galaxies and accelerating them to speeds faster than the speed of light. In order to explain this phenomenon, scientists have proposed the existence of negative matter, dark energy, and a host of other exotic concepts.

This new evidence suggests, at least theoretically, that an entirely new form of space travel might be developed—one that requires no mechanical reaction force. If the physics involved is ever understood, then perhaps designers will one day be able to build a spacecraft that generates a small space–time bubble around itself. As the ship moves forward, space–time would warp, allowing the ship to travel at speeds faster than the speed of light. (This is possible because, although no object in space–time can travel faster than the speed of light, there seems to be no limit to the speed at which space–time itself can travel within space–time.)

Entering a bubble universe would be like entering an elevator car. Inside the bubble universe, you would remain stationary relative to your universe (the world of the elevator car) and thus continue to obey all the laws of physics. Even if the bubble universe containing you exceeds the speed of light, *inside* the bubble you would not.

Such a bubble would move by surfing space–time—that is, by expanding the space–time behind the ship, contracting the space–time in front of the ship, and riding the crest of the generated "wave." The Alcubierre drive, described by Mexican physicist Miguel Alcubierre in a 1994 paper, employs a very similar strategy.

There are many such unexplained phenomena in the universe, and in one of these rocket scientists may eventually find a way to the stars. Limited to current physics, however, the stars remain closed to us.

Astronomers have discovered *a pushing force in the universe, which may be caused by negative matter and dark energy. If such things exist, then perhaps they can be harnessed for propulsion.*

XVIII. MARX'S INFLUENCE

BY THE TIME OF MARX'S DEATH IN 1883, there were already political parties and workers' movements identifying themselves by his name. Some adhered faithfully to what he had written, while others took advantage of his lack of specificity to read their own thoughts into his discussions of the political future. For this reason, even though the increasingly wild business fluctuations that Marx predicted never came about, his vision of the future inspired a great deal of political activity during the late nineteenth and early twentieth centuries.

Ironically, the first revolutions in Marx's name were staged not by the industrialized workers, in whom he had placed his faith, but by peasants, whom Marx considered anachronistic and lacking a political future. First in Russia and later in China and elsewhere, peasant revolutions changed the political topography of the world, eventually producing the Cold War that dominated global politics for half a century.

In the West, Marxist thought became largely academic. Marx's writings were analyzed in universities, and the interplay between his thought and the political events it inspired was discussed. In the East, however, most of the Marxists belonged to political parties, which struggled to adapt Marxist thinking to the exigencies of governance and economic development.

Clearly, nothing that emerged in Russia, China, or anywhere else matched Marx's vision of the future under communism. While many elements of his political platform have become commonplace—public education and the abolition of child labor, for example—key elements, such as the nationalization of production, have proven largely unsuccessful. Most obviously, the overthrow of the capitalist order never took place in industrialized Europe, where Marx insisted it was imminent. Instead, the worker uprisings of the late nineteenth and early twentieth centuries turned out to be merely a stage in the evolving relationship between capital and labor, which has since become much more quiescent. Today, Marxist political parties are few, and most economic trends point to liberalization, which Marx would have seen as bourgeois consolidation.

For this reason, people who continue to see value in Marx's work tend to emphasize his analytical insights. Even though nearly all of the world's Marxist states have collapsed in failure, it remains a testament to Marx's influence that few can hear his name mentioned without thinking of his call for radical political change in the name of economic equality.

In the West, *Marxism became primarily an academic pursuit; while in the East, it became the basis for a series of successful peasant revolts.*

XVIII. POST-IMPRESSIONISM

LIKE *IMPRESSIONISM*, the term *post-impressionism* is fundamentally vague. Coined by British critic and artist Roger Fry in 1910, it has been used to describe several styles, closely following on impressionism, that dominated the French avant-garde during the 1890s. In contrast to the empirically grounded impressionists, post-impressionists favored symbolism, idealism, and romanticism. In other words, they preferred subjectivity (the conceptual) to objectivity (the perceived).

Georges Seurat (1859–91) and Paul Signac (1863–1935), both of whom exhibited in the final impressionist show of 1886, painted in a style called pointillism because it used distinctive "points" of color to build form and image. The idea was based on the work of Michel-Eugène Chevreul, an early-nineteenth-century chemist who worked for the Gobelin tapestry company. Chevreul's job was to study the way different colors contrasted so that his firm could design more attractive tapestries. Eventually, he published his findings in a treatise, which described the way that colors imposed their complements on adjacent colors. For example, a red dot placed next to a blue dot will make the blue dot appear greenish because green is red's complementary color. (For the same reason, the red dot will now seem to be tinted orange, because orange is blue's complementary color.) Using this principle and building upon the color experiments of the impressionists, Seurat and Signac created large compositions entirely with small, dotlike brushstrokes that finely juxtaposed complementary colors. The most famous painting in this style, also known as divisionism (Seurat's term) and neo-impressionism, is Seurat's *Sunday Afternoon on the Island of La Grande-Jatte* (1884).

George Seurat, *Sunday Afternoon on the Island of La Grande-Jatte* (1884)

Paul Gauguin (1848–1903) and Vincent Van Gogh (1853–90), on the other hand, were symbolists who grounded their work not in observations of nature but in their own emotions. Color was very important to them, often an end in itself, and so they used it wildly. To the uninitiated eye, the colors in symbolist paintings can seem arbitrary, but this is only because Gauguin and Van Gogh saw no need for the color of a painted object to resemble the color of its antecedent in the world outside the canvas. Two hallmark paintings in this highly intuitive style, based largely on contemporary developments in French literature, are Gauguin's *Vision After the Sermon* (1888) and Van Gogh's *The Night Café* (1888).

With the disbanding *of impressionism, new post-impressionist styles began to emerge—such as pointillism and symbolism—signaling new directions for modern art.*

XVIII. THE AGRICULTURAL REVOLUTION

BEGINNING BETWEEN twelve thousand and ten thousand years ago, another major shift in human evolution took place, as agriculture replaced hunting and gathering among many human populations. The practice of growing food for harvest appeared first in a swath of the Middle East known as the Fertile Crescent. Not long afterward, agriculture developed in other regions of the world as well. Today, most humans depend on agriculture for their food supply, although a few populations still rely on hunting and gathering.

Prehistoric hunting and gathering populations tended to be small and mobile, because the plant foods that they gathered were often limited in supply and the animals that they hunted moved around. Agricultural populations, however, could be much larger and more settled, because they were able to produce relatively large quantities of food in a single place. This development proved hugely advantageous, but it didn't improve all aspects of human life.

The spread of infectious disease, for example, became a major problem for agricultural populations. Their large size and sedentary (as opposed to nomadic) lifestyle meant that virulent diseases could spread easily and quickly among many people. Furthermore, the food raised by agricultural communities often had a lower nutritional content than the food eaten by hunting and gathering populations.

Overreliance on a single crop could lead to further nutritional deficiencies, which caused other diseases; and if that single crop failed, the population could starve. Human skeletal remains also show that, as agriculture increased the percentage of starch in the human diet, cavities and tooth decay became much more prevalent. Nevertheless, the sedentary lifestyle made possible by the agricultural revolution paved the way for modern civilization and its high population densities, surpluses of food, social classes, towns and cities, and written records.

Having now examined human origins through several different lines of evidence—especially the fossil, archaeological, and genetic records—we can see that, as a species, humans have developed exceptional capabilities for cognitive thought, learning, and symbolic representation. Yet we shouldn't forget that we carry within every cell of our bodies the history of our evolution in the form of ancestral DNA sequences. This tangible link to our evolutionary past should serve as a reminder that, despite our amazing adaptations, we remain part of a much larger biological continuum and are still evolving.

Agriculture revolutionized human society, *making possible the concentration of large numbers of people in a single place and paving the way for modern civilization.*

XVIII. THE HOLOCAUST LEGACY

Slave laborers at Buchenwald after its liberation.

AT FIRST, the genocide undertaken by the Nazis was considered a part of the history of World War II. Gradually, however, it came to be seen as a discrete historical event. This process was aided by the work of Raphael Lemkin, who in 1933 had petitioned the League of Nations to condemn genocide following the slaughter that year of Assyrians in Iraq and the earlier killings of Armenians by Ottoman Turks during World War I. Although Lemkin's prewar efforts failed, his 1944 book, *The Axis Rule in Occupied Europe*, brought the issue before the new United Nations, which passed a resolution against genocide that was used during the 1945–49 Nuremberg war crimes trials.

The rise of the US civil rights movement also contributed indirectly to a growing awareness of the Holocaust among American Jews. Witnessing the struggle of African Americans to claim their own identity, many young American Jews became dissatisfied with the assimilationist choices made by their parents. Further encouraged by Israel's victory in the 1967 Six-Day War, they reconsidered what being Jewish meant to them; and many, believing that too much had been sacrificed, returned to a more particularistic Jewish identity. Among these people, the Holocaust came to be seen as one of the most important formative experiences of modern Jewish life.

Since the early 1980s, awareness of the Holocaust has increased rapidly. All over the world, museums and memorial sites have been established to preserve the memory of the event. In many parts of the world, Holocaust education has become mandatory in schools, and Holocaust Remembrance Day has become a cornerstone in the lives of many religious Jews—even though a few theologians have expressed concerns about giving the Holocaust such a prominent role in Jewish religious life at the expense of Judaism's rich historical heritage.

Some scholars have also complained of an emerging "Holocaust industry" that seeks to manipulate the event for economic gain. The most disturbing outcome, however, has been the campaign to deny that the Holocaust ever took place. In a famous 2000 libel trial, British judge Charles Gray ruled against anti-Semitic historian David Irving, finding that Irving had "for his own ideological reasons persistently and deliberately misrepresented and manipulated historical evidence." In December 2006, Iranian president Mahmoud Ahmadinejad hosted a gathering of Holocaust deniers in Teheran at which he called the killing of six million Jews "a myth." Ahmadinejad's comments were subsequently condemned by much of the world.

The Holocaust, *once considered part of World War II history, is now seen as a discrete event and is considered by many one of the formative experiences of modern Jewish life.*

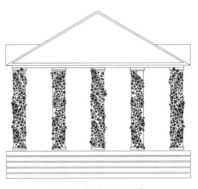

SYLLABUS

IV

I. THE MOVEMENT BEFORE BROWN

WHEN MOST PEOPLE THINK of the civil rights movement, they picture Martin Luther King, Jr., speaking at the Lincoln Memorial or languishing in a Birmingham jail. Yet the struggle for African American equality began long before King was even born. The *modern* civil rights movement began in 1954, when the Supreme Court issued its landmark ruling in *Brown v. Board of Education*, but no history of that movement can proceed without some reference to the events that came before *Brown*.

With the passage of the Thirteenth Amendment in 1865, the last remaining slaves were freed, but little was done for them. After the Civil War (and especially after federal troops left the South in 1877), the freed people found themselves in a new condition of economic slavery. With neither land of their own nor the skills to survive in an urban economy, most had no choice but to remain agricultural laborers on the same plantations that they had once worked as slaves.

Racial segregation also became a burden. Although it had never been rigidly observed in the antebellum South, it was elevated after the war to the status of a long-standing southern "folkway," which whites used to justify the passage of Jim Crow laws further restricting black opportunity. (*Jim Crow* was the name of a stock character in nineteenth-century minstrel shows, and it gradually became a racial epithet.)

In search of relief, many African Americans turned to the "accommodationism" being preached by Booker T. Washington. According to Washington, blacks needed to accept their political humiliation and look beyond it to economic advancement. Middle-class accommodationists considered political agitation both futile and needlessly confrontational. A much more prudent course, they thought, was to forgo their political rights (at least temporarily) in favor of material self-improvement and the cultivation of white goodwill. The resulting gains would eventually allow Negroes to claim the same citizenship rights as whites—or at least that was the plan.

Of course, not all blacks thought like Washington. W. E. B. Du Bois notably chastised the accommodationists for abandoning black political rights and urged African Americans "to complain loudly and insistently" because "persistent manly agitation is the way to liberty." In 1909, Du Bois helped found the National Association for the Advancement of Colored People (NAACP), which quickly became the nation's leading civil rights organization.

An antilynching flag outside the NAACP offices in 1936.

The roots of the civil rights movement *go all the way back to Reconstruction, with Booker T. Washington and W. E. B. Du Bois emerging as the two major leaders.*

I. WHAT IS EMPIRICISM?

EMPIRICISM IS THE IDEA THAT knowledge is based on experience. The word *empiricism* comes from the Greek *empeiria*—whose Latin equivalent, *experientia*, is the source of our word *experience*. The opposite of empiricism is rationalism, according to which knowledge is based not on experience but on thinking or reasoning.

What is experience? The word has at least two different meanings. First, it can refer to a form of conscious awareness. To experience something is to be in a certain kind of mental state. Sense experience is experience of this sort. But experience can also mean a series of events you live through or undergo, and perhaps learn from, such as a religious experience or job experience.

Of course, no one thinks we simply read off all our beliefs directly from experience. What experience is the immediate source of my belief that bears hibernate in winter, that slavery is immoral, or that the earth orbits the sun? Empiricists claim instead that our beliefs form a kind of hierarchy, a tree whose trunk supports its higher branches. Our most basic beliefs, that is, arise more or less directly from experience, and those beliefs in turn form the basis of other, more general and abstract beliefs, including the huge number of things I believe only because others have told me so.

The philosophical problems with empiricism all boil down to the problem of how to identify which beliefs are the truly basic, rock-bottom ones and how to derive or infer all our other beliefs from them. A deeper problem has to do with beliefs that don't seem to have any basis in experience at all. Is my belief that 1 + 1 = 2 based on experience? Should I doubt that belief if I see someone "add" one drop of water to another drop, or push one pile of sand into another, to make *one*? Obviously not. There are other equally puzzling beliefs that pertain to experience without seeming to be based on it—for example, my belief that objects or even people I see remain identical across time as their properties change. A piece of wax melts—changing shape, color, and texture; I believe it's still the same piece of wax, but is it my experience that tells me so?

Empiricism is the claim that knowledge is based on experience. Rationalism is the claim that knowledge is based on reason.

Albert Einstein as a young man.

I. EINSTEIN'S EARLY YEARS

ALBERT EINSTEIN was born in Ulm, Germany, on March 14, 1879. His parents were Jewish but not observant. Initially, they were concerned about his intelligence because he was slow to speak, but these worries passed quickly.

Because his father was an electrical engineer with a manufacturing business in Munich, Einstein was exposed to science at an early age. The needle of his father's compass held particular interest for him. He understood intuitively that if two objects were in contact, one could exert a force upon the other. But the idea that the earth could exert a force upon the compass needle *without touching it* amazed him.

When Einstein was ten years old, a family friend introduced him to some important texts on math and science, and Einstein began studying them, teaching himself geometry and calculus. Particularly important was his study of logic, especially the deductive reasoning associated with Euclidean geometry. Deductive reasoning is the process by which one moves from general premises to specific conclusions. To create his system of geometry, Euclid began with a set of statements, called postulates, that he asserted as true, even though they were unprovable. From these, Euclid made a series of deductions to arrive at his theorems. If one accepts the truth of the postulates that form the basis of the system, then the theorems must also be true because they follow logically from the postulates. Einstein used a similar method when developing his own work on relativity.

As a teenager, Einstein attended the prestigious Luitpold Gymnasium, a secondary school considered quite progressive for its time. Even so, he disliked the rote memorization at the heart of the school's curriculum and tended to ignore assignments that he considered unnecessary. His impatient attitude toward restrictions on his creativity persisted throughout his entire life, and though it sometimes caused him trouble, it also freed up his mind to challenge established scientific orthodoxy.

When Einstein was fifteen, his father's company failed, and the family moved to Italy. At first, Einstein remained in Munich to finish his schooling, but he disliked the gymnasium so much that he withdrew and finished his secondary education in Switzerland. Next, he attended the Swiss Federal Institute of Technology, from which he obtained a physics degree in 1900. For the next two years, Einstein searched for a teaching position but found none, eventually accepting employment as an assistant examiner with the Swiss patent office in Bern.

Einstein's early exposure *to science and mathematics, especially his study of deductive reasoning, greatly influenced his later work.*

I. THE NATURE OF THE SUNNI-SHI'ITE SPLIT

LIKE CHRISTIANITY, the Islamic faith has historically been divided into a number of different communities, or sects, that disagree on basic issues of doctrine, ritual, and religious authority. In the case of Christianity, these disagreements, while perhaps political in nature, have ostensibly been about theology. In the Islamic world, however, the disputes, while sometimes expressed in theological language, have been fundamentally about who possesses the legitimate authority to lead—that is, they have been about politics. The divisions date all the way back to the time of Muhammad, when rival factions competed for control of the fledgling Islamic community after the Prophet's death.

The *Oxford English Dictionary* defines *sect* as "a system differing from what is deemed the orthodox tradition; a heresy." But the term *heresy*, while quite common in Christian parlance, is out of place in any discussion of Islam because it presupposes an existing orthodoxy that sectarians have distorted or corrupted. As we will see, there is no such orthodoxy in Islam.

A Shi'ite shrine in Najaf, Iraq.

In fact, Islam's main "heretical" sect emerged well before the consolidation of its current "mainstream" community. Thus, when discussing Islam, we must abandon the idea that sects are somehow deviant. Instead, we need to be mindful of the fact that the Islamic mainstream has historically been defined by political dominance, and that Islamic "orthodoxy," like most history, has been written by the winners.

Within the Islamic faith, the two most important branches are the *Ahl al-sunna*, or Sunni, and the more disparate communities collectively known as the Shi'a (whose name in Arabic means "party" or "faction"). The Sunnis are the largest and most politically powerful sect in Islam, while the Shi'a comprise a number of smaller groups, some of which are nearly as distinct from one another as they are from the Sunni mainstream.

Although there exist a number of sects in Islam not properly termed either Shi'ite or Sunni, we are focusing exclusively on these two because of their great historical and numerical importance. Although the Shi'a make up only 10 percent of the worldwide Muslim population, which now exceeds one billion people, they have been particularly important in the history of the Middle East and make up about half of the Muslim population in that region. Moreover, in the countries immediately surrounding the geopolitically important Persian Gulf, Shi'ites may actually constitute a majority.

Unlike Christian sects, *which are distinguished primarily by doctrine, the main Islamic sects are separated by a political divide that reaches all the way back to Muhammad.*

I. THE TWO RUSSIAS

Peter the Great

WHEN RUSSIAN TSAR Peter the Great began building St. Petersburg in 1703, he had very practical considerations in mind. He wanted to establish a port city on the Baltic that could open trade with the West and serve as a naval base against the Swedes. Yet he also had an important symbolic purpose. The new Russian capital would be his country's "window onto Europe" (a phrase made famous by Alexander Pushkin, the founder of modern Russian literature). It was Peter's goal to transform Russia into a modern state that could compete militarily and economically with Europe. To this end, he ordered the construction of a new Russian fleet and also insisted that the members of his court shave their beards (because beards weren't the current European fashion). Peter's commitment to this plan and his city were absolute. When his son mentioned that, upon ascending the throne, he would likely move the capital back to Moscow, Peter tortured him to death for insubordination. The ordeal took place in the Peter and Paul Fortress, the city's first structure and later its most infamous prison.

In Peter's time, there were actually two Russias: one in which the aristocracy lived and another in which the peasantry resided. Russian peasants were known as serfs because their status was even lower than that of the European peasantry. In fact, serfs were little more than slaves, bound to the land of their feudal master and utterly subject to his will. Under Peter's influence, Russia's French-speaking aristocrats, German-inspired intellectuals, and urban civil servants soon became Europeanized, but the country's serfs remained steeped in feudal traditions, forced to work the land with technologies that were equally outdated.

Over time, a backlash against Peter's Europeanizing emerged; and during the early nineteenth century, members of the educated classes began searching for a new, more authentically Russian national identity. Not surprisingly, they turned to "the Russian people" of the countryside for inspiration. The vast majority of the people they found, however, were serfs—who made the educated classes feel, by turns, moved, repulsed, alienated, and guilty. Meanwhile, it became clear to all that the anachronism of serfdom was blocking Russia's path to modernity, because the agricultural practices ingrained in serfdom (such as the division of farmland into a patchwork of tiny plots) were highly inefficient. Yet what to do with the serfs was anyone's guess, and the question became hotly debated.

Russia during the early nineteenth century *was a patriarchal society divided, almost unbridgeably, between wealthy Europeanized aristocrats and anachronistic feudal serfs.*

II. THE NAACP'S LEGAL STRATEGY

In 1935, Charles Hamilton Houston, dean of the Howard University Law School, took a leave of absence to become the NAACP's first chief counsel. Since its founding in 1909, the NAACP had occasionally hired lawyers to defend Negroes unjustly accused of sensational crimes. Houston, however, had little interest in such criminal work. He wanted instead to develop civil cases that could gradually undermine the legal basis for racial segregation.

Segregation was legal in 1935 because in 1896 the Supreme Court had ruled in *Plessy v. Ferguson* that racial separation was not inherently discriminatory. As long as equal accommodations were provided, the practice was constitutional, the Court said. Houston's plan was to attack this "separate but equal" doctrine by demonstrating that blacks were not being treated equally.

Focusing on public education, Houston brought cases against southern school districts that paid black teachers far less than their white counterparts. He won many, but each decision applied only to the school district being sued. Also, raising the pay of black teachers didn't eliminate the vast inequalities of the South's segregated education system—well-funded schools for whites, poorly funded schools for blacks. Following Houston's return to private practice in 1938, the NAACP appointed a new chief counsel, Thurgood Marshall, who adopted a new legal strategy.

While Houston had focused on the *equal* in "separate but equal," Marshall attacked the *separate*, arguing that racially segregated facilities could never be equal. He began by suing school systems that provided graduate-level education for whites but none for blacks. His point was not merely that such arrangements were unequal; more importantly, he argued that the opportunities available at white professional schools (such as networking) could never be matched at segregated black schools.

Marshall (left) and Houston (right) with a client in 1935.

During the litigation of *Sweatt v. Painter* (1950), the State of Texas offered to build a new law school for blacks rather than admit Heman Sweatt to the segregated University of Texas. Marshall won the case by persuading the Court that an all-black law school, no matter how well funded, could never match the advantages available at the existing school.

Marshall's victory, however, was incomplete. He had hoped that *Sweatt v. Painter* would set a precedent he could use to desegregate undergraduate, secondary, and even elementary education. But the Court wouldn't bite, explicitly limiting its opinion to graduate education and leaving *Plessy* the law of the land.

The NAACP decided *to attack the "separate but equal" legal basis for segregation, with Houston first taking on "equal" and Marshall then going after "separate."*

II. ARISTOTLE, THE FIRST EMPIRICIST

A Roman copy of a ca. 350 BCE
Greek bust of Aristotle.

WHO WAS THE FIRST EMPIRICIST in the history of philosophy? It's difficult to say, but a good candidate is Aristotle (384–22 BCE). Aristotle was—with his teacher, Plato (ca. 428–347 BCE)—one of the two greatest philosophers of antiquity. Plato was not an empiricist, but a rationalist. He taught that the "visible" world, which is to say the world available to the senses, is not fully real and so not an object of knowledge at all. Why not?

First, because visible things are constantly in flux, always changing. The same *river* is never the same *water* from one moment to the next. Second, visible things are always only visible from different, often conflicting, perspectives. A beautiful horse is beautiful from some points of view, but not others—not from underneath, say, or from too far away. Finally, visible things are never perfect. Circles and triangles drawn in sand are never perfect geometrical figures. What we have genuine knowledge of in all these cases, Plato said, is not something *visible* but something *intelligible*, something we know not by *looking* but by *thinking*. Purely intelligible objects are what he called ideas or forms. They are nonperspectival, rational, fully real, and outside of space and time. True knowledge, Plato concluded, is knowledge of forms, not of visible things.

Aristotle rejected Plato's theory, not by denying the existence of intelligible forms outright but by insisting that they are not separately existing, timeless entities. Instead, they are aspects of concrete things, which we know through sense experience. Aristotle argued that we acquire knowledge by being affected by what he called the sensible forms of things. For him, this meant that our souls take on formal aspects of those things themselves. Some have understood this to mean that when I see a red apple, my soul literally turns red. Others have interpreted the doctrine as meaning only that something in my soul has some kind of correspondence with the object but doesn't necessarily come to resemble it. Unlike Plato, Aristotle believed that things are (more or less) the way they appear in perception; the visible world just *is* the real world.

According to Plato, *knowledge is not based on sense experience, but on rational apprehension of invisible forms. Aristotle rejected Plato's theory and insisted that knowledge is based on sense experience.*

II. **THE MIRACLE YEAR**

EINSTEIN'S JOB AT THE SWISS PATENT OFFICE turned out to be a great boon. Reading through applications for electromagnetic devices sharpened his understanding of the concepts involved, and because he worked quickly, he was able to spend several hours a day pursuing his own research.

During 1905, Einstein published four major papers in the German physics journal *Annalen der Physik*. Each had an instant and dramatic impact on the scientific world because it explained a concept that had been puzzling other scientists for some time. In fact, Einstein's work was so remarkable that word quickly spread beyond the scientific community, and Einstein became an international celebrity. To this day, the ideas contained in the four papers are still being explored and developed, which is why 1905 is sometimes referred to as Einstein's *annus mirabilis*, or miracle year.

The first paper concerned the photoelectric effect by which photovoltaic cells convert light into electricity. Although scientists had been discussing this effect for sixty years, none was quite sure how it worked, and experimental results kept contradicting established theories about light. Einstein's explanation began with the postulate that light, which generally behaves like a wave, interacts with matter on the subatomic level as discrete packets of energy called quanta. Using deductive reasoning, he then accounted for the confusing experimental results. The work had great relevance to the new theory of quantum mechanics, which attempted to account for the unusual behavior of subatomic particles, and it won Einstein the 1921 Nobel Prize in Physics.

The 1905 issue of *Annalen der Physik* in which Einstein's first relativity paper appeared.

The second paper discussed Brownian motion, a term describing the random movement of particles suspended in a fluid. Again, this phenomenon was well known but poorly understood. Einstein explained that the motion resulted from molecular activity and thus reinforced the atomic theory of matter (the idea that all matter is composed of discrete atoms).

His third paper, ostensibly on electrodynamics, included the presentation of his Special Theory of Relativity, which reconciled Isaac Newton's laws of motion with the laws of electricity and magnetism recently developed by James Clerk Maxwell. In order to accomplish this feat, however, Einstein had to propose a model of the world radically at odds with human sensory perception. In his fourth paper as well, Einstein made a related but equally incredible argument: that mass and energy were actually two aspects of the same fundamental thing.

In 1905, *Einstein published four papers of such impressive thought and creativity that the ideas contained within them are still being explored and developed today.*

II. THE FOUNDING OF THE MUSLIM COMMUNITY

THE CAREER OF THE PROPHET MUHAMMAD (CA. 570–632) is unique in world history: He founded not only a major religion but also a political order that quickly came to dominate the Middle East. Within the annals of Islam itself, Muhammad is also unique because within the Muslim community, or *umma*, he remains the only leader to have exercised both political and religious authority.

At the age of forty, when Muhammad began receiving the divine revelation that became the Quran (or Koran), he was a petty merchant living in the Arab town of Mecca (in present-day Saudi Arabia). He belonged to the Hashimite clan of the Quraysh tribe, which was then dominant in Mecca. Slowly, Muhammad began to

A page from a Quran created by a Baghdad calligrapher ca. 1000.

build a new community, based on the teachings of the Quran, that distinguished itself both by belief and by lifestyle. The majority of Muhammad's kinsmen in Quraysh were polytheists who lived relatively lawless lives, guided primarily by a code of honor. While this code dictated that hospitality should be shown to guests and strangers, it also demanded that offenses against one's honor be avenged through violence. As a result, cycles of aggression and retaliation regularly spun out of control, causing prolonged blood feuds among tribes and clans.

Those who accepted Muhammad's monotheistic faith took on a new code of behavior based on social justice, prayer, fasting, and other devotional practices. The members of the fledgling Muslim *umma* thus came to resemble Arabian Jews and Christians more than their own polytheist kinsmen—a similarity that was hardly accidental. In fact, Muhammad consciously placed himself within the line of great Israelite prophets because he perceived his scripture to be the culmination of a long process of revelation, beginning with the Jews and continuing with the Christians.

In 622, after a dozen years of persecution in Mecca, Muhammad's community was forced to flee the town by some of the Prophet's hostile Quraysh kinsmen, especially the leading clan of Umayya. The Muslims found refuge in Yathrib (later renamed Medina), where the local tribesmen chose to accept Muhammad's leadership. Thus, the Prophet's mission entered a new phase. The addition of so many converts transformed the *umma* overnight from a persecuted minority into a strong military force. Over the next several years, while continuing to recruit converts, Muhammad successfully engaged the Quraysh in a series of battles. Finally, in 630, the increasingly outnumbered Quraysh capitulated and surrendered the city of Mecca to the Prophet.

Muhammad's unique role *as both religious prophet and political leader established a new model for authority and leadership in the Middle East.*

II. THE GOLDEN AGE BEGINS

IN ORDER TO APPRECIATE FULLY the flowering of Russian literature during the nineteenth century, one must first understand how unexpected it was. After touring Europe in 1789 and meeting some of the Continent's greatest writers, Russian court historian Nikolay Karamzin wondered in a subsequent travelogue whether Russia would ever produce a single writer the world would bother to read. Ten years later, Alexander Pushkin (1799–1837) was born.

Pushkin reinvented every genre of Russian literature, from drama to verse to the short story, and in doing so developed a literary language of unprecedented richness. He made use not only of Church Slavonic, the Russian liturgical language, but also of colloquialisms that seemed quite shocking in their new literary context. Overall, Pushkin's work was known for its classical simplicity of phrase and for the romantic passions that swirled beneath its serene surface.

As an intellectual, Pushkin was concerned with Russia's volatile social divisions and especially its harsh autocratic political structure. Because he flirted constantly with political rebellion, he was exiled from St. Petersburg in 1820. Five years later, following the December 1 death of Tsar Alexander I, a group of soldiers in St. Petersburg refused to swear allegiance to the new tsar (Nicholas I) and instead demanded a constitutional monarchy. Their Decembrist Revolt was quickly suppressed, but its effects lingered. Although Pushkin had been confined to his mother's estate at the time, his sympathies were well known, and his poems were later found among the Decembrists' papers, prompting the imperial government to subject his work to even greater scrutiny and censorship.

In early 1837, Pushkin was killed in a duel over anonymous letters mocking him for the alleged infidelity of his wife. Many regarded these letters as a pretext for the murder of a man whose genius threatened the status quo. Pushkin's premature and tragic death, however, merely reinforced his status as a Russian prophet. His poem "The Prophet" describes a man wandering in the desert, "tormented by a spiritual thirst," who receives from a "six-winged seraph" the gift of poetry. The poem's closing lines would inspire generations of future Russian authors: "Corpse-like I lay in the desert, / And God's voice called out to me: / 'Arise, O prophet, and see, and listen; / Fill yourself with my will, / And, traveling over many lands and seas, / Burn men's hearts with the word.'"

Pushkin revolutionized Russian literature *while establishing, through his life and death, a model of the prophetic role that authors would play in Russian society.*

III. **THE BROWN DECISION**

THE COURT'S NARROW DECISION in *Sweatt v. Painter* left Thurgood Marshall with a difficult choice: Should he bank his winnings or go for the big payoff? Bringing more pressure to bear might finally force the Court to reverse *Plessy v. Ferguson*, but such an effort could also fail, resulting in a decision that reaffirmed segregation and condemned yet another generation of African Americans to the oppression of Jim Crow. Despite advice to the contrary, Marshall decided to move strongly ahead. Again, the terrain would be public education.

Seven-year-old Linda Brown lived in Topeka, Kansas. Every day, she had to cross the tracks of a railroad switching yard to reach the bus that took her to a segregated elementary school on the other side of town. Her father, Oliver, decided to sue the school district because he couldn't bear the risk to his daughter when a perfectly good public school, albeit one for white children only, operated within safe walking distance of his home.

Oliver Brown's NAACP lawyers emphasized new sociological evidence that made clear the harm being done to black children by segregation. The lawyers cited, most

Kenneth Clark conducts his doll test.

famously, a doll test used by psychologist Kenneth B. Clark to measure children's self-esteem. Clark had shown a group of black children dolls made from the same mold and dressed alike but with different skin colors. He then asked the children to pick out "the nice doll," "the doll that looks bad," and so on. The results showed that black children consistently associated the white doll with "good" and the black doll with "bad." In other words, Clark's test showed that segregation produced in black children a sense of inferiority that undermined their self-esteem.

On May 17, 1954, Chief Justice Earl Warren read the Supreme Court's unanimous decision in *Brown v. Board of Education*. "Does segregation of children in public schools solely on the basis of race, even though the physical facilities and other 'tangible' factors may be equal, deprive the children of the minority group of equal educational opportunities?" Warren asked. "We believe that it does....We conclude that in the field of public education the doctrine of 'separate but equal' has no place. Separate educational facilities are inherently unequal."

In arguing **Brown**, *Thurgood Marshall used new sociological evidence to persuade the Supreme Court that "separate" could never be "equal."*

III. THE RISE OF RATIONALISM

ARISTOTLE'S PHILOSOPHY dominated Western thought throughout the Middle Ages. By the sixteenth century, however, the Scientific Revolution posed a radical challenge to Aristotelianism, including its empiricist account of knowledge.

René Descartes

It's tempting to identify the rise of modern science with the triumph of observation and experience. Even more important, however, was a new willingness to reject sensory appearances as superficial and misleading. Modern science, that is, arose not just with more and better observations, but with a new emphasis on controlled experimentation and mathematics. The result was a profound realization that the world is often *not* as it appears to be. The sun seems to orbit the earth, but Copernicus and Galileo demonstrated that just the opposite is true. Naive observation got things exactly backward.

It shouldn't be surprising, then, that the first three great philosophers of the early modern period—René Descartes (1596–1650), Baruch de Spinoza (1632–77), and Gottfried Leibniz (1646–1716)—weren't empiricists but rationalists. Impressed by the discoveries of the "new science," as it was then called, they rejected Aristotelian empiricism and stressed the importance of abstract thought and deductive reasoning.

The advent of modern science gave a new boost to rationalism—the idea that we can know the world only though reason, not the senses. Think again of the melting wax, an example of Descartes's. In liquid form, it has hardly any of the properties it had as a solid object. Your senses tell you it's different now, but you *judge* it to be the same thing. What you know is the enduring object itself, and you know it with your intellect, not with your eyes. What we call *seeing* is really *judging*. Do I *see* a book on the table? No, for Descartes (as for Plato), what I see is a flux of shifting shapes and colors, and I *think*, "Aha, a book!"

Descartes concluded that we cannot literally acquire our ideas from sense experience. That would be like thinking there are voices echoing through telephone lines—whereas, of course, the lines themselves merely relay electrical impulses that then trigger the sounds of voices in telephones. So, too, although many of our ideas are sparked or activated by experience, the ideas themselves must already lie dormant in our minds. Ideas, Descartes argued, must be innate.

At the heart of *the Scientific Revolution was the rationalist principle that objects in the visible world are often not what they seem to be.*

III. NEWTONIAN MECHANICS

Isaac Newton

DURING THE ENLIGHTENMENT, also known as the Age of Reason, a revolution took place in the way that researchers investigated and explained the physical sciences. Beginning in the early seventeenth century, observation and experimentation replaced scholasticism, a medieval method of learning that arrived at scientific truth by comparing authoritative texts (such as the Bible) rather than by studying the natural world. Perhaps the greatest of the many pioneering scientists who emerge during this period was the English mathematician Isaac Newton. With the publication of his 1687 treatise *Philosophiæ Naturalis Principia Mathematica*, Newton transformed physics from an intellectual backwater into a bold new discipline with great predictive power.

In the *Principia*, Newton articulated three laws that he used to describe the relationship between forces acting on an object and the resulting motion. Newton's first law stated that an object at rest, unless acted upon by a force, will remain at rest. (Similarly, an object in motion, unless acted upon by a force, will continue to move in the same direction at the same rate of speed.) Newton's second law stated that, for any given object, force and acceleration are proportional. That is, a larger force will produce a greater acceleration (the rate at which an object's speed increases or decreases). Finally, Newton's third law stated that for every action, there is an equal and opposite reaction. In other words, when force is applied to an object, the object exerts an equal force in the opposite direction.

Elsewhere in the *Principia*, Newton presented his groundbreaking theory of universal gravitation. According to the famous story, the sight of an apple falling from a tree led the twenty-nine-year-old Newton to wonder whether the same force that caused the apple to fall straight down also held the planets in their orbits around the Sun. The equation that he published in the *Principia* two decades later described this force so well that it accurately predicted the results of any experiments he could think to try.

For more than two centuries, Newton's model of the universe prevailed, and his theories sufficed to answer all questions posed to them. In fact, during the late nineteenth century, one prominent scientist publicly advised ambitious young men not to pursue a career in physics because all of the important questions had been answered. Within a few years of this remark, however, new research into light and radioactive decay posed some new questions that Newtonian mechanics couldn't answer.

The model of the universe *that Newton constructed using his laws of motion and theory of universal gravitation held sway, unchallenged, for more than two hundred years.*

III. A CRISIS OF LEADERSHIP

MUHAMMAD'S AUTHORITY was both religious and secular. He offered spiritual guidance and governed the community's economic and social affairs, even leading its warriors into battle. All matters related to the *umma* were decided on the basis of the teachings in the Quran or according to the inspired example set by the Prophet.

Because of his divinely ordained status as a prophet, Muhammad's authority was absolute. Following his death in 632, however, the Prophet's unique mode of leadership turned out to be a problem for his successors, who couldn't claim the same kind of authority, especially in religious matters.

The Shi'a–Sunni split can be traced directly back to the moment of Muhammad's death, because the central dispute between these two branches of Islam

A sixteenth-century Persian painting of Muhammad ascending into the heavens.

concerns the Prophet's legacy. In polytheistic Arabian culture, the *shaykh*, or head of a tribe, usually ruled not as an absolute dictator but as the head of a council of notables—that is, as the *primus inter pares*, or first among equals. According to Sunni tradition, the Prophet made no specific provisions for an heir or successor to lead the community after his death. Instead, Sunnis believe, he (and thus God) intended that the *umma* henceforth be ruled in accordance with the older tribal tradition of the *shaykh* who was first among equals. As it turned out, this is exactly what happened: Following Muhammad's death, his father-in-law and most trusted confidant, Abu Bakr, assumed leadership of the community as head of a council of tribal notables.

Shi'ites, however, tell a very different story. They believe it was Muhammad's (and thus God's) will for the Prophet's cousin and son-in-law, Ali, to succeed him as ruler of the *umma*. (Ali was the young son of Muhammad's uncle Abu Talib and also the husband of Muhammad's daughter Fatima.) According to Shi'ite tradition, Muhammad announced his decision to make Ali his heir during a public sermon at Ghadir Khumm, stating that "He whose master I am, Ali is his master as well; O God, befriend anyone who is his friend, and show enmity to anyone who is his enemy!" The Sunnis accept that the sermon took place, but they dispute the meaning of Muhammad's words, denying Ali's exclusive claim to leadership of the community.

The Prophet's death *resulted in a leadership crisis that planted the seed of future sectarian division.*

III. THE BRONZE HORSEMAN

THE TITLE OF PUSHKIN'S long narrative poem "The Bronze Horseman" refers to a famous monument to Peter the Great in St. Petersburg. It depicts the tsar astride a rearing horse, his eyes glaring and his right arm outstretched imperiously above the Neva River. Mounted on a massive rock, the statue intimidates as it inspires.

Like the statue, Pushkin's poetic monument to Peter tells the heroic story of the founding of the modern Russian state. Indeed, the poem opens with the sort of hyperbolic praise commonly found in the work of eighteenth-century Russian court poets. Peter stands godlike in a swampy wilderness, deciding to build a city where none believed one could be built. "On the shore of a wilderness of waves, / He stood, full of great thoughts, / And gazed into the distance." Then, in a miraculous transformation, Peter's thoughts become clothed in granite, and the city seems to appear almost instantly before him. (Buried beneath this founding myth, of course, are the thousands of anonymous convicts who died raising Peter's new capital from the mud.)

Within the body of the poem however, the deep irony of Pushkin's opening salute becomes apparent. The poem's principal character, a poor clerk named Yevgeny, dreams modestly of marriage to a girl named Parasha. Sadly, his dream is swept away by one of Petersburg's periodic, cataclysmic floods. Pushkin casts this flood as the "vengeance" of natural elements angered by the imposition of Peter's will on nature; and Yevgeny, struggling with the floodwaters, also comes to see the tsar (symbolized by his monument) in a demonic light.

Later, the broken Yevgeny finds himself once again standing before Peter's statue. Pathetically but defiantly, he raises a fist at the monument. Yet in the moment of his resistance, he goes mad and suddenly takes fright. Turning and fleeing, he believes that the statue is pursuing him, its galloping bronze hooves echoing off the cobblestone pavement. With his brief but symbolic rebellion crushed, Yevgeny soon dies; and his body is later found on the doorstep of his drowned fiancée's shack, which has been carried by the flood into the same watery wilderness out of which Peter's accursed city grew. Although Pushkin wrote "The Bronze Horseman" in 1833, imperial censors prevented its publication during his lifetime.

Pushkin's "The Bronze Horseman" *opens in typical praise of Russian autocratic power but more importantly depicts the suffering of a petty clerk whose life is destroyed by that power.*

IV. **THE MURDER OF EMMETT TILL**

IT TOOK THE JUSTICES of the Supreme Court a full year to decide how *Brown v. Board of Education* would be implemented. Not until May 1955 did they settle on a gradual approach, using the intentionally vague phrase *with all deliberate speed.* Because of this timidity and the emergence of a southern backlash to *Brown*, another fifteen years passed before meaningful school desegregation began in the South.

The successful resistance to *Brown* has led some scholars to belittle the Court's decision and instead credit the mass protests that followed with forcing the South to integrate. Yet such an argument misses the point that *Brown* changed the way young African Americans thought about themselves and the world. Whites might still treat them unfairly, but after *Brown*, such treatment was no longer legal—an important distinction.

Another event that changed the way young blacks thought about the world was the August 1955 murder of fourteen-year-old Emmett Till. The killing took place in Mississippi, indisputably the most racist southern state. When Till—acting on a dare—whistled at a white woman in the small town of Money, everyone but the Chicago-born eighth-grader knew that there would be trouble.

Because Till wasn't a southerner, he was only dimly aware of the strict code governing race relations in Mississippi. His uncle Mose Wright, whom Till was visiting, told the white men who came for the boy a few nights later that Till hadn't known what he was doing. But Roy Bryant (the woman's husband) and J. W. Milam (her brother-in-law) didn't care. They took Till away, and the next time Wright saw his nephew was three days later, when his mutilated corpse was pulled from the Tallahatchie River.

Newspaper accounts inspired national outrage at the brutality of the murder. Even so, white Mississippi lined up dutifully behind Bryant and Milam. It took the all-white jury just sixty-seven minutes to return a not-guilty verdict, and it would have taken even less time, one juror said, "if we hadn't stopped to drink pop."

John Lewis was just seventeen months older than Till. Five years later, as a college student in Nashville, Lewis became a leader of the emerging sit-in movement. According to Lewis, Till's murder "galvanized the country. A lot of us young black students in the South later on, we weren't sitting in just for ourselves—we were sitting in for Emmett Till."

Although there was successful resistance to Brown, the decision nevertheless altered the worldview of young blacks, as did the murder of Emmett Till.

Emmett Till with his mother.

IV. LOCKE'S CRITIQUE OF INNATE IDEAS

MODERN EMPIRICISM began with John Locke (1632–1704), who was not just a philosopher but also a government official, a medical researcher, an economic theorist, and a political activist. An enemy of superstition and authoritarianism, Locke was politically allied with the forces that overthrew James II in the Glorious Revolution of 1688 and established a parliamentary democracy in England. In addition to his main philosophical work, *An Essay Concerning Human Understanding* (1690), Locke also wrote *Two Treatises of Government* (1689), the second of which became the foundation of modern liberal political theory.

The core of Locke's empiricism lies in his attack on the rationalist doctrine of innate ideas, or nativism, according to which ideas cannot derive from experience but must already lie dormant in the mind. Nativism is not the absurd claim that babies are born aware of all the ideas they will ever have. Rather, Descartes meant that these ideas are latent, ready to be activated or triggered, either by external stimuli or by other conscious ideas. Locke (who may or may not have been addressing Descartes directly) argued, to the contrary, that the mind is a *tabula rasa* ("blank slate").

What Descartes objected to was the Aristotelian notion that the soul soaks up its ideas from the external world like a sponge. Ideas are always only in the mind; they don't float around in the air. Locke was no Aristotelian, and he didn't believe that ideas seep into the mind from the outside any more than Descartes did; but he did think the doctrine of innate ideas was absurd. It's like saying that when you strike a match, the flame must somehow be innate in the match before the strike.

John Locke

David Hume, the third and greatest of the three classical British empiricists, later dismissed the controversy over innate ideas as a product of verbal obscurity and confusion. If *innate* merely means "mental," then all ideas are innate. If it means "original" (rather than derived from other ideas), then immediate sensory ideas (what Hume called impressions) are innate, while other more abstract ideas are not.

Locke criticized the rationalist doctrine of innate ideas, which held that all ideas are present in the mind at birth and remain latent until triggered by a thought or sense experience.

IV. GALILEAN RELATIVITY

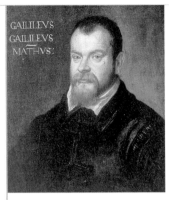

Galileo Galilei

IN PHYSICS, *relativity* refers to the concept that measurement depends on one's frame of reference. The basic idea is simple: Imagine a car traveling along a straight highway at sixty miles per hour. To an observer on the side of the road, the driver is moving at sixty miles per hour. However, to an observer in the backseat of the car, the driver isn't moving at all. During the early seventeenth century, Galileo Galilei formalized this notion into a set of equations known as Galilean relativity.

The key to Galilean relativity is the observer, who defines the reference frame. In Galilean relativity, the observer must be moving at a constant speed. (This includes the speed of zero, meaning the observer is at rest.) An observer moving at a constant speed is said to have an inertial frame of reference because *inertia* is the tendency of matter to continue moving at a constant velocity until acted upon by a force. (Newton stated this in his first law of motion.)

Using the example of the car, both the observer on the side of the road and the observer in the backseat represent inertial frames of reference. The velocity of the former is sixty miles per hour; the velocity of the latter is zero. It's important to note, however, that Galilean relativity does not apply if the frame of reference is accelerating.

According to Galilean relativity, correct measurement depends on the observer's relative velocity with respect to the object being observed. Suppose the observer in the backseat tosses a ball forward at five miles per hour. To the observer in the backseat, the ball is moving at five miles per hour. To the observer on the side of the road, however, the ball is moving at sixty-five miles per hour (the speed of the car plus the additional speed of the ball within the car). Both measurements are correct, yet the values differ because of relativity.

For three hundred years, Galilean relativity functioned perfectly well, and it still does at the low velocities one encounters in everyday life. But when scientists at the turn of the twentieth century began contemplating frames of reference moving at speeds approaching the speed of light, Galilean relativity broke down, which is why Einstein set about fixing it.

Since 1905, *the term* relativity *has been indelibly associated with Einstein, but even then the idea was nothing new. Galilean relativity had been around for centuries.*

IV. THE RIGHTLY GUIDED CALIPHS

THE MEN WHO SUCCEEDED MUHAMMAD as leaders of the early Muslim community were known as caliphs, from the Arab word *khalifa* (meaning "successor"). The first caliph, Abu Bakr, governed for just two years, during which he successfully prosecuted the *ridda* wars, which were fought against Arab tribes who had left the faith (and shed Muslim political control) following the death of the Prophet. Although Muhammad's followers were generally tolerant of other monotheists (such as Christians and Jews), this tolerance didn't extend to pagan Arabs, who were compelled to accept Islam.

Following Abu Bakr's death in 634, the tribal leaders chose Umar bin al-Khattab to serve as the second caliph. A tireless crusader for Islam, Umar was so successful in spreading the faith that he is sometimes called "the Paul of Islam." For ten years, he presided over an astonishing expansion of Muslim power in the Middle East. Then, in 644, he died, but not before appointing a council to determine his successor.

By this time, Muslims enjoyed political hegemony over most of the Middle East, as well as parts of the eastern Mediterranean and North Africa. For this reason, a great deal of wealth and power was at stake in the council's decision. Its job was to mediate disparate interests and determine peacefully which should prevail. Even so, the work proved highly acrimonious. In fact, the bitter rivalries that developed during this period would dominate Muslim politics for centuries. Ultimately, Ali was passed over again, and Uthman bin Affan, one of the Prophet's close companions, was chosen as the third caliph.

Uthman, who belonged to the Umayya clan, reigned for twelve years, during which time political tensions increased dramatically. Rebellions broke out, and blood was shed. Uthman's greatest sin appears to have been nepotism. He rewarded large numbers of his Umayyad kinsmen with positions of influence, even though many were late converts who had accepted Islam only under threat of force. Uthman was finally assassinated in 656 by dissidents who proclaimed Ali the new caliph. Many Muslims subsequently accepted Ali, and he reigned until his death in 661.

To later Shi'a, Ali's ascent represents a final realization of legitimacy after two decades of rule by usurpers. Sunni accounts, however, make no such distinction. Thus, in the Sunni tradition, we find the doctrine of the Rashidun, or Four Righteous Caliphs—Abu Bakr, Umar, Uthman, and Ali—all of whom are considered equally legitimate.

According to Sunni tradition, *the first four caliphs exercised legitimate authority, but the Shi'ites dispute this claim, believing that only Ali had the right to lead.*

IV. THE SUPERFLUOUS MAN

PUSHKIN GAVE THE NAME *YEVGENY* (meaning "well born") to two of his most enduring creations, the doomed clerk of "The Bronze Horseman" and the jaded aristocratic hero of *Yevgeny Onegin*. The title character of this revered novel in verse, written before "The Bronze Horseman," lives an emotionally empty existence that leaves him cynical and cold. The story opens with the world-weary Onegin, once a Petersburg dandy, retiring to the countryside, where he meets the hopelessly idealistic young poet Lensky. Together, they become involved with the Larin sisters. The beautiful though vapid Olga becomes Lensky's muse, while the more contemplative Tatyana falls for Onegin. A devoted reader of English romance novels, Tatyana breathlessly interprets Onegin's arrival as the beginning of her own romantic adventure—with Onegin, of course, as the hero. However, like many other characters in imperial Russian literature, Tatyana tragically confuses fiction with real life.

Alexander Pushkin

After Tatyana reveals her feelings to Onegin, he rejects her, but comforts her with the assurance that he's incapable of love. Soon afterward, annoyed and bored, Onegin provokes Lensky by dancing with Olga. The impulsive poet rises to the bait and challenges Onegin to a duel, during which Onegin kills him. The novel ends several years later when Onegin encounters Tatyana, now married and a renowned Petersburg lady. Stunned by the transformation, he declares his love for her, only to be rejected in turn.

Together, Pushkin's two Yevgenys established an enduring literary archetype: the superfluous man. The term refers to men who, all too commonly in Pushkin's Russia, failed to find a meaningful place in society and instead gave themselves over to philosophical musings, idleness, and sometimes pointless destruction.

Many of the authors who followed Pushkin—Nikolay Gogol and Ivan Turgenev, in particular—interpreted the superfluous man in slightly different ways. The dubious heroes of Gogol's Petersburg stories, for instance, are economically marginal people who rebel against their existence by seeking refuge in dreams, if not madness. In Turgenev's novels, the superfluous men are troubled radicals who can't reconcile their visions for reform with Russia's ossified reality. Even later, making a profound metaphysical leap, Fyodor Dostoevsky reconceived the superfluous man as the even more rebellious Underground Man, who refuses to obey rational laws of any kind. Although superfluous men often display a captivating idealism, they're also deeply flawed and can be isolated, vicious, petty, or deranged.

Yevgeny Onegin's title character *was the first in a long line of marginalized Russian anti-heroes known as superfluous men because they couldn't find a place in society.*

V. THE MONTGOMERY BUS BOYCOTT

THE JIM CROW LAWS that dominated southern life extended well beyond public education. In Montgomery, Alabama, for example, Chapter Six, Section Ten, of the City Code required public bus companies to "provide equal but separate accommodations for white people and Negroes." But these accommodations were hardly equal. Blacks were allowed to sit only in the back of the bus, and they often had to get up so that white passengers could sit.

On the evening of December 1, 1955, forty-two-year-old seamstress Rosa Parks boarded a Cleveland Avenue bus at a stop near the department store at which she worked. Two stops later, the bus driver noticed that a white man was standing, so he ordered a row of seated black passengers to give up their seats and move farther back, even though the rest of the seats in the crowded rear of the bus were taken. When Parks refused, the driver called the police and had her arrested.

Rosa Parks in a mug shot taken by Montgomery police.

The African American community responded on Monday, December 5 with a one-day bus boycott that proved 90 percent effective. At a mass meeting that night, it voted to continue the boycott until three demands were met: greater courtesy to black passengers, the hiring of Negro bus drivers, and first-come, first-served seating. The bus company refused.

To manage the boycott, the city's black leadership (many of them Baptist ministers) formed the Montgomery Improvement Association (MIA), choosing as its president the twenty-six-year-old Martin Luther King, Jr. The MIA raised funds, sponsored weekly mass meetings to keep up morale, and organized a car-pool system that carried thousands of people to work each day.

Montgomery's white authorities tried everything they could think of to crush the boycott, including harassment, arrests, and even a hoax (announcing that the boycott had been settled to trick black riders back onto the buses). On January 30, 1956, King's house was dynamited. No one was hurt, but the MIA responded with a federal lawsuit challenging the constitutionality of bus segregation. In November 1956, the case reached the Supreme Court, which upheld a lower court ruling prohibiting the segregation. The yearlong boycott ended on December 21, 1956, when blacks returned to the buses and took seats in the front rows.

The Montgomery bus boycott *sought an end to segregation through direct mass political action.*

V. PRIMARY AND SECONDARY QUALITIES

ARISTOTLE BELIEVED that material objects are more or less as we perceive them to be. That is, in addition to size, shape, and motion, they have color, flavor, texture, and odor, and they also make sounds. Like Descartes, Locke rejected this view as naive and instead drew a distinction between real physical properties and qualities merely apparent in our ideas. The former he called primary qualities; the latter, secondary qualities.

Imagine a snowball. One of the primary qualities of the snowball is its spherical shape. My visual experience of that shape and the shape itself are different things, but they *resemble* each other. The snowball's white appearance and coldness to the touch, by contrast, are secondary qualities. They do not exist in the snowball itself as properties resembling my ideas of them.

Locke did not deny that objects have secondary qualities; only that those qualities resemble our ideas of them. Just as there is nothing *in* fire that resembles the sensation of pain I feel when I touch fire, there is nothing *in* the snow that resembles my visual experience of its whiteness. Our experiences of secondary qualities do not resemble the qualities themselves. Instead, according to Locke, a secondary quality is merely the power of an object to produce an idea in us. It is that object's power to impress upon us sensations of color, sound, texture, flavor, and odor. Fire, for example, causes pain in us, but our pain does not resemble anything in the fire.

Secondary qualities, Locke observed, are also variable and observer-relative in ways that primary qualities are not. We see things as remaining the same size and shape as we move closer to them, whereas the fire feels warmer the closer we get to it. Similarly, lukewarm water feels hot to a hand previously in cold water and cold to a hand previously in hot water. So, is the water itself hot or cold? Conveniently, Locke's distinction between primary and secondary qualities excuses us from answering such awkward questions. Regarding warmth as a subjective *feeling*, rather than an objective *property*, allows us to say that the fire itself is no more warm than it is "painy."

According to Locke, *primary qualities are real physical properties, whereas secondary qualities are merely the ability of things to cause in us subjective ideas that do not resemble the objects themselves.*

V. THE LIMITS OF GALILEAN RELATIVITY

DURING THE MID-NINETEENTH CENTURY, Scottish mathematician James Clerk Maxwell proposed four stunning equations that succinctly described the intimate relationship between electricity and magnetism. Most importantly for other scientists, these equations became extraordinarily powerful tools for solving electromagnetic problems. For our purposes, however, they are relevant because they demonstrate that light acts as an electromagnetic wave with a constant speed (designated by the symbol c).

Unfortunately, this discovery begat a problem: Maxwell's equations specified no frame of reference—that is, they failed to identify who was doing the measuring. In a world of Galilean relativity, where all measurement depends on the observer's frame of reference, this made no sense. How could the speed of light be the same for a moving observer as for a stationary one?

James Clerk Maxwell

This paradox plagued Einstein, who considered both Galilean relativity and Maxwell's equations to be absolutely true. Unable to create a relevant laboratory experiment, he devised what he called a "thought experiment" to play with the problem and clarify his ideas. The thought experiment went something like this: Suppose you are traveling at the speed of light, and you hold up a mirror in front of your face. Would you see your reflection?

In a Galilean world, the light would leave your face at c (relative to you). Therefore, to an observer at rest, it would be traveling at $2c$ (relative to him). But this can't be, according to Maxwell's equations. On the other hand, if the light is traveling at c relative to the observer at rest (as Maxwell would have it), then its speed relative to you would be zero (according to Galileo) because you are already moving at c. This speed of zero would also violate Maxwell's equations, and it would mean that you never see your reflection because the light never reaches the mirror.

Obviously, Galileo and Maxwell couldn't both be right, but Einstein couldn't understand why until he decided to apply some deductive reasoning. He chose Maxwell's equations as his postulate and saw where it led. In such a world—where light always traveled at c, no matter the reference frame—you would see the light travel from your face to the mirror and back again at c relative to you (thus seeing your reflection), while an observer at rest would also see the light traveling at c relative to him. Now all Einstein had to do was revise Galilean relativity so that it conformed to this prediction.

Maxwell's equations *predicted a constant speed for light, but this contradicted Galilean relativity, which held that all measurement depends on the reference frame.*

V. THE CALIPHATE OF ALI AND THE FIRST CIVIL WAR

NOT SURPRISINGLY, the ousted Umayya clan refused to accept Ali as caliph, and the ensuing struggle for power quickly led to armed conflict. After suppressing one rebellion that included among its leaders A'isha (one of the Prophet's wives and the daughter of Abu Bakr), Ali faced an even more substantial challenge to his authority.

While Medina continued to serve as the capital of the expanding Muslim caliphate, several other large cities, taken by the Arabs from the Byzantine and Persian empires, became rival power centers in the Muslim world—Damascus, in particular. The ruler of that city was the Umayyad governor Mu'awiya bin Abi Sufyan, who refused to recognize Ali's legitimacy.

Because Mu'awiya had been governing the rich province of Syria since the time of Umar, he commanded vast economic and military resources and could not be easily removed. Nor could he easily remove Ali, who enjoyed considerable support elsewhere in the empire, especially within Iraq. For several years, these two men competed for ultimate authority. Finally, in 657, they faced off against each other at Siffin on the banks of the Euphrates in Syria. The fighting was inconclusive, however, and in the end, in accordance with long-standing Arab tradition, arbitrators were appointed to settle the matter. This decision disgusted some of Ali's supporters, who were appalled that the caliph would allow such a crucial matter to be decided by arbitration rather than by God's will on the battlefield. As the negotiations dragged on interminably, some of these unhappy partisans abandoned Ali's cause and became Islam's first sectarians.

Called Kharijites (meaning "those who secede"), they rejected both claimants to the caliphate, although Ali became their particular nemesis after 658, when his forces confronted, defeated, and massacred the Kharijites at Nahrawan. As one might expect, the few who survived became even more zealous in their beliefs. In 661, one of these Kharijites assassinated Ali, after which the caliphate fell to Mu'awiya. Sunnis recognize this transition as the end of the era of the Rashidun and the legitimate beginning of the Umayyad caliphate of Syria, which endured for nearly a century. The Shi'a, however, never accepted this interpretation and instead remained loyal to Ali and his heirs. In fact, the name *Shi'a* derives from *shi'at Ali,* meaning "partisans of Ali." Shi'ites view Mu'awiya as merely one more usurper in the long tradition of illegitimate rule that has characterized Islamic history since the death of the Prophet.

The struggle between *the fourth caliph, Ali, and the Umayyad leader Mu'awiya produced a deep and lasting rift in the Muslim community.*

V. A HERO OF OUR TIME

PERHAPS THE MOST NOTORIOUS superfluous man was Pechorin, the protagonist of Mikhail Lermontov's 1840 novel *A Hero of Our Time*. Pechorin made such an impression on contemporary readers that Lermontov (1814–41) felt compelled to write a foreword to the second edition upbraiding his wealthy but unsophisticated audience for its inability to detect the irony in the novel's title. Meanwhile, Lermontov also used the foreword to distance himself from Pechorin, because many Russians were reading the novel as autobiography. Although such an interpretation was crude, it was also understandable because of the obvious similarities that existed between Lermontov's life and Pechorin's.

Unable to find a productive outlet for his energies, the isolated and brooding Pechorin pursues women while amusing himself against an exotic Caucasian backdrop by killing acquaintances in duels. After romancing (that is, kidnapping) a local girl, Pechorin cynically seduces a Russian princess and then shoots a hapless young rival named Grushnitsky—all while flaunting his total ambivalence toward life. As he muses on the eve of his duel with Grushnitsky, "So what? If I die, I die! No big loss for this world—and I myself am already pretty bored." Overall, the novel is structured as a series of frames in which the narrator, traveling through the Caucasus, hears accounts of Pechorin's exploits before finding Pechorin's diaries, which expose the man's tortured inner life, prefiguring the works of Dostoevsky.

Like Pechorin, Lermontov also found fame in the Caucasus. In 1837, while a young soldier in Petersburg, he wrote a poem clearly charging members of Nicholas I's court with complicity in Pushkin's murder. Displeased, the tsar transferred Lermontov from the capital to the distant Caucasus, where he expected Lermontov to die taming the region for the empire. In fact, Lermontov survived his encounters with the local population but died, like Pechorin, in a pointless duel at the age of twenty-six.

The confusion of life with literature that many Russian readers experienced at this time can be traced mostly to their inexperience. *A Hero of Our Time* was the first Russian prose novel of note, and there was widespread ignorance of the literary devices that Lermontov used. So Russians read as they always had—that is, literally. As a result, efforts by early writers such as Lermontov to make use of irony and metaphor were commonly misinterpreted, often laughably so.

Because of their inexperience, *Russian readers of the 1830s and 1840s often confused literature with life—Mikhail Lermontov and his character Pechorin being prime examples.*

VI. MARTIN LUTHER KING, JR.

MARTIN LUTHER KING, JR. (known to his closest friends as Mike), first became acquainted with the strategy of "passive resistance" during his undergraduate years (1944–48) at Morehouse College in Atlanta. An indifferent student at Morehouse, King nevertheless followed closely the nonviolent struggle of Indian leader Mohandas K. Gandhi to win independence from British rule. Even so, he was never the Gandhian that many journalists made him out to be. His interest in nonviolence was rather that of a Christian pacifist—always rooted in the biblical directive to match hate with love.

When the Montgomery bus boycott began, King had been pastor of the Dexter Avenue Baptist Church for less than two years, and his wife, Coretta, had just given birth to their first child. For these reasons, King's election as MIA president caught him "unawares," he explained. "It happened so quickly that I did not even have time to think it through. It is probable that if I had, I would have declined the nomination."

Martin Luther King, Jr., at a March 1960 press conference.

Yet King's performance at the first mass meeting on December 5, 1955, was mesmerizing. Although he never raised his voice, he preached as though he wanted to shout, and this made his voice sound electric. "You know, my friends," he told the standing-room-only crowd, "there comes a time when people get tired of being trampled over by the iron feet of oppression. There comes a time, my friends, when people get tired of being flung across the abyss of humiliation, where they experience the bleakness of nagging despair. There comes a time when people get tired of being pushed out of the glittering sunlight of life's July and left standing amidst the piercing chill of an Alpine November. We are here this evening because we're tired now."

The bus boycott began without King and would have continued without him, but his leadership was nonetheless irreplaceable. Without it, the boycott would never have become the truly *mass* movement that it did. "There was no other leader with the humility, with the education, with the know-how of dealing with people who were angry and poor and hungry," one MIA insider recalled. Certainly the media, with its insatiable appetite for personalities, singled King out and highlighted his role, but the attention was justified, and King's importance was not lost on the civil rights movement's white antagonists.

Martin Luther King, Jr., *was, at first, a reluctant leader, but the role fit him so well that he quickly became both indispensable to and inseparable from the movement.*

VI. LOCKE ON ESSENCE AND SUBSTANCE

WHEREAS RATIONALISTS like Descartes believed that reason could reveal the way the world is in itself, Locke's empiricism made him much more skeptical about our ability to know the true essence of things. Why?

Descartes equated matter with space, which he believed was ubiquitous, continuous, and infinitely divisible. Thus, there can be no *empty* space (because space is matter) and no basic unit of matter (because matter is infinitely divisible). Locke, by contrast, embraced the corpuscular theory of matter, according to which physical objects are composed of minuscule discrete units known as corpuscles, or atoms.

For Locke, experience has the same atomistic structure as the world itself. Like corpuscles, that is, ideas are discrete units, and the way we combine and arrange them determines the way we experience and understand the world. This understanding is in part stipulated by the linguistic terms we use to describe objects. Fish, for example, are just those things we have decided to call *fish*. The nature or essence of *fish* is what Locke calls a *nominal* essence—that is, an essence corresponding to a name. The *real* essences of things, the natures they have independent of our language and concepts, are, Locke believed, forever beyond our grasp.

Locke also conceived of matter as substance—which he called a substratum, an "I know not what" that underlies and "supports" the properties of things. What exactly is substance? On one reading, it is what all particular things—all particular substances—have in common. The notorious "I know not what" is, on this view, the unknown real essence of things, possibly different for different kinds of things. What the substratum "supports" would then be merely the observable properties of things.

Another, more standard reading holds that substance is not the same as real essence, but the underlying support for all properties, including both real and nominal essences. On this reading, substance as such, strictly speaking, lacks properties of its own. But what is a "propertyless" thing? Is that notion even intelligible?

Locke believed *that human knowledge is limited because the real essences of things are beyond our grasp. It is unclear in his account whether material substance coincides with or underlies the real essence of things.*

VI. EINSTEIN'S POSTULATES OF RELATIVITY

EINSTEIN'S WORK modifying Galilean relativity began with two postulates. The first, known as the principle of relativity, he merely borrowed from Galileo. It stated that the laws of physics apply in the same way across all inertial frames of reference. To understand this, let's consider our previous example of the car traveling down the highway—except that this time, rather than tossing a ball forward, the observer in the backseat simply lets it drop. Both the observer in the backseat and the observer on the side of the road then measure its acceleration due to gravity. According to Einstein's first postulate (and Galilean relativity), both values will be the same, because the law of gravity doesn't change relative to one's frame of reference.

Einstein's second postulate, known as the invariance of the speed of light, stated that light travels in a vacuum at a constant speed independent of the motion of its source. In other words, if I am traveling at the speed of light (designated by the symbol c, as noted previously), and I shine a flashlight around myself, I am going to observe the light from that flashlight traveling at c no matter what direction I choose to point the light. An observer at rest will similarly witness the light from my flashlight traveling at c no matter the direction in which I point the beam. It is this second postulate that was truly revolutionary because it meant that light, unlike a thrown ball, doesn't share the inertial momentum of its source.

Having established these two postulates, Einstein next devised a series of provocative thought experiments to test them out. Employing the tools of deductive reasoning, he worked out theorems based on the postulates. Then he used the theorems to predict results for the various thought experiments. The predictions were astonishing, counterintuitive, and also, as it turned out, entirely correct. When Einstein was satisfied with the work, he published it in his third *annus mirabilis* paper, calling it the Special Theory of Relativity.

Einstein based *his Special Theory of Relativity on two postulates: that the same physical laws apply in all inertial frames of reference and that the speed of light never changes.*

Einstein as a Swiss patent clerk.

VI. THE BATTLE OF KARBALA

WITH MU'AWIYA AS CALIPH, the Umayyads in Syria quickly came to dominate the rest of the increasingly diverse Muslim empire. Governing with energy and efficiency, Mu'awiya aggressively favored Arab tribal elites over other sectors of society and broke with established precedent regarding the choice of his successor. Specifically, he wanted to establish a new dynastic pattern of succession, naming his son Yazid as the next caliph.

In southern Iraq, however, resistance to Mu'awiya's rule was growing, led by members of the Hashimite clan, to which both Ali and the Prophet had belonged. Many discontented Iraqis saw the Hashimites, especially the Alid Hashimites (the direct descendants of Ali and their families), as a viable alternative to Umayyad rule.

The conflict surrounding the ascent of Ali that began with the assassination of Uthman in 656 is often referred to as the first *fitna*, or Islamic civil war. The second *fitna* began in a similar manner when Mu'awiya died in 680 and Yazid tried to consolidate his father's power. Although not the only Muslims to resist Yazid's succession, the dissident Iraqis in Basra and Kufa exploited this moment of uncertainty by inviting Ali's son Husayn to lead their revolt against the Syrians. Husayn had become de facto leader of the Hashimites after his older brother, Hasan, reached an accommodation with Mu'awiya several years earlier. Husayn rejected his brother's quietism, and so, when the Iraqi invitation came, he set out from Medina with a small group of followers to lead a rebellion against the Umayyads.

On October 10, 680, however, Husayn and the rest of his party were intercepted at Karbala by a vastly superior Umayyad force. Husayn and most of his family were massacred, but a few members of the party survived, including Husayn's young son Ali. At the time, the death of Husayn amounted to little more than a minor incident in the second *fitna*, which lasted twelve years and expanded well beyond the Iraqi revolt against the Umayyads.

For later Shi'ites, however, the battle of Karbala represents perhaps the most important event in human history. In Shi'ite remembrance, Husayn knows that he will be killed yet chooses to sacrifice himself and his family so that humanity may be saved. Just as Christians believe that the death of Jesus provides salvation for the Christian faithful, so do many Shi'ites believe that their own faithful will be redeemed through Husayn's intercession on Judgment Day.

The martyrdom of Husayn at Karbala *in 680 was a minor event in the bloody second* fitna, *yet it took on enormous significance for the Shi'a in later years.*

VI. THE PETERSBURG TALES

NIKOLAY GOGOL (1809–52) was born in Ukraine, but his genius didn't blossom until he reached the troubled metropolis of St. Petersburg. Gogol arrived in the capital in 1828, bringing with him grandiose fantasies of immediate anointment by the city's (albeit small) literary elite. Instead, his earliest efforts were failures, even by his own admission. His full talent didn't become apparent until around 1836, when the settings of his stories changed from his native Ukraine to Petersburg itself—the city's dark, oppressive atmosphere inspiring him to write darkly comic stories that satirized a society in which social rank meant everything. From these stories, Gogol's fame finally came, but the conflict between dreams and reality that he had until recently felt continued to haunt his writing.

Nikolay Gogol

Although comical on their surface, Gogol's Petersburg tales were, at their core, deeply disturbing works, filled with a sense of life's strangeness and absurdity. In "The Nose," a vainglorious major wakes up one morning to discover that his nose is missing. He finds it later, walking around Petersburg in a more impressive uniform than his own. In "Nevsky Prospekt," a young artist catches a fleeting glimpse of a woman he finds incomparably beautiful. Following her home, he discovers that she's actually a prostitute who lives in a hovel. Unable to accept less than his idealized vision of the girl, he escapes into the world of dreams, at first with the help of opium and ultimately through suicide. In "The Overcoat," a poor clerk endures months of deprivation to save enough money buy a new overcoat, only to have it stolen on the first day he wears it.

Yet the most moving of all Gogol's tales is "Diary of a Madman," the first-person account of a superfluous man whose only escape from his troubles is insanity. The author of the titular diary is another petty clerk, who becomes obsessed with the daughter of a superior. Her social class is completely closed to him, yet he won't give up his obsession. Instead, he expands his campaign to reach her, even to the point of intercepting what he believes to be the secret correspondence of her pet dog. By this time, of course, he's gone mad, a fact that Gogol makes clear in the dates of the diary entries that make up the story. These move from October 3 to April 43 to Martober 86 to "days without dates."

Nikolay Gogol's *darkly comic Petersburg tales explore the divide between literature and life by investigating in detail the gap that often exists between dreams and reality.*

VII. INTEGRATING LITTLE ROCK

TODAY, IT'S FAIRLY EASY to see that the momentum of history favored civil rights. But government leaders of the 1950s had to act without such hindsight, and this made the choice between moral leadership and political opportunism much more problematic.

At the time, Arkansas was considered a racially moderate state because it seemed to have taken desegregation in stride. The University of Arkansas had voluntarily admitted its first black law student in 1948, and the Little Rock bus system had also been integrated without incident. After *Brown*, the Little Rock schools superintendent announced without much fanfare that token integration would begin at Central High School in the fall of 1957.

Like Pres. Dwight D. Eisenhower, Arkansas governor Orval Faubus had been content after *Brown* to let others tackle the thorny desegregation issue. During his 1956 reelection campaign, however, Faubus realized that the political winds were shifting toward the segregationists, and he decided to shift with them. On Labor Day 1957, he called out the Arkansas National Guard to cordon off Central High and block the admission of the first black students, known as the Little Rock Nine.

Although Faubus's action defied a federal court integration order, Eisenhower remained silent, hoping that the crisis could be resolved without his intervention. He thought that Faubus, having made such a dramatic gesture, would now withdraw the troops and blame Central's subsequent integration on the federal government.

In fact, Faubus did remove the Guard after federal judge Ronald Davies issued another order on September 20. But the withdrawal didn't end the crisis because a violent mob of enraged segregationists quickly took the Guard's place. Although the city police did manage to sneak the Little Rock Nine into school on Monday, September 23, the students had to be evacuated when the crowd outside threatened to overrun the building. Later that day, state NAACP president Daisy Bates announced that the students would not return to Central until Eisenhower personally guaranteed their safety.

The next morning, Little Rock's mayor sent the president a telegram formally requesting federal troops. By this time, Eisenhower had no choice. He ordered one thousand soldiers of the 101st Airborne and used these troops on the morning of September 25 to disperse the mob at bayonet point so the Little Rock Nine could attend classes. The segregationists called it "an invasion."

A white woman harasses one of the Little Rock Nine.

Resistance to school integration *in Little Rock, especially the violent defiance of a federal court order, forced a reluctant President Eisenhower to send in federal troops.*

VII. BERKELEY'S CRITIQUE OF ABSTRACT IDEAS

DURING HIS LIFETIME, George Berkeley (1685–1753), the bishop of Cloyne in Ireland, was most famous for his book *Siris* (1744), which both extolled the curative powers of tar water (water mixed with pine tar) and explained how to contemplate the mind of God. Berkeley's enthusiasm for God and tar water are by now mere historical curiosities, but he remains important for his *Treatise Concerning the Principles of Human Knowledge* (1710) and *Three Dialogues Between Hylas and Philonous* (1713), which put forward arguments denying the existence of material substance.

To understand why Berkeley (pronounced "BARK-lee") would make such a bizarre and counterintuitive claim, it's important to see that his denial of the existence of material substance rests on a more general critique of abstract ideas. Like Locke, Berkeley was a nominalist. That is, he thought there are no natural groupings in the world—no species, no types, no categories. There are only particulars—that is, individual objects. The way we group ordinary objects into kinds—for example, by calling them *fish* or *trees*—is entirely artificial.

Applying Locke's nominalist argument to ideas, Berkeley claimed that ideas, too, exist only as particulars—*this* pain, *this* sensation of red, *this* smell of coffee. We are able to speak and think in general terms about pains and sensations and odors, but we don't do so by having ideas that are themselves abstract, which is to say outside of space and time like Platonic forms. Instead, we have particular ideas, and we let them represent other particulars. When I think about triangles, I visualize a particular triangle and let it stand in for *any* triangle. We have no abstract idea of triangles in general, only ideas of the particular triangles we imagine.

On this point, Berkeley may be guilty of conflating two different features of ideas: their status as concrete mental states on the one hand, and the role they play in representing or signifying objects on the other. Berkeley seems to argue from the premise that ideas are themselves concrete particulars to the conclusion that they can only represent concrete particulars. But is that right? A photograph of a tree is always a photograph of a particular tree, but does the word *tree* refer to one tree in particular? Which one?

Berkeley's seemingly bizarre *claim that there is no such thing as material substance is based on his critique of abstract ideas. An abstract idea, like material substance, is empty. We have only particular ideas of particular things.*

VII. SIMULTANEITY

ONE OF THE FIRST PUZZLES that Einstein encountered in his work on relativity involved the concept of simultaneity. By definition, two events that are observed to occur at the same time are said to be simultaneous. For example, suppose that I am riding in the middle of a glass-walled train car moving down a straight track at sixty miles per hour. Just as I pass an observer at rest, lights flash at both ends of the train car. Because the flashes of light appear to reach me at the same time, I observe them to be simultaneous. Because they also appear to reach the observer at rest at the same time, he observes them to be simultaneous. So much for the Galilean world of slow speeds.

Now let's suppose that the train speeds up to 0.9c, or nine-tenths the speed of light. The same flashes occur—which, for clarity's sake, we'll call event A (front-end flash) and event B (rear-end flash). The light from event A travels toward me at c, and because I am traveling toward the light source at 0.9c, I observe this event rather quickly. The light from event B is also traveling toward me at c, but because I am moving away from the light source at 0.9c, it takes a longer time for the flash to reach me. Therefore, I observe event A before I observe event B and, as a result, judge them to be not simultaneous. From the point of view of the observer at rest, however, the events are simultaneous. Here's why: The observer at rest is equidistant from the two ends of the train car at the moment the lights flash; therefore, each flash travels the same distance at the same speed to reach him.

So which one of us is correct? According to Einstein, both of us are. If one accepts the truth of the postulates of relativity, then it follows logically that two events occurring simultaneously in one inertial reference frame may not occur simultaneously in another. Neither view is more correct than the other.

Not surprisingly, this conclusion pushed Einstein to think more about time. If the train's speed determines the time lag between event A and event B, then time must move at different rates in different inertial reference frames. No one had ever considered this before.

Two events *occurring simultaneously in one inertial frame of reference frame may not occur simultaneously in another.*

VII. **THE ABBASID REVOLUTION**

AROUND 692, Abd al-Malik, a distant cousin of Mu'awiya, reconstituted the Umayyad caliphate, and the dynasty went on to enjoy decades of relative stability until factionalism led to its gradual decline during the 740s. Meanwhile, a revolutionary movement gestated in the Iranian province of Khurasan on the eastern edge of the empire. Although its background and exact nature were unclear, its agents claimed to be working on behalf of *al-rida min Al Muhammad*, the "chosen one from the family of the Prophet."

The backbone of this revolutionary movement was the *mawali*, a disaffected class of non-Arab Muslims— usually of Christian, Jewish, or Iranian descent—who were being systematically exploited and deprived of their rights by the Arabs, whom they outnumbered in many parts of the empire. In fact, by the mid-eighth century, the *mawali* were so numerous in Iran and elsewhere that their demands for equal treatment

A decorated stone box from the Abbasid period.

couldn't simply be ignored. Allied with them, and nearly as important to the revolution, were disgruntled Arab elements—including the early Shi'a, who strongly supported the continuing claims of the family of Ali.

It is believed that most supporters of the revolution assumed that the new caliph, the "chosen one from the family of the Prophet," would be a member of the house of Ali. When Umayyad rule was finally overthrown in 750, however, the vagueness and secrecy of the movement turned out to be a serious liability. Rather than the Alids, the actual beneficiaries of the revolution were the Abbasids, Hashimite cousins to the Alids, who took advantage of the political chaos and quickly seized power.

Under Abbasid rule, the peace and social justice that the *mawali* had been promised also turned out to be illusory. The chief architect of Abbasid power, al-Mansur, reigned ruthlessly from 754 until 775, methodically pursuing and eliminating the scions of the Umayyad royal house as well as those of the house of Ali. One account describes an enormous mausoleum, discovered after Mansur's death, in which the caliph had ghoulishly piled high the many corpses of Alid men, women, and children he had murdered.

The Alids' response was hopelessly ineffectual, and their sporadic rebellions against the Abbasid regime typically went nowhere. Meanwhile, the Abbasids shifted the empire's center of gravity from Syria to Iraq and built on the Tigris the glorious new city of Baghdad.

The popular revolt *that overthrew Umayyad rule in 750 was supposed to restore the Alids to power, but this didn't happen, leading to more disappointment for the early Shi'a.*

VII. DEAD SOULS

DURING THE EARLY 1840S, a new school of Russian literary criticism emerged, which held that literature's primary purpose should be to portray social injustice as scathingly as possible. Not surprisingly, these critics enjoyed the satirical humor of Gogol's Petersburg tales immensely, but they often failed to appreciate the depth of Gogol's work and especially its irony. Such was the case with *Dead Souls*, Gogol's masterful 1842 novel, which concerned the painful topic of serfdom.

Gogol's plan for *Dead Souls* included three sections, but he lived to complete only one. The section that he did finish presents a peculiarly Russian hell. It begins in a provincial town with the arrival of Chichikov, a mysterious man brimming with ambition yet spiritually hollow. After establishing himself in a squalid inn, Chichikov begins visiting the wealthiest local landowners, each of whom he flatters with small talk before asking whether any of their serfs have died since the last census. Later, it becomes clear that Chichikov's scheme is to acquire title to these officially registered people who may be dead in God's eyes but not in the government's. Once transferred to his own estate, these "dead souls" can be used by Chichikov as phantom collateral in future swindles. In one remarkable scene, however, suddenly inspired by the lists of names and other details the landowners have provided, Chichikov resurrects the serfs in his mind and begins conversing with them.

After reading an early draft of *Dead Souls*, Pushkin famously remarked, "God, how sad Russia is!"— and Gogol himself often wondered whether things would ever change. Probably for this reason, the novel's first section ends with an enigmatic metaphor: Russia as a speeding troika (a team of three horses that pulls a carriage). To where, Gogol asks, is this troika racing? He offers no answer.

Gogol had designed *Dead Souls* to be a modern Russian counterpart to Dante's *Divine Comedy*, with the first section representing the Inferno. In the second section, corresponding to Purgatory, Chichikov was to be purified and transformed; but Gogol couldn't figure out how to do this. Try as he might, he simply couldn't imagine a redeemed, transfigured Russia. In the end, growing artistic despair combined with a nascent religious fanaticism drove Gogol mad. Under the influence of a priest who told him that his writings were sinful, Gogol burned the incomplete second section of *Dead Souls* and starved himself to death.

In his novel *Dead Souls, Gogol attempted to escape Russia's hellish reality. His description of the Inferno won him great praise; but after that, his art failed him, and he died unredeemed.*

VIII. MALCOLM X AND THE NATION OF ISLAM

IN THE SOUTH, nonviolent, church-based organizing made sense because most of the prominent civil rights leaders were Christian ministers with deep roots in the pacifist tradition. Up North, however, conditions were different. Many blacks living in urban ghettos were neither ideologically nonviolent nor Christian, and they sought a different path.

Malcolm Little was six years old when his father was run over by a streetcar under mysterious circumstances. Eight years later, after his mother was declared insane, fourteen-year-old Malcolm was placed in a series of foster homes. At sixteen, he became a pimp, drug dealer, and petty thief in Boston. At twenty, he was sent to state prison, where he became a member of the Nation of Islam (NOI). Also known as Black Muslims, NOI believers followed the teachings of the Honorable Elijah Muhammad, who said the white man was the devil and urged blacks to separate themselves from whites in order to save their souls.

When Malcolm emerged from prison in August 1952, Muhammad gave him the new surname *X* (to represent the lost surname of his African ancestors) and sent him to Harlem, where Malcolm charismatically proclaimed the divinity of the black man and predicted the impending destruction of the "blue-eyed white devil." Quickly he became the second most powerful NOI leader and Muhammad's heir apparent, although he remained largely unknown outside the black community.

Then, in 1959, a sensational television documentary, "The Hate That Hate Produced," introduced Malcolm X and the Nation of Islam to a shocked national audience. The resulting publicity made Malcolm a national figure, and white reporters began hounding mainstream black integrationists to state where they stood on the issue of "black supremacy." In the meantime, Malcolm's growing fame was making Elijah Muhammad jealous. In December 1963, Muhammad "silenced" Malcolm for making disparaging remarks about the late President Kennedy.

Three months afterward, anticipating his expulsion, Malcolm quit the Nation and began moving beyond the NOI's black–white dualism to embrace a more humanistic vision of the world. As Malcolm moved farther and farther away from NOI orthodoxy, the rift grew worse, and in February 1965, Malcolm (now El-Hajj Malik El-Shabazz) was killed by NOI assassins at the Audubon Ballroom in Harlem.

Through its spokesman, *Malcolm X, the Nation of Islam rejected the integrationist agenda of the King-led civil rights movement and vowed to meet violence with violence.*

Malcolm X addressing a rally in Harlem, July 1963.

VIII. IMMATERIALISM

BERKELEY'S DENIAL of the existence of material substance rests on his rejection of abstract ideas. The idea of material substance is an abstract idea, hence empty and illegitimate.

What then are physical objects if not material substance? Mere collections of ideas. An object, after all, is a collection of properties, which are present to the mind in the form of ideas. Objects cannot be distinct from yet resemble ideas in our minds, because only an idea can resemble another idea. Berkeley also argues that the very idea of an independently existing material world is, in effect, the idea of a perceived thing without a perceiver perceiving it, which is absurd.

What about objects that no one is currently perceiving? Berkeley gave two replies. First, he said that God constantly perceives everything, so that the enduring

George Berkeley

existence of things just consists in their occurrence as ideas in God's mind. Second, he proposed that to say some unperceived object exists is really to say that *if* you were in the right place at the right time, *then* you would have the ideas that constitute it.

Berkeley's idealism has struck many readers as preposterous. Notable among them was the great eighteenth-century English literary critic Samuel Johnson, who famously kicked a stone and proclaimed, "I refute it thus!" Berkeley insisted, however, that his doctrine is, in fact, closer to common sense than the indirect realism of Descartes and Locke, according to which objects are hidden behind a veil of ideas. On Berkeley's view, objects just are ideas, so we can be said to perceive them directly, with no obstructions or intermediaries. Moreover, because my finger is, like my pain, just an idea in my mind, Berkeley's theory allows me to say that the pain I feel in my finger really is in my finger, just like the bones and muscles.

Berkeley's immaterialism may best be understood as the counterintuitive, perhaps absurd, result of failing to distinguish an idea's subjective qualities from its objective reference—that is, what the idea is an idea of. Berkeley tends to equate "idea of red" with "idea, [namely] red." But sensations of secondary qualities differ from sensations of pain in just this way, for whereas a sensation "of" pain just is the pain, a sensation "of" red is itself no more red than a sensation of wet is wet.

Berkeley argued *that physical objects are not material substance, but mere collections of ideas.*

VIII. TIME DILATION

BEFORE 1905, scientists believed that time moved at a constant rate of speed. With the Special Theory of Relativity, however, time became another changeable physical dimension, akin to height and width and depth. Instead of three-dimensional space, scientists now speak of four-dimensional space–time.

The realization that time moves at different rates of speed in different frames of reference led Einstein to the idea of time dilation. This idea can be more easily understood if we return to our glass-walled train car moving straight ahead at $0.9c$. Still standing in the middle of the car, I place a laser on the floor. When I turn it on, it sends a beam of light up at a mirror on the ceiling at height h. The mirror reflects the beam down to a detector on the floor. From my point of view, the light travels straight up and straight down, a distance of $2h$.

On the side of the track, however, the observer at rest sees something different. Instead of watching the beam move straight up, he sees it travel along a forward diagonal line. This is because, from his point of view, the train and the mirror move forward during the time it takes for the beam to travel from floor to ceiling. By the time the beam returns to the floor, the train has moved farther still, resulting in a similarly diagonal return path. Therefore, from his point of view, the light travels a total distance somewhat greater than $2h$.

Velocity is defined as distance divided by time. If both of us observe the velocity of the laser beam to be c (which it must be according to the second postulate of relativity), then different distances must mean different times. In other words, because the light travels a shorter distance in my frame of reference, the trip up and down must also take a shorter time (if the velocity is to remain constant). Therefore, from the point of view of the observer at rest, time must be passing more slowly in my frame of reference than in his.

Imagine a clock on a spaceship. The faster the spaceship travels, the more time dilates, and the slower the hands on the clock turn—but this applies only to observers in different inertial frames of reference. From the point of view of the astronauts aboard the spaceship, the hands of the clock turn just as fast as they always have.

According to the Special Theory of Relativity, *time dilates, which means that it moves more slowly as the frame of reference speeds up.*

VIII. **THE CONSOLIDATION OF THE SHI'A**

IT WAS DURING THE LATE Umayyad and early Abbasid periods that the first indications of Shi'ite self-awareness began to emerge. The harsh and steady persecution that the

Shi'a suffered under the Abbasids encouraged both a quietism and a sense of resignation. Yet, as the Shi'a became more accustomed to oppression, they also began to develop communal institutions and religious doctrines that helped them articulate a more distinct Muslim identity.

Meanwhile, the ninth and tenth centuries witnessed the slow attenuation of Abbasid power. Once the absolute masters of an empire stretching from southern Europe to the borders of China, the Abbasid caliphs gradually weakened.

A mural from a palace of the Abbasid caliphs near Baghdad.

Their authority became more and more nominal as viceroys, governors, and other imperial surrogates increasingly took matters into their own hands. Eventually, independent principalities formed. Some, like the Tulunids in Egypt, recognized the nominal authority of the caliph; others, like the Umayyads in Spain, refused even this gesture. As a result, by the year 1000, the Abbasid caliphate had become politically superfluous.

This development benefited the Shi'a, who took advantage of diminished imperial control to establish several autonomous communities of their own. Although all shared the same key doctrines and institutions, each followed a different lineage of imams. (In this specific Shi'ite sense, the term *imam* refers to the religious head of the entire Muslim community; more generally, it refers to a prayer leader in a mosque.) These Shi'ite imams, however, were all direct descendants of the Prophet through Ali and Fatima, Husayn, and then Ali bin Husayn (the son of Husayn who survived the massacre at Karbala).

Earlier, a son of Ali by another wife (not the Prophet's daughter Fatima) and a grandson of Ali through Hasan (not Husayn) had asserted claims to Alid leadership and gathered something of a following. By the ninth century, however, nearly all Shi'ites believed that no imam could be legitimate unless he was a direct descendant of the Prophet through Ali and Fatima and then through Husayn—a doctrine actively promoted by Ja'far al-Sadiq (702–65), Husayn's great-grandson and the sixth in the most prevalent line of Shi'ite imams (with Ali being the first imam and his sons Hasan and Husayn the second and third, respectively). Recognized by all the major branches of Shi'ism that came later, Ja'far is considered the intellectual architect of the faith—the developer of its key theological ideas as well as its jurisprudence.

Under Abbasid persecution, *the early Shi'a coalesced into a distinct sectarian group.*

VIII. NIHILISM

IN 1855, the highly repressive tsar Nicholas I died, and his son, the much more liberal Alexander II, came to power. Like Peter the Great, Alexander was acutely aware of the economic backwardness of his country compared with Europe, and he recognized that the core of the problem was serfdom. Therefore, in 1861, Alexander freed the serfs, distributing to each of them a plot of land.

Alexander II

Whatever the tsar's intentions, the Great Liberation produced a nearly apocalyptic sense of social upheaval, further exacerbated by Alexander's push for industrialization. Many newly freed serfs, unable to support themselves on the small plots of land they'd been given, left the countryside to take jobs in the new urban factories. Meanwhile, Russian reform politics took a radical turn. During the early 1860s, young intellectuals began viewing the established order as so depraved that nothing of value could be built until the status quo was leveled. They believed that Alexander's reforms didn't go far enough (especially with regard to land redistribution), and some were prepared to use terrorism to speed history on its way.

A curious aspect of Alexander's liberalism was that, during his reign, imperial censorship eased considerably, allowing Russian authors much greater latitude in their writings. In his 1862 novel *Fathers and Sons*, for instance, Ivan Turgenev wrote not only of the tension between generations but also of the tension between social classes trapped within a society deeply in flux. The lens that Turgenev used to view these issues was the Kirsanov family. As the novel opens, Nikolay Petrovich (the patriarch of the family) and the defiantly aristocratic Pavel Petrovich (Nikolay's brother) welcome home Nikolay's son Arkady, who is accompanied by his university friend Bazarov. Scandalized by Bazarov's iconoclastic rejection of every existing social value, Pavel Petrovich challenges the young man to a duel.

To describe Bazarov's ideas, Turgenev used the term *nihilist*, a word he didn't invent but did popularize. From the Latin *nihil* (meaning "nothing"), nihilism is the philosophical position that there is no God; therefore, there are no divinely prescribed values, and each person is free to create his or her own. Although *Fathers and Sons* is largely sympathetic to nihilism, Turgenev outraged many young nihilists when he allowed Bazarov to fall in love—a turn of events irreconcilable with nihilist rationalism. In fact, falling in love proves too much for Bazarov, and he dies, perhaps by suicide—his rational revolution checked by his irrational, emotional human nature.

The sense of social upheaval *that accompanied the emancipation of the serfs contributed to the growth of nihilism, a radical movement that rejected all existing social values.*

IX. THE SIT-INS

THE GENERATION THAT BUILT the NAACP saw the 1954 *Brown* decision, quite correctly, as the culmination of decades of patient legal block-building. Not so the children of that generation, mere adolescents at the time of *Brown*, who considered school desegregation an obvious call and, lacking historical perspective, expected many more changes to follow.

Five years later, as these young adults settled into college, they found themselves staying up late at night, discussing why so little had changed. The idea of racial segregation seemed almost silly to them. What sense did it make for blacks and whites to go to school together and ride buses together but not eat together in restaurants or drink from the same water fountains?

Ezell Blair, Jr.; Franklin McCain; Joseph McNeil; and David Richmond entered North Carolina Agricultural and Technical College as freshmen in the fall of 1959. They became fast friends, ate together, studied together, and talked together about whatever was on their minds. After watching a television show on Gandhi's use of nonviolence to achieve his political ends, the four classmates decided to visit a downtown Greensboro lunch counter, where, by custom, blacks weren't served. On February 1, 1960, they bought some toiletries at the Woolworth's on North

A Negro student sits in at a Nashville lunch counter.

Elm Street, sat down at its lunch counter, and nervously ordered coffee. Although the waitress refused to serve them, they remained in their seats until closing time in protest.

Word spread quickly, and before the freshmen returned to the A&T campus, students there were already talking about what they had done. The next morning, they led a group of twenty-seven A&T students back to the Woolworth's, where, observed by several members of the local press, they sat in again. Day by day, the sit-in movement expanded, first throughout Greensboro, then across North Carolina, and finally—within just two weeks—across the entire Upper South.

The sit-in movement demonstrated that young blacks could protest effectively without the guidance of older leaders, and it led directly to the April 1960 student conference at Shaw University, where the Student Nonviolent Coordinating Committee (SNCC) was founded.

Youth moved to the forefront *of the civil rights movement when college students began sitting in at whites-only lunch counters in the South.*

IX. BERKELEY'S THEORY OF VISION

AMONG HIS MANY OTHER scientific, mathematical, and philosophical ideas, Descartes advanced a theory of vision that Berkeley regarded as implausibly rationalistic. According to Descartes, in addition to color, shape, magnitude, and position, we also literally see distance. This is because, for Descartes, vision is a form of thinking.

We see distance, he argued, by gauging the angle at which our binocular lines of sight converge—like the sides of an isosceles triangle or like two sticks held by a blind man, one in each hand, converging on an object.

In his first published book, *An Essay Towards a New Theory of Vision* (1709), Berkeley objected to Descartes's theory by pointing out that people are perfectly capable of judging distances

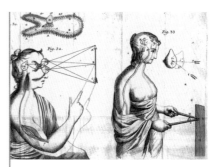

An illustration from a 1729 book showing Descartes's theory of vision.

without knowing anything about the geometry of isosceles triangles. More to the point, geometrical angles and lines are not real physical things, but mere mathematical idealizations. Berkeley concluded that we don't literally perceive distance at all but merely judge it on the basis of what we do perceive, which is just two-dimensional visual input. What I see are the visual ideas in my mind, and I impute depth to them—just as when I see people smile, I impute or ascribe happiness to them. But I don't see depth any more than I see happiness.

Berkeley borrowed much of this theory from the Irish scientist and politician William Molyneux (1656–98), who posed a famous question now known as Molyneux's Problem. Suppose a man who is blind from birth learns to distinguish a cube from a sphere by touch. He then gains sight. Could he distinguish a cube from a sphere merely by looking at the two objects? Molyneux, Locke, and Berkeley all said no, while the rationalist Leibniz answered yes. Interestingly, in 1728, the British surgeon William Cheselden successfully restored the vision of a fourteen-year-old boy, blind nearly from birth. Unfortunately, the boy still had great difficulty seeing things properly. Many therefore concluded that the negative answer the empiricists gave to Molyneux's question had been empirically vindicated.

Contrary to Descartes's *rationalist theory of vision, Berkeley maintained that we do not literally see depth but merely impute it to the two-dimensional array of visual data we do see.*

IX. LENGTH CONTRACTION

IN THE SAME WAY THAT moving frames of reference dilate time, they also physically contract length. Think again of the laser beam on the train car, and remember that velocity is defined as distance divided by time. Because the velocity of the beam is fixed at c, a decrease in time (caused by time dilation) must also mean a corresponding decrease in distance. As a general rule, objects moving at relativistic speeds contract proportionally in the direction of their motion.

Suppose you and your friend board identical spaceships. (The spaceship's length at rest with respect to you is called its proper length.) Now suppose your friend passes you at a very high speed. As he passes, you measure the length of his ship. You find that it is shorter than yours because it has length-contracted. (The width and height of his ship remain unchanged because length contraction occurs only with respect to the direction of travel.)

An equally interesting aspect of length contraction is that, if he measures your ship as he flies by, he will find that your ship has length-contracted relative to him. This is because, relative to him, you are traveling at a relativistic speed backward.

There is a famous paradox associated with length contraction, which is often stated this way: A farmer has a long ladder that he wants to store in his barn. Unfortunately, the ladder is longer than the barn is wide. After learning of length contraction, he decides to accelerate the ladder to a relativistic speed and send it through the front door of the barn, into which it will now fit because its length will be contracted relative to the stationary barn. At this point, the farmer plans to shut the barn doors, trapping the ladder inside. The farmer's plan seems ingenious until one considers it from the ladder's frame of reference, according to which it is the barn that becomes length-contracted.

The resolution to this paradox is found in the idea of simultaneity. Consider the front end of the ladder leaving the barn as one event and the back end of the ladder entering the barn as another. From the farmer's point of view, these events occur simultaneously, and the ladder fits inside the barn. From the ladder's point of view, however, the events are not simultaneous, and the front end leaves the barn before the back end enters.

According to the Special Theory of Relativity, *length contracts, which means that objects traveling at relativistic speeds contract in the direction of their motion.*

IX. *ZAYDIS, ISMA'ILIS, AND IMAMIS*

DESPITE THE MANY COMMONALITIES among Shi'ite groups during the ninth and tenth centuries, there was also considerable disagreement about who should provide leadership within the community and what its relationship to non-Alid governmental authority should be.

For some believers, the legacy of Abbasid oppression was the transformation of Shi'ism from a political movement to a religious sect. For others, however, political dissent remained a core principle, and active opposition to regimes considered unjust or illegitimate continued to be obligatory. This latter category of Shi'ites believed that *khilafa* (caliphate) was legitimate only when merged with *imama* (imamate). In other words, no allegiance could be given to a caliph unless he was also an imam of the house of Ali.

The choices that believers made with regard to these issues helped define the three distinct branches of Shi'ism that emerged during this period, all of which still exist today. These three branches were the Zaydis, Isma'ilis, and Imamis. The ways they differentiated themselves from one another were (and remain) meaningful to Shi'ites, yet they can seem subtle to outsiders. The most obvious difference involved the imams they followed.

The Zaydis followed a line of imams descending from Zayd—a son of the fourth imam, Ali bin Husayn. For this reason, they were called Fivers because the Isma'ilis and Imamis followed a different fifth imam: Zayd's older brother Muhammad al-Baqir. The Zaydis were also unusual among Shi'ites in that they recognized the legitimacy of the first three caliphs—a position that reflected their more nuanced and accommodating view of non-Shi'ite authority.

The Isma'ilis were called Seveners because they followed a line of imams descending from Isma'il—son of Ja'far al-Sadiq, whom both the Isma'ilis and the Imamis considered the true sixth imam. The Imamis, who comprise the vast majority of modern Shi'ites, were called Twelvers because they followed a different line through Ja'far's younger son Musa al-Kazim—a lineage that ended in the late ninth century with the disappearance of the twelfth imam, Muhammad al-Mahdi.

Unlike the Zaydis, the Isma'ilis and the Imamis are both known as *rafida* ("refusers") because they refuse to accept the legitimacy of the first three caliphs—or any non-Alid authority, for that matter. However, while the Isma'ilis are distinguished historically by their excessively militant attitude toward non-Shi'ite authority, Imami opposition to the Abbasids was always much more theoretical than practical.

The three Shi'ite branches *that emerged during the Abbasid period are distinguished by the lineage of their imams and their attitudes toward governmental authority.*

IX. THE EMERGENCE OF DOSTOEVSKY

FYODOR DOSTOEVSKY (1821–81) grew up in a blighted area of Moscow near the hospital for the poor where his father worked. Neighborhood landmarks included an insane asylum, an orphanage, and a graveyard for criminals. When he was nine, he suffered his first epileptic seizure, and subsequent attacks occurred periodically throughout his life. Typically, they were preceded by moments of euphoria—in exchange for which, according to Dostoevsky, a person would trade his entire life. This sentiment later became something of an idée fixe, and it motivated Dostoevsky's lifelong search for meaning and fulfillment in a dark and seemingly hopeless world.

As a young man, Dostoevsky departed Moscow for St. Petersburg, where he studied at the Military Engineering Academy. He was more taken with German literature than with mathematics, however, and soon began writing fiction of his own. In 1845, he published his first novel, *Poor Folk*.

Fyodor Dostoevsky as a military engineer.

Like most Russian literature of the nineteenth century, the novel appeared serially in a literary journal—whose editor reportedly exclaimed that "a new Gogol" had arisen. Yet the success was short-lived. In 1849, Nicholas I's police arrested Dostoevsky for attending underground meetings of a reformist political group known as the Petrashevsky Circle. Dostoevsky was imprisoned for several months in the Peter and Paul Fortress before being subjected to a horrifying mock execution. His death sentence was then commuted to four years in a Siberian labor camp; but even after his release, he was forced to remain in Siberia for another five years.

Three years after his 1859 return to St. Petersburg, Dostoevsky published *Notes from the Dead House*, a thinly fictionalized account of his life in prison. With unforgiving realism, he described the filth, lack of privacy, and spiritual oppression that he experienced in the labor camp and how it had offered him startling insights into the human soul at its best and worst.

Having passed through this crucible, Dostoevsky's creative genius became fixed on the most pressing dualities of human existence: life and death, freedom and imprisonment, faith and despair. What gives life meaning? Under what circumstances is it worth living? Can morality exist if God does not? Most importantly, how can the suffering of the innocent be reconciled with the idea of a loving and omnipotent Creator? These were a few of the so-called cursed questions that inspired the philosophical dialogues for which Dostoevsky's novels are justly famous.

The insights into the human condition *that Dostoevsky gained while imprisoned in Siberia deepened his lifelong search for meaning in a dark, seemingly hopeless world.*

X. THE FREEDOM RIDE

AS PRES. JOHN KENNEDY TOOK OFFICE in 1961, civil rights was not on his agenda. He and his brother, Attorney General Robert Kennedy, personally supported the cause, but they were much more concerned with foreign policy and were willing to let racial justice develop slowly. James Farmer was not.

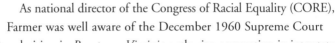

As national director of the Congress of Racial Equality (CORE), Farmer was well aware of the December 1960 Supreme Court decision in *Boynton v. Virginia* outlawing segregation in interstate bus travel. Nevertheless, WHITE and COLORED signs remained in place above waiting room doors throughout the South.

To compel federal action, Farmer organized the Freedom Ride. His plan was to send interracial volunteers on a bus trip through the South, during which they would exercise their rights under *Boynton*. The thirteen original Freedom Riders left Washington, DC, on May 4, 1961, in two buses, one a Greyhound and the other a Trailways. The whites sat in the back of each bus; the blacks, in the front. At each stop, the Freedom Riders ignored the WHITE and COLORED signs, and—in the Upper South, at least—the locals ignored them.

On Mother's Day, May 14, however, the Greyhound bus carrying half of the Freedom Riders from Atlanta to Birmingham passed through the Ku Klux Klan stronghold of Anniston, Alabama, where a mob of angry whites broke the bus's windows, slashed its tires, and—when the bus was forced to pull over—firebombed its interior. Meanwhile, the Trailways bus carrying the other half of the Freedom Riders reached Birmingham unscathed, but its passengers were attacked in the terminal building and severely beaten. (There were no Birmingham police present because city officials had promised the Klan fifteen minutes alone with the riders.)

President Kennedy first learned of the Freedom Ride when a story about the attacks appeared on the front page of the next day's *New York Times*. The last thing he wanted was well-publicized racial violence in the South, which the Soviet Union could use to embarrass the United States, its Cold War foe. Kennedy was also eager to avoid what he called the "Little Rock method." He wished the matter would simply go away. But, as Farmer had intended, the publicity forced a reluctant government to act. Meanwhile, the small, dramatic, vanguard action that was the Freedom Ride so inspired part-time student activists that many left school to become full-time SNCC organizers.

While putting the Kennedy administration *to the test, the Freedom Ride dramatized southerners' violent determination to flout federal law and retain segregation.*

X. HUME, THE NEWTON OF THE MIND

David Hume

BORN IN EDINBURGH, Scotland, David Hume (1711–76) was the last and greatest of the early British empiricists. In his own day he was famous as an essayist and historian, having written a best-selling six-volume history of England. He also influenced the economic and moral theories of his friend Adam Smith.

Precocious like Berkeley, Hume was in his mid-twenties when he wrote *A Treatise of Human Nature* (1739–40), the work on which his philosophical reputation rests. His later books *An Enquiry Concerning Human Understanding* (published in 1748 under a different title) and *An Enquiry Concerning the Principles of Morals* (1751) restate the central views of the *Treatise*, though with some modifications.

Hume could be called the first modern psychologist. His ambition was to understand the human mind as part of nature rather than as a distinct nonnatural substance—which is what Descartes, Locke, and Berkeley all thought it to be. His project had both a negative, critical side and a positive, constructive side. Negatively, Hume's aim was to discredit the rationalist theory of belief formation, according to which we are free to choose our beliefs on the basis of purely rational considerations. Descartes maintained, for instance, that the intellect is infallible and that all errors of judgment are errors of will—that is, choosing to believe something in the absence of sufficient evidence or argument. Hume maintained that belief is involuntary; that the mind forms beliefs just as the heart beats and the eye blinks. After all, drop a book and try to believe that it will float up rather than fall down. You can't. According to Hume, we can't help having the beliefs we have. Moreover, our beliefs have no rational foundation. We have no good reason to believe what we believe, but we can't help believing it.

The positive side of Hume's project was to do for the human mind what Isaac Newton had done for the physical world—namely, describe its fundamental laws of operation. Such laws would be principles governing what Hume called the association of ideas. According to Hume, the mind involuntarily associates ideas (puts them together) in three basic ways: by resemblance (a picture of Sally makes us think of Sally), by contiguity (noses make us think of mouths and eyes), and by cause and effect (where there's smoke, there's fire).

Because Hume viewed thought *as a natural psychological process, he believed that he could discover the laws governing it, just as Newton had discovered the laws of motion.*

X. THE IMPLICATIONS FOR SPACE AND TIME TRAVEL

SCIENCE-FICTION AUTHORS have long noticed the interesting implications time dilation and length contraction have for space and time travel. For instance, suppose that you and I leave Earth in a spaceship traveling at $0.995c$. Our destination is a star ten light-years away. This is the distance that light travels in ten years from the point of view of an observer on Earth. But Earth is not our frame of reference. Because our spaceship is traveling at near-light speed, the world outside our ship becomes length-contracted, which shortens the distance of our trip to just one light-year. As a result, according to our onboard clock, we reach the star in a little over a year (because we are traveling at just under the speed of light). To an observer on Earth, however, the distance we travel is still ten light-years, and our trip still requires about ten years to complete.

Both observations are, of course, correct and consistent with time dilation. From the point of view of an Earth observer, the time inside our spaceship is moving much more slowly than time on Earth. Therefore, we are aging much more slowly than if we were still on Earth. Even though the Earth observer ages ten years in the time it takes us to reach the star, we age only one year.

As for time travel, suppose that once we reach our destination, we immediately turn around and return to Earth. The round trip, within our frame of reference, will take about two years. On Earth, however, about twenty years will have passed. Therefore, when we return, our identical twins (if we have any) will be eighteen years older than we are. This effect seems like time travel, because we are returning to a future world, but it is time travel only in one direction. Nothing about relativity suggests a way to travel backward in time.

A common misconception is that moving at relativistic speed can somehow extend the human life span. To understand why this isn't so, think about our round trip to the star. Although twenty years pass on Earth, only two years pass on the spaceship. We can spend our entire lifetimes in whatever frame of reference we choose, but from our perspective, we will always live the same number of years we would have on Earth—no more, no less.

Although time dilation *and length contraction shorten significantly the time required for space travel at relativistic speeds, they do not permit travel backward in time.*

X. THE ASCENDANCE OF THE ISMA'ILIS

THE FIRST SHI'ITES to achieve significant political success were the Isma'ilis, whose militancy strongly challenged Abbasid rule. The breakthrough came in North Africa, where a powerful group of Isma'ilis founded the Fatimid dynasty. Over time, their empire came to incorporate Egypt and many lands beyond. In 969, the Fatimids founded the city of Cairo and for the next two centuries presided over a brilliant, cosmopolitan culture that rivaled and eventually eclipsed the Abbasid society in Baghdad. Promoting this Fatimid efflorescence was an alliance of heterogeneous groups, including Isma'ili propagandists and Berber warriors; later, Turks and Bedouins joined as well. As the Fatimids extended their hegemony into Palestine and Syria, their imams even took the title of caliph to demonstrate that their wealth and power far exceeded anything of which the dwindling Abbasid regime could boast. Shi'ite ascendancy, it seemed, had finally arrived.

During the twelfth century, after the Fatimids began to weaken and decline, Isma'ilis of a very different sort became quite influential in Iran and Iraq. These Isma'ilis, known as Nizaris, combined esoteric religious teachings with a radically activist political philosophy. Because they lacked numerical strength and thus couldn't survive direct confrontations with the governments they opposed, the Nizari Isma'ilis had to develop new techniques to support their political program of violent resistance to non-Shi'ite authority. Their principal innovation was to sequester themselves in a chain of fortresses, from which they occasionally emerged to commit brutal acts of violence against officials working for the dominant regime.

A fragment of a bowl decorated with peacocks produced in Fatimid Egypt during the twelfth century.

According to legend, the grand master of the Nizari Isma'ilis, Hasan-i Sabbah, would often order young men abducted and brought to the great Nizari stronghold at Alamut, where he would ply them with intoxicants and sex. Then, when they were sufficiently sated, the grand master would instruct these young men to martyr themselves in order to earn similar rewards in Paradise. The Nizari thus became notorious as the Hashishin (meaning "those intoxicated with hashish"), which is the source of the English word *assassin*. Mongol invaders finally conquered the Nizari strongholds during the thirteenth century.

The Fatimid Isma'ilis *brought an intellectual, cultural, and economic efflorescence to North Africa, while the later Nizari Isma'ilis brought terror to Iran and Iraq.*

X. NOTES FROM THE UNDERGROUND

DOSTOEVSKY'S SHORT BUT POWERFUL *Notes from the Underground* (1864) is the first-person confession of a reclusive forty-year-old former clerk, who has sought refuge from a society he despises by going "underground." Dostoevsky's use of the word *underground* suggests the sense of being buried alive, but it also implies the irrational, the subconscious, and a cynical view of everything going on "aboveground."

In the first of the novel's two parts, the Underground Man explains, "I am a sick man....I am an evil man. I am a most unattractive man. I think I have a liver illness." Having thus introduced himself, he launches into a blistering attack on modernist values, especially the delusional belief that humanity is progressively marching toward a society governed by rational laws. Such a reduction of life to a few principles of math and science is, to the Underground Man, a sort of living death. The key symbol for him of the triumph of modern rationalism is the Crystal Palace, a vast structure of glass and steel built in London for the Great Exhibition of 1851. The Underground Man denounces the Crystal Palace as nothing more than a prison for the human spirit, which he asserts is fundamentally irrational.

The Underground Man's claim that humanity loves freedom above all else was hardly new, but Dostoevsky's readers were nonetheless shocked by the ways in which the Underground Man expressed his freedom—specifically, through irrationality and often self-destruction. According to the Underground Man, human nature insists on being irrational, because an essential part of being free is rebelling against the dictates of reason. Otherwise, people couldn't take pleasure from activities they know to be "bad" for them. While Enlightenment thought had encouraged the idea that freedom and rationality were closely related, the Underground Man rejected all such thinking, preferring to endure the suffering that freedom entailed rather than accept enslavement by materially prosperous but spiritually emaciated rationalism.

Less overtly philosophical than the first section, the novel's second section recounts the Underground Man's former life among society. Years of humiliation and hatred finally produce, near the end, a glimmer of hope. A prostitute named Liza sees through the Underground Man's abrasive exterior and recognizes how unhappy he is. She offers him gestures of love, but he responds heartlessly by lashing out at her and shoving money in her direction. This insult drives Liza away, leaving the Underground Man alone in his underground.

According to Dostoevsky's *Underground Man, freedom requires individuals to rebel against the dictates of reason—even if doing so is, in the end, self-destructive.*

XI. THE INTEGRATION OF OLE MISS

THE KENNEDY ADMINISTRATION'S reaction to the Freedom Ride set a pattern for its future behavior with regard to civil rights. The president did everything he could to keep the issue from hijacking his Cold War agenda. He cajoled the parties involved, threatened them, and even made secret deals with them. But, when pressed, he ultimately enforced the law, albeit with reluctance.

Kennedy's most difficult racial crisis came to a head in September 1962, when a federal court ordered the immediate admission of black student James Meredith to the all-white University of Mississippi, known as Ole Miss. On September 13, playing to Mississippi's segregationist electorate, Gov. Ross Barnett announced that he was ordering the university to defy the federal court order.

A student confronts police at Ole Miss.

Barnett's rhetoric was all show, however, because he was at the same time conducting secret talks with the Kennedy administration. Both sides understood that Meredith would have to be enrolled, and each had its own reasons for wanting to minimize the political consequences. The sticking point was the federal show of force: The president wanted to appear to be using minimal force to fulfill his constitutional obligations, while Barnett wanted Meredith to be admitted at federal gunpoint so that he could maintain his charade of defiance. Barnett held out too long, however, forcing Kennedy's hand.

By Sunday, September 30, the college town of Oxford was in a state of near hysteria. Klansmen were arriving from all over the South to defend white supremacy, and radio stations were counting down the hours until Monday, when Meredith was to be registered and bloodshed seemed likely. Barnett and Kennedy thought they could avoid violence by registering Meredith unexpectedly on Sunday night—and Meredith was brought to the campus about 6 PM for that purpose—but an angry crowd gathering in front of the administration building to threaten the federal marshals there made that plan impossible.

Racial slurs—such as "Marshal, where is your wife tonight? Home with a nigger?"—escalated into brick and bottle throwing. Federal vehicles were overturned and set on fire, and soon there was gunfire. One marshal was hit in the leg; another was shot in the neck. Permission to fire back was refused by the president, who didn't want further escalation. But the rioting proved impossible to ignore, and eventually Kennedy had to send in sixteen thousand federal troops to restore order.

Just as Eisenhower did in Little Rock, *President Kennedy found in Mississippi that he had no choice but to respond to white violence with federal force.*

XI. IMPRESSIONS AND IDEAS

HUME BUILT HIS PSYCHOLOGICAL THEORY on a distinction between impressions and ideas. Impressions, the most vivid or forceful of our perceptions, come from the five outer senses and from our own inner psychological states. So, for example, when I look at the sky, I have an outer impression or sensation of blue. Similarly, when I am provoked or insulted, I have an inner impression or feeling of anger.

Ideas, by contrast, are derived from impressions and thus, Hume said, are "more feeble" by virtue of being derived. They differ from impressions as judgments differ from sensations, or as what we think differs from what we feel. Such distinctions are notoriously difficult to draw sharply, yet it seems clear that there is a difference. A toothache or the smell of tobacco is nothing like my judgment that 2 + 2 = 4, which has no qualitative "feel" about it.

Being an empiricist, Hume believed that all knowledge comes from experience—or, more precisely, from impressions. Logical and mathematical knowledge, which might seem to be entirely independent of experience, is merely a function of what he called relations of ideas. So, for example, experience gives me impressions of green and blue, from which I derive the more general idea of color. My knowledge that everything green has a color doesn't come to me from a source other than experience; it's just a consequence of the way those two ideas are related to each other. That all green things are colored is true by definition of the words *green* and *color*.

Recall that one of the three principles of the association of ideas is cause and effect. That is, one of the ways we put ideas together is to consider what comes before and what comes afterward. For example, when I drop a book (cause), I expect it to fall (effect). When I see smoke (effect), I expect fire (cause). But from what impression does my idea of *cause* itself derive? This question troubled Hume deeply and motivated his famous skeptical account of causal necessity.

Hume drew a distinction *between impressions, which are vivid outer sensations and inner feelings, and ideas, which are thoughts derived from impressions.*

XI. THE LORENTZ TRANSFORMATIONS

LET'S RETURN TO Einstein's initial thought experiment, in which a person traveling at *c* holds up a mirror in front of his face. According to Galilean relativity, the light moving from this person's face to the mirror should be traveling at *c* relative to him and at 2*c* relative to an observer at rest. Einstein invented the Special Theory of Relativity to explain why this couldn't be so, but he didn't have to work out all the related mathematics because most of the necessary equations had already been developed by Hendrik Lorentz. Along with a few other physicists, Lorentz had spent much of the late 1890s seeking a way to transform quantities in accordance with Maxwell's equations. Einstein simply adopted Lorentz's work, making only a few minor modifications.

The Lorentz Transformations allow physicists to make predictions based on changing frames of reference. For example, if I know the space–time coordinates of an event in one inertial frame of reference and also the relative velocity between that frame of reference and another, I can calculate the space–time coordinates the event would have in the second frame of reference. (Space–time coordinates include the three usual dimensions plus time.) At low speeds, the Lorentz Transformations reduce to the Galilean-style equations of Newtonian mechanics. At relativistic speeds, however, only the Lorentz Transformations produce accurate results.

Here's how the equations work: Suppose I witness a spaceship approaching Earth at velocity *V*, and it emits a flash of light. The coordinates of that flash in space–time within my frame of reference are *x*, *y*, *z*, and *t*. Using this information, I can calculate x', y', z', and t', which are the coordinates of the flash within the spaceship's frame of reference. (The symbol x' is pronounced "x prime.") Next, I observe a satellite passing the spaceship at velocity *u*. I can also use the Lorentz Transformations to calculate u', which is the satellite's velocity from the point of view of an observer on the spaceship.

Now let's plug in some actual values: Let's say that the spaceship is approaching Earth at 0.8*c* and that it launches a probe toward our planet at a speed of 0.7*c* relative to the spaceship. Simple Galilean relativity would tell us that the probe is moving at 1.5*c* relative to Earth, but this can't be so, because nothing can exceed the speed of light. Using the Lorentz equations, however, I obtain a probe speed of 0.96*c* relative to Earth, which is the correct value.

The Lorentz Transformations *are equations that allow physicists to calculate changes in position and velocity between one frame of reference and another.*

XI. THE MATURATION OF SUNNI IDENTITY

THERE IS NO TELLING what proportion of the Muslim community was Shi'ite during the late Abbasid period. Yet there is also no question that Shi'ites appeared to dominate Muslim society for much of that time, which is why the advent of a militantly anti-Shi'ite empire during the late eleventh century is often called the Sunni Revival.

As early as the ninth century, *Sunni* was a term used by various non-Shi'ite groups who rejected the claim of the Shi'ites that political power could be vested only in the descendants of Ali. However, during the late Abbasid period, even as the caliphate remained the focus of non-Shi'ite identity, a more coherent religious and ideological definition of *Sunni* began to emerge.

A tile panel showing Mecca.

The roots of the first Sunni communities are to be found in major imperial cities such as Baghdad, Kufa, Basra, Mecca, and Medina, where early religious scholars congregated to learn the *sunna* ("way of the Prophet") as communicated by the *hadith* (oral traditions relating the words and deeds of Muhammad). Whereas the Shi'a relied on their imams for religious guidance, these non-Shi'ite scholars sought to base Islamic law and ritual on the *hadith*. Over time, they became spokesmen for other non-Shi'ite Muslims, who came to call themselves the *Ahl al-sunna wa'l-jama'a* (meaning "the people of the way of the Prophet and the [legitimate] community").

While Sevener and Twelver Shi'a clung to the ideal of *rafd* ("refusal")—that is, refusing to accept non-Alid caliphs—Sunnis promoted a corresponding doctrine, *irja'*, or "returning" judgment to God. According to the Sunnis, anyone who has become caliph is inherently legitimate because God would not allow a usurper to become caliph. From this doctrine, in turn, the Sunnis developed the concept of the Rashidun, or Four Rightly Guided Caliphs. That the Sunnis believe the era of the Rashidun was a golden age of justice in Islamic history is a key distinction between them and the Shi'a. In a sense, the Sunnis chose to ignore complex questions of legitimacy and instead follow whomever God elevated to the caliphate.

By the time the Turkish Seljuks arrived in Baghdad late in the eleventh century, however, the Sunnis had taken the next step: coming to view the caliph's authority as primarily symbolic while vesting ultimate authority in the consensus of the religious scholars. This made it easy for the declining Abbasids to retain the title *caliph* while ceding actual political authority to the Seljuk warlords, who took the title *sultan*.

Sunnism, *which rejected Shi'ite beliefs about political and religious authority, became an increasingly dominant concept during the tenth and eleventh centuries.*

XI. CRIME AND PUNISHMENT

WRITTEN IN 1866, *Crime and Punishment* is perhaps Dostoevsky's most approachable novel, because its tortured existential discourses are presented in the form of a detective story. At the same time, *Crime and Punishment* is hardly a whodunit, because the reader knows the killer's identity (and every thought) from the start. The murderer is Raskolnikov, a poor student who slays an old pawnbroker with an ax and then steals some of her valuables. When the pawnbroker's sister unexpectedly walks in on the crime, Raskolnikov kills her, too. Then, after a few tense moments, he escapes more or less undetected.

Dostoevsky in 1879.

After quickly dispensing with these plot points, Dostoevsky devotes the rest of the novel to a game of psychological cat and mouse between Raskolnikov and Porfiry Petrovich, the police detective in charge of the case. Well versed in criminal psychology, Porfiry quickly realizes, despite the lack of physical evidence, that Raskolnikov is the murderer. But rather than arrest and interrogate Raskolnikov, he's content to let the murderer remain free—certain that he will, like a "moth to a flame," be driven to confess in the end.

Initially, Raskolnikov rationalizes his crime as extraordinary (rather than petty) theft. The crime is extraordinary because he, as a man, is extraordinary. Using some philosophically grandiose arguments, he persuades himself that his genius places him above the laws of good and evil. This status justifies his decision to "step across blood" in order to seize the means (the pawnbroker's valuables) that he needs to rise from obscurity and "speak a new word." Raskolnikov reasons that he can take the liberty of killing the pawnbroker, a "louse" of a human being, because his rise is in humanity's best interest and because men such as himself aren't bound by moral standards.

For Dostoevsky, of course, reason alone is always suspect. Unless bridled by the heart's compassion, its deranged mathematics can lead to monstrous atrocities. Raskolnikov's willingness, for example, to condone the "useful" killing of a human being, even out of a professed love for humanity, leads not to redemption but to bloodbaths of historical proportions.

Dostoevsky's Crime and Punishment *is a psychological detective story in which the mystery is not the killer's identity but his motive.*

XII. PROJECT C

DURING THE SUMMER OF 1962, Martin Luther King, Jr., suffered his worst setback yet. The desegregation movement that he had joined in Albany, Georgia, ended without achieving any of its goals. Cleverly, Albany's police chief, Laurie Pritchett, had studied King's methods (as well as Birmingham's response to the Freedom Ride) and concluded that the best way to counter nonviolence was to be nonbrutal. He arrested and jailed hundreds of demonstrators but allowed no beatings and thus avoided federal intervention.

The lesson King learned was that, in the absence of violence, the federal government would not act to protect Negro civil rights, nor would the American public pay much attention. After a lengthy internal debate, King decided that his organization, the Southern Christian Leadership Conference (SCLC), would need to raise the stakes. He targeted Birmingham because he knew that its ruthless public safety commissioner, Eugene "Bull" Connor, would likely react with such outrageous brutality that public opinion would shift King's way.

The campaign began on April 3, 1963, but languished until early May, when James Bevel suggested that Project C (for "confrontation") enlist the children he had been training in nonviolence workshops. Adults had proven increasingly reluctant to risk arrest and the loss of their jobs, but "a boy from high school has the same effect in terms of being in jail, in terms of putting pressure on the city, as his father," Bevel told King.

The Children's Crusade began on May 2. At first, Connor wasn't sure what to do with the youngsters, some as young as six, but he eventually decided to arrest them, imprisoning six hundred in a makeshift jail at the local fairgrounds. The next day, another thousand marched. With no place to put these

Birmingham firemen train their hoses on young Negro demonstrators.

additional children, Connor ordered them dispersed rather than arrested. His firemen trained hoses on the marchers; and when some refused to yield, the firemen turned up the pressure until the jets of water lifted marchers off the ground. Angry parents began throwing rocks and bricks at the firemen, prompting the police to loose German shepherds on the crowd.

That night, network news programs broadcast footage of the violence, and instantly white and black Americans all over the country unified behind King. According to Kennedy aide Arthur Schlesinger, even the president was persuaded that he would now have to take on southern intransigence with regard to civil rights.

With the movement flagging, *King decided to risk everything on a confrontation in Birmingham, betting that the local authorities wouldn't be able to resist violence.*

XII. CAUSAL NECESSITY

HUME BEGAN HIS SEARCH for the origin of the idea of cause by observing that it cannot be derived from mere impressions of events, because events as we observe them are simply one thing happening followed by another thing happening. That is, nothing in our impressions of events contains the idea of one thing *causing* another thing to happen. Nor, Hume continued, can our idea of cause be derived from reason, because nothing in the mere relations of ideas requires that one event must bring another about. For example, the idea of a cue ball coming into contact with an eight ball doesn't logically require that the eight ball should then move.

Because Hume couldn't locate the idea of causal necessity either in observation or in reason, he concluded that causal necessity doesn't exist. Causality, he decided, isn't a *necessary connection* between events but merely a *constant conjunction* of one kind of event with another. The act of dropping a book doesn't "make" it fall; instead, whenever I drop a book, it just *does* fall. You might ask, doesn't the force of gravity make it fall? Well, what is the force of gravity? Do you have an impression of it? No. The force of gravity is an abstract theoretical idea enlisted to explain the observable fact that when you drop something, it falls. To say that there is a force causing this to happen is akin to Molière's "imaginary invalid" proclaiming that opium puts people to sleep by means of its "dormitive power"—that is, its power to put people to sleep. The explanation is vacuous.

According to Hume, we are not entitled to our idea of causal *necessity*, but only to the notion of causal *regularity*—that is, similar effects regularly following similar causes. And yet, although we are not entitled to the idea of causal necessity, we can't help but have it. So, the psychological question remains: What impressions does the idea of cause come from? Hume's answer was that the originating impression is the *expectation* of the effect given the cause, or the cause given the effect. As you let go of the book, you feel (involuntarily) that it will fall, and the intensity of that expectation leads you to suppose that there is a force in the world making it happen. Notice, of course, that the psychological "force" of your expectation is no more a real force than the force of gravity, but merely the vividness of your feeling.

Hume argued that *our idea of causal necessity derives neither from observation nor from reason; therefore, it is illegitimate. Causality is mere regularity: When one kind of thing happens, another kind of thing regularly follows.*

XII. MASS-ENERGY EQUIVALENCE

BY THE EARLY TWENTIETH CENTURY, the conservation of mass and the conservation of energy were well-established physical principles. According to the conservation of mass, the total quantity of matter measured before a chemical reaction must equal the total quantity of matter measured after the reaction. Conservation of energy similarly held that energy could be neither created nor destroyed. Scientists believed in both of these principles just as firmly as they believed in Galilean relativity, until some strange experimental results challenged their faith.

In his fourth *annus mirabilis* paper, Einstein explained these results by asserting the equivalence of mass and energy. According to Einstein, mass and energy were merely different manifestations of the same thing. Furthermore, mass could be converted into energy, and energy converted into mass. To describe this conversion process, Einstein created his most famous equation, $E = mc^2$. In other words, mass and energy are proportional quantities differing by a factor equal to the square of the speed of light. Actually, according to Einstein, only mass-energy is conserved.

The $E = mc^2$ equation has a number of important applications in nuclear physics. Radioactive elements are naturally unstable. Over time, they break down, or decay, into more stable elements through a process called nuclear fission. When a radioactive nucleus decays, however, the total mass of its pieces does not equal the mass of the original nucleus. A little matter is lost and converted into energy. From $E = mc^2$, we can see than even a little bit of mass converts into a great deal of energy (because of the c^2 factor). This is why nuclear weapons are so powerful.

The first test of a nuclear bomb at Alamogordo, NM, July 1945.

Nuclear reactors create and control the energy produced by nuclear fission. Inside a fission reactor, many radioactive nuclei decay simultaneously, emitting a huge amount of energy. Nuclear power plants capture this energy, which they use to boil water. The resulting steam spins turbines, which generate electricity.

Nuclear fusion is similar to nuclear fission, but the process moves in reverse. During nuclear fusion, smaller nuclei are fused together to form larger nuclei. This process requires a great deal of energy to overcome the electrostatic force keeping the two nuclei apart—which is why fusion takes place only under extreme conditions, such as those found in the core of a star. However, because nuclear fusion also converts some of the matter into energy, the process produces more energy than it consumes.

Einstein resolved contradictions *relating to the conservation of mass and energy by proposing that mass and energy are different manifestations of the same basic thing.*

XII. RELIGIOUS MINORITIES AND THE SUNNI MAJORITY

FROM THE DEATH OF THE PROPHET until about 900, there was, more or less, a single, dominant caliphal power. Beginning early in the tenth century, however, the decline of the Abbasid caliphate led to a splintering of political authority and the development of numerous autonomous communities organized around different political, social, and religious principles. Some paid nominal allegiance to the caliph in Baghdad; others ignored or challenged his authority outright. Still, all were equal participants in a common Islamic civilization that flourished in the Mediterranean and the Middle East throughout the High Middle Ages.

In some respects, Islamic society of this period was marked by a high degree of tolerance, especially of the *dhimmi* communities (non-Muslim monotheists). Arabized though not necessarily assimilated, these Jews and Christians were allowed to maintain their religious identities while making important contributions to the common "Islamicate" civilization. The Shi'a also contributed, though under less favorable

A scene of thirteenth-century village life in Iraq.

conditions. Although Shi'ites may have constituted a significant proportion of the population at the start of this period, over the next few centuries they were steadily reduced in status to an oppressed minority.

During the twelfth and thirteenth centuries, in particular, a distinct "Sunnification" of political discourse took place. In many contexts, the Sunnis and the Shi'a continued to cooperate and coexist peacefully, but there were regular instances of violence and persecution as well. More importantly, the Sunnis gradually became accustomed to wielding power over (and sometimes against) the Shi'a, who became more and more entrenched in a subordinate position.

This imbalance was temporarily rectified when the Mongols invaded in the thirteenth century. Initially, both Sunnis and Shi'ites suffered terribly from the slaughter that accompanied the Mongols' arrival in the central Islamic lands. For the Sunnis, the worst moment may have come in 1258, when Hulagu Khan, grandson of Genghis Khan, put the last Abbasid caliph to death. On the other hand, the Shi'a, who had never accepted the Abbasid caliphate, gradually came to benefit from the new Mongol order. For example, Nasir al-Din al-Tusi, one of the most important Shi'ite scholars of the Middle Ages, was offered royal patronage. The Mongols also began favoring other minorities in an effort to prevent a reassertion of Sunni power.

Along with some *assimilated Christians and Jews, both Sunnis and Shi'ites participated in the flourishing Muslim civilization of the High Middle Ages.*

XII. THE BROTHERS KARAMAZOV

DOSTOEVSKY HAD JUST BEGUN writing his final novel, *The Brothers Karamazov* (1880), when his three-year-old son, Alyosha, died in May 1878. The cause of death was the epilepsy the boy had inherited from his father. As a result, in addition to its other strong religious themes, *The Brothers Karamazov* dwells often and in detail on the suffering of innocent children. Appropriately, the novel's hero is named Alyosha.

A more distant but nearly as inspirational biographical event was the mysterious death of Dostoevsky's father, who passed away while Dostoevsky was attending the Military Engineering Academy in St. Petersburg. The speculation at the time was that Mikhail Dostoevsky had been murdered by his serfs. Although this now seems doubtful, Dostoevsky himself believed the story was true.

Like Turgenev's *Fathers and Sons*, *The Brothers Karamazov* concerns generational conflict, but on a much deeper metaphysical level. It tells the story of a father's neglect for his sons and the consequences of that neglect. The dubious patriarch of the Karamazov family is the skirt-chasing, blaspheming Fyodor Pavlovich. The titular brothers are Fyodor's sons. The oldest, Dmitry, is the child of Fyodor's first marriage; he's impulsive, robust, and headstrong like his mother. Fyodor's second wife, however, has a much more religious disposition, bordering on madness. Her sons are Ivan, a brooding intellectual, and the compassionate Alyosha, who finds his calling in a monastery. Later, Dostoevsky reveals that Smerdyakov, a pompous lackey in the Karamazov household, is also a son to Fyodor, the result of his shameful liaison with a village mendicant nicknamed Stinking Lizaveta.

The plot of this sprawling philosophical novel is set in motion by the murder of Fyodor Pavlovich, and it culminates with the trial of Dmitry, to whom all the evidence points. In fact, Dostoevsky carefully arranged the rational evidence so that it would "prove" Dmitry's guilt, and yet still be wrong. The point is that objective truth and higher truth are dissimilar things. For Dostoevsky, the rational thought that governs objective truth is coercive, enslaving, and easily deceived. Higher truth, on the other hard, is sensed by the heart—that is, by intuition and by faith—which can't be tricked quite so easily.

For *The Brothers Karamazov*, *Dostoevsky drew on the murder of his father and the death of his young son to create a tale of filial revolt that distinguishes objective truth from higher truth.*

XIII. THE MARCH ON WASHINGTON

BEFORE THE PROJECT C DEMONSTRATIONS, President Kennedy didn't want to introduce new civil rights legislation because he was sure that no bill would pass and he didn't want to needlessly antagonize southern Democrats, whose support he needed in Congress.

The violence in Birmingham, however, changed his mind, and on June 11, 1963, in a nationally televised speech, Kennedy announced his intention to introduce a new equal accommodations bill. "We preach freedom around the world, and we mean it," the president said, "and we cherish our freedom here at home, but are we to say to the world and, much more importantly, to each other that this is a land of the free except for the Negroes; that we have no second-class citizens except Negroes; that we have no class or caste system, no ghettos, no master race except with respect to Negroes?"

Meanwhile, labor leader A. Philip Randolph had begun planning a massive march on Washington to focus national attention on civil rights. The last thing that Kennedy wanted was tens of thousands of demonstrating Negroes roiling the waters of Congress, but when Randolph—supported by Martin Luther King, Jr., and James Farmer—refused to call off the march, the president had no choice but to cooperate (in order to maximize his influence on the plans being made).

Administration officials, who were quietly channeling hundreds of thousands of federal dollars into the event, were able to persuade the organizers to hold the march on a weekday—specifically, Wednesday, August 28—so that most of the marchers would have to come late and leave early (not being able to take two days off work). They also arranged for the rally to be held at the Lincoln Memorial, conveniently surrounded on three sides by water and thus ideal for crowd control.

As it turned out, of course, the quarter of a million marchers couldn't have been more orderly. The last orator of the day, King, mounted the speakers' platform shortly before 4 PM. Like the others before him, he had agreed to limit his remarks to seven minutes, but in the end King ignored this commitment and spoke for nineteen. "I have a dream," he said, "my four little children will one day live in a nation where they will not be judged by the color of their skin but by the content of their character."

Martin Luther King, Jr., organized a vast interracial coalition to pressure Congress into passing President Kennedy's new civil rights bill.

XIII. HUME'S SKEPTICISM

HUME'S CRITIQUE of the idea of causal necessity is so powerful that it threatens to undermine virtually all of our beliefs about the world beyond our immediate experience. This is because most of what we believe depends on the assumption of causal regularity, or what is also known as the uniformity of nature. When I look away from the book on my desk, does it momentarily pop out of existence? Only by taking for granted a causally stable world can I dismiss that idea as absurd.

But what is the basis of our belief in the uniformity of nature? Recall that our idea of causal necessity is based on our expectation that things will continue to behave as they have in the past. That expectation is not based on reason but is merely habitual, like a reflex. Beliefs about the future are instilled in us by our past experience, but past experience doesn't justify those beliefs. This is known as the problem of induction. In logic and mathematics, sound deductive arguments guarantee the truth of one's conclusions, whereas inductive inferences are empirical and can always go wrong.

Hume's view of induction was relentlessly skeptical. He thought that nothing justifies our beliefs about the future. You might be tempted to say that the assumption of the uniformity of nature is surely justified by being reliable. But that amounts to saying that we can know that the future will resemble the past because *in the past* the future has reliably resembled the past. But that begs the question, will it continue to do so?

Hume was similarly skeptical about the identity of objects across time. Think again of Descartes's example of the melting wax. How do we know it to be the very same piece of wax in its solid and liquid states? Hume thought that we don't. In fact, Hume thought that it isn't. Of course, if Hume thought he knew that, you could fairly ask him *how* he knew it. Maybe things remain identical across time, though we can never know that they do.

Happily, nature has made us incapable of sustaining this sort of rationally irrefutable skepticism for very long. We may be skeptics for a few minutes in a philosophy seminar, but we are natural-born believers throughout the rest of our lives.

Hume was the first *philosopher to raise the problem of induction. He believed that neither experience nor reason justifies our natural assumption that the future will resemble the past.*

XIII. THE ATOMIC BOMB

ALTHOUGH EINSTEIN and others realized early on the implications of $E = mc^2$ for advanced weaponry, there were a number of rather large hurdles that had to be overcome before a practical fission bomb could be built. To begin with, radioactive decay happens irregularly and spontaneously, whereas a bomb could hardly be effective if no one knew when it would go off.

During the 1930s, it was discovered that fission could be induced in otherwise stable radioactive nuclei if those nuclei were bombarded with neutrons. Bombarding uranium-235, for example, produces uranium-236, which is much less stable and therefore decays much more quickly. As U-236 decays, it releases energy and also neutrons. If enough U-235 atoms are located nearby, these neutrons will create more U-236, leading to more decay and even more neutrons. The result is a chain reaction.

Chain reactions will occur spontaneously if the quantity of nuclear fuel present exceeds an amount known as the critical mass. Critical mass varies depending on the nuclear fuel being used. For U-235, the critical mass is about fifty kilograms. Naturally occurring uranium ore, composed mostly of relatively stable U-238, contains only minimal amounts of U-235 (typically less than 1 percent). Therefore, a physicist interested in creating a chain reaction must first "enrich" (that is, refine) the ore until a critical mass of U-235 is produced.

In 1942, émigré physicist Enrico Fermi initiated the first artificial chain reaction in a makeshift reactor built inside a squash court beneath the University of Chicago football stadium. Fermi's experiment made it clear that such reactions, if controlled by the insertion of neutron-absorbing carbon rods, could produce usable nuclear energy. If the reactions weren't controlled, however, they could lead to massive explosions.

The final step in the creation of the atomic bomb was the development of a trigger mechanism. One method, the gun-type assembly, divided the bomb's fissile material into two isolated halves. Individually, neither possessed enough U-235 to initiate a chain reaction. When a small chemical explosion inside the bomb forced the two halves together, however, their combined mass was more than sufficient for a chain reaction to begin, quickly producing a nuclear explosion. A second method, used primarily with plutonium and known as the implosion assembly, arranged the fissile material in a hollow (or not very dense) sphere. A chemical explosion compacted the sphere, increasing its density and triggering the chain reaction.

A scale model of the atomic bomb dropped on Nagasaki.

Controlled chain reactions *produce usable nuclear energy. Uncontrolled chain reactions are the basis of atomic bombs.*

XIII. SUNNIS AND SHI'ITES IN THE EARLY MODERN ERA

ALTHOUGH IRAN HAD BEEN home to various Shi'ite communities over the years, the Nizari Isma'ilis among them, it wasn't until the sixteenth century that the Safavids converted the country as a whole to Imami Shi'ism. Safi al-Din al-Ardabili, who lived near Tabriz in northwestern Iran, founded the Safavid dynasty early in the fourteenth century, when he combined Imami Shi'ism with elements of Sufism (Islamic mysticism) and initiated a Twelver crusade against rival Iranian regimes.

A Safavid courtier.

Safi al-Din claimed descent from the seventh imam of the Twelver line, Musa al-Kazim, and his religiosity was infectious. Many followers joined his cause, and he rapidly built a power base for himself among the Qizilbash, a confederacy of Turkic nomads. Under Safi al-Din's leadership, the Qizilbash spread their hegemony eastward, eventually controlling all of Iran.

During the sixteenth and seventeenth centuries, the Safavid shahs built a brilliant and flourishing empire in Iran with Twelver Shi'ism at its core. Imami scholars from all over the Muslim world were brought to the court of the Safavids and given patronage, as were many Twelver institutions of higher learning. As one might expect, the well-supported Iranian *ulama*, or community of scholars, quickly rose to positions of leadership within the Twelver movement, and their ideas were exported back to Shi'ite communities throughout the Middle East.

Inevitably, a bitter rivalry arose between the Shi'ite Safavids and the militantly Sunni Ottoman Turks, who had succeeded the Seljuks in Egypt, Syria, Palestine, and elsewhere. The resulting war, fought over the heart of the Middle East, was as ideological as it was political, and there were severe domestic repercussions. While the Safavids spread Twelver Shi'ism throughout Iran by coercion as well as conversion, the Ottomans nearly eradicated Shi'ism from the Anatolian heartland.

Furthermore, the Ottomans weren't the only rivals with which the Safavids had to contend. The other great Islamic power of the early modern era, the Mughal dynasty in South Asia (modern-day India and Pakistan), was also Sunni and traced its lineage back to the Mongol ruling house (whose anti-Sunni bent had gradually dissipated). Over time, the Ottomans, Safavids, and Mughals divided the Islamic world into Sunni and Shi'ite spheres of influence, but these boundaries were largely permeable, and the influence of the Iranian Twelver *ulama* continued to be felt in Shi'ite communities that were otherwise under Ottoman or Mughal domination.

During the sixteenth century, *the Middle East was divided between militantly Sunni Ottoman Turks and Safavids, under whose rule Iran was converted to Shi'ism.*

XIII. THE LEGEND OF THE GRAND INQUISITOR

Dostoevsky in an 1872 portrait by Vasily Perov.

NEAR THE MIDPOINT OF *The Brothers Karamazov*, two of the brothers—Ivan, the thinker, and Alyosha, the novice monk—meet in a tavern, where they engage in a discussion of such intensity and length that this section of the novel is often published separately as *The Legend of the Grand Inquisitor*. Its core is a tale, composed by Ivan, in which Christ returns to earth during the time of the Spanish Inquisition. After raising a girl from the dead, Christ is arrested and sentenced by the Inquisition to burn at the stake. However, before the punishment is exacted, Christ receives a visit from the Grand Inquisitor, who is angry that Christ has returned to "interfere with us." While the Grand Inquisitor defends the Inquisition, Christ significantly remains silent.

According to the Grand Inquisitor, Christ misunderstands humanity. The spiritual freedom that Christ offers isn't a gift but an unbearable burden, of which humanity longs to rid itself. Although Christ's way may appeal to the few who are spiritually strong, the masses yearn not for freedom but for material happiness. They crave enslavement by "bread and miracles." Christ, meanwhile, comes to them "with empty hands."

In an important way, Ivan behaves like the Grand Inquisitor, using rationality to "prove" an argument. Introducing his tale, Ivan explains that, while he doesn't necessarily deny the existence of God, he rejects on moral grounds the universe that God has created. As support for this conclusion, he lists a series of atrocities committed against children. Dismissing the notion that some "eternal harmony" awaits these innocent victims, Ivan insists that nothing can redeem the unjust suffering of a child. Alyosha, however, resists Ivan's rationalism and holds to his faith, despite all the logical evidence marshaled against it. Like Christ in Ivan's story, Alyosha remains largely silent until the close of the novel, when he stands beside the grave of an innocent child and professes his faith that all suffering will be washed away in eternity.

Compared with the brilliance of Ivan's rhetoric, Alyosha's position is unconvincing; but it's not meant to convince, because only rational argument can do that. In fact, critics have marveled at the fearlessness shown by Dostoevsky (who clearly sympathizes with Alyosha) in creating a foil of Ivan's power. Indeed, many readers of *The Brothers Karamazov* are seduced by Ivan's logic into dismissing Alyosha's faith, but—in Dostoevsky's view at least—the faith that remains silent triumphs in the end.

As he recounts the tale *of the Grand Inquisitor, Ivan makes a persuasive argument against faith. His brother Alyosha, however, like Christ in the story, remains silent.*

XIV. THE CIVIL RIGHTS ACT OF 1964

ALTHOUGH DRAMATIC AND INSPIRING, the March on Washington had little effect on the congressmen then at the heart of the civil rights debate. The House Judiciary Committee approved the administration's civil rights bill (which ended discrimination in public accommodations such as restaurants) on October 22, 1963, but thereafter the bill languished in the Rules Committee chaired by Howard Smith, a Virginia Democrat strongly opposed to integration. Smith was still sitting on the bill a month later when President Kennedy was shot in Dallas.

When Lyndon Johnson became president, he made the stalled civil rights bill his top priority. Johnson badly wanted to remain in the White House after the 1964 election, and he knew that to do so he would have to win over the Democratic party's powerful liberal wing. Passing the martyred president's civil rights bill would, he calculated, do just that.

Johnson could never match John Kennedy's oratorical skill, nor his ability to inspire people, but as a legislator he was without peer in twentieth-century American history. He knew that his first task was to get the bill out of the Rules Committee, which he did by criticizing

King (left) and other civil rights leaders meet with Preisdent Johnson (center) in early 1964.

Howard Smith for his refusal even to hold hearings. This pressure forced Smith to schedule nine days of hearings, after which the politics of the bill became impossible for Smith to control. On January 30, HR 7152 was voted out of committee, and eleven days later it passed the House, 290–130.

The key figure in the Senate turned out to be Minority Leader Everett Dirksen, an Illinois Republican who supported civil rights but was troubled by the bill's enforcement provisions, which he considered a federal overreach. "The bill can't pass unless you get Ev Dirksen," Johnson told Majority Whip Hubert Humphrey. "You get in there to see Dirksen. You drink with Dirksen! You talk with Dirksen! You listen to Dirksen!"

A compromise on trial-by-jury language resolved Dirksen's concerns; in the meantime, however, Richard Russell of Georgia began a filibuster on March 9 that became the longest in Senate history, climaxing on June 9 with a fourteen-hour monologue by Robert Byrd of West Virginia. Byrd's nightlong performance was the South's last gasp. Less than an hour after he finished, Humphrey won the cloture vote, and on July 2 President Johnson signed the Civil Rights Act of 1964 into law.

The Civil Rights Act of 1964, *which outlawed Jim Crow segregation in the South, might have been John Kennedy's bill, but it was Lyndon Johnson's law.*

XIV. MORAL SENTIMENT

IN HUME'S DAY, moods and emotions were called sentiments, because they were felt (or sensed), and passions, because they were undergone passively rather than undertaken actively. Reason, Hume famously said, is "the slave of the passions." By this he meant two things: First, what moves us to act is always a sentiment of some kind, rather than mere reasoning. Second, what justifies our moral and aesthetic judgments are ultimately the sentiments that give rise to them.

Hume criticized moral rationalists, who argued that moral judgments are based on reason, and ethical egoists, who either dismissed morality as an illusion or maintained that people really act only out of self-interest. Hume considered the rationalist account of moral judgment not just false but barely intelligible. In his view, reason deals only with facts and inferences among relations of ideas. It therefore cannot generate value judgments of good and bad or right and wrong. Morality involves praise or blame, which spring from feeling and not from reasoning. At best, reason informs us about the means to an end; it doesn't tell us which ends we ought to pursue.

Whereas rationalism is incoherent, egoism, in Hume's view, is just false. Experience shows that people do not always act selfishly. Besides, even if there is more self-interest in our actions than we suppose, that doesn't mean that we aren't also motivated by sympathy for others. Helping you might also make me feel good, but your advantage isn't the same thing as my good feeling, even if the two go together.

Morality, according to Hume, rests on sentiments of approval and disapproval—which we feel when we observe people's actions, principally with regard to benevolence and justice. Those virtues are useful and agreeable to society, so we applaud actions expressing them. If we didn't share the same basic sentimental response to such actions, agreement about basic moral matters would dissolve. Sympathy, according to Hume, not reasoning or naked self-interest, is "the foundation of morals."

Moral judgment, *according to Hume, is based on sentiment, not reason. In morality, as in all matters, reason is "the slave of the passions."*

XIV. GENERAL RELATIVITY

IN 1916, Einstein published another paper in *Annalen der Physik* that expanded his ideas on relativity. The limitation of his Special Theory of Relativity had been that it applied only to inertial frames of reference. His new General Theory of Relativity applied to accelerating frames of reference as well.

In Newtonian physics, gravity is described as a force that exists between two masses. For example, the gravity that existed between Newton's apple and Earth is what caused the apple to fall down, accelerating as it went. In the General Theory of Relativity, however, Einstein described gravity in an entirely different way. According to General Relativity, mass causes space–time to bend, with the amount of curvature depending on the size of the mass. The curvature is gravity.

Imagine a tarpaulin stretched tightly over an empty crate. Suppose you place a marble on the tarpaulin. It makes a small indentation. Now imagine placing a bowling ball on the tarpaulin. It makes a much larger indentation. Finally, you roll a marble across the tarpaulin with the bowling ball still in place. As the marble passes near the bowling ball, its path is affected by

A model of a gravity well.

the depression caused by the bowling ball. One of two things happens, depending on the speed of the marble and its distance from the bowling ball. If the marble is moving fast enough, or if it doesn't approach the bowling ball too closely, it will bend toward the bowling ball but still continue past it. On the other hand, if the marble isn't moving very fast, or if it gets too close to the bowling ball, it will fall into the well created by the bowling ball.

Space–time behaves similarly, except that it is much stiffer than a tarpaulin. Only masses the size of planets can curve it significantly. If a smaller mass (such as an asteroid) approaches a planet, it will bend toward the planet because the planet has curved space–time. Depending on the asteroid's speed and distance from the planet, it may simply bend in its path, or it may fall into the gravity well created by the planet.

Stars curve space–time even more. In fact, planets orbit stars because they are traveling neither fast enough to escape the star's gravity well nor slow enough to fall into it. One way to think about this relationship is to understand that mass tells space–time how to curve, and space–time tells mass how to move.

Einstein's General Theory of Relativity *described gravity in an entirely new way: not as a force existing between two masses but as the curvature of space–time.*

XIV. SUNNI AND SHI'ITE DOCTRINE

ALTHOUGH ONE SHOULD NOT downplay the very real divisions that have marred Sunni–Shi'ite relations through the ages, there is, in fact, much more that unites these two sects than divides them. Because of their shared histories, their mutual devotion to the Prophet, and the common basis of their faith in the Quran, their religious doctrines have developed along remarkably similar lines.

Regarding what constitutes "true" Islam, the Sunnis and the Shi'a agree on the most fundamental points: There is but one God, and Muhammad was His prophet. The Quran is a divine work, virtually an aspect of God Himself, and it represents His final revelation to humanity (following earlier revelations in the Torah and the New Testament). Both communities also assert the importance of moral accountability and the certainty of reward or punishment after death.

With regard to leadership and authority, important doctrinal differences do exist, but even these have become less relevant over time. The Sunni *ulama* have

Scholars in a medieval Arabic library.

historically claimed leadership based on their surpassing knowledge of the Quran and the *sunna*. The Shi'a, in contrast, have looked to various imams as living sources of religious guidance, at least in the distant past. During the last thousand years, however, the role played by Shi'ite imams has become less direct. In the most extreme case, that of the Twelver Shi'a, the disappearance of their twelfth imam, Muhammad al-Mahdi, made him physically inaccessible. (Twelvers believe that he continues to exist in a state of occultation, hidden from view.) As a result, the Imami *ulama* have since acted as mediators of his will to the living faithful. Nevertheless, the distinction remains that Sunni *ulama* are thought to articulate the divine will themselves by virtue of their scholarly consensus, while Shi'ite *ulama* merely mediate the divine will of their imam.

Another notable point of difference relates to the question of intercession. Citing specific portions of the Quran, strict Sunni interpreters deny the possibility of any power intervening on a sinner's behalf on Judgment Day. Among the Shi'a, however, intercession is recognized, and the doctrine is celebrated in popular culture. Almost always, it is Husayn who is portrayed as the great intercessor, guaranteeing salvation to the faithful and thus vindicating their suffering on his behalf.

Although the Sunnis and the Shi'a are *separate communities, their long contact and common devotion to the Prophet have led to profound similarities in their beliefs.*

XIV. WAR AND PEACE

LEO TOLSTOY (1828–1910) was born into one of Russia's most prestigious noble families. As a young military officer, he saw action in the Crimean War of 1853–56 and took part in the harrowing fight for Sevastopol—an experience that produced some of his first short stories. Later in his career, Tolstoy addressed war on a much grander scale in his monumental novel *War and Peace*, which was published (and written) serially between 1865 and 1869.

Tolstoy as an army officer in 1854.

Set against the backdrop of the 1812 Napoleonic invasion of Russia, *War and Peace* is the story of two aristocratic families. The exuberant, impulsive Rostovs have a lively daughter, Natasha, and two sons, Nikolay and Petya, who join the war against Napoleon. (Petya, the younger son, is killed in the fighting.) The Bolkonsky family, on the other hand, is decidedly more sullen. The aged, domineering father, Prince Bolkonsky, has two children: the devoutly religious Maria and the cynical but remarkably brave Andrey. (Disillusioned by society, Andrey, a soldier, seeks meaning on the battlefield.) Another important character is the socially clumsy Pierre Bezukhov, a quiet and observant but sometimes reckless man who wanders through the "war" and the "peace" in a confused search for truth.

There is irony to be found in the historical aspects of *War and Peace*, because Tolstoy often expressed skepticism about works of history. He believed that historians misguidedly sought to weave unconnected, highly complicated events into pleasingly uniform narratives. Out of necessity, they focused their accounts on recognizable leaders, rather than the anonymous masses who are the true driving force of history.

Napoleon, who famously considered himself a "great man" of history, is depicted by Tolstoy in the early chapters of *War and Peace* as the master of armies and nations. Yet the French emperor is humbled, in fiction as in life, by the Russian general Kutuzov—who, like Tolstoy, appreciates the unpredictable nature of battle and the impotence of individual men to direct the course of history.

Tolstoy's skepticism about history also manifests itself in *War and Peace* as a more general skepticism about storytelling. Although routinely hailed as one of the greatest novels ever written, the book is actually a highly unconventional antinovel—fragmented, impressionistic, and lacking a coherent storyline. Later, as Tolstoy's doubts became more extreme, his work came to be dominated by the idea that all stories are, by definition, lies.

The manner in which Tolstoy wrote War and Peace *reflected his relentless skepticism toward history in particular and coherent narrative in general.*

XV. FREEDOM SUMMER

MARTIN LUTHER KING, JR.'S, shrewd manipulation of his personal fame greatly extended the reach of his minimal staff. But the SCLC never did put many boots on the ground. In general, the foot soldiers of the movement worked for SNCC, especially in Mississippi, where Robert Moses ran the show. A young mathematics teacher from New York City, Moses typically kept himself in the background while encouraging others to become empowered.

As King traveled the country, holding press conferences and leading marches, Moses remained in Mississippi, methodically building his organization county by county. The repression was brutal, so the work went poorly. After King's triumph in Birmingham, Moses became particularly aware that, for a breakthrough to take place in Mississippi, he needed to attract some national attention. He was searching for an idea when Allard Lowenstein, a thirty-four-year-old New York lawyer, gave him a call in July 1963, offering to recruit northern white student volunteers. A successful pilot project in the fall persuaded Moses and Lowenstein to propose a broader Mississippi Summer Project for 1964.

Some SNCC staffers opposed the move, arguing that importing inexperienced white students would undermine SNCC's primary mission to empower local blacks. On the other hand, the many benefits of the idea included free labor, financial support, and national attention. In the end, the decision was made to go ahead with Freedom Summer.

The primary goal was to challenge the legitimacy of the all-white Mississippi Democratic party by expanding black voter registration; organizing a new, integrated Mississippi Freedom Democratic party (MFDP); and sending an MFDP delegation to the Democratic national convention in Atlantic City to supplant the white "regulars." When the MFDP delegates arrived in Atlantic City, however, they found the northern party establishment lined up against them. Not wanting the MFDP challenge to spoil his coronation, President Johnson used his considerable influence to impose a "compromise": Each Mississippi regular would have to sign a loyalty oath before being seated, while the MFDP would receive two at-large seats.

Deeply disappointed, the MFDP members refused to take these leavings from the table. "Never again," wrote one SNCC organizer, "were we lulled into believing that our task was exposing injustices so that the 'good' people of America could eliminate them. We left Atlantic City with the knowledge that the movement had turned into something else. After Atlantic City, our struggle was not for civil rights, but for liberation."

The student movement *recruited volunteers to spend the summer of 1964 in Mississippi, organizing a challenge to the exclusively white state Democratic party.*

XV. THE ENLIGHTENMENT

THE ENLIGHTENMENT was the historical period, roughly coinciding with the eighteenth century, during which empiricism spread throughout European intellectual culture. This took place thanks largely to the efforts of a group of French writers known as *philosophes*, who championed a spirit of free inquiry and extended Locke's philosophy to a wide range of moral, historical, social, and political issues. Prominent among the *philosophes* were Voltaire (1694–1778), Denis Diderot (1713–84), the marquis de Condorcet (1743–94), and Jean d'Alembert (1717–83).

The title page from the first edition of Voltaire's *Candide*.

The Enlightenment is most closely associated with France, but there was also a Scottish Enlightenment, which featured such figures as Hume, Francis Hutcheson (1694–1746), Adam Smith (1723–90), and Thomas Reid (1710–96). Sometimes the terms *Enlightenment* and *Age of Reason* are used interchangeably, but the latter term more properly refers to both the seventeenth and eighteenth centuries and thus includes the European rationalists (Descartes, Spinoza, and Leibniz) along with the British empiricists and the French *philosophes*.

Voltaire's novella *Candide* (1759) is in many ways a paradigmatic Enlightenment text. One of the central characters, the pedantic rationalist Dr. Pangloss (whose name literally means "always talking"), is a parody of Leibniz, who confidently proclaimed that this is "the best of all possible worlds," all appearances of widespread disaster and unhappiness notwithstanding. Through Pangloss, Voltaire caricatures Leibniz's attempt to reconcile the idea of an omnipotent, omniscient, benevolent God with the existence of evil in the world. What appear to readers to be genuine instances of evil—disease, famine, natural disasters, murder—are, to Pangloss, mere details in a picture that would be less beautiful without them. God, he says, sees the "big picture," and we can see it, too, provided we step back far enough from the spectacle of human misery. The first Europeans to explore the New World returned with syphilis, for instance, but they also brought back chocolate, so all's well.

The absurd, gratuitous suffering endured by the characters in *Candide* can be read as a stark empirical challenge to Leibniz's blindly optimistic doctrine. For a rationalist such as Pangloss, all observable evidence of human misery vanishes before reason, which guarantees both divine justice and cosmic order. For an empiricist such as Voltaire, by contrast, the gruesome evidence of the misery all around speaks for itself and can't simply be dismissed or explained away.

During the Enlightenment, *the principles of empiricism were further applied and defended by Voltaire and the other French* philosophes.

XV. GRAVITATIONAL LENSING

LIKE ALL BOLD THEORIES, General Relativity predicted the existence of many unfamiliar phenomena. Some were verified experimentally during Einstein's lifetime, others have been verified since, and some are still beyond our ability to observe. Among the most interesting is the effect called gravitational lensing. The basic premise is simple: Light travels in space–time. Therefore, it should follow the curvature of space–time. If it passes close to a massive object, it should bend toward that object.

The effect was first observed during a 1919 solar eclipse, when scientists carefully recorded the positions of stars near to the Sun. These positions were then compared with data recorded during a time of year when Earth was on the other side of the Sun, giving astronomers an unobstructed view of these stars. The comparison revealed small discrepancies in the star's positions, exactly as General Relativity had predicted. The light emanating from them had, in fact, been bent by the Sun, causing them to appear slightly shifted. Newspapers worldwide published the news on their front pages, championing it as proof that the General Theory of Relativity was correct.

Since 1919, work on gravitational lensing has become much more ambitious. As far as astronomical objects go, our Sun's mass isn't very great. For this reason, its lensing effect is rather subtle. A black hole or a galaxy with billions of stars should produce a much more noticeable effect. A famous example confirming this view involved the 1979 discovery of "twin" quasars. (A quasar is a type of young, active galaxy that emits an enormous amount of light.) These quasars intrigued astronomers because they were very close together and apparently identical. As it turned out, they were actually two images of the same quasar. The effect was caused by an intervening galaxy, which was bending the quasar's light. Some of this light was traveling around one side of the galaxy to reach Earth, and some light was traveling around the other side, hence the double image.

This cluster of galaxies is so massive that its gravitational field bends light passing through it in the same way that an optical lens does.

Astronomers are currently using the principle of gravitational lensing to create a new generation of telescope. Just as optical lenses focus light by bending its path, so should gravitational "lenses" be able to focus (and thus enhance) the light coming from distant objects. Already, this method has proved useful in locating planets in other solar systems as well as distant galaxies.

One of the more interesting *effects predicted by General Relativity is gravitational lensing, or the bending of light along the curvature of space–time.*

XV. **SUNNI AND SHI'ITE PRACTICE**

AS WITH DOCTRINE, the basic religious practices of the Sunnis and the Shi'a are fundamentally the same. Both communities recognize the Five Pillars of Islam: profession of faith in God and the Prophet, prayer five times daily, performance of the Hajj (pilgrimage to Mecca), fasting during the holy month of Ramadan, and payment of *zakat* (religious alms). Both Sunnis and Shi'ites also observe a code of ritual purity that demands, among other things, ablution before prayer and strict adherence to dietary restrictions, such as the well-known prohibition regarding pork.

With regard to matters of law, the two groups also have much in common. Both are governed by *shari'a*, a form of law based on the Quran and other sources. There does exist some variation in *shari'a*, however. Within the Sunni tradition, for example, debate among the four major *madhhabs* (schools of law) has produced some divergences, but all of these are considered acceptable and equally legitimate.

One telling difference between Sunni and Shi'ite traditions involves the Shi'ite practice of *mut'a*, according to which marriages are contracted, consummated, and dissolved within a specified (usually short) period of time. Even though the Quran seems to approve of this practice, Sunnis have criticized it as legalized prostitution.

The Sunnis and the Shi'a also practice different sorts of pilgrimage. For Shi'ites, the practice of *ziyara* (pilgrimage to Alid shrines) is central to their faith. The most sacred of these sites—including Najaf, the burial place of Ali; Karbala, where Husayn was martyred; and Mashhad, where the eighth Twelver imam is buried—may even hold greater importance for some Shi'a than Medina or Mecca. Sunni ideologues have often excoriated the Shi'a for this "idolatrous" and "deviant" practice—although, in fact, some Sunnis visit the tombs of Sufi saints whom they revere and believe may intercede on their behalf come Judgment Day.

Pilgrims on their way to Mecca in a thirteenth-century illustration.

With regard to holidays, the Sunnis and Shi'ite religious calendars are largely the same, but there is one important Shi'ite holiday for which no Sunni equivalent exists. Ashura commemorates the martyrdom of Husayn, and for the Shi'a this is a day of extreme sorrow and penitence, marked by processions and public rites of mourning. Ashura thus evokes the historical victimization of the Shi'a and demonstrates the extreme degree to which martyrdom and persecution form the distinctive core of Shi'ite identity.

Sunni and Shi'ite practices *tend to overlap, but the differences that do exist help to clarify the individual character of each sect.*

XV. ANNA KARENINA

TOLSTOY'S *ANNA KARENINA*, published serially between 1873 and 1877, begins with a deceit, an act of adultery, committed by the titular heroine. From the start, the author makes it clear that God will see through and punish such falsehood. "Vengeance is mine: I will repay, sayeth the Lord," reads the book's epigraph; and, indeed, Anna is punished harshly for her sins. But as the book unfolds, Tolstoy's ire becomes increasingly focused on the hypocritical aristocratic society in which Anna lives.

Anna is married to Aleksey Karenin, a perfectly respectable man by all social standards but not respectable by the moral standards that Tolstoy imposes. Although Karenin provides materially for the support of his wife and child, he is cold and keeps his emotional distance from Anna, which makes her feel unhappy with her life. Seeking warmth and affection, she begins an affair with Count Vronsky. Later, she confesses the relationship to her husband and is appalled to learn that he cares less about her infidelity than he does about the harm it may do to his reputation if revealed. Realizing that Karenin is concerned only with appearances, Anna denounces her husband's hypocrisy and concludes that "his food is falsehood."

Her newfound hatred of lies elevates Anna morally above the hypocrites surrounding her, but this does her little good once the affair with Vronsky

An 1884 portrait of Tolstoy at his desk by Nikolay Ge.

becomes public knowledge. Although the count's social life is unaffected, Anna is banished from her home and child and shunned by society. Frustrated and angered by this double standard, she succumbs to despair and, in the end, throws herself under a train.

Anna's fate is prefigured by a string of encounters, both innocent and ominous, with trains, which often suggest death and fate in Russian literature. For example, Anna first meets Vronsky at a train station, only moments after learning that a railway worker has just died gruesomely beneath a train. From that moment on, Anna herself seems to be speeding down a predetermined track—which ends, ineluctably, in her death, fulfilling the prophecy voiced in the epigraph. Ultimately, Anna is a sacrificial lamb, punished by fate for the guilt of an entire society.

Anna Karenina is a scathing critique of Russia's aristocratic social order—against which Anna revolts, but to which she eventually falls victim, both deservedly and undeservedly.

XVI. THE SELMA-TO-MONTGOMERY MARCH

AFTER THE CIVIL RIGHTS ACT of 1964 was passed, Martin Luther King, Jr., quickly turned his attention to voting rights. President Johnson wanted to wait before introducing a bill, complaining to King that the country was "tired" of civil rights. But the SCLC leader wouldn't wait, deciding to force the issue in Selma, Alabama, where only 1 percent of eligible blacks were registered.

King chose Selma for the same reason he chose Birmingham: Like Bull Connor, Dallas County sheriff Jim Clark was redneck, overbearing, and quick to lose his temper—the sort of man who could be counted on to resort to violence. Selma's mayor favored a Laurie Pritchett–style approach to the SCLC protest marches, which began on January 18, but the sheriff couldn't control himself. After just one day, he began manhandling the demonstrators, assaulting a few of them and arresting hundreds.

King leading the Selma march.

Racial tension in Selma gradually escalated until February 18, when state and local police attacked a group of marchers in nearby Marion. While panicked demonstrators fled, Jimmie Lee Jackson stopped to help his beaten, bleeding grandfather. Several state troopers followed them into a local café, where one trooper attacked Jackson's mother. As the twenty-six-year-old army veteran leaped to her defense, another trooper shot him in the stomach.

At Jackson's funeral, an emotional James Bevel proposed that the body be taken to Montgomery and placed on the steps of the state capitol to confront the governor with the evil being done in his name. Although the idea of transporting Jackson's casket was soon dismissed, the larger goal of seeking redress took hold, and on March 3 the SCLC announced a five-day march from Selma to Montgomery. When the first marchers crossed the Edmund Pettus Bridge on Sunday, March 7—now known as Bloody Sunday—they were met by a phalanx of state and county police, who used clubs and tear gas to literally beat them back.

King wanted to try again on March 9, but a federal court order held the march up until March 21. Meanwhile, on March 15, President Johnson sent a strong voting rights bill to Congress. Supported by public opinion (and the many liberal Democrats elected on LBJ's coattails in 1964), the bill became law on August 6. In November 1966, with more than half of Selma's eligible blacks now registered, Jim Clark was voted out of office.

With the passage *of the Civil Rights Act of 1964, the movement turned its attention to voting rights, which became a pressing national issue after Bloody Sunday in Selma.*

XVI. KANT'S CRITIQUE OF REASON

Immanuel Kant

FROM THE MID-SEVENTEENTH CENTURY to the late eighteenth, rationalism and empiricism together dominated Western philosophy. Then, in 1781, the German philosopher Immanuel Kant (1724–1804) published his groundbreaking *Critique of Pure Reason*, which challenged both traditions.

According to Kant, rationalism's faith in the transcendent power of reason had led some philosophers to make extravagant claims about transcendent matters such as God, free will, the immortality of the soul, and the nature of space and time. Unfortunately, every rationalist doctrine seemed to refute every competing rationalist doctrine, so that nothing could be demonstrated with certainty. Such excesses led to the empiricist backlash, which worked itself out ever more skeptically in the writings of Locke, Berkeley, and Hume.

In *Critique of Pure Reason*, Kant sought a middle way between the dogmatism of the rationalists and the skepticism of the empiricists. His work was thus a defense of reason within the bounds of experience and a critique of reason as applied beyond those bounds. According to Kant, knowledge is not *based on* experience, but is *limited by* it. Neither intellect nor experience is alone sufficient for knowledge; instead, we need both sense experience and thought to have objective knowledge of the world. "Thoughts without content are empty," Kant wrote, and "intuitions [sensations] without concepts are blind."

For example, all experience is experience of a world in space and time, but our ideas of space and time can't be gleaned from our sensations. Kant also agreed with Hume that concepts such as substance and cause can't be derived from sense experience. Nevertheless, Kant argued, we are entitled to those concepts because without them, we couldn't be aware of objects or ourselves. Moreover, without the concept of causal necessity, we wouldn't be able to see changes over time as lawlike and irreversible (as opposed to arbitrary and reversible, as Hume saw them).

According to Kant, the world we know is a world shaped by human sensibility and human understanding. Our world is not a world of *things in themselves* but of *appearances*. However, this is not to say, as Berkeley and Hume supposed, that all experience is subjective. Rather, objects exist objectively in space and time, which is held together not by mere constant conjunctions of ideas but by real causal laws. Recognizing this, Kant said, required a radical reorientation of philosophy akin to the Copernican revolution that replaced geocentrism with heliocentrism.

Rejecting both *the dogmatism of the rationalists and the skepticism of the empiricists, Kant believed that knowledge isn't based on, but is limited by, experience.*

XVI. GRAVITATIONAL COLLAPSE

STABILITY EXISTS IN THE UNIVERSE to the extent that opposing forces balance each other. For instance, a white dwarf star holds its shape because the gravitational forces that would otherwise cause it to compress are balanced by electrostatic forces that push its atoms apart. According to Newtonian physics, the greater an object's mass, the more it will tend to compact; but sufficient repulsive force will always exist to keep an object from compacting completely.

In the world of General Relativity, however, no such emergency brake exists. On the contrary, there is a definite point beyond which electrostatic forces cannot resist the deep curvature of space–time. This point is called the Chandrasekhar limit because it was calculated (using Einstein's General Relativity equations) by Indian physicist Subrahmanyan Chandrasekhar. The Chandrasekhar limit describes the maximum mass whose gravitational pull can be balanced by electrostatic forces. Above this limit, the object collapses almost into nothingness. What happens is that the object keeps collapsing in on itself until it becomes an incredibly dense single point in space. Scientists call this a singularity. More commonly, it is known as a black hole.

Objects whose mass falls below the Chandrasekhar limit can still become singularities if they are compressed beyond a point known as the Schwarzschild radius. This value, which depends on an object's mass, was first calculated by German physicist Karl Schwarzschild shortly after he read Einstein's 1916 paper on General Relativity in *Annalen der Physik*. Once an object contracts beyond the Schwarzschild radius, it becomes so dense and curves space–time so deeply that no known force can prevent the formation of a black hole. For a star such as the Sun, the Schwarzschild radius is about three kilometers.

Once a black hole forms, an event horizon is established at the Schwarzschild radius. The event horizon blocks our view of the central singularity because no light within the event horizon can escape the gravity well produced by the singularity. As a result, all we see is blackness.

Initially, many physicists scoffed at the idea that an object as massive as a star could collapse into a single point. English astrophysicist Arthur Eddington, director of the 1919 eclipse research that had confirmed gravitational lensing, dismissed the idea as absurd. Since that time, however, it has become apparent that black holes do exist. They cannot be seen directly, of course, but they can be detected indirectly through observation of the effect they have on nearby matter.

Another prediction of General Relativity *was that massive objects sometimes collapsed in on themselves to form singularities, also known as black holes.*

XVI. SHI'ISM IN CONTEMPORARY IRAN

SEVERAL CENTURIES OF DELIBERATE Shi'ification in Iran produced an Imami *ulama* with deep roots in Iranian society. Because the Safavid shahs weren't imams themselves, the Twelver clergy couldn't recognize them as fully legitimate rulers; however, the *ulama* supported the Safavids because the Safavids, in turn, protected Shi'ite interests. This accommodationism prevailed until the early twentieth century, when the *ulama*, who typically identified themselves with the interests of the masses, began championing populist and anticolonial causes in direct opposition to government policy.

The *ulama* supported the 1905 constitutional revolution that sought to limit the shah's power, but in 1925 they changed sides and backed the coup led by army officer Reza Pahlavi, who subsequently declared himself shah. The idea seems to have been that the new monarchy would act as a bulwark against the modernizing secularism that had already infected Turkey. During the 1950s, again fearing secularism, the *ulama* sided with the US Central Intelligence Agency in ousting the nationalist government of Mohammad Mossadegh and restoring the Pahlavi dynasty. Of course, the new shah, Mohammad Reza Pahlavi, turned out to be the most Westernizing influence of all, and it was his rule that was overthrown by the *ayatollahs* (the most senior members of the Iranian *ulama*) in 1979.

Although the proximate cause of the 1979 revolution was the oppressive rule of the shah, the Iranian *ulama*, led by the Ayatollah Ruhollah Khomeini, had been campaigning against the shah for many years. This was made possible by the reconstruction of Twelver Shi'ism into a revolutionary ideology, using Husayn's revolt against Umayyad tyranny as a compelling paradigm for resistance. The politicization of Shi'ite symbolism that characterized this period is most vividly exemplified by the famous dictum, "Every day is Ashura, every place is Karbala."

Khomeini's personal contribution was the doctrine of *vilayet-i faqih*, or "government of the jurist." His idea was that only direct rule by the *ulama* could safeguard true Islam. For this reason, he can hardly be seen as a traditionalist, because the changes he brought about in Shi'ism were radical indeed, with no precedents in Islamic history. More accurately, he should be viewed as a fundamentalist. Itself an invention of the modern period, fundamentalism draws its strength from the idealized notion of a pristine faith that has become corrupted and must be restored to its "original" state.

The Iranian Revolution of 1979 *was made possible by the new Twelver doctrine of* vilayet-i faqih, *or government by the clerics.*

XVI. TOLSTOY AND THE END OF LIFE

AS HIS SEARCH for moral truth intensified, Tolstoy moved away from literature—which, like all stories, was full of lies—and instead took up moral activism. He wrote pamphlets advocating self-denial, pacifism, and vegetarianism, as well as readers for the peasant children attending a school he had established on his estate. Tolstoy even composed a version of the New Testament, purging it of miracles and retaining only the pure moral instruction. By the time of his death, he had developed a worldwide following, not only for his novels but also for his moral teachings.

Tolstoy with his wife in 1910.

As an aristocrat, Tolstoy enjoyed a great many privileges, but he often yearned for a simpler, more genuine existence. What he really wanted to be, especially in his later years, was a peasant, and so he eventually adopted the ways of a peasant, dressing simply and working in the fields. But strive as he might to live like one, the count was no peasant and could never authentically be one. This paradox ate away at Tolstoy and ultimately caused him to despair that he would never find truth in his lifetime. Instead, he came to hope for it in death.

Some of the most powerful moments in Tolstoy's writings concern the end of life. Memorable instances of characters confronting the beyond include a soldier having a final flash of consciousness before being shot down in one of the early Sevastopol stories, Anna Karenina's suicide, and the death of Andrey Bolkonsky in *War and Peace*. In one of his last works, *The Death of Ivan Ilych* (1886), Tolstoy revisits this theme, describing the mundane demise of an all-too-ordinary man, whose life has passed him by almost unnoticed. The process of dying, however, brings him into collision with the meaning of life, stripping away the trifles and practicalities that had busied him previously. Sadly for Ivan Ilych, he must endure his passing alone—because, although relatives and doctors attend him, these people are largely indifferent to his plight.

In November 1910, Tolstoy set out secretly from his estate, intending never to return (in large part because of his tumultuous relationship with his wife). He didn't get very far, collapsing and dying at a nondescript local train station. He was subsequently buried on his estate in a simple, unmarked grave.

Tolstoy ultimately concluded *that authenticity was impossible in life and that only in death could transcendent meaning be found.*

XVII. BLACK POWER

THE SELMA-TO-MONTGOMERY MARCH, like the civil rights movement itself, is generally remembered for its nonviolence. But the specter of violence was never too far away. As marchers passed through deeply racist Lowndes County, for example, they acquired a federal escort so that Lyndon Johnson could be sure none were shot.

Accompanying the column were SNCC organizers Stokely Carmichael and Bob Mants, who wrote down the names and addresses of locals brave enough to cheer the marchers on. A few weeks later, they returned to the county with more SNCC organizers to begin the work of registering black voters.

Stokely Carmichael

Although a SNCCer since 1961, Carmichael generally spoke for the newer, younger, more militant staffers, who respected John Lewis's courage but considered his willingness to be beaten foolish or, even worse, an anachronism. Recent killings of civil rights workers in Mississippi and Alabama had cast doubt upon the efficacy of nonviolence, and when Jonathan Daniels, a white seminary student volunteering with Carmichael, was murdered in August 1965, the Lowndes County team made two decisions: They would no longer accept white volunteers, and they would henceforth arm themselves.

By May 1966, when SNCC's national staff met for the annual leadership election, the questioning of nonviolence had spread to the point that it imperiled John Lewis's reelection as national chair. Carmichael was persuaded to run against him, and after hours of debate lasting long into the night, Carmichael won.

A month later, the new SNCC chair was arrested during a protest march in Greenwood, Mississippi. Later that night, he appeared at a rally, telling the crowd, "This is the twenty-seventh time I have been arrested, and I ain't going to jail no more!" Carmichael had to wait for the cheers and clapping to subside before continuing, "The only way we're gonna stop them white men from whupping us is to take over. We been saying freedom for six years, and we ain't got nothing. What we gonna start saying now is black power!" At this point, advance man Willie Ricks shouted out, "What do you want?" "Black power!" the crowd yelled back.

The introduction of the phrase *black power* took Carmichael's militant style to an entirely new level. In his mind, *black power* signified little more than the acquisition of political power by black people. But hostile press reports relentlessly equated the phrase with black nationalism, racism, and violence, all of which frightened whites.

Carmichael's rise to SNCC leadership *and his subsequent introduction of the phrase* black power *signified a new black assertiveness that badly frightened many whites.*

XVII. LOGICAL POSITIVISM

KANT'S PHILOSOPHY posed a powerful challenge to classical empiricism. More than a century later, in the 1920s, a new school of empiricism emerged, informed by radical developments in modern logic and inspired by the early work of Ludwig Wittgenstein (1889–1951). The logical positivists (or logical empiricists) of the Vienna Circle held that Locke, Berkeley, and Hume were right that knowledge rests on experience but wrong to suppose that it springs directly from sensation through mere association, selection, abstraction, and reflection. Instead, there are independent logical constraints on the organization of knowledge that have no basis in sense experience.

The central tenet of logical positivism is a theory of meaning known as verificationism. Like Kant, the positivists wanted to banish all speculative claims that go beyond the limits of experience. For a proposition to be meaningful, they argued, it must be either empirically verifiable or true by definition (true, as Hume would have said, by virtue of mere relations of ideas). Propositions that meet neither of these conditions can be neither true nor false and therefore have no meaning.

Yet there are several problems with verificationism. One fairly obvious problem is that verificationism itself is neither empirically verifiable nor true by definition—hence, by its standard, meaningless. Another problem with verificationism has to do with the very idea of verification itself. Recall Hume's problem of induction: How does past experience justify beliefs about the future? More specifically, how can empirical evidence ever confirm a theory? Karl Popper (1902–94) attempted to solve this problem by arguing that science doesn't proceed inductively by the accumulation of evidence but rather by bold conjecture. Empirical evidence never confirms a theory as true, according to Popper; instead, it disconfirms and eliminates theories as false. The best scientific theories, therefore, are those that haven't yet been disconfirmed.

Thomas Kuhn (1922–96) and others took Popper's reasoning even farther, arguing that empirical evidence figures into scientific inquiry only after it has been thoroughly sifted, selected, and interpreted. For this reason, they believed that there is no such thing as "raw" data, either in science or in ordinary life.

The logical positivists, *who revived empiricism, believed that for a proposition to be meaningful, it has to be either empirically verifiable or true by definition.*

XVII. GRAVITY WAVES

ANOTHER INTERESTING PHENOMENON predicted by General Relativity is gravitational radiation. Think of the waves that ripple outward in a pool when it's disturbed, as by a stone falling into it. According to General Relativity, an analogous disturbance in space–time should produce similar ripples, called gravity waves, traveling outward from the disturbance at the speed of light. (Newtonian physics doesn't allow for gravity waves because space, in the Newtonian sense, has no physical structure and thus can't serve as a medium for the transmission of waves.)

As with black holes, the idea of gravity waves was met with a great deal of initial skepticism. The ever-doubtful Arthur Eddington reportedly joked that "gravitational waves propagate at the speed of thought." One reason for this skepticism was that gravity waves were impossible for scientific instruments of the early twentieth century to detect. Because space–time is so stiff, the amplitude (height) of any gravity wave passing through it would be extremely small.

Scientists estimate the amplitude of gravity waves to be on the order of 10^{-21} of the length of the objects through which they pass. In other words, if you built a device to record gravity waves that was one meter long, the ripples that would register on that device would be about one-billionth of an atom high. Even now, the best measuring devices are unable to detect vibrations that faint, although a lot of work has recently gone into making them more sensitive.

One experimental method for detecting gravity waves involves a resonant bar. When disturbed by a gravity wave, the bar resonates, or "rings," in response. The problem with resonant bars is that seismic activity and thermal motion also cause them to ring, masking the gravity waves they were designed to detect. Keeping the bars at very cold temperatures reduces the thermal motion of the particles inside them, but eliminating seismic interference will probably await a space-based installation.

Another strategy for detecting gravity waves makes use of interferometers to split beams of light in two. A set of mirrors then recombines the beams, at which point the paths they have taken are compared. A certain kind of difference would indicate the presence of gravity waves. Like resonant bars, however, interferometers are not yet sensitive enough to detect the gravity waves that should be all around us. They're also susceptible to seismic interference, which is why a space-based interferometer is currently under development.

General Relativity predicts *the existence of gravity waves, which should ripple space–time the way a tossed stone ripples water.*

XVII. THE EMERGENCE OF HEZBOLLAH

THE INDEPENDENT STATE OF LEBANON was created by the French after World War I to safeguard the interests of the large Christian community living in the Levant (the region of the Middle East bordering the Mediterranean). The constitutional system established there after World War II enshrined Christian control of the government, but during the 1960s, increasing resentment on all sides led to the growth of sectarian militias, which protected and promoted the interests of various groups. Finally, in 1975, open warfare broke out—not merely between Christians and Muslims, but also among the many subgroups within each community.

Into this political maelstrom came the Palestine Liberation Organization (PLO). As early as 1969, the PLO was permitted to establish bases in southern Lebanon, from which it launched regular attacks against Israel. Although welcomed by Lebanese Sunnis, the PLO had an extremely negative impact on the many Twelver Shi'a living in southern Lebanon, who suffered from Israeli retaliation, especially the 1978 and 1982 Israeli invasions meant to curb PLO activity.

Meanwhile, the politics of Lebanon's large Twelver community had become increasingly intertwined with those of Iran. During the 1970s—that is, before the shah's overthrow—many radical members of the Iranian *ulama* sought refuge in Lebanon, which was provided mostly by the Lebanese Shi'ite party Amal. After the 1979 Iranian revolution, the strong bond between Amal and these Iranians paved the way for a reciprocal influence, as members of the Iranian Revolutionary Guard began exporting Khomeini's ideology to the Shi'a in Lebanon. Some members of Amal, however, refused to accept Khomeini's fundamentalism, and there was a schism in the party, leading to the emergence of Hezbollah during the early 1980s.

The flag of Hezbollah.

Particularly influential in the development of Hezbollah was the cult of martyrdom promoted by Khomeini using the model of Husayn. This led directly to Hezbollah's most significant contribution to Middle Eastern politics: the suicide bomber. While car bombings had proliferated during the first stage of the Lebanese civil war, Hezbollah achieved much greater tactical success when it began utilizing believers who were willing to die in order to maximize the destructive impact of their attacks. Although Hezbollah has long denied responsibility for the twin suicide bombings of October 23, 1983, which destroyed the French and American military barracks in Beirut, they were almost certainly executed by Hezbollah agents with Iranian support.

Influenced by their Iranian allies, Twelver Shi'ites in Lebanon have embraced a more active role in Lebanese politics through the formation of Hezbollah.

XVII. THE CHERRY ORCHARD

Anton Chekhov about 1900.

ALTHOUGH ANTON CHEKHOV (1860–1904) was an unsurpassed master of the Russian short story, he is best known in the West for his plays, four of which have become staples of the international theater: *Uncle Vanya*; *The Seagull*; *Three Sisters*; and, finally, *The Cherry Orchard*.

Staged for the first time in January 1904, *The Cherry Orchard* depicts social change in imperial Russia on the eve of revolution. Perhaps expressing his own ambivalence toward the disintegration of the old social order, Chekhov described the play as a comedy, even though its themes—the passage of time and the decay of a family—are essentially tragic. What's unmistakable is his sharp critique of Russia's erstwhile ruling class, tempered only by his dislike for the uncouth bourgeoisie replacing it.

The cherry orchard of the title is located on the ancestral estate of the aristocratic widow Ranevskaya, who associates the blossoms that appear each spring with her youth, home, and family. They remind her especially of her late son, who drowned tragically on the estate five years earlier. As the play begins, Ranevskaya returns to the estate after several years abroad in time to see the cherry trees bloom again. She learns, however, that she is deeply in debt and risks losing the estate. Incapable of taking any practical action, which she considers beneath her dignity as an aristocrat, she prefers to daydream and escape into the haze of memory. Having lived with privilege all her life, she simply can't conceive of life without it and so denies even the possibility.

Ranevskaya's rival of sorts is Lopakhin, once her serf and now a member of the rising merchant class. Practical to the point of crudity, he offers to help Ranevskaya by arranging for the sale of the cherry orchard in order to pay down her debt. (His plan is to raze the orchard and turn it into plots for dachas, the small country homes then becoming popular among the emerging middle class.) Ranevskaya refuses even to discuss the matter and ultimately loses the estate, which Lopakhin buys at auction. In the final act, Ranevskaya leaves her home forever. Only Firs, the caretaker, remains to live out his final days in the mansion. As the play ends, Firs hears the sound of axes cutting down the cherry orchard.

In *The Cherry Orchard*, *Chekhov depicts a family of ruined aristocrats forced to sell their estate to a new class of merchants, which have arisen to take their place.*

XVIII. THE DISINTEGRATION OF THE MOVEMENT

THE POLITICAL STRATEGY employed by Martin Luther King, Jr., from 1955 until his death in 1968 focused on white public opinion. If whites could be persuaded to pay more attention to the oppression of blacks, King believed, then the resulting public disgust would compel the federal government to pass new laws mandating racial justice. The two great accomplishments of this strategy were the Civil Rights Act of 1964 and the Voting Rights Act of 1965.

Laws can be ignored, however, and the nation's attention, though capable of producing breakthroughs, can't be held indefinitely. As King himself realized near the end of his life, lasting change requires constant grassroots pressure. The field secretaries of SNCC had been pursuing this difficult, largely thankless work for years. Unfortunately, by the time King finally came to appreciate its worth, the student movement was already falling apart. SNCC had become a pressure cooker, asking staff members to work harder (and with fewer resources) than was bearable. Resentment grew, and radicalism took hold.

Most white Americans could support sit-ins, freedom rides, and marches on Washington because these were nonviolent dramatizations of black oppression. But the riots that took place in Watts, Newark, and Detroit between August 1965 and July 1967 were neither dramatizations nor nonviolent. These revolts, along with the appearance of armed groups such as the Black Panthers, deeply frightened white America, and fear rarely inspires racial harmony.

King and several of his aides on the balcony of his Memphis hotel the day before he died.

King's assassination in Memphis ultimately crippled the civil rights movement, or at least that part of it still committed to nonviolence. The work continued after 1968, but on an ad hoc basis, with different groups pursuing disparate agendas. Some leaders (notably Jesse Jackson) turned to electoral politics for the fulfillment of their goals, wrapping themselves in the rhetoric of the movement but only rarely re-creating its remarkable moral energy.

At its height, the civil rights movement served as a model of political action for all Americans. It showed how wrongs can be made at least partially right and how good intentions can overcome institutionalized hate. Its history teaches what should (but not always does) matter in life and how a great cause can bestow purpose at the same time it dispenses pain, anger, and disappointment.

The assassination of Martin Luther King, Jr., *crippled the civil rights movement, which had been on a downward trajectory since the Selma-to-Montgomery march.*

XVIII. THE COGNITIVE REVOLUTION

AROUND THE MIDDLE of the twentieth century, the cognitive revolution in linguistics and psychology dealt empiricism another serious blow. Behavioral psychologist B. F. Skinner (1904–90) had advanced an empiricist theory of language acquisition, according to which children learn language by observing the verbal behavior of others and then drawing inferences concerning the proper use and meaning of words. Linguist Noam Chomsky (1928–), however, raised a simple but devastating objection. As Chomsky pointed out, the inductive process described by Skinner can't possibly explain the remarkable ease with which two-year-olds produce and understand such an enormous range of verbal constructions, given their extremely limited experience.

It is an astonishing mathematical fact that nearly every sentence we utter consisting of more than a few words has never been uttered in the entire history of the language. Yet from an early age, children produce such unprecedented sentences effortlessly while also distinguishing grammatical from ungrammatical constructions. Obviously, children learn the vocabulary and the grammatical idiosyncrasies of particular languages from observation and mimicry. Yet the ability to generate new sentences can't plausibly be ascribed to learning and must instead be innate, or "hardwired," in our brains. Language thus has more in common with puberty than with table manners; that is, it's a biological, rather than a cultural, inheritance. Chomsky didn't mean that children were born with particular languages (such as English, Chinese, or Swahili) already loaded into their brains. Instead, he meant that they were born with an understanding of the universal, or "generative," grammar common to all human languages. (In arguing for the innateness of universal grammar, Chomsky was self-consciously reviving the spirit, if not the letter, of seventeenth-century rationalism, which is why he titled his 1966 book on the subject *Cartesian Linguistics*.)

During the second half of the twentieth century, philosophy moved in a broadly rationalist direction, giving birth to the interdisciplinary study of cognitive science— which includes such fields as psychology, linguistics, and vision research. Meanwhile, philosophical and scientific debate continues, oscillating periodically between rationalist and empiricist tendencies. The social, behavioral, and cognitive sciences are all in relatively rationalistic phases now, but empiricism is by no means dead. Although it no longer dominates as it did in the eighteenth century, and more recently in the first half of the twentieth century, empiricism remains a deep and vital current in contemporary intellectual life.

Inspired in part by Chomsky's linguistic theory, philosophy and psychology have recently tended toward rationalism, yet empiricism remains vital and will likely reassert itself.

XVIII. THE SEARCH FOR A GRAND UNIFIED THEORY

SCIENTIFIC THEORY currently describes the world in terms of four fundamental forces: the gravitational force, the electromagnetic force, the strong nuclear force, and the weak nuclear force. The persistent goal of many scientists has been to develop a Grand Unified Theory that, in a simple and universal way, explains all of these forces. Einstein himself spent the last decades of his life working to reconcile gravity with electromagnetism. He never completed this work, and the search continues.

The strongest of the four fundamental forces is the strong nuclear force, which holds protons and neutrons together within atomic nuclei. Although incredibly powerful, it has a very limited range. Beyond the radius of an atomic nucleus, it quickly drops to zero. The second strongest force is the electromagnetic force, which operates between electrically charged particles, causing opposite charges to attract and like charges to repel. Unlike the strong and weak nuclear forces, the electromagnetic force has an extremely long range, estimated at about 10^{45} meters, which means that it can be felt over intergalactic distances.

The next strongest force is the weak nuclear force, which causes neutrons to disintegrate into protons and electrons through a radioactive process called beta decay. The weak nuclear force has an even shorter range than the strong nuclear force, exerting its influence only within a radius about one-hundredth the size of a proton. Although the gravitational force is the weakest of the four fundamental forces, it acts over the longest distance, which is why the effects of gravity are so noticeable throughout the universe.

It has been theorized that, during the earliest moments of the universe, the four fundamental forces acted as a single force. The support for this speculation is that all four forces behave differently under conditions of high energy, such as those that prevailed at the birth of the universe, than they do under the low-energy conditions of today. If the four fundamental forces were indeed once a single force, then perhaps there is hope that they can be recombined, at least mathematically. A little progress has already been made. The theory of quantum mechanics discussed earlier, for instance, successfully describes the three strongest forces.

Einstein believed strongly that a single theory could be found to unite all of the universe's four fundamental forces.

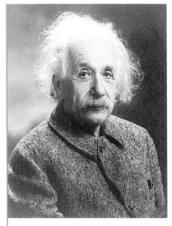

Einstein in 1947.

XVIII. SUNNIS AND SHI'ITES IN CONTEMPORARY IRAQ

THROUGHOUT THE HISTORY of the Iraqi republic established by the British in 1947, the Iraqi Shi'a were systematically persecuted, even though they made up a majority of the country's Arab population. When the socialist-leaning Ba'athists seized power in 1968 following a succession of nationalist regimes dominated by military juntas, they articulated an explicitly secular political program, which gave the Shi'a hope that their long persecution might soon be ending. Unfortunately, Saddam Hussein quickly rose to dominate the Ba'athist regime, and despite a great deal of nationalist and egalitarian rhetoric on his part, he nevertheless continued a policy of state discrimination against the Shi'a.

Overall, the sectarian divide in Saddam's Iraq was most keenly felt in the wide economic and political gap that existed between the privileged Sunni minority and the marginalized Shi'ite majority. For this reason, the legacy of his brutal rule can be most easily seen in the fierce competition for influence and resources that followed the American invasion of Iraq in 2003.

Further complicating this Sunni–Shi'ite rivalry is the ambivalent attitude most Iraqi Shi'ites have toward Iran. Although they certainly feel a sense of fraternity with their coreligionists to the east, many Iraqi Shi'ites also remain resistant to Iranian theocratic principles and surprisingly loyal to the Iraqi nationalist ideal. During the Iran–Iraq War of 1980–88, for instance, despite the Ayatollah Khomeini's call for Iraqi Shi'ites to desert Saddam, the great majority chose to side with their country instead.

The Iraqi clergy have also resisted Iranian control. Even though he was himself of Iranian extraction, Abu'l-Qasim Kho'i, an Iraqi ayatollah based in Najaf, attacked Khomeini's revolutionary doctrines as aberrant, and this criticism was later carried on by Kho'i's protégé, the Ayatollah Ali Sistani, who pressed in the aftermath of the American invasion for a constitutional solution to Iraq's political crisis.

Meanwhile, as Shi'ite militias jockeyed for power and influence over the masses, groups such as Al-Qa'ida in Iraq played on Sunni anxieties about Shi'ite reprisals—fears that were only intensified by the continuing radical rhetoric of groups such as Muqtada al-Sadr's Mahdi Army. The scion of an influential family of Shi'ite *ulama* with branches in Iran, Iraq, and Lebanon, al-Sadr's deliberate invocation of messianic symbolism echoed similar tactics used by the Iranian and Lebanese *ulama* in previous decades. It remains to be seen whether Iraq's conflicting religious ideologies and old political grievances can be transcended and a path to reconciliation found.

The struggle between Sunni and Shi'ite factions in post-Saddam Iraq have demonstrated the continuing relevance of sectarian divisions in Middle Eastern politics.

XVIII. THE EVE OF REVOLUTION

ANDREY BELY'S 1913 novel *Petersburg* departs radically from its Russian predecessors. Throughout the nineteenth century, realism had dominated Russian prose, but *Petersburg* is daringly modern. As a symbolist, Bely (1880–1934) described things not as they appeared (as realists did), but as representations of a higher realm of meaning.

Full of wordplay, Bely's intricately patterned, highly stylized prose resembles James Joyce's more than Turgenev's or Dostoevsky's. However, the novel's subject is classically Russian: the troubled relationship between a father and his son. In this case, the protagonists belong to a family named Ableukhov, whose decrepit patriarch is a prominent member of the Duma (the Russian legislature). Revolutionaries have recently assassinated his close friend; now they are plotting with Ableukhov's son, the shiftless intellectual Nikolay, to kill the senator in his own home, where Nikolay has agreed to plant a time bomb. From the moment that the bomb starts ticking, the pace of the novel accelerates to an almost unbearable intensity.

Completed just four years before the 1917 revolutions, *Petersburg* weaves familiar literary symbols of the imperial city into an apocalyptic fugue, prefiguring some sort of urban cataclysm. Pushkin's Bronze Horseman rides again, while Gogol's surrealistic Petersburg and Dostoevsky's conception of the capital as "the most artificial city in the world" combine to create, in Bely's hands, a view of the city as a Western cancer, whose boulevards and railroads stretch with hostile intent into the Russian countryside.

After Russia's defeat in the 1904–5 Russo-Japanese War, which demonstrated to many the vulnerability of the old imperial regime, past schisms flared up, especially the divisions between rich and poor and East and West. Rebellious undercurrents, long suppressed by the aristocratic social order (not to mention the imperial censors), erupted for good in 1917, when Peter's royal line finally ended and the Bolsheviks took over, abandoning Peter's city and establishing their new capital in Moscow. As Bely might have imagined the scene, Peter's stone city sinks back into the swamp whence it came, vanishing as suddenly as it had appeared.

Demonstrators being shot in St. Petersburg during the February 1917 revolution.

Bely's novel Petersburg *revisits in a relentlessly avant-garde and genuinely twentieth-century way the major themes of nineteenth-century imperial Russian literature.*

FURTHER READING

GENERAL GRANT'S CIVIL WAR

McFeely, William S., and Mary D. McFeely, eds. *Ulysses S. Grant: Memoirs and Selected Letters.* New York: Library of America, 1990.

McPherson, James M. *Battle Cry of Freedom.* New York: Oxford University Press, 2003.

Simpson, Brooks D. *Ulysses S. Grant: Triumph Over Adversity, 1822–1865.* Boston: Houghton Mifflin, 2000.

GLOBALIZATION

Bhagwati, Jagdish. *In Defense of Globalization.* New York: Oxford University Press, 2007.

Chanda, Nayan. *Bound Together.* New Haven, CT: Yale University Press, 2007.

Easterly, William. *The White Man's Burden: Why the West's Efforts to Aid the Rest Have Done So Much Ill and So Little Good.* New York: Penguin, 2007.

Rodrik, Dani. *One Economics, Many Recipes: Globalization, Institutions, and Economic Growth.* Princeton, NJ: Princeton University Press, 2007.

Stiglitz, Joseph E. *Making Globalization Work.* New York: W. W. Norton, 2007.

THE HUDSON RIVER SCHOOL

Bermingham, Peter. *American Art in the Barbizon Mood.* Washington, DC: Smithsonian Institution Press, 1975.

Millhouse, Barbara Babcock, and Kevin J. Avery. *American Wilderness: The Story of the Hudson River School of Painting.* Hensonville, NY: Black Dome Press, 2007.

Wilmerding, John, ed. *American Light: The Luminist Movement, 1850–1875.* New York: Harper & Row, 1980.

Wilton, Andrew, and Tim Barringer. *American Sublime: Landscape Painting in the United States, 1820–1880.* London: Tate Publishing, 2002.

THE ASTRONOMICAL UNIVERSE

Berman, Bob. *The Secrets of the Night Sky: The Most Amazing Things in the Universe You Can See with the Naked Eye.* New York: Harper Perennial, 1996.

Hawking, Stephen. *A Brief History of Time: From the Big Bang to Black Holes.* New York: Bantam, 1998.

Raymo, Chet. *365 Starry Nights: An Introduction to Astronomy for Every Night of the Year.* Englewood Cliffs, NJ: Prentice Hall, 1990.

Terzian, Yervant, and Elizabeth Bilson, eds. *Carl Sagan's Universe.* New York: Cambridge University Press, 1997.

MYTHS OF ANCIENT GREECE AND ROME

Buxton, Richard. *The Complete World of Greek Mythology.* New York: Thames & Hudson, 2004.

Lefkowitz, Mary. *Greek Gods, Human Lives: What We Can Learn from Myths.* New Haven, CT: Yale University Press, 2003.

Trzaskoma, Stephen, R. Scott Smith, and Stephen Brunet, eds. *Anthology of Classical Myth.* Indianapolis, IN: Hackett Publishing, 2004.

Vernant, Jean-Pierre. *Myth and Society in Ancient Greece.* Brooklyn, NY: Zone Books, 1990.

EMERSON AND TRANSCENDENTALISM

Richardson, Robert D. *Emerson: The Mind on Fire.* Berkeley, CA: University of California Press, 1996.

Sacks, Kenneth S. *Understanding Emerson: "The American Scholar" and His Struggle for Self-Reliance.* Princeton, NJ: Princeton University Press, 2003.

Schreiner, Samuel A., Jr. *The Concord Quartet: Alcott, Emerson, Hawthorne, Thoreau, and the Friendship That Freed the American Mind.* New York: Wiley, 2006.

THE HISTORY OF THE EARTH

Cattermole, Peter. *Building Planet Earth.* New York: Cambridge University Press, 2000.

Dixon, Dougal. *The Practical Geologist: The Introductory Guide to the Basics of Geology and to Collecting and Identifying Rocks.* New York: Simon & Schuster, 1992.

Sagan, Carl. *Cosmos.* New York: Ballantine, 1985.

REVOLUTIONARY FRANCE

Darnton, Robert. *The Great Cat Massacre.* New York: Basic, 2000.

Doyle, William. *The French Revolution: A Very Short Introduction.* New York: Oxford University Press, 2001.

Hunt, Lynn. *The French Revolution and Human Rights: A Brief Documentary History.* New York: Bedford/St. Martin's, 1996.

Palmer, R. R. *Twelve Who Ruled: The Year of Terror in the French Revolution.* Princeton, NJ: Princeton University Press, 2005.

Woloch, Isser. *Napoleon and His Collaborators: The Making of a Dictatorship.* New York: W. W. Norton, 2002.

THE SEARCH FOR ALTERNATIVE ENERGIES

Gibilisco, Stan. *Alternative Energy Demystified.* New York: McGraw-Hill Professional, 2006.

Inslee, Jay, and Bracken Hendricks. *Apollo's Fire: Igniting America's Clean Energy Economy.* Washington, DC: Island Press, 2007.

Smil, Vaclav. *Energy at the Crossroads: Global Perspectives and Uncertainties.* Cambridge, MA: MIT Press, 2003.

Vaitheeswaran, Vijay V. *Power to the People: How the Coming Energy Revolution Will Transform an Industry, Change Our Lives, and Maybe Even Save the Planet.* New York: Farrar, Straus and Giroux, 2004.

Yergin, Daniel. *The Prize: The Epic Quest for Oil, Money, & Power.* New York: Free Press, 1993.

SCHOOLS OF BUDDHIST THOUGHT

Aitken, Robert. *Taking the Path of Zen.* Berkeley, CA: North Point Press, 1982.

Dalai Lama. *The Meaning of Life.* Somerville, MA: Wisdom Publications, 2000.

Gethin, Rupert. *Foundations of Buddhism.* New York: Oxford University Press, 1998.

ROCKET SCIENCE

Bate, Roger R., Donald D. Mueller, and Jerry E. White. *Fundamentals of Astrodynamics.* Mineola, NY: Dover Publications, 1971.

Hill, Philip, and Carl Peterson. *Mechanics and Thermodynamics of Propulsion.* Englewood Cliffs, NJ: Prentice Hall, 1991.

Vallado, David A. *Fundamentals of Astrodynamics and Applications.* New York: Springer, 2007.

THE WORLDVIEW OF KARL MARX

Bottomore, Tom. *A Dictionary of Marxist Thought.* Malden, MA: Blackwell Publishing, 1998.

D'Amato, Paul. *The Meaning of Marxism.* Chicago: Haymarket Books, 2006.

Martin, Randy. *On Your Marx: Rethinking Socialism and the Left.* Minneapolis, MN: University of Minnesota Press, 2001.

THE IMPRESSIONISTS

Adams, Stephen. *The Barbizon School and the Origins of Impressionism.* New York: Phaidon Press, 1994.

Herbert, Robert L. *Impressionism: Art, Leisure, & Parisian Society.* New Haven, CT: Yale University Press, 1988.

Moffett, Charles. *The New Painting: Impressionism, 1874–1886.* Seattle, WA: University of Washington Press, 1986.

Thompson, Belinda. *Impressionism: Origins, Practice, Reception.* New York: Thames & Hudson, 2000.

HUMAN ORIGINS

Diamond, Jared. *Guns, Germs, and Steel: The Fates of Human Societies.* New York: W. W. Norton, 1999.

Johanson, Donald, and Blake Edgar. *From Lucy to Language.* New York: Simon & Schuster, 2006.

Relethford, John H. *Genetics and the Search for Modern Human Origins.* New York: Wiley, 2001.

Rowe, Noel. *The Pictorial Guide to the Living Primates.* Charlestown, RI: Pogonias Press, 1996.

THE HOLOCAUST IN EUROPE

Bergen, Doris L. *War and Genocide: A Concise History of the Holocaust.* Lanham, MD: Rowman & Littlefield, 2003.

Borowski, Tadeusz. *This Way for the Gas, Ladies and Gentlemen.* New York: Penguin, 1992.

Hillesum, Etty. *Etty Hillesum: An Interrupted Life and Letters from Westerbork.* New York: Holt, 1996.

THE CIVIL RIGHTS MOVEMENT

Branch, Taylor. *Parting the Waters: America in the King Years, 1954–63.* New York: Simon & Schuster, 1989.

——————. *Pillars of Fire: America in the King Years, 1963–65.* New York: Simon & Schuster, 1999.

——————. *At Canaan's Edge: America in the King Years, 1965–68.* New York: Simon & Schuster, 2007.

Rubel, David. *The Coming Free: The Struggle for African-American Equality.* New York: DK, 2005.

Williams, Juan, and Julian Bond. *Eyes on the Prize: America's Civil Rights Years, 1954–65.* New York: Penguin, 1988.

EMPIRICISM

Ayers, Michael. *Locke.* New York: Routledge, 1999.

Bennett, Jonathan. *Locke, Berkeley, Hume: Central Themes.* New York: Oxford University Press, 1971.

Berman, David. *Berkeley.* New York: Routledge, 1999.

Quinton, Anthony. *Hume.* New York: Routledge, 1999.

Scruton, Roger. *A Short History of Modern Philosophy.* New York: Oxford University Press, 2001.

EINSTEIN AND RELATIVITY

Gamow, George. *Mr. Tompkins in Paperback.* New York: Cambridge University Press, 1993.

Geroch, Robert. *General Relativity from A to B.* Chicago: University of Chicago Press, 1981.

Kaku, Michio. *Einstein's Cosmos: How Albert Einstein's Vision Transformed Our Understanding of Space and Time.* New York: W. W. Norton, 2004.

Thorne, Kip. *Black Holes and Time Warps: Einstein's Outrageous Legacy.* New York: W. W. Norton, 1995.

Wheeler, John Archibald. *A Journey into Gravity and Spacetime.* New York: W. H. Freeman, 1999.

THE SECTS OF ISLAM

Aghaie, Kamran Scot. *The Martyrs of Karbala: Shi'i Symbols and Rituals in Modern Iran.* Seattle, WA: University of Washington Press, 2006.

Momen, Moojan. *An Introduction to Shi'i Islam.* New Haven, CT: Yale University Press, 1987.

Nasr, Vali. *The Shia Revival: How Conflicts within Islam Will Shape the Future.* New York: W. W. Norton, 2007.

Norton, Augustus Richard. *Hezbollah: A Short History.* Princeton, NJ: Princeton University Press, 2007.

Rogerson, Barnaby, *The Heirs of Muhammad: Islam's First Century and the Origins of the Sunni–Shia Split.* New York: Overlook Press, 2007.

MASTERWORKS OF IMPERIAL RUSSIA

Billington, James H. *The Icon and the Axe: An Interpretive History of Russian Culture.* New York: Vintage, 1970.

Figes, Orlando. *Natasha's Dance: A Cultural History of Russia.* New York: Picador, 2003.

Frank, Joseph. *Dostoevsky: The Mantle of the Prophet, 1871–81.* Princeton, NJ: Princeton University Press, 2003.

Mirsky, D. S. *A History of Russian Literature: From Its Beginnings to 1900.* Evanston, IL: Northwestern University Press, 1999.

Nabokov, Vladimir. *Lectures on Russian Literature.* New York: Harcourt, 1982.

Volkov, Solomon. *St. Petersburg: A Cultural History.* New York: Free Press, 1997.

Wilson, A. N. *Tolstoy: A Biography.* New York: W. W. Norton, 1998.

ACKNOWLEDGMENTS

The Agincourt Press team that created this book included Julia Rubel (photo research), Laura Jorstad (proofreading), and Jon Glick and Miwako Nishizawa (design and production).

IMAGE CREDITS

ABOUT THE CONTRIBUTORS

Taylor Carman (EMPIRICISM) is Associate Professor of Philosophy at Barnard College. He is the author of *Heidegger's Analytic: Interpretation, Discourse, and Authenticity in "Being and Time"* (2003). He specializes in nineteenth- and twentieth-century European philosophy, phenomenology, and existentialism—especially Kierkegaard, Nietzsche, Heidegger, and Merleau-Ponty.

Bill Danielson (THE HISTORY OF THE EARTH) is a professional naturalist and environmental researcher who has worked for the National Park Service, the US Forest Service, and the Massachusetts Department of Environmental Management. Since 1997, he has written a popular newspaper column titled "Speaking of Nature."

Susan DiFranzo (THE ASTRONOMICAL UNIVERSE, EINSTEIN AND RELATIVITY) is Assistant Professor of Physics at Hudson Valley Community College and also teaches at the State University of New York at Albany. She has previously taught physics and astronomy at Rensselaer Polytechnic Institute and Siena College. Her field of research is information theory, and she is currently at work deriving some of the postulates of quantum mechanics using the method of consistent amplitudes.

Kirk Dombrowski (THE WORLDVIEW OF KARL MARX) is Associate Professor of Anthropology at John Jay College and the City University of New York Graduate Center. His work on Marxist theory, which relates to the intersection between culture and class, has been published in *Historical Sociology* and *International Labor and Working Class History*. He is the author of *Against Culture* (2001), which concerns the emerging class differences among the indigenous peoples of Alaska, and sits on the editorial board of the Marxist e-journal *New Proposals*.

Can Erbil (GLOBALIZATION) is Assistant Professor of Economics at Brandeis University and also teaches at Harvard. He specializes in international trade and development economics with a focus on trade liberalization, tax reform, and macroeconomic policy. His other areas of scholarly interest include the effects of instability on bilateral foreign trade and ethnic and sectarian tensions.

Delano Greenidge-Copprue (EMERSON AND TRANSCENDENTALISM) is a professor of humanities at the Manhattan School of Music. After a brief minor-league baseball career, he earned his doctorate from Columbia University, where his dissertation concerned the jazz cadence of nineteenth- and twentieth-century American literature from Herman Melville to Toni Morrison. He continues to write about the interdisciplinary nature of jazz.

Daniel Gremmler (MYTHS OF ANCIENT GREECE AND ROME) is a lecturer at the State University of New York at Albany, where he completed his dissertation on Greek tragedy. His other areas of scholarly interest include Aegean prehistory, comparative mythology, and the Elizabethan stage.

Paul G. Hackett (SCHOOLS OF BUDDHIST THOUGHT) is a lecturer at Columbia University, where he completed his dissertation on Tibetan Buddhism. He is the author of *Tibetan–English Dictionary of New Words* (2001), *A Tibetan Verb Lexicon: Verbs, Classes, and Syntactic Frames* (2003), and *Classical Tibetan Reader: A Progressive Reader in the Traditional Language and Topics of the Tibetan Buddhist Educational System* (forthcoming).

Mark Hoff (THE SEARCH FOR ALTERNATIVE ENERGIES) is a vice president at Energy Intelligence, a global energy company specializing in news, analysis, and data with offices in New York City, Houston, London, Moscow, and Singapore. Previously, he was a director at Cambridge Energy Research Associates, where he specialized in issues relating to energy technology and environmental strategy.

Kirsten Jensen (THE HUDSON RIVER SCHOOL, THE IMPRESSIONISTS) is an art historian specializing in nineteenth- and twentieth-century American art and architecture. She has worked at the Andrew W. Mellon Foundation, the National Academy of Design, and Yale University. She currently chairs the curatorial committee at the Thomas Cole National Historic Site in Catskill, New York.

Charles R. Justiz (ROCKET SCIENCE) is a NASA Doctoral Fellow and adjunct associate professor at the University of Houston who has spent more than thirty years in aviation and rocketry. As a test pilot, he has accumulated over thirteen thousand flight hours in more than one hundred different types of aircraft. As a professor of aerospace engineering, he has authored more than twenty technical papers on flight simulation and more than thirty technical papers on ionized plasma flows around charged spacecraft. He has taught many college-level classes to astronauts and mission controllers, including graduate-level astrodynamics and graduate-level spacecraft mission design.

Nira Kaplan (REVOLUTIONARY FRANCE) is an independent scholar who specializes in eighteenth- and nineteenth-century French history. Her publications include several articles for *Eighteenth-Century Studies,* and she helped prepare the ninth edition of the textbook *The Western Experience.* She has taught European history at Princeton, NYU, Columbia, and Hunter College.

Mark Pettus (MASTERWORKS OF IMPERIAL RUSSIA) recently received his doctorate (on Dostoevsky's influence on modern literature) from Princeton University, where he has taught classes on the nineteenth-century Russian novel. He is currently living in St. Petersburg, where he earlier spent a year as a Fulbright Scholar. In addition to Russian literature, his scholarly interests include Russian history and European intellectual history.

Michael Pregill (THE SECTS OF ISLAM) is Distinguished Emerging Scholar and Assistant Professor of Religious Studies at Elon University. He has previously taught at Hofstra, Columbia, and NYU. His area of specialization is the Quran and Islamic exegetical literature. His current research focuses on Muslim perceptions and portrayals of Jews in the early Islamic period, as well as on the cross-cultural ramifications of prophecy in late antiquity.

Thomas R. Rein (HUMAN ORIGINS) recently received his doctorate in physical anthropology from NYU, where he has taught on the early hominin fossil record. His academic specialties are early hominin evolution, the rise of bipedalism, and the comparative morphology of extant human and nonhuman primates. His research includes projects at the American Museum of Natural History (examining the relationship between cranial shape and climate in macaque species) and at NYU's Population Genetics and Molecular Anthropology Laboratory (extracting, amplifying, and sequencing primate DNA). His field experience includes fossil collection and identification at the Manonga Valley and Laetoli sites in Tanzania.

David Rubel (GENERAL GRANT'S CIVIL WAR, THE CIVIL RIGHTS MOVEMENT) is the author of more than a dozen book of American history. His recent books include *The Coming Free: The Struggle for African-American Equality* (2005); *The Story of America: Freedom and Crisis from Settlement to Superpower* (2002), coauthored with Archivist of the United States Allen Weinstein; and *The Civil War Chronicle* (2000), coedited with Russell Shorto. He is also president of Agincourt Press, a book production company in Chatham, New York, and appears regularly on Northeast Public Radio.

Barry Trachtenberg (THE HOLOCAUST IN EUROPE) is Assistant Professor of European Jewish Studies at the State University of New York at Albany. He was trained in Jewish history at UCLA, the Hebrew University of Jerusalem, and Oxford University. He is the author of *The Revolutionary Roots of Modern Yiddish, 1903–1917* (2008), which examines the importance of the 1905 Russian Revolution in the formation of Yiddish scholarship.

INDEX

geological history of, *see* Syllabus II *passim*
   magnetic shield, 129, 275
   mantle, 124, 134, 144
   oceans, 129, 149
ecolabeling, 82
École des Beaux-Arts, 202, 207, 242, 247,
   267, 277
Eddington, Arthur, 369, 374
Edison, Thomas, 126, 136
effective exhaust velocity, 235, 245, 260
Eichmann, Adolf, 259
Eightfold Path, 122, 147
Eileithyia, 45
Einsatzgruppen, 244, 254, 259
Einstein, Albert, 74, 104; *see also* Syllabus IV
   passim
Eirene, 45
Eisenhower, Dwight D., 322
electricity, 82, 126, 299, 349
   biomass-generated, 161, 191
   coal-generated, 111, 121, 126
   fuel cell–generated, 181
   geothermal-generated, 171
   solar-generated, 111, 121, 131, 151, 191
   tidal-generated, 176
   wind-generated, 111, 121, 156, 191
electromagnetic force, 379
electromagnetic spectrum, 275, 34, 39, 54
electromagnetism, Maxwell's equations concerning,
   299, 314, 344
electrostatic force, 349, 369
elements,
   definition of, 114
   heavy, formation of, 64, 109
Emerson, Ralph Waldo, *see* Syllabus II *passim*
   and British romanticism, 113, 118, 123
   and German idealism, 118, 123
   influence on the Hudson River School, 73, 83
   and Unitarianism, 108, 113, 128
empiricism, 216; *see also* Syllabus IV *passim*
   and causal necessity, 343, 348, 353, 368
   and causal regularity, 348, 353
   and induction, 353, 373
   and morality, 358
   and the uniformity of nature, 353
Enabling Act of 1933, 234
endocasts, 283
energy,
   conservation of, 349
   economics of, 111, 186, 196
energy companies, 111, 121, 131, 136, 141,
   146, 191
energy independence, 111, 131, 141, 186
energy infrastructure, 126, 131, 146, 186
energy technologies,
   alternative, *see* Syllabus II *passim*
   conventional, *see* Syllabus II *passim*
Engels, Friedrich, 201, 221, 231, 236, 241, 271
Enlightenment, 23, 108, 113, 125, 130, 206, 209,
   304, 363
Enquiry Concerning Human Understanding
   (Hume), 338
Enquiry Concerning the Principles of Morals
   (Hume), 338

environment,
   effect of energy technologies on, 111, 121, 126,
   131, 176, 186
   effect of globalization on, 82, 97, 102
epicycles, 19
Erinyes, *see* Furies
Eris, 49
Eros, 35
escape velocity, 215
Essay Concerning Human Understanding (Locke), 308
"Essay on Prints" (Gilpin), 23
Essay Towards a New Theory of Vision (Berkeley), 333
essence,
   nominal, 318
   real, 318
Estates General, 115, 130
ethanol, 121, 166, 191
Etruscans, 100, 105
Euclid, 294
Eudoxus of Cnidus, 19
Eunomia, 45
Eurystheus, 65, 95
event horizon, 74, 369
evolution, theory of, 213
"Exploration of the Universe with Reaction
   Machines" (Tsiolkovsky), 230
Exposition of My System of Philosophy (Schelling), 118
external combustion engine, 116
extraterrestrial life, 99

Fair Oaks, battle of, *see* Seven Pines, battle of
fair trade, 17
Farmer, James, 337, 352
Fates, 45
Fathers and Sons (Turgenev), 331, 351
Fatima, 305, 330
Fatimids, 340
Faubus, Orval, 322
Fermi, Enrico, 354
Fertile Crescent, 288
fêtes galantes, 242
feudalism 115, 125, 135, 246, 261, 266, 296
Feuerbach, Ludwig, 211, 216
Feuillants, 145
Fichte, J. G., 118
Final Solution, *see* Holocaust
fire,
   as a gift of the gods, 60
   hominin control of, 116, 273
First International, 201, 271
First Turning of the Wheel of Dharma, 122
fitna, 320
Five Ages of Mankind, 55
Five Forks, battle of, 96
Five Pillars of Islam, 365
Fivers, *see* Zaydis
flex-fuel engines, 166
Floyd, John B., 36
Ford, Henry, 166
foreign aid, 47, 92
foreign direct investment (FDI), 47
foreign loans, 47, 72
Forrest, Nathan Bedford, 51
Fort Donelson, 36, 41

Fort Henry, 36, 41
fossil fuels, 116, 121, 126, 136, 141, 161, 186, 191, 196
fossils, 174, 179, 184; *see also* Syllabus III *passim*
dating of, 184, 223
formation of, 184, 208
Four Foundations of Mindfulness, 157
Four Noble Truths, 122, 132, 137
Four Rightly Guided Caliphs, *see* Rashidun
Fourier, Charles, 148
Fragonard, Jean-Honoré, 242, 262
Francis, Convers, 128
Franco-Prussian War, 237, 247, 252, 257, 271, 272
Frank, Anne, 279
Frank, Otto, 279
Fredericksburg, battle of, 66
free fall, 215, 275
Freedom Ride, 337, 342, 347
Freedom Summer, *see* Mississippi Summer Project
Freikorps, 219
French Revolution, 206, 236; *see also* Syllabus II *passim*
and the ancien régime, 115, 120, 125, 165, 175, 185
and the rise of the bourgeois, 120, 125, 130, 140, 195
and the role of religion, 175
and the role of women, 165, 185, 195
and the spread of revolutionary values, 190, 195
and the Terror, 155, 160, 175, 180
From the Earth to the Moon (Verne), 230
fuel cells, 181, 196
Fuller, Margaret, 128, 143
Furies, 40, 65

Gaia, 35, 40
galaxies, 79, 84, 94, 364
Galileo Galilei, 29, 39, 210, 303, 309
gamma rays, 34, 39
Gandhi, Mohandas K., 193, 317, 332
gas giants, *see* planets, jovian
gasoline, *see* petroleum
Gauguin, Paul, 287
geist, 206, 211
General Agreement on Tariffs and Trade (GATT), 67
General Theory of Relativity (Einstein), *see* relativity
Generation of 1914, 224
geocentrism, 19
geological time, 144, 169, 194
scale, 174, 179, 223
geothermal energy, 121, 136, 146, 171
Germany,
defeat in World War I, 219, 224, 229
Nazi party, *see* Nazi party
nonaggression pact with Soviet Union, 244, 254
Weimar Republic, 219, 229, 274
Gettysburg, battle of, 66, 91
Gifford, Sanford Robinson, 53, 73, 78, 83
Gilpin, William, 23
Girondins, 150, 155
glacials, 169
Gleyre, Charles, 242, 247, 257
global warming, 82, 121, 141, 146, 186, 191, 196, 216

globalization, *see* Syllabus I *passim*
and corruption, 77, 92, 102
and environmental impacts, 82, 97, 102
and the race to the bottom, 17, 97, 102
winners and losers, 62, 102
glucose, 159, 174
Goddard, Robert, 230
Gogol, Nikolay, 311, 321, 326, 336, 381
Gorge in the Mountains (Gifford), 78
Göring, Hermann, 229
Grand Canyon of the Yellowstone (Moran), 88
Grand Unified Theory, 379
Grant, Ulysses S., *see* Syllabus I *passim*
gravitation, theory of universal (Newton), 29, 210, 304, 359, 369
gravitational collapse, 369
gravitational force, 379
gravitational lensing, 74, 364, 369
gravity waves, 104, 374
gravity well, 280, 369
Great Britain, war with revolutionary France, 150, 155, 170, 180, 190
Great Fear, 135
Great Liberation, 331
Great Picture, 63, 68
Greece, ancient,
astronomers, 19
historical timeline of, 20
myth as an element of culture, 25, 30
mythology of, *see* Syllabus I *passim*
greenhouse gases, *see* carbon emissions
Grundrisse der Kritik der Politischen Ökonomie (Marx), 241
Guizot, François, 236
gunpowder, invention of, 225
Guth, Alan, 89
Gypsies, inclusion in the Holocaust, 204, 264, 274

Hades, 65, 70, 95
hadith, 345
Haiti, *see* Saint Domingue
Hajj, 365
half-life, 114, 189, 223
Halleck, Henry W., 41
Halley, Edmond, 210
handicapped, inclusion in the Holocaust, 204, 239, 274
haplorhines, 218
Harris, Thomas, 31
Harvard College, 108, 118, 133, 138, 173
Harvard Divinity School, 108, 128, 138
Hasan, 320, 330
Hasan-i Sabbah, 340
Hashimites, 300, 320, 325
Hassam, Childe, 103
Haussmann, Georges-Eugène, 237
Hawthorne, Nathaniel, 128, 148, 188
Hayden, Ferdinand V., 88
Heade, Martin Johnson, 73, 83
Heart of the Andes (Church), 63
Hebe, 45
Hedge, Frederic Henry, 128
Hegel, G. W. F., 118, 206, 211, 246

evolution of, 64, 69
formation of, 59, 69, 79, 119
main sequence, 64, 69
neutron, 69, 104
red giants, 64, 69
spectral types, 54, 64, 69
supernovas, 24, 59, 69, 104, 109, 119, 124
white dwarfs, 64, 69, 369
steady state theory, 89
stellar wind, *see* solar wind
Stone Age, 273
stone tools, 208, 238, 258, 273, 283
  Acheulean, 273
  Aurignacian, 268
  Châtelperronian, 253
  Mousterian, 253, 273
  Oldowan, 273
stratigraphic superimposition, 223
strepsirhines, 218
Stuart, Gilbert, 18
Student Nonviolent Coordinating Committee
  (SNCC), 332, 337, 362, 372, 377
Sturmabteilung (SA), 229, 234
subduction zones, 144
sublime (aesthetic), 23, 28, 33, 38, 48, 53, 68, 83
substance, material, 318, 323, 328, 368
suffrage, 140, 150, 180, 195, 212, 236
Sufism, 355, 365
suicide bombers, 375
Sun, 54, 64, 129, 151, 161 275, 280
Sunday Afternoon on the Island of La Grande-Jatte
  (Seurat), 287
Sundown (Inness), 98
Sunni, *see* Syllabus IV *passim*
superfluous man, 311, 316, 321
supernovas, *see* stars, supernovas
supply and demand, 17, 111, 256
Supreme Court, 292, 297, 302, 307, 312, 337
surplus value, 241, 251, 261, 266
Sweatt v. Painter (1950), 297, 302
Swedenborg, Emanuel, 98
symbolic representation, 258, 278, 283
symbolism, 287, 381
Syria, Umayyad caliphate of, 315, 320, 325, 330
System of Transcendental Idealism (Schelling), 118

Tantalus, 65
tantrism, *see* Buddhism, tantric tradition
Taoism, 192, 225
tariffs, 27, 67
Tarquin, 105
Tartaros, 35, 40
Taung Child, 233
telescopes,
  early, 24, 29, 39
  gravitational, 364
  radio, 39, 99
  reflecting, 39
  refracting, 39
  space-based, 39, 44, 230, 285
Tennis Court Oath, 130, 135
Tethys, 45
Thailand, Buddhism in, 147, 187
"Thanatopsis" (Bryant), 38

Theia, 134, 139
Themis, 35, 45, 75
Theogony (Hesiod), 30, 35
Theravāda, *see* Buddhism, Theravādan tradition
Theses on Feuerbach (Marx), 281
Thomas, George H., 51
Thompson Dorothy, 284
Thoreau, Henry David, 128, 173, 178, 183, 193
  influence on the Hudson River School, 73
Three Dialogues Between Hylas and Philonous
  (Berkeley), 323
Three Jewels, 127
Three Poisons, 152, 157, 182
Three Sisters (Chekhov), 376
Thyestes, 65
Tibet,
  Buddhism in, 147, 197
  Chinese control of, 197
  influx of Indian Buddhists, 142, 197
  Mongol invasions of, 197
tidal energy, 176
tidal turbines, 176
Till, Emmett, 307
time dilation, 329, 334, 339
time travel, 339
Titans, 40, 45, 50, 60, 75, 95
Tolstoy, Leo, 361, 366, 371
tonalism, 103
tools, stone, *see* stone tools
Toussaint L'Ouverture, 170
trade,
  barriers to, 17, 22, 27, 67, 77
  benefits of, 37, 62
  liberalization, 22, 67, 77
  sanctions, 27, 87
Transcendental Club, 128, 138, 143, 148
transcendentalism, *see* Syllabus II *passim*
  influence on the Hudson River School, 73, 83
transmigration, 112
*Treatise Concerning the Principles of Human
  Knowledge* (Berkeley), 323
Treatise of Human Nature (Hume), 338
Treblinka, 259
Triassic period, 179
trilobites, 174
Trojan War, 55
Troyon, Constant, 207
Trumbull, John, 28, 38
Tryon, Dwight, 103
Tsiolkovsky, Konstantin, 230, 240
Tsong-kha-pa, 197
Tulunids, 330
Turgenev, Ivan, 311, 331, 351, 381
Turner, J. M. W., 23, 33, 63, 73, 88, 207, 252
Twachtman, John, 103
Twelvers, *see* Imamis
Twilight in the Wilderness (Church), 53
Two Treatises of Government (Locke), 308

ulama,
  Imami, 355, 360, 370, 375, 380
  Iranian, *see* ulama, Imami
  Shi'ite, 360, 380
  Sunni, 360